Olive Logan

THE

MIMIC WORLD,

AND

PUBLIC EXHIBITIONS.

THEIR HISTORY,

THEIR MORALS,

AND

EFFECTS.

BY OLIVE LOGAN.

PHILADELPHIA, PA.:
NEW-WORLD PUBLISHING COMPANY.
MIDDLETOWN, CONN.: PARMELEE & CO.
BURLINGTON, IOWA: R. T. ROOT.
1871.

Entered according to Act of Congress, in the year 1871, by

NEW-WORLD PUBLISHING COMPANY,

(John C. Copper.—S. J. Vandersloot,)

In the Office of the Librarian of Congress at Washington, D. C.

PREFACE.

THERE is little need of a preface to such a book as this. It is such a big book—it holds so much—that I have been able to express myself pretty fully, and I do not find, in giving a last look at the pages as they lie before me, that I have forgotten to say anything I wanted to say.

And if I had, I should not drag it into the preface and half say it, for fear of never getting a chance to say it anywhere else.

I don't believe this book will be my last. I don't expect to get through writing on my favorite subjects for a good while yet—a statement which some of my critics will receive, I fear, with indescribable anguish.

The book is the result of many years of careful preparation, during which I have been gathering, from experience and from study, the material here presented. I have scorned no source from which reliable and worthy material could be derived—from the most ponderous volumes to the most ephemeral newspapers—from the reminiscences of the most cultivated and scholarly play-goers to the gossip of the humblest of the player-folk—from the experiences of the most celebrated actresses, actors and managers, to the experiences of my humble self, from girlhood to womanhood, through a life which has been full of strange vicissitudes.

I give my work to the world in the sincere and earnest hope that it will do good. If it strips off some of the "gauze and vanity" from the "show world," I hope it also exhibits that world in a fairer and juster light to many who have hitherto looked on it with ungenerous and unenlightened eyes.

OLIVE LOGAN.

AUTHORS' UNION, 264 PEARL ST., N. Y.

CONTENTS.

CHAPTER I.

CHAPTER II.

CHAPTER III.

CHAPTER IV.

CHAPTER V.

CHAPTER VI.

CHAPTER VII.

CHAPTER VIII.

CHAPTER IX.

CHAPTER X.

CHAPTER XI.

CHAPTER XII.

CHAPTER XIII.

CHAPTER XIV.

CHAPTER XV.

CHAPTER XVI.

CHAPTER XVII.

CHAPTER XVIII.

CHAPTER XIX.

CHAPTER XX.

CHAPTER XXI

CHAPTER XXII.

CHAPTER XXIII.

CHAPTER XXIV.

CHAPTER XXV.

CHAPTER XXVI.

CHAPTER XXVII.

CHAPTER XXVIII.

CHAPTER XXIX.

CHAPTER XXX.

CHAPTER XXXI.

CHAPTER XXXII.

CHAPTER XXXIII.

CHAPTER XXXIV.

CHAPTER XXXV.

CHAPTER XXXVI.

CHAPTER XXXVII.

CHAPTER XXXVIII.

CHAPTER XXXIX.

CHAPTER XL.

LIST OF ILLUSTRATIONS.

THE MIMIC WORLD.

CHAPTER I.

Recollections of Early Life.—Cornelius A. Logan, Comedian, Critic, and Poet.—Vicissitudes of a Strange Career.—How a Family of Girls took to the Stage.—Reminiscenes of Cincinnati.

My earliest recollections are of the city of Cincinnati, whither I was borne while yet an infant, and where I spent the "happy days of childhood."

There are many magnificent monuments at the cemetery of "Spring Grove," in Cincinnati, but for me it contains but one grave. A simple headstone, with name and date of death, and then only the solitary line:

"Our Father who art in heaven."

This is the grave of Cornelius A. Logan, "Comedian, Critic and Poet."

My father's domestic circle was a large one, and composed principally of those troublesome members of the human family,—girls. Six girls, two boys, father and mother,—ten persons whose livelihood was to come from the dusty precincts of behind the scenes! It is not, perhaps, in the best taste to put forward biographical details when not writing a biography, but my father's history has always seemed to me so full of romance, so much out of the beaten track of ordinary life, that without further apology I will here jot down some of its salient events.

My father's family were people of rank in Ireland, who

had once owned large estates, and held important offices in Church and State; but misfortune having overtaken them, the younger members of the family resolved to leave the green hills and the emerald lakes of the unfortunate Island, and see if Fate would not have better things in store for them in this far-distant land.

Soon after their arrival, my father was born. In early years his family decided that he should enter the priesthood, and placing him in a Catholic College, near Baltimore, they looked forward fondly to the day when he should emerge from this educational and religious sanctuary with the greatest honors.

But these bright dreams were never to be realized. Whether from a restless disposition, on my father's part, or from undue severity on the part of the priests who had his body and mind in charge, he chafed under his bondage, and finally ran away from the college,—escaping at night, like a prisoner from jail.

After this his life was like a boat drifting on an open sea. Eighteen years of age, with magnificent health and peculiar personal beauty, an indignant family, outraged tutors, a classical scholar, and not a cent in his pocket.

He went to sea. Shipwreck, mutiny, horror, rat-eating, China! He came back again. Poverty,—family still angry,—nothing to do. Nothing to do, that is, but fall in love and marry.

Then children, and the universal problem which so troubled the old woman who lived in a shoe.

First, the literary life—notorious for its starving pay, —then tutorship—more starvation,—then to writing newspaper criticisms on the actors; then, with a profound conviction that he could act better than the men he was writing about, he went on the stage,—and did act better.

And in this way the theatrical life—the hard battle with the world, with unjust prejudice, with many professors of religion, whose hearts, beyond any one's else in the world, should be open to the woes and the weaknesses of all,—began not only for father and mother, but, in course of time, for six innocent and pure-minded girls.

The boys were, like all boys, more fortunate than their sisters; all the trades and professions are open to boys. One chose to be a doctor, the other a lawyer. But what medical college, or what law office, would graduate *girls*, fifteen or twenty years ago?

And so, one by one, as necessity urged, myself and every one of my sisters were made familiar with the hardships and the pleasures, the jealousies, the vanities, the wit, the jollity, and the toil of life behind the scenes.

But my recollections of Cincinnati are not altogether of a theatrical character. In the earliest years of my girlhood my own connection with the stage was very slight. My father was ambitious that his children should be thoroughly prepared for the battle of life, and to the full extent of his ability furnished every educational facility to them. I attended the Wesleyan Female Seminary in Cincinnati during a portion of my girlhood; and memory says much that is pleasant to me in that connection. Still, I have never been one of the sort who look back upon their school-days through a rose-colored pair of spectacles. To me, the fairy tales of youth are told chiefly in connection with the Ohio river, whose boatmen's song was once so popular with the negro minstrels:—

"Oh—ho! On we go!
Floatin' down de O-hi-o!"

I mind me well during the months favorable for navigation, how much the fashion it was for the gilded youth of Cincinnati, male and female, to take boat at the spacious wharf of their Queen City, and—not because they wanted to go there, but only because they enjoyed the trip,—be off to Louisville early in the morning—"Off to Louisville afore de broke ob day."

The gilded youth took boat—and such boats as they were. The *Ben. Franklin*, the *Lady Washington*, the *Fashion—que-sais je!* These were the boats, my friends, you have read about.

The jolly Captain, red of face, flush of pocket, heavy with antique watch-fob and glittering diamond pin, with a curious golden tail spreading over the snowy shirt front; he who interested himself personally in the comfort of every traveler—especially of every lady traveler—and made himself beloved by every creature in or out of his service. Oh, where is he?

What merry, merry parties have sailed down that muddy old Ohio, landed at the towns on its shores, waved handkerchiefs to passing craft, laughed, danced, and sung! The beautiful Sallie Ward, whose loveliness was renowned from the sources of the Ohio to the Gulf; Therese Chalfant, the belle of the Queen City for many a long day; Olivia Groesbeck, who married Gen. Hooker some years ago, and died, a short time since, at Watertown, N. Y.; all these were frequent passengers by the "Lou*ee*-ville packets."

I was only a child when I used to see these fair women come aboard—come aboard with their cavaliers, who were dressed "up to the nines," as the saying went; regular "bucks" you know; for a "swell" was a "buck" some ten or fifteen years ago.

I have questioned memory since I began writing this, how it happened that *I* came to be a passenger so frequently on the "Lou*ee*ville packets," and memory has answered that I went to school with a girl whose father was a river captain, and whom (for he loved her passing well) he allowed to bring her schoolmates for the "trip and back" on the river. We lived on the boat while we lay in port, I remember, and very good living it was.

I was a child of the most uninteresting age when all

this happened. A tall, scraggy girl, with red elbows, and salt-cellars at my collar-bones, which were always exposed, for fashion at that time made girls of this age uncover neck and arms. It also made them put on "pantalettes," the ugliest garment that ever rendered a girl hideous.

I think twelve or thirteen is a very trying age for a girl. Too old to play with dolls, too young to play with love, she looks with disdain on her juniors, and with burning envy on her seniors; and when the Sallie Wards and the Theresa Chalfants, and the Olivia Groesbecks came aboard with their "bucks," it is not strange that the girl should stare at them wonderingly, admiringly, and then rush off in despair and go make faces at herself in the glass because she is not pretty, and sees no prospect of ever becoming so.

What luscious fare was provided on those boats, it is almost unnecessary to say. The thing has passed into a proverb. When, as frequently happens, we are told that such or such a hotel is kept by an old ex-steamboat captain, we know at once that at that place the inner creature will be succulently pandered to.

Such steaming hot corn-bread, such tough hoe-cake, such overdone beefsteak, sailing in rich, brown gravy! Ah, those days of gravy! How we partook of it again and again, and soaked our hot biscuit in it, and drank strong coffee along with it, and never once stopped to think that we had such a thing as a digestion.

Alas! those days are past, and gravy is now a matter for grave consideration.

But the evening sports were best of all. After "supper" everything would be cleared away, tables and chairs ranged snugly along the sides of the boat, and the long narrow cabin would be ready for the mazy dance. No opera bouffe indecencies, no improper Germans, nor shocking round dances, but the good old time cotillion, when all we had to do was to stand up and "jine in," no prior instruction by dancing masters being necessary, for the "figures" were called out, and easily followed.

The musicians on the boat were generally "niggers:" they were summoned from their other occupations by the captain with a "Here, you black nigger, come up and play for the ladies and gentlemen," and grinning red lips and a cracked fiddle would soon appear.

The fiddler on "our" boat was one "Wash" by name, but not by nature; for cleanliness was not taught to the negroes then any more than the alphabet was.

"Wash" not only called the figures and played the fiddle, but he also kept time with his feet, and sang words to the tune he was playing. What made it most amusing was that the words were extemporaneous and apposite to the occasion, and often very shrewd hits at the company assembled. Many a bashful swain or "buck" has been helped on to his avowal by Wash's lyric assistance, given in such style as this, for instance:

"Massa Dick he lub Miss Sallie well.

(*Keeping time with both feet and calling the figure very loudly.*)

FORWARD FOUR!

But he ain't got courage for to tell.

SET TO YOUR PARTNERS, AND DOSEY DOE!"

It is true, life on the Ohio wave was not at all rose-coloured. Explosions were frequent; to bu'st a b'iler was next door to an every day occurrence. Professional gamblers, "sporting men" (sad sport!) took up a local habitation on the packets, and fleeced verdant passengers traveling southward. Rows, where the dreadful bowie was flourished and fatally used, were often seen. But such dangerous diversions seemed only to add zest to the dish, and I fancy travel was never interrupted for any length of time by these "unpleasantnesses."

Now, all this is changed. Traveling by boat has become quite as hum-drum as traveling by rail. The captain is still the leading spirit of the boat; but he lets you come aboard and go off with as much nonchalance as the proprietor of a hotel does when you occupy one of his rooms over night. Black men have more serious business now than fiddling; sporting men are at a discount; and bowie knives are vulgar.

In Cincinnati itself are to be seen very great changes. Fourth-st., which was once a sort of Broadway and Fifth-ave. combined, is now only Broadway in its character: the Fifth-avenue part is dead and dull, deserted by all save the old and quiet families who would be glad to surrender their places to trade, only trade objects, and says property eastward is not worth anything for business purposes; and the city moves in the other direction.

Longworth's fine property—surrounded by grounds which used to be called the "Garden of Eden," and which, in early days, I really thought had some direct connection with Paradise—stands still intact; but to the eye of one who knew it of yore, and loved it (and half believed that Adam and Eve had once lived there), the modern elegances of bronze lamps from Paris are a hateful innovation.

And year by year the population of Cincinnati increases, while that of Spring Grove—especially in cholera seasons—keeps fair pace.

Ay, turn where we will, to the West or to the East, this spectacle meets our eyes. Death stalking grim and gaunt, hand in hand with teeming birth—smiting the aged, the youthful, the Therese Chalfants, the Olivia Groesbecks, their bucks and beaux, and making the talk of their beauty and brilliancy as much a matter of indifference as the loveliness and wit of Louise de la Valliers and Lady Mary Wortley Montague.

Thus, day by day, we build and build, and hour by hour we rot and rot, and thereby hangs a tale.

CHAPTER II.

Residence in Philadelphia.—The Comedian as his Contemporaries saw Him.—The Critic and the Poet as his Works show Him.—His defense of the Stage.—How the Theatre can be Purged of Vice.

The correspondent of a Philadelphia journal recalls the period of our father's early residence in that city in these words: "I remember, as if it were but yesterday, my first introduction to Cornelius A. Logan, Esq., the eminent comedian, now, alas, no more. He resided, at the period alluded to, (embracing the years from 1825 to '30), either in Willow or Noble Street, I forget which, below Second. He had around him a small family of children—children that have now become men and women."

This was several years before the date of my birth—which took place in the village of Elmira, N. Y., in the summer of 1839, when my father was filling a professional engagement there.

The reputation of Cornelius A. Logan as an actor is confined to comedy; but, like many others who, have mistaken their *forte*, he commenced his theatrical career as a tragedian. There can be no doubt that his powers as a comedian were extraordinary. His contemporaries seem to have had but one opinion of his ability to stir the merriment of an audience irresistibly. The critic of the New Orleans *Delta* declared that "his dry quaint manner would almost elicit laughter from a dead elephant." The Nashville *American* of Oct. 15, 1851, said: "He stands at the head of his profession—a position he has maintained for many years—and the ablest and most practiced critics in all the Atlantic cities have universally accorded to him the position of almost the highest and most original genius on the American stage." His chief popularity was in the West and South.

Of his poetical works, my father neglected to make any collection. He was singularly careless of literary renown. One of his noblest poems, undoubtedly, was "The Mississippi," written at the mouth of the Ohio river. This poem was copied into the *Edinburg Review* with a handsome tribute to the author, and was favorably reviewed in several other European publications of high critical character.

Of his critical essays, one of the most erudite and able was his reply to a distinguished divine who had preached against the stage. This production is so well suited to the pages of the present work that I have a double satisfaction in extracting largely from it—pride in the literary work of a loved and honored father, and the pleasure which it ever gives me to furnish earnest defence of an honorable stage against its enemies both from within and from without.

"In the remoter ages of the world," wrote my father, "the Drama was the *only* medium of human worship. Bacchus, and Mammon, and the whole host of heathen deities were imaginations of a much later date. The shepherds and husbandmen of the Nile—the earliest worshipers that tradition reaches—invented a sort of sacred Drama, of which the priests were the actors. The 'God of the Overflow' was adored in a secondary character—that is, as represented by a sage, whose duty it was to watch the march of the heavenly bodies, and to predict the period of the inundation of the valley. A malignant spirit was also introduced upon the scene, who was crowned with a dead serpent of the Nile, and whose dress was composed of the leaves of the withered lotus. This mystery, like the melodrama of the present day, was interspersed with music, and the most magnificient temples were erected for its representation. These were the first churches. Thus it appears that Religion and the Drama were at first identical, but time has divided them. God has assigned to the one the high and holy mission of promulgating throughout the world his ineffable glory, and to the other he has delegated the power to sway the human heart by striking its subtle and intangible chords—to soften, to refine, and to elevate. 'Tis true that Thespis on his car at Athens chanted odes to Bacchus; but Bacchus was not held by the Athenians as the God of Drunkenness, as many imagine. He was the God of the Vine, doubtless, but he was honored for qualities distinct from ideas of sensual indulgence. Solemn temples were erected to his worship by a temperate people, and it is thus that with the name of this god the performances of the earliest professional actor are associated. As civilization advanced Æschylus rose—the father of the Drama. He was, like Shakspeare, an actor as well as a poet, and 'no Athenian of his day was so honored as Æschylus, for he created the Drama.' They bound his brows with laurel, and when he walked forth at noon they sprung arches of oak over his head. Sophocles, Euripides. and Aristophanes followed Æschylus, and some of their works live yet, unapproached by human effort—an imperishable and somewhat humiliating proof that whatever strides science may have taken in the world, the sublime genius of letters—mature at its birth—has denied the honor to succeeding generations of adding any thing to its brilliancy. This divine tells us that 'the Drama has commenced its retreat, and will soon pass away.' Nothing can be more evidently opposite to the truth than both the assertion and the prediction. At no period of the world were theatres and actors so numerous as now. In most of the civilized nations of Europe the Drama is under the special protection of the crown, and in those countries where letters are most cultivated, and where refinement has attained its highest polish, the theatre is supported by the government. In this country, 'tis true, the recent commercial distress, pervading as it did all classes of the community, reached theatrical amusements, and prostrated several establishments whose capital was too slender to bear the shock. * * * * 'The claims of the theatre to holiness will not be insisted on.' No; the theatre lays as few claims to holiness as the Church does to comedy—each has its appropriate sphere. The Church is built upon the Rock of Ages, and the Drama is built upon the human heart; the divine truth of the one, and the sublime morality of the other, will find a living response in that heart as long as it beats with a single attribute of the Deity. The doctor complains that ministers of religion are brought upon the stage to be ridiculed as 'dolts, pedants, or dullards.' The reply is that *there exist* ministers who *are* stupid, pedantic, and dull; and should these be exempt from censure or ridicule more than the rest of mankind? Should 'such divinity hedge' *all* who wear the black robe, that they should not be held amenable to the laws by which other men are governed? If there *are* reverend gentlemen who disgrace their holy calling by seduction, adultery, forgery, simony, or hypocrisy, should our awe of the cloth they pollute screen them from the punishment with which the law should visit their crimes, or the satire with which the stage should lash their vices? * * * * * 'What school-houses, academies, or colleges has it (the theatre) built?' If the theatre added to its other important powers the building or endowing of educational institutions, it would surpass as an instrument of good all human inventions. But, unhappily, its ability is not equal to such attempts. Its means of doing good are crippled by the pulpit. * * * * * * 'What streams of knowledge has it diffused? What science cultivated or explained?' Plays, for the most part, are founded on remarkable events in history, ancient and modern. Of the thirty-seven written by Shakspeare, twenty-four may for our present purpose be called poetical versions of well-authenticated historical passages. From no single historian can a tenth part of the truth of any event dramatized by Shakspeare be gathered. The immortal poet frequently drew his knowledge from sources which have not come down to our day. We can nowhere obtain so clear an insight into the characters, motives, passions, and politics of the men who fought the wars of the Roses as in the plays of this author. Who ever *saw*, except their own contemporaries, the heroes of antiquity, until Shakspeare introduced them to us face to face—the living, breathing, speaking inhabitants of Greece and Rome,—their warriors, sages, orators, patriarchs, and plebians? To the man who reads history only, Marius, Sylla, Nero, and Caligula have none of the features of humanity about them. The chief acts of their lives being exhibited unrelieved by a statement of the means by which their deeds were accomplished, they appear like the grotesque figures in a phantasmagoria—fearful from their indistinctness, horrible from their mysterious burlesque on human nature, and alike hideous whether we laugh or shudder at the monstrous chimera. Turn to the page of Shakspeare, or behold his swelling scene at the theatre, and these men—seen, arriving at natural ends by natural means,—teach the eternal truth that the heart of man is the same in all ages, and that vice has produced misery and virtue happiness, from the beginning of the world. The doctor quotes Plato as averse to the theatre. Every man who has not forgotten his school-boy classics can quote passages in Plato which would make the doctor feel that he calculated too much on the ignorance of his hearers. And Aristotle, too, the divine drags into the argument. Why, every tyro knows that the only laws acknowledged, even to this day, for constructing comedies are those of this philosopher, who declares that 'tragedy is intended to purge our passions by means of terror and pity.' And 'Tacitus says the German manners were guarded by having no play-houses among them.' If that be true, the Germans have thought better on the subject since the time of Tacitus; for one of the modern writers of that nation (Zimmerman) says, 'We are greatly a dramatic people. Nothing but good can result from the widest indulgence of this taste among us, unless it happen that the sedentary and imaginative student should, through his diseased appetite, draw poison from the stage, as the serpent distils venom from the nutritious things of nature.' The doctor next invokes Ovid to his aid. Surely nothing but a design to frighten us with an array of classical names could induce the preacher to bolster his argument with the opinion of the most licentious poet of ancient or modern times. Ovid calling the theatre dissolute! and advising its suppression! Why, 'tis like Satan denouncing heaven from the burning lake, or like a pickpocket advising the suppression of the penal code. Next we have a list of the formidable opinions of the early fathers of the Church, who were unanimous in the condemnation of the theatre. Doubtless. So they were in the condemnation and burning of martyrs and witches. However pious were many of them, according to their unchristian and ferocious notions of piety, their sentiments on the subject of the Drama are not worth a moment's discussion. The doctor here arrives at a point where the stage seems indeed vulnerable. He alludes to the bars for the sale of liquors, and to the third row. * * * Bars are no more necessary to the theatre than to the pulpit. I am old enough to remember the time when men would assemble at the tavern nearest the church as soon as the service was over, and there discuss the merits of the sermon and of brandy and water at the same time. The Temperance movement, however, wrought wonders, and I believe the same men do not drink now,—at least not until they reach home. The other charge is a graver one—the third tier. This evil is no more essential to the Drama than the bars; nor is it 'an inseparable concomitant of the theatre.' The separation has taken place in many towns of this country." And at the present time, I may add, the separation is complete throughout the whole land. In a future chapter I shall refer more at length to this subject, and show how the theatre *can* be purged of vice and indecency, by proper effort. My father concludes: "Those periods in history in which the Drama declined are marked by bigotry, violence, and civil war. All the theatres in London were closed by order of Oliver Cromwell, and ten days afterward the head of Charles the First rolled from the block! Terror and gloom hung over the kingdom. The Drama was interdicted—the arts perished—the woof rotted in the loom—the plow rusted in the furrow, and men's hearts were strung to the ferocity of fanaticism. Fathers and sons shed each other's blood; and in the intervals of lust and murder, wild riot howled through the wasted land. Even if permitted by the laws, the theatre could not exist amid such horrors. But the actors were outlawed, and the bigoted Roundheads fixed that stigma upon the profession of a player which illiterate and narrow-minded people attach to it even to this day. The Pulpit too often depicts Virtue in austere and forbidding colors, and strips her of every attractive grace. The path of duty is made a rugged and toilsome way—narrow and steep; and the fainting pilgrim is sternly forbidden to turn aside his bleeding feet to tread, even for a moment, the soft and pleasant greensward of Sin, which smiles alluring on every side. The Stage paints Virtue in her holiday garments; and though storms sometimes gather round her radiant head, the countenance of the heavenly maid, resigned, serene, and meek, beams forth, after a season of patient suffering, with ineffable refulgence. Vice constantly wears his hideous features, and in the sure, inevitable, punishment of the guilty we behold the type of that Eternal Justice, before whose fiat the purest of us shall tremble when the curtain falls on the Great Drama of Life."

CHAPTER III.

My First Visit Behind the Scenes, an Infant in Long Clothes.—My First Appearance Before an Audience, a Child of Five Years.—Children as Actors.—Ristori's Debut as a New-born Babe.—Drilling Children in the Art of Acting.—Early Distaste for the Life.—Precocious Dramatic Children.—The Bateman Sisters.—Amusing Anecdotes of Children on the Stage.—A Healthy Infant.

I cannot remember the time when I was not familiar with that curious place known both to theatricals and the outer world as behind the scenes. I know I was not born there; but I think I must have been carried there when I was a baby in long clothes. I cannot remember when the musty stage trappings, the pasteboard goblets, the wooden thrones, the canvas tombs, were unfamiliar sights to me.

I think I could not have been more than four or five years old when I made my first appearance on the boards —very much against my will,—and from that period until within five years ago, when I bade farewell to the mimic stage, I hope forever, I have played, off and on, sometimes with an intermission of years, sometimes every night in the year, from babyhood up.

My childhood debut was made in the character of Cora's child in Pizarro, and subsequently as the child of Damon in the play of Damon and Pythias.

My father, if I remember rightly, was stage manager of the theatre in Cincinnati at the time.

Madame Ristori began her dramatic career earlier than this. When she was less than three months old, she was carried on the stage in a basket, to personate a new-born infant.

Cora's child and Damon's child have nothing to say;

but I can recall this day the shudder of terror with which I received the news that I would be obliged to go on the stage at night, as Cora's child. For fancy a girl baby being fought over with broad swords by a party of actors! One of them (Rolla) seizes the child, flings it upon his shoulder, and rushes across a shaking bridge, which, after he has crossed, he knocks down with his sword, holding the unhappy child high in the air with his left hand, while he is engaged in these playful diversions with his right.

I was always sadly frightened when I was called upon to play these little parts; and although the actress who played Cora generally gave me sugar plums for being "good," I could not reconcile myself to it. My mother tried her best to relieve me from the irksome task. Sometimes they succeeded in finding another child, whose parents would hire her out for the night; but it often happened that at the last moment these people would fail to appear, and I was sent for, routed out of my first sleep to go on again to personate Cora's child.

By and by I got into "speaking parts," such as the Duke of York in Richard the Third; the child in the Rent Day, a touching domestic drama, now little played, and others.

Of course, a child has to be instructed in these speaking parts. It could scarcely be expected that the immature intellect of childhood could grasp the subtle wit of Shakspeare.

For instance, the young Duke of York says to Gloster (afterwards Richard the Third), after his brother has said:

"My Lord of York will still be cross in talk;—
Uncle, your grace knows how to bear with him."

DUKE OF YORK—"You mean to bear me, not to bear with me.
Uncle, my brother mocks both you and me;
Because that I am little, like an ape,
He thinks that you should bear me on your shoulders."

The last line alludes to the hump on Gloster's back, which the boy seems to think would be convenient for carrying burdens.

Now, it is of course evident that no actor comes to the morning rehearsal with a padded hump on his shoulders. Therefore, to the narrow intellect of a child it seems a stupid thing to say "This gentleman will have a hump on his shoulder at night; and you are to lift up your shoulders as if to imitate his deformity, and lay great stress on the line

"'You should bear me on your shoulders.'"

All of which I remember thinking very stupid and tiresome.

I never see a child on the stage without experiencing a throb of sympathetic pity; for it does not seem to me as if any child could really like it.

Among precocious dramatic children may be named the Bateman sisters, Ellen and Kate; two sweet little playmates of mine. These little girls—with father and mother both celebrated in the theatrical world—were thrust upon the stage as early as the children of most theatrical people are. Their father (who was an excellent manager and tutor) conceived the idea of instructing them in the most difficult tragic and comic parts, hitherto only attempted by grown people; such parts as Richard the Third and Richmond, Iago, King Lear, and many others.

Their success was very surprising. They appeared in all the principal cities of the country, attracting crowded houses; then went to England, played before the Queen, who expressed herself delighted with them, and finally returned to their home in St. Louis with a snug sum of money acquired by their cleverness.

During the entire time they remained the same pretty, sweet, unaffected, truth-loving children they had always been; never puffed up by their success, nor vain of the adulation they received.

Although the theatrical life naturally absorbed much of the time of these children, it was curious to see how nicely the moments were parceled off by their careful mother, that as little detriment as possible to the health and education of the children should result.

For instance, every morning they pursued their educational studies, their mother acting as instructress. At noon they dined, and soon after they went to bed. It was funny to see them put on their night-dresses while the sun was still shining, and go to bed, dropping off to sleep almost immediately. At night they were fresh and wide awake for their performances.

One of these little girls—Ellen—married a wealthy gentleman, and never returned to the stage; the other—Kate—now celebrated as Miss Bateman—returned to the stage on reaching womanhood, and renewed the successes of her youth.

Many amusing incidents are related about child actors. One of the latest relates to a performance of "Dora,"—a pretty play founded on Tennyson's poem of that name. When the lady who plays the part of *Mary Morrison* made her exit to bring on her little *Willie* of four years, she was shocked to find a lubberly boy of at least fourteen, and as he was the only *Willie* at hand, on he must go, though he was well nigh as big as his mother. The *Farmer Allen* of the play, being equal to the emergency, instead of inquiring, "How old are you, my little man?" endeavored to remedy the matter by saying, "How old are you, my strapping boy?" But he failed, for the boy, who was instructed to say "*four to six*," said it in such a coarse, sepulchral tone as to drive the good-natured grandfather to exclaim, "*Forty-six!* You look it, my boy, you look it."

Mrs. Mowatt relates an incident which occurred to her at Savannah, Ga., where she was playing. The play announced for the evening was "The Stranger." "I was informed at rehearsal that the two children who usually appeared as Mrs. Haller's forsaken little ones, were ill. No other children could be obtained. Yet children were indispensable adjuncts in the last scene. The play could not be changed at such hasty notice. What could be done? I was walking up and down behind the scenes, very much annoyed, and wondering how the difficulty could be overcome, when the person who temporarily officiated as my dressing maid accosted me. She was an exceedingly pretty mulatto girl. She saw that I was distressed about the absent children, and, with a great deal of hesitation, offered to supply the deficiency. I brightened at the prospect of deliverance from our dilemma, telling her that I would be much obliged, inquired to whom the children belonged. 'They are mine, ma'am,' she answered, timidly. 'I have a couple of pretty little ones, very much at your service.' 'Yours?' I answered, aghast at the information. 'Yours? why, Mrs. Haller's children are supposed to be white. I am afraid yours won't very readily pass for mine;' and I could hardly help laughing at the supposition. The young woman took my distressed merriment good naturedly, and replied, 'Oh, my children are not so *very* black, seeing as how their father is altogether white!' 'Do you really think they would pass for white children?' 'Why the little girl has blue eyes, and they have both got hair nearly as light as yours; then you might *powder* them up a bit if you thought best.' I sent her for the children. They were really lovely little creatures, with clear cream-colored complexions, and hair that fell in showers of wavy ringlets. I decided at once that they would do, and told her to bring them at night in their prettiest dresses, to which I would make any needful additions. The children do not make their appearance on the stage until the last act. After retouching their toilets, instructing them in what they had to do, and feeding them with sugar-plums, I told their mother to make them a bed with shawls in the corner of my dressing-room. She did so, and they slept quietly through four acts of the play. We gently awakened them for the fifth act. But their sleep was too thoroughly the sweet, deep slumber of happy childhood to be easily dispelled. With great difficulty I made them comprehend where they were, and what they must do. Even a fresh supply of sugar-plums failed to entirely arouse them. The sleepy heads would drop upon their pretty round shoulders, and they devoured the *bon-bons* with closed eyes. The curtain had risen, and the children must appear upon the stage. I led them to the wing, and gave them in charge of Francis. Francis walked on the stage, leading a child by each hand. The trio hardly made their appearance when the little girl, thoroughly wakened by the dazzling light, gave one frightened look at the audience, broke away from Francis, and, shrieking loudly, rushed up and down the stage, trying to find some avenue through which to escape. The audience shouted with laughter, and the galleries applauded the sport. The poor little girl grew more and more bewildered. Francis pursued her, dragging her brother after him. The unexpected exercise, added to his sister's continued cries, alarmed the boy. He screamed in concert, and, after some desperate struggles, obtained his liberty. Francis had now both children to chase about the stage. The boy he soon captured, and caught up under his arm, continuing his flight after the girl. She was finally secured. The children, according to stage direction, are to be taken through a little cottage door, on the left of the stage. Francis, panting with his exertions, dragged them to the door, which he pushed open with his foot. The struggling children looked in terror at the cottage. They fancied it was the guard-house, in which colored persons are liable to be confined if they are found in the streets after a certain hour without a 'pass.' Clinging to Francis, they cried out together, 'Oh, don't ee put me in ee guard-house! Don't ee put me in ee guard-house!' The accent peculiar to their race, and their allusion to the 'guard-house,' at once betrayed to the audience their parentage. The whole house broke forth into an uproar of merriment. Francis disappeared, but the audience could not be quieted. I was suffering not a little at the contemplated impossibility of producing the children at the end of the play. But nobody cared to listen to another line. *Mrs. Haller's* colored children had unceremoniously destroyed every vestige of *illusion*. I made my supplication to 'kiss the features of the father in his babes,' in the most suppressed tone possible, yet the request produced a fresh burst of laughter. We hurried the play to a close. The entrance of the children, and the excitement produced upon the parents by their presence, we left to the imagination of the spectators. The play ended without the re-appearance of the juvenile unfortunates."

My sister, Eliza Logan, during her brilliant theatrical career, was very popular in Savannah. Once, after enacting the character of *Mrs. Haller*, the little creature who had just figured as her child ran into her dressing room to return a pocket handkerchief which my sister had dropped as she fell at the feet of the unrelenting husband. Observing the child carefully, she detected her *color*, and inquired who her mother was. The reply was that her mother was a colored woman.

"Singular, but I remember hearing that Mrs. Mowatt, when she played this part here, had a colored child for the part of William."

"Dat's so, missis; I is de bery chile."

"You? why it's ten years ago."

"Yes missis, but I is a Quadroon Dwarf, an' I been playin' de Stronger's chile for all de Stronger's wot been comin' to Sawannah for de last *twelve years.*"

So it is clear that, whatever the vicissitudes of her debut, the frightened little heroine of "ee guard-house" was not driven from the stage thereby.

CHAPTER IV.

Training for the Stage.—False Notions about "Genius."—The Road to Success a Road of Hard Work.—How Fanny Kemble Studied Walk, Gesture, and Accent for Years before Making a Public Appearance.—The Severe Training of Rachel, the Tragedienne.—A Woman's Criticism of Rachel.—Her Wonderful Powers, her Serpent-like Movements, her Thrilling Intensity.—Brief Sketch of Her Life.—Kate Bateman's Training.—Anecdote of Julia Dean.—Mrs. Mowatt's Training.—Betterton, the Great English Actor.—The Severe Discipline by which He Overcame the Most Extraordinary Disadvantages, an Ugly Face, a Grotesque Figure, a Grumbling Voice, and Great Awkwardness.

I know that many people claim that actors, like poets, are "born, not made;" but so far as my own experience goes, I must say that I never knew an actor or actress to reach distinction without having passed through many long and weary years of study and toil. Of course the natural genius must be there, or all the study and toil would go for nothing; but as well might you expect a painter or a sculptor to bring forth perfect works of art without learning the rudiments, as to expect any man or woman to give, without study, a perfect delineation of a part. On the other hand, all the study in the world will not *make* a genius,—dramatic or other.

That is a very prevalent error in regard to "genius," which believes it capable of rising superior to the mechanical appliances of art. No more dangerous a fallacy can the mind, gifted by nature, but uncultured by art, labor under, than that of easy reliance on the intangible thing called genius; and there can be no doubt that many great intelligences, in every department of learning, art, and science, have defeated their own noble missions from their very self-sufficiency as regards their native power, and their culpable neglect of the practical methods by which alone that power can be fostered and developed. This is especially true of the dramatic art, and yet the fact is far from being recognized by the world at large, or even the exponents of Shakspeare themselves.

It is willingly conceded that genius, and that, too, of a very high order, is indispensable to a great actor, but like the gift of the poet, it is expected to be all-sufficient,—indeed, there are many people who would be amazed to learn that there is any regular apprenticeship to be served to the trade of acting. It seems to be tacitly agreed that great actors spring, Minerva-like, into the full possession of their histrionic powers at a single bound.

We often hear the remark, "Oh, what a splendid actress Miss C. would make!" or, "If John would go on the stage he'd make his fortune!"

Now, in nine cases out of ten, the individuals in question, if put to the test, would fail signally. I remember a case in point:

A young married lady, who had two years before, when she was a girl of seventeen, vainly urged her family to allow her to go on the stage, took a sudden resolve to relieve her pecuniary embarrassments by becoming an actress.

She called on an actress for instruction; but so well assured was she that she possessed inherent tragic power that it was out of the question to teach her much. She was a genius,—everybody said it, and if further proof were needed, she *felt* it!

Mysterious feeling,—it was in her!

She was little, to be sure, but so was Kean. Stage-fright had no terrors for her; oh, no, the illusion would carry her far beyond and above the reach of anything like that!

The important night arrived, but, as may be expected, she failed to establish herself as a worthy successor of the

Keans and the Kembles. With the *feeling* and the *assurance* as strong as ever, she had no voice, no presence, no power; in other words, she had not the stage-training.

When she gained it, as she afterwards did by accepting, with the martyrdom of a crushed genius, a small situation in a stock-company, it made of her a very good serio-comic and soubrette actress, in the course of some years.

A young lady of good standing in society had from childhood evinced the most ardent liking for the stage, and it is probable she would have adopted it but for the scruples of her family. As it was, she contented herself with committing to memory passages from Shakspeare and the poets, and reciting them for the edification of an admiring circle of friends.

On the occasion of a re-union at her house, an ex-actress of great ability was present. Recitations were the order of the day. The young lady declaimed. Her enthusiasm was perceptible in every vibration of her voice, in every flash of her brilliant eyes; her feeling was genuine; her emotion carried her far away from her every-day surroundings.

Surely, here was a case of self-asserting genius!

Not so; the feeling was all in herself; she had not the art to impart it to her audience of admiring friends, who saw in her merely a pretty girl, with large, luminous eyes, laboring under strong excitement, and reciting in a hurried tone familiar lines.

But when the trained actress arose, how different! She may have differed from the impulsive girl in not feeling herself, but she certainly imparted the feeling to others.

Her practiced, methodical use of her eye alone, held the spectators spell-bound, and her assumption of passion and pathos carried away their feelings as if by some subtle magnetic force.

The voice should be skilled for speaking as it is for

singing, and it is capable of almost as many fine gradations in one as in the other. A young friend of mine, on the stage, felt the necessity of having a marked course of instruction to pursue, and expressed a wish to learn elocution.

"Elocution!" exclaimed a young and "promising" actor; "Oh, that's all played out; be natural, and let elocution go."

Natural! Look at the people all around you—sensible, educated, and intellectual people, no doubt,—but just fancy every one of them on the stage, *acting naturally*, each retaining his or her individual peculiarities or deficiencies!

"Be natural! let elocution go!" As well say to an uneducated singer, "You have a voice—be natural—let instruction go."

It is as absurd to assume that innate dramatic force and fire take proper shape unaided, as it would be to assert that a brilliant conversationist is indebted to nature alone for his powers. If Madame de Stael had one of the most striking and original minds of the age, she also had one of the most highly polished.

Unfortunately, nature, does not often bestow upon the votaries of the dramatic art the ready requisites for its highest interpretation, and the history of its great exponents proves this beyond a doubt.

I can recall but few instances of actors having achieved great distinction, who had not previously served an apprenticeship to toilsome drudgery; and the sudden flashes of genius which electrify the world are generally the carefully prepared result of long and arduous endeavor.

Fanny Kemble, who belonged to the greatest dramatic family that ever lived, walked about her house every day, in England, for *three years*, in the dress of a tragedy queen

—the trailing shoulder robe, the crown, the long train,—that she might acquire perfect ease in the management of these unusual garments. The consequence was, the very first moment she stepped on the stage, she looked every inch a queen; and was as unconcerned about her costume as if it had consisted of a calico gown and sun-bonnet.

This minute training extended to every part of her performances. Every word, every gesture, every syllable, was carefully studied; and yet so skilfully had this perfection been attained, that every word fell from her lips in what seemed to be a charmingly natural way—in short, the "art which conceals art" was here in its perfection. When she first appeared on the stage, it was said of her, that the mantle of her renowned aunt (Mrs. Siddons) had fallen upon her shoulders, and that she had never trod the boards in any inferior capacity.

One of the most striking examples of the value of training, that the world has ever known, is furnished in the case of the great French actress, Rachel—who certainly could afford to dispense with training if any one ever could—for in her case the dramatic ability was so marked, so conspicuous, that there is little doubt she would have shone as a very bright star even without the aid of training. Her empire as dramatic queen would not, of course, have been the undisputed one it now is, but *genius* was in that woman's breast, if it ever was in the breast of woman.

Rachel studied with the greatest of French tutors from childhood, and consequently the prevailing supposition that she, an ignorant girl of eighteen, interpreted with original perception the greatest dramatists of her own or any age, and blazed before the astonished world, a self-asserting, an untutored genius, is wholly without foundation.

It is said that she was but an echo of her great master,

a grand and magnificent echo, truly, yet but an echo; and it has been added that even were this undeniable, the master had many pupils, and the world had but one Rachel!

Undoubtedly; but without her master and their joint labors for years, would the genius of Rachel ever have found a perfect utterance?

Mrs. Jameson, the English authoress, has drawn a picture of Rachel which so vividly illustrates the effect of training and practice on the artist that I quote it—premising, however, that Mrs. Jameson was very far from being a partisan or even an admirer of Rachel. With most English women, the possibility of anything French being worthy of mention in the same breath with anything English, is not admissible; and Mrs. Jameson shares the peculiarity so far as to deny Rachel a place as an artist alongside of the tragedy queens of England. "The parts in which Rachel once excelled—the *Phedre* and the *Hermione*, for instance—have become formalized and hard, like studies cast in bronze; and when she plays a new part it has no freshness. I always go to see her whenever I can. I admire her as what she is—the Parisian actress, practised in every trick of her *métur* trade. I admire what she does, I think how well it is all done, and am inclined to clap and applaud her drapery, perfect and ostentatiously studied in every fold, just with the same feeling that I applaud myself.

As to the last scene of 'Adrienne Lecouvreur,' (which those who are *avides de sensation*, athirst for painful emotion, go to see as they would drink a dram, and critics laud as a miracle of art;) it is altogether a mistake and a failure. It is beyond the just limits of terror and pity—beyond the legitimate sphere of *art*. It reminds us of the story of Gentil Bellini and the Sultan. The Sultan much admired his picture of the decollation of John the Baptist, but informed him that it was inaccurate—surgically—for the tendons and muscles ought to shrink where divided; and then calling for one of his slaves, he drew his scimitar, and striking off the head of the wretch, gave the horror-struck artist a lesson in practical anatomy. So we might possibly learn from Rachel's imitative representation, (studied in a hospital as they say,) how poison acts on the frame, and how the limbs and features writhe unto death. I remember that when I first saw her in *Hermione*, she reminded me of a serpent, and the same impression continues. The long meagre form, with its graceful undulating movements, the long narrow face and features, the contracted jaw, the high brow, the brilliant supernatural eyes which seem to glance every way at once; the sinister smile; the painted red lips, which look as though they had lapped, or could lap, blood; all these bring before me, the idea of a Lamia, the serpent nature in the woman's form. In *Lydia*, and in *Athalia*, she touches the extremes of vice and wickedness with such a masterly lightness and precision, that I am full of wondering admiration for the actress. There is not a turn of her figure, not an expression in her face, not a fold in her gorgeous drapery, that is not a study; but withal such a consciousness of her art, and such an ostentation of the means she employs, that the power remains always extraneous, as it were, and exciting only to the senses and the intellect."

A glance at the life-history of Rachel will show more fully how gradual was her progress toward perfection, how thorough was her training, how laborious the means by which she "clutched the dramatic diadem." She was the daughter of a Jewish pedler, who pursued his calling in various parts of Switzerland and Germany, and was followed in his wanderings by his family, consisting of his wife, four daughters, of whom Rachel was the second, and a son. At Lyons, where they took up their residence temporarily, Rachel and her sister Sarah contributed to the common support by singing at the cafés and other public resorts; and at Paris, whither the family removed in 1831, the two sisters similarly employed themselves on the boulevards. Choron, the founder of the institution for the study of sacred music, struck by their performance, took them both under his instruction; but finding that the talent of Rachel, to whom he gave the name of Eliza, was dramatic rather than vocal, he transferred her to the care of M. St. Aulaire, a teacher of declamation, who carefully grounded her in the chief female parts of the standard classical drama. Her admirable personation of *Hermione*, at a private performance of "Andromaque" procured her admission in 1836 as a pupil of the conservatoire; and shortly after she obtained an engagement at the Gymnase, where on April 24, 1837, she made her public debut under the name of Rachel, in a vaudeville. Whether the part was not adapted to her, or she had not yet acquired confidence in her own powers, the performance attracted little attention, and for upwards of a year she did not again appear prominently before the public.

In the meantime she studied assiduously under Samson, an actor and author of great experience, and on September 7, 1838, startled the Parisian public by a personation of *Camille* in "Les Horaces" at the Theatre Francais, so full of originality and tragic intensity as almost to obliterate the traditions of former actresses in the same part. At her third appearance the receipts rose from about 300 francs on the first night, to 2,040, a fabulous sum for a performance of a classical drama; and thenceforth she stood alone on the French stage, confessedly the first actress of the day, and never probably rivaled in her peculiar walk of tragedy. The long neglected plays of Corneille, Racine and Voltaire, were speedily revived for her, and she appeared with peculiar success in the leading characters. "In personating these characters she paid little regard to the cherished traditions of the stage, and the actors performing with her were frequently confused and even startled by tones and gestures so different from those established by custom as to appear to them wholly foreign to the play. The studied declamation of the old school was exchanged for an utterance at once natural and impressive, and the expression of her face, her gesture or attitude, scarcely less eloquent than her voice, conveyed a fullness and force of meaning which made each part a new creation in her hands. She excelled in the delineation of the fiercer passions, but jealousy and hatred were so subtly interpreted, that the mind was even less affected by what she expressed than by what she left to the imagination."

No actress owes more to training than Kate Bateman. Her severe discipline began, as I have shown, in earliest childhood, at the hands of a father whose skill in this regard is second to that of no man I ever met. But even when Miss Bateman attained to more mature powers, she never considered herself fully competent to play even the simplest part that fell to her lot without severe study and practice.

An actress who played with her in Boston during the engagement in which she produced "Leah" for the first time on any stage—(a character in which she has since obtained world-wide celebrity)—told me that she practised the one single feature of rushing on the stage pursued by the town rabble, during two long hours every day regularly for a week, before she trusted herself to do it before the public on the first night. The consequence was that the effect was magnificent—the persecuted and lovely Jewess flying with swift feet before the vile rabble of a bigoted German town, hooting at her, stoning her—she as a climax turning and defying them—that one effect was enough to carry the weight of the entire play and make it a success.

Julia Dean, who obtained great celebrity, especially in the Western and Southern States, is another actress who was severely drilled by her father. She found it difficult to overcome a certain listlessness which was of course a great drawback to the truthful character of certain passionate scenes.

On one occasion, while she was playing *Julia* in "The Hunchback," her father, annoyed at her listless manner, advanced close to the edge of the scene, and cried out to her in a hoarse whisper, "Fire, Julia, fire!"

The poor girl, taking him at his literal meaning, gave an agitated shriek, and, to the blank amazement of the audience exclaimed, "Where, father? where?"

Mrs. Mowatt relates that for months before she made her *debut*, she took fencing lessons, to gain firmness of position and freedom of limb; used dumb-bells to overcome the constitutional weakness of her arms and chest; exercised her voice during four hours every day, to increase its power; wore a voluminous train for as many hours daily, to learn the graceful management of queenly or classic robes; and neglected no means that could fit her to realize her beau ideal of Campbell's lines:—

> "But by the mighty actor brought,
> Illusion's perfect triumphs come;
> Verse ceases to be airy thought,
> And sculpture to be dumb."

Betterton, who was perhaps the greatest actor the English stage ever possessed, with the sole exception of Garrick, furnishes one of the most extraordinary examples of the value of training that the world has ever known. Almost incredible accounts remain to us of the effects produced by his performance. The magnetic influence of tone and expression seemed to mesmerise an audience, and make them the followers of his slightest intonation. Almost without speaking he could let them into the workings of his mind, and anticipate his next motion, as if it arose from their own volition. And yet, cheer up, my dumpy friend with the passionate will to tread the boards! If you have only the tremendous energy which likes to surmount difficulties rather than glide along without an obstacle, never mind your inelegant figure and utterly ungracious face—your scrambling walk and clod-hopping calves. If you feel the divine fury in your heart, and know it to be no exhalation from the stagnant marshes of your self-conceit, but the genuine fire that warmed the stuttering Demosthenes till he became an orator, and the skeleton Luxemburg till he rivaled the Cæsars and Alexanders of ancient story, be not afraid of external deficiencies. We don't see them when our eyes are filled with tears. We don't believe in them when the pulse is stopped in terror and surprise. Read the following description of Betterton, and take courage. It is quoted from a pamphlet by Anthony Aston, called "A Brief Supplement to Colley Cibber, Esquire, his Lives of the Famous Actors and Actresses." "Mr. Betterton, although a superlative good actor, labored under an ill figure, being clumsily made, having a great head, short thick neck, stooped in the shoulders, and had fat short arms, which he rarely lifted higher than his stomach. His left hand frequently lodged in his breast, between his coat and waistcoat, while with his right he prepared his speech. His actions were few but just. He had little eyes, and a broad face, a little pockpitten, a corpulent body, and thick legs, with large feet. He was better to meet than to follow, for his aspect was serious, venerable and majestic—in his latter time a little paralytic. His voice was low and grumbling; yet he could time it by an artful climax, which enforced universal attention even from the fops and orange-girls. He was incapable of dancing, even in a country-dance, as was Mrs. Barry, but their good qualities were more than equal to their deficencies."

Surely this is the picture of a chawbacon, qualifying, by a long course of awkward stolidity of look and attitude, to grin successfully through a horse collar at a fair! Yet this quintessence of the sublime and beautiful threw the brazen Duchess of Cleveland into hysterics, and moved the talkative Nell Gwynne to silence. Of him also Addison wrote a criticism distinguished by his usual refinement:

"Such an actor as Mr. Betterton ought to be recorded with the same respect as Roscius among the Romans. I have hardly a notion that any performer of antiquity could surpass the action of Mr. Betterton in any of the occasions in which he has appeared upon our stage. The wonderful agony which he appeared in when he examined the circumstance of the handkerchief in the part of Othello, the mixture of love that intruded upon his mind upon the innocent answers Desdemona makes, betrayed in his gesture such a variety and vicissitude of passions as would admonish a man to be afraid of his own heart, and perfectly convince him that it is to stab it to admit that worst of daggers—jealousy. Whoever reads in his closet this admirable scene will find that he cannot (except he has as warm an imagination as Shakspeare himself) find any but dry, incoherent, and broken sentences. But a reader that has seen Betterton act it, observes there could not be a word added—that longer speeches had been unnatural, nay impossible, in Othello's circumstances. This is such a triumph over difficulties, that we feel almost persuaded that the deficiencies themselves contributed to the success."

CHAPTER V.

The Memory of Actors.—How the Memory Strengthens by Practice.—How a Distinguished Actor Committed a Whole Play to Memory, by Simply Listening to it Once as Played on the Stage.—Marvelous Feats of Memory.—"Winging" a Part.—Modes of Memorizing.—Learning a Whole Newspaper by Heart.—Treacherous Memories.—Instances of Parts being taken at Short Notice.

By dint of practice, the memory of actors becomes remarkable for its quickness.

Not to have "a good study," as it is technically called, would be an almost fatal drawback to the success of a histrionic aspirant, and such cases are rare.

Even a poor memory becomes wonderfully improved by the practice of memorizing stage parts, while the exploits of some actors whose memories must have been naturally good, and which have been strengthened by practice, are almost beyond the reach of credibility.

One actor, I remember, not a very long time ago, while in London, saw a play presented at one of the theatres; and returning to his room sat down, and *aided by memory alone*, wrote it all down, word for word, from beginning to end, three lengthy and complicated acts, with long and diversified parts for as many as a dozen persons, running through the piece.

His copy was brought to New York and played. So completely identical was it with the author's manuscript, that it was of course supposed that he had obtained a written copy from some person who was not authorized to sell it. When he took oath that he had written it out from memory, many uninitiated people were inclined to doubt the statement; but any actor or actress could easily testify to its entire credibility.

The practice of "winging a part" is one so common among actors as to excite no surprise whatever among those who have been bred to the stage.

This consists in going on the stage to play a part without having studied it at all. The actor carries the part in his pocket, and when he vanishes from the sight of the audience, pulls it out and falls to reading the words, standing in the "wings" to do so. When his cue is called, he pockets the part again, goes on, and speaks it as well as he is capable of doing.

Of course, under these circumstances he is not expected to speak the part correctly. It is one of the shifts of necessity which sometimes arise in theatres, and an actor gets over it as well as he can,—speaks the words as far as he remembers them, and substitutes words of his own when he don't remember,—any way to get through the part, and enable the other actors to go on properly with theirs.

An old writer, in a quaint work, now obsolete, gives some interesting particulars relating to this subject. He says: "In provincial theatres, instances of memory occur nightly that are little short of marvelous. Mr. Munroe, now of the Haymarket Theatre, has on several occasions studied twelve to fourteen lengths from rehearsal until night; and I remember his playing *Colonel Hardy* quite perfect, having received notice of it at four o'clock, and going to the theatre at half-past six—the part is at least five hundred lines. I have known others study a hundred lines per hour, for five or six hours in succession, but these are extraordinary instances. Most actors find that writing out a part greatly facilitates the acquisition of it. Slow writers impress the words more on their memory than rapid ones; and it is said that you study more perfectly from an ill-written copy than a good manuscript, as the pains taken to ascertain the sentences impress them indelibly on the memory. This is carrying matters perhaps a little too far. Cathcart (late of the Coburg,) never wrote out a part, or kept a book; once studied, he never forgets a line. Munroe never wrote out a line in his life, and will repeat parts at one reading that he has performed a dozen years before. Mr. Bartley, of Covent Garden, posesses a wonderful memory, and advocates repeating the part aloud, as the best means of study. Knight always learned the entire scene in which he was engaged, and not the words of his part alone. My readers are familiar with the story of Lyon, a country actor, learning the contents of a newspaper by heart in one night. The thing seems incredible; but it will be remembered that when this feat was performed, newspapers did not contain one-third of the matter they do at present, and their contents were not half so miscellaneous. A member of the present Covent Garden Company, while sojourning at Greenwich, a few years back, undertook to get by heart a copy of the *Times* newspaper; in the course of that week he had also to study seven parts for the theatre, yet he completed his task, and won his wager, delivering the whole of the journal, from the title and date to the end. This was averaged at six thousand lines; but the wonder consists more in the perplexing nature of the thing studied than the quantity."

Dr. Abercrombie mentions an instance of treacherous memory, which was communicated to him by an able and intelligent friend, who heard it from the lips of the individual to whom it relates. A distinguished theatrical performer, in consequence of the illness of another actor, had occasion to prepare himself, on very short notice, for a part which was entirely new to him, and the part was long and rather difficult. He acquired it in a very short time, and went through it with perfect accuracy, but immediately after the peformance, forgot every word of it.

Characters which he has acquired in a more deliberate manner he never forgets, but can perform them without a moment's preparation; but in the character now mentioned there was the further and very singular fact that, though he has repeatedly performed it since then, he has been obliged each time to prepare it anew, and has never acquired in regard to it that facility which is familiar to him in other instances. When questioned respecting the mental process which he employed the first time he performed this part, he says that he lost sight entirely of the audience, and seemed to have nothing before him but the pages of the book from which he had learned it; and that if anything had occurred to interrupt this illusion, he should have stopped instantly.

There are great numbers of interesting stories afloat concerning feats of memory of actors, in taking parts at short notice, and performing them. A year or two since, it is said, Mr. J. W. Wallack, Jr., went on at a theatre in Washington entirely perfect in the part of *Brierly*, in the "Ticket-of-Leave Man," having acquired the words in thirty minutes. It is related that Mr. Edwin Booth once, when a boy, got through *Richard III*, in the illness of his father, without having studied it.

One evening, when my father was playing in a Canadian city, several years ago, he was suddenly called upon to take the powerful part of *Black Ralph*. The performer who was expected to enact this part was taken ill at six o'clock in the evening, and *some* one must play his part, or the performance could not go on. *Black Ralph* is a very long tragic part, and my father was the "funny actor" of the company; yet, in spite of this fact, he agreed to take it and do his best with it.

It was six o'clock when the part was placed in his hands. At half-past-seven o'clock the curtain rang up. In this short interval my father memorized the part from beginning to end, besides changing his dress, and making up his laughter-provoking and genial face into the aspect of fierce and brutal villainy.

He went on the stage, and proceeded for some time with perfect ease, while a gentleman who sat in the audience followed him, word by word, by means of a printed copy of the play, which he held in his hand.

Suddenly father caught sight of this gentleman with the play-book. He stopped short, stammered, and was barely able to proceed.

As soon as he got behind the scenes, he sent word round to the gentleman in the audience, requesting him to put the book out of sight, for it so confused and annoyed him that he could not go on with his part.

The gentleman very obligingly did as he was desired, and my father played the part to the end without making a single mistake. To this the prompter testified,—he having, of course, followed the part through, word by word.

Few people realize what little things can throw an actor off his guard at times, and make him forget his part, or so stumble through it as to make it a hopeless mess. The rustling of a newspaper, the crying of a baby, the getting up and going out of a squeak-booted man,—these and other such trifles have at times had the effect of disconcerting the performer completely.

CHAPTER VI.

Erroneous Ideas of the Gayety and Ease of Life Behind the Scenes.—An Actor's Daily Duties.—Studying Parts, attending Rehearsals, and Performing at Night.—The Mental Labor.—The Physical Labor.—The Mockery of Stage Glitter.—False Jewels and Flaring Gaslight.—How Actors Go Astray.—The Stern Rules which Govern Life Behind the Scenes.—Waiting for the Cue.—A Curious Incident in the Life of a Celebrated Actress.—Asleep on the Stage.

I have met a great many people who had a fixed idea that theatrical life was an idle life; one in which there was positively nothing to do but to carouse away the time in frivolous nonsense, in chatting and merrymaking, if not in actual debauchery!

Nothing can be farther from the truth.

Recreation is the incident in the life of an actor or an actress; work—hard work—is the rule.

"Work! an actor work?" I hear you say, as I have heard many say.

Ay, and hard work. Read what the *American Cyclopedia* says on this point:

"The profession of the stage is perhaps the *most laborious* of all crafts, requiring an almost unceasing mental and physical effort."

Both mental and physical, you observe. The lawyer works hard with his brain, so does the editor, the bank-clerk, the book-keeper; but all of these are nearly free from physical labor.

On the other hand, the carpenter, the mason, the hod-carrier, earn their bread by sweating brow and fatigued limbs; but every one knows that this is the heaviest part of a mechanic's toil. There is little or no brain-work to torture him.

"Well, if an actor works, what in the name of goodness does he work at?"

"The duties of an actor comprise a study of new parts, and recovery of old ones, occupying, on an average, from two to *four* hours a day; an attendance at rehearsal in the morning, occupying, on an average, *two* hours a day; and a performance each evening, occupying in winter *four*, and in summer about *three* hours."

This, you perceive, gives an average of six hours' daily labor, and four hours' evening labor for the actor, the year round. But even this conveys little idea of the specially fatiguing character of his work.

If any of my readers would like to test it somewhat, in the privacy of their own homes, let them draw down a volume of Shakspeare, and try to commit to memory in a hurry any one of his important male or female characters, —*Richard the Third*, or *Queen Catharine*, *Othello*, *Lady Macbeth*, *Juliet*, or *Hamlet*.

Every word must be exact, remember; the interpolation or dropping out of a single syllable is enough to lay an actor open to the charge of inexcusable ignorance, or impertinent singularity.

This will give you an idea of an actor's daily mental labor; for, except in the larger cities, where plays frequently have long "runs," (that is, are repeated night after night for weeks, or even months,) it is the rule in theatres for the play to be changed every night, and consequently for every actor or actress to study each night a new part—long or short, as the case may be.

So much for the mental labor of the actor. Now for the physical.

This includes *standing up* the most of the time he is in the theatre. On the stage, of course, he must never sit down, except when it is so indicated in the play. Fancy

Hamlet sitting down comfortably while talking to the ghost of his father; or *Macbeth* inquiring—

> "Is this a dagger that I see before me,
> The handle towards my hand?"

from amidst the soft cushions of a parlor sofa!

A great many male tragic parts require the actor to fence, and that this is hard work for a slender man (or a stout one either, for that matter,) any one will testify who has seen Edwin Booth in *Hamlet*, or *Romeo*, or *Richard the Third*, or Forrest in the *Gladiator* or *Jack Cade*.

The frequent changes of dress made while the actor is off the stage, and many perhaps suppose him to be resting, also tend to increase his physical fatigue. The rushing up and down of delineated fury, the stamping of feet, the loud and hurried speaking,—all this is what goes to make up the physical fatigue of the actor's life.

It is strictly forbidden to place chairs in the "wings," as the space at the side of the theatre, between the scenery, is called. Obliged thus to be standing up waiting for their "cue," it is no uncommon thing to hear the poor players moaning with sad lamentations of weariness.

I have seen tears in the eyes of actresses, wrung from them entirely by physical fatigue.

If human machinery always worked well, there would be less cause for this standing about the wings; for it is the prompter's duty to prepare notes for the call-boy, with which to notify the players during the evening, a few minutes previous to the time they are wanted; and it is the call-boy's duty to call out these written notes at the door of the green-room at stated intervals; thus enabling the players, who leave the green-room directly they are "called," to arrive at the wing in good season for their cue to go on the stage, without unnecessary fatigue of waiting.

But between prompter and call-boy this often goes wrong, and the player not unfrequently has the mortification of being late on the stage; a fact which is perfectly clear, and always annoying, to an audience.

There is little use of quarreling about this; the call-boy (generally an impertinent little imp) will always be ready to beat you down that he *did* call you, and while you are calmly replying that "if you had been called you should certainly have come on," the stage-manager quietly marks you down for a fine for having kept the stage waiting. So the safest plan is to stand around the wings, waiting through everybody's scenes, until your own cue comes.

The rules governing the conduct of actors and actresses vary greatly, according to the theatre, and according to circumstances. The best-conducted theatres, I need hardly say, are the most strict in enforcing their rules, and preserving the discipline of the green-room and coulisses.

The following may be considered a specimen set of rules, and every well-conducted theatre in the land may be expected to have a set of a very similar character, though not perhaps precisely on this pattern. Events are continually occurring to cause changes to be made in every theatre, and as the power of changing the rules is an arbitrary one with the manager (or the stage-manager, as the case may be,) the change can be effected without holding a council of war on the subject.

GREEN-ROOM RULES.

1. Gentlemen, at the time of rehearsal or performance, are not to wear their hats in the Green Room, or talk vociferously. The Green Room is a place appropriated for the quiet and regular meeting of the company, who are to be called thence, *and thence only*, by the call boy, to attend on the Stage. The Manager is not to be applied to in that place, on any matter of business, or with any personal complaint. For a breach of any part of this article, fifty cents will be forfeited.

Schell

2. The calls for all rehearsals will be put up by the Prompter between the play and the farce, or earlier, on evenings of performance. No plea will be received that the call was not seen, in order to avoid the penalties of Article Fifth.

3. Any member of the company unable, from the effects of stimulants, to perform, or to appear at rehearsal, shall forfeit a week's salary, and be liable to be discharged.

4. For making the Stage wait, Three Dollars.

5. After due notice, all rehearsals must be attended. The Green Room clock or the Prompter's watch is to regulate time; ten minutes will be allowed, (*the first call only*) for difference of clocks; forfeit, twenty-five cents for each scene—every entrance to constitute a scene; the whole rehearsal at the same rate, or four dollars, at the option of the Manager.

6. A Performer rehearsing from a book or part, after proper time has been allowed for study, shall forfeit Five Dollars.

7. A Performer introducing his own language, or improper jests not in the author, or swearing in his part, shall forfeit Five Dollars.

8. Any person talking loud behind the scenes, to the interruption of the performance, to forfeit Five Dollars.

9. Every Performer, concerned in the first act of a play, to be in the Green Room, dressed for performance, ten minutes before the time of beginning, as expressed in the bills, or to forfeit Five Dollars. The Performers in the second act to be ready when the first finishes. In like manner with every other act. Those Performers who are not in the last two acts of the play, to be ready to begin the farce, or to forfeit Five Dollars. When a change of dress is necessary, ten minutes will be allowed.

10. Every Performer's costume to be decided on by the Manager, and a Performer who makes any alteration in dress without the consent of the Manager, or refuses to wear the costume selected, shall forfeit Three Dollars.

11. If the Prompter shall be guilty of any neglect in his office, or omit to forfeit where penalties are incurred, by non-observance of the Rules and Regulations of the Theatre, he shall forfeit, for each offense or omission, One Dollar.

12. For refusing, on a sudden change of a play or farce, to represent a character performed by the same person during the season, a week's salary shall be forfeited.

13. A Performer refusing a part allotted by the Manager, forfeits a week's salary, or may be discharged.

14. No *Prompter*, *Performer*, *or Musician* will be permitted to copy any manuscript belonging to the Theatre without permission of the Manager, under the penalty of Fifty Dollars.

15. Any Performer singing songs not advertised in the bill of the play, omitting any, or introducing them, not in the part allotted, without first having consent of the Manager, forfeits a week's salary.

16. A performer restoring what is cut out by the Manager, will forfeit Five Dollars.

17. A Performer absenting himself from the Theatre in the evenings when concerned in the business of the stage, will forfeit a week's salary, or be held liable to be discharged, at the option of the Manager.

18. Any Performer unable, from illness, to fulfil his or her duties, either at rehearsals or in the evening performances, must in every case give a written notice, certified by a Physician, within a reasonable time, to enable the Management to provide a substitute; and where a Performer's duties are unattended to from repeated illness, it will be at the option of the Management to cancel the engagement. Any neglect to furnish the written notice and certificate, as above named, will be deemed tantamount to a resignation. The Manager reserves the right of payment or stoppage of salary during the absence of the sick person.

19. No person permitted, on any account, to address the audience, but with the consent of the Manager. Any violation of this article will subject the party to a forfeiture of a week's salary, or a discharge, at the option of the Manager.

20. Any member of the company causing a disturbance in any part of the establishment, will be liable to a forfeiture of a week's salary, or to be discharged, at the option of the Management.

The rules in vogue in English theatres are very nearly the same, as may be seen from the following resume of them: "1. Every member of the company required to assist in the national anthem; also to give their services for the music of 'Macbeth,' masquerade and dirge of 'Romeo and Juliet,' music of 'Pizarro,' &c. 2. Ten minutes allowed for change of dress. 3. Ten minutes grace allowed for difference of clocks, for the first rehearsal only. 4. No performer allowed in front of the house before or after performing the same evening. 5. Any member of the company going on the stage, either at rehearsal or at night, in a state of intoxication, to forfeit one week's salary, or to receive immediate dismissal, at the option of the manager. 6. For addressing the audience without the sanction of the management, to forfeit five shillings. [In some theatres this is a guinea forfeit.] 7. For using bad language, or being guilty of violent conduct, one guinea. 8. For neglecting stage-business, as arranged by the stage-manager at rehearsal, five shillings. 9. For being absent at rehearsal—for the first scene, one shilling; for every succeeding scene, sixpence. 10. For crossing the stage during performance, five shillings. 11. For loud speaking at the wings and entrances during business, two shillings. 12. For being imperfect at night, sufficient time having been allowed for study, five shillings. 13. For refusing to play any part, such character being in accordance with the terms of engagagement, one guinea. 14. For keeping the stage waiting, two and sixpence. 15. For detaining prompt-book beyond the time arranged by the stage-manager, two shillings. 16. On benefit occasions, pieces selected to be submitted for the approval of the management, before issuing bills or announcements." In addition to these reasonable rules there are others of a more stringent and arbitrary character. One is given which must have been invented by a wag: "Rule twelve: Actors are requested not to grumble and stay, but to grumble and go." This must be regarded as a downright suspension of the constitutional privileges of petition and complaint of grievances, but was doubtless only aimed at the chronic grumblers who infest every profession.

And now no doubt the question will present itself to many minds, "Why do people leave other pursuits to rush to the stage, if there are so many hardships there?"

The answer is that most people are ignorant of these hardships. They see the glitter of an actor's life, and idly fancy that an actor's only care is to strut up and down a stage, dressed in fine clothes, decked with false jewels, and bellowing high heroics for an admiring crowd.

The consequence is that idle apprentices, dissatisfied grocers' clerks, and many other people who have not the smallest conception of the real duties of a conscientious actor, rush into the theatrical profession and swell the already large army of good-for-nothings, who bring down upon the heads of decent members such shame and obloquy.

These people, once they have been initiated in the very first steps of an actor's life, usually see very clearly that fifty times more talent, tact, perseverance, and self-denial are required to make the smallest headway as an actor than to be the most successful grocer or tape-seller that ever lived. Thereupon they become discouraged at the prospect; fancy themselves neglected geniuses; grumble at the world; hang around drinking saloons all day; go upon the stage drunk at night, ill-dressed, imperfect in their parts—the very meanest specimens of the human family extant.

Then people cry, "Ah, yes—see what actors do!"

But candid and just persons will acknowledge that it is *not* usually those who confer credit upon their profession who do this. No one ever saw Mr. Joseph Jefferson hanging around the bar of a drinking saloon; nor Lester Wallack; nor Edwin Booth.

One of the most striking illustrations of the weariness occasioned by the severe toil of a player, is furnished by Mrs. Anna Cora Mowatt. She relates that often after a protracted rehearsal in the morning, and an arduous performance at night, she returned home from the theatre wearied out in mind and body; yet she dared not rest. The character to be represented on the succeeding night still required several hours of reflection and application. Sometimes she kept herself awake by bathing her heavy eyes and throbbing temples with iced water as she committed the words to memory. Sometimes she could only battle with the angel who

'Knits up the ravelled sleeve of care,'

by rapidly pacing the room while she studied. Now and then she was fairly conquered, and fell asleep over her books. Strange to say, her health, instead of failing entirely, as was predicted, visibly improved. The deleterious effects of late hours were counteracted by constant exercise, an animating, exhilarating pursuit, and the all-potent *nepenthe* of inner peace. She gained new vigor and elasticity. With the additional burden came the added strength whereby it could be borne.

As may be readily imagined, she was often weary to exhaustion, even during the performance. On one occasion her fatigue very nearly placed her in a predicament as awkward to her as it would have been amusing to the audience. She was fulfilling a long engagement at Niblo's, New York. She was playing *Lady Teazle*, in the "School for Scandal." When *Lady Teazle*, at the announcement of Sir Peter, is concealed behind the screen in Joseph Surface's library, she is compelled to remain a quarter of an hour, or perhaps twenty minutes, in this confinement. Mrs. Mowatt was dreadfully fatigued, and glad of the opportunity for rest. There was no chair. At first she knelt for relief. Becoming tired of that position, she quietly laid herself down, and, regardless of *Lady Teazle's* ostrich plumes, made a pillow of her arm for her head. She listened to Placide's most humorous personation of *Sir Peter* for awhile; but gradually his voice grew more and more indistinct, melting into a soothing murmur, and then was heard no more. She fell into a profound sleep. When *Charles Surface* is announced, *Sir Peter* is hurried by *Joseph* into the closet. *Lady Teazle* (according to Sheridan) peeps behind the screen, and intimates to

Joseph the propriety of locking *Sir Peter* in, and proposes her own escape. At the sound of *Charles Surface's* step, she steals behind the screen again. The cue was given, but no *Lady Teazle* made her appearance. She was slumbering in happy unconsciousness that theatres were ever instituted.

Mr. Jones, the prompter, supposing that Mrs. Mowatt had forgotten her part, ran to one of the wings from which he could obtain a view behind the screen. To his mingled diversion and consternation, he beheld the lady placidly sleeping on the floor. Of course, he could not reach her.

Mrs. Mowatt continues: "I have often heard him relate the frantic manner in which he shouted, in an imploring stage whisper, 'Mrs. Mowatt, wake up! For goodness' sake, wake up! Charles Surface is just going to pull the screen down! Wake up! You'll be caught by the audience asleep! Wake up! Good gracious, *do* wake up!' I have some confused recollection of hearing the words 'wake up! wake up!' As I opened my heavy eyes, they fell upon Mr. Jones, making the most violent gesticulations, waving about his prompt book, and almost dancing in the excitement of his alarm. The hand of *Charles Surface* was already on the screen. I sprang to my feet, hardly remembering where I was, and had barely time to smooth down my train, when the screen fell. A moment sooner, and how would the slumbering *Lady Teazle*, suddenly awakened, have contrived to impress the audience with the sense of her deep contrition for her impudence! how pursuaded her husband that she had discovered her injustice to him during her pleasant nap!"

CHAPTER VII.

How Rehearsals are Conducted.—The Stage by Daylight.—Queens in Calico Dresses.—Kings in Threadbare Trowsers and Coats out at Elbows.—Ball-room Belles in India Rubber Overshoes.—Fairies in Thick Boots and Demons in Stovepipe Hats.—The World Upside down.—How to make a Crowd of Democrats Yell.—The Rehearsal a School.—Humorous Account of a Rehearsal in California.

All plays have to be carefully rehearsed by the actors before they are presented to the eagle eye of the critics and the admiring eye of the public.

These rehearsals take place, of course, in the day time. It is customary for the stage manager to make out beforehand a list of the characters, assigning the performance of each character to some member of the company; then each member is notified that he (or she) is "cast" for such or such a part in the forthcoming play of so-and-so. In badly regulated theatres this is neglected, however, and no actor knows whether he is to play in the piece until he comes to the first rehearsal.

The notice or "call" for rehearsal is hung up in a conspicuous place—generally in two places—behind the scenes, so that no one employed about the theatre shall possibly miss seeing it.

Obedient to the call, the players gather on the stage—usually about ten o'clock in the morning—for rehearsal.

With them come the scene-shifters, the musicians, and everybody who has to do with the production of the piece at night.

But where, oh! where is that which so charms us in the evening when the gas is alight? Instead of the brilliant flickering of innumerable jets of light from grand chandeliers or sparkling dome, there is a dull, drowzy, dirty daylight streaming in from nooks and corners of the theatre, through ventilators, and cobwebbed windows away up in the gallery walls,—lighting up a huge cave-like place, reeking with the odors of escaping gas, and suggestive of everything else but gayety.

Of course no one wears, at the rehearsal, the costume of the night; but all the actors come in the everyday clothes which they are accustomed to wear—and as they are not always able to dress as well as they would like—the necessities of out-door costume always ranking second with a conscientious actor, to the requirements of the stage—the effect is often most incongruous.

This is especially so on a rainy day. It seems funny to see an actor stalking about the stage in a water-proof over-coat, carrying an umbrella in one hand, and remarking, in a very unconcerned tone, "A horse! a horse! my kingdom for a horse!" Or to see a lady in a last year's bonnet and wearing a pair of overshoes, pirouette across the stage, saying as she does so, "Ah, mamma, how happy I am to-night! How beautifully the lamps are shining on this gaily attired company of fair women and brave men! It seems like fairy-land!"—while not three feet away from her, a couple of begrimed men in shirt-sleeves, and smelling of tar and things are kneeling on the floor hammering away at the gas arrangements or something about the scenery.

Or to see a bevy of girls representing fairies, trip upon the stage with thick boots clattering, while from the other side a "demon" comes on in a stovepipe hat and goes through an excited pantomime.

Or to see a middle-aged lady, in a calico dress, sitting on a shaky chair, and addressing the other actors as "My faithful servitors," and promising, as she is queen, to see them righted.

Or to behold a well-dressed person kneeling at the feet

of a seedy-looking man in a coat out at elbows, and saying, "Your majesty! I am your slave!"

A spectator sitting in the auditorium and looking on, would certainly think the world was upside down.

It is related of a well-known actor, distinguished in the profession for his particularity at rehearsals, that upon one occasion when rehearsing the play of Coriolanus, in the scene where those representing the citizens are expected to cheer loudly on some information which they are supposed to receive, the poor supes who were hired to represent the Romans did not at all satisfy the Coriolanus of the occasion. For fully half an hour did he make them yell at the top of their voices. At length, pausing for a while, he addressed them, "I want you men to seem in earnest about this. If you can't imagine yourselves Romans, why—why, confound it, consider you're all Democrats, and you've just heard the election returns, and if that don't make you yell loud enough, I don't know what will."

On another occasion it is told of an actor whose name stands among the highest in the dramatic annals of America, that observing a young actor, in an important scene apparently inattentive to the business of the situation, he stopped speaking, and addressing himself to the young man, he said: "My young friend, if you desire to progress in your profession, you should be more attentive. A rehearsal is *your school*, sir, and inattention to what's going on on the stage, while you are engaged in the scene, is wrong, sir."

A journalist who witnessed a rehearsal in a California theatre, gives the following amusing account of his sensations and observations:

You may get as perfect an idea of a play by seeing it rehearsed as you do of Shakspeare from hearing it read in Hindoostanee. The first act consists in an exhibition of great irritability and impatience by the stage manager, at the non-appearance of certain members of the troupe.

At what theatre? Oh, never mind what theatre. We will take liberties, and mix them thus:—

Stage Manager. (Calling to some one at the front entrance,) "Send those people in!"

The people are finally hunted up, one by one, and go rushing down the passage and on to the stage like human whirlwinds.

Leading Lady. (Reading) "My chains a-a-a-a rivet me um-um-um (carpenters burst out in a tremendous fit of hammering) this man."

Star. "But I implore—buz-buz-buz—*never*—um-um" (great sawing of boards somewhere).

Rehearsal reading, mind you, consists in the occasional distinct utterance of a word, sandwiched in between large quantities of a strange, monotonous sound, something between a drawl and a buz, the last two or three words of the part being brought out with an emphatic jerk.

Here Th——n rushes from the rear:

"Now my revenge."

Star. (Giving directions,) "No, you Mr. H—s—n, stand there, and then when I approach you, Mr. B—r—y, step a little to the left; then the soldiers pitch into the villagers, and the villagers into the soldiers, and I shoot you and escape up into the mountain."

Stage Manager, (who thinks differently,) "Allow me to suggest, Mr. B——s, that"—(here the hammering and sawing burst out all over the stage, and drown everything.)

This matter is finally settled. The decision of the oldest member of the troupe, the patriarch of the company, having been appealed to, is adopted. Then Mr. Mc——h is missing. The manager bawls "Mc——h!" Everybody bawls "Mc——h!" "Gimlet! Gimlet!"

This is the playful rehearsal appellation for *Hamlet.* Gimlet is at length captured, and goes rushing like a locomotive down the passage.

Stage Manager. "Now, ladies and gentlemen. All on!"

They tumble up the stage steps, and gather in groups. H—l—n fences with everybody. Miss H—w—n executes an imperfect *pas seul.*

Leading Lady. "I-a-a-a love-um-um-um—and-a-a-a another"——

Miss H—l—y, Miss M—d—e, or any other woman. "This engage-a-a-a my son's um-um-um Bank Exchange."

A—d—n raises his hands and eyes to heaven, saying, "Great father! he's drunk!"

Leading Lady. (Very energetically.) "Go not, dearest Hawes! The Gorhamites are a-a-a-um-um devour thee."

Mrs. S—n—s. "How! What!!"

Mrs. J——h. "Are those peasantry up there?" (Boy comes up to the stage and addresses the manager through his nose), "Mr. G., I can't find him anywhere."

H——y J——n. "Forasmuch as I"——(terrible hammering).

Nasal Boy. "Mr. G., I can't find him anywhere."

L—c—h. "Stop my paper!"

Manager. "Mr. L., that must be brought out very strong; thus, *Stop my paper!*"

L—c—h. (Bringing it out with an emphasis which raises the roof of the theatre,) "STOP MY PAPER!"

The leading lady here goes through the motion of fainting, and falls against the Star, who is partly unbalanced by her weight and momentum. The Star then rushes distractedly about, arranging the supernumeraries to his liking. Ed——s and B——y walk abstractedly to and fro. S—n—r dances to a lady near the wings. These impromptu dances seem to be a favorite pastime on the undressed stage.

Second Lady. "Positively a-a-a Tom Fitch um-um amusing a-aitch, a-aitch, a-aitch."

It puzzled me for a long time to find out what was meant by this repetition of a-aitch. It is simply the reading of laughter. A-aitch is where "the laugh comes in." The genuine peals of laughter are reserved for the regular performance. Actresses cannot afford to cachinnate during the tediousness and drudgery of rehearsal. Usually they feel like crying.

Stage Manager. "We must rehearse this last act over again."

Everybody, at this announcement, looks broadswords and daggers. There are some very pretty pouts from the ladies, and some deep but energetic profanity from the gentlemen.

Much more than this is said and done at rehearsal, but it is all equally tedious and monotonous. Daily do these unfortunate people go through such a performance, from ten A. M. to one or two P. M. And then they go home for a few hours, perhaps to study their parts and get up their wardrobes. I have no aspirations. Have you, Mr. Pea Green? If so, go—go on the stage, but let it be one that carries the mail and passengers.

CHAPTER VIII.

Stage Dresses.—Hair Dressers and the Like.—Exigencies of Attire.—The Art of Dressing a Part to Suit the Character and the Period.—Ristori's Attention to such Details.—Mistaking Dress for the Chief Requirement of an Actor.—Absurd Anachronisms by Ignorant or Careless Actors.—The Wardrobe Keeper.—Curious Instances of Effect in Costume.—A Living Pack of Cards.—Exaggerated Idea of Value of Stage Jewels. The Mountain Robbers.—The Stolen Crown.—My Jewel Bag in a Western Town.

All theatres of any importance have "dressers." Male dressers for the actors, and women dressers for the actresses. These help the players in change of dress, and fold up and put away their stage clothing after the piece is over. The leading players, I should say; for the poor ballet girls, who are most tired of all, are not vouchsafed the luxury of a dresser.

In French theatres a hair dresser is also furnished for the players' convenience, and a useful person he is. It is his duty to dress the heads of all the leading players in every piece each night; and to be sure that he shall dress it in the style worn at the time the play represents. Thus he must dress it fashionably if it is a modern play, or in the style of the Cavaliers, Round Heads, Greeks, or Roman, or powder it *a la* Pompadour, as the case may be. This useful person has not been adopted in American theatres, and we often see very stupid anachronisms committed on the stage by a character appearing in a style of head-dress not worn perhaps for a hundred years after the individual he is representing was dead and buried.

This matter of costuming has been in some cases carried so far as almost to reach a fine art.

In some theatres, where much attention is given to the

costumes worn, the name of the costumer is printed on the evening playbill. This causes him to be known to the public, and his services are often sought by persons who are desirous of hiring or having made costumes for masquerade balls, private theatricals or charades.

Ristori was inimitable in her careful attention to details in dress. Macaulay himself could scarely have had a better knowledge than she of the different peculiarities of the epochs in which her plays were laid. Her costumes in Marie Antoinette were copied from pictures taken from life; and her court dress in Elizabeth was one which it was asserted old Queen Bess had actually worn.

Those who saw Ristori in this play will not easily forget her wearing clumsy white cotton gloves. Kid gloves were not known in Elizabeth's time.

It is a great mistake, however, for a player to suppose that attention to dress will compensate for inattention to matters of even greater importance; and, as has been remarked, it must be extremely galling to a bad and imperfect performer to have a warm reception given him entirely on that score, as it sometimes happens, and to hear the gallery-gods shout heartily, "Brayvo the dress!" One should try to hit the happy medium in this respect, and to pay due regard to propriety of costume, without neglecting other essentials. The style and cut of a stage garment are of more consequence than the quality or nature of the material of which it is composed, and the correct dress of the period certainly enhances the beauty of the play; yet in the "School for Scandal" and other elegant comedies of the same date the gentlemen generally sport moustaches; and a "star" appears in "Guy Mannering" without previously shaving off his whiskers and imperial. But carelessness in these and other such instances is not half so censurable as the downright ignorance that is occasionly to be met with in the profession.

All sorts of anachronisms do manage to creep in, even at the best theatres, at times. In a leading London theatre one of the most celebrated actors of his day once made the blunder of wearing spectacles in a piece, the time of which was one century antecedent to their invention; Kean, as *Crichton*, played on a modern pianoforte; and pistols and guns are used in all our theatres, in many pieces, the supposed dates of which are prior to the invention of fire-arms.

At the Fifth Avenue Theatre in New York, a short time ago, Mr. James Lewis played the part of *John Hibbs* a London dry-goods drummer, in Robertson's comedy of "Dreams." The scene is of course laid in England; but at one point it was funny to see the generous-hearted *Hibbs*, take out his pocket-book, and present the suffering hero with a liberal donation of *greenbacks*, instead of notes of the Bank of England. This mistake—trifling as it seems —was amply sufficient to destroy the stage illusion for the moment; for the idea of a London cockney presenting a fellow foreigner with American greenbacks was a little too ridiculous.

The costumer or wardrobe keeper is generally a very humble individual of either sex.

It is not an unusual occurence for the wardrobe keeper to have lodgings in the theatre. These are of course furnished gratis by the manager, who gets his reward in their adding one more watchman to those specially engaged for the purpose. But I may here remark that *I* should have to be placed pretty low on fortune's ladder before I would consent to pass my days and nights sleeping or waking with the lugubrious surroundings of musty stage duds,—odds and ends of a more multifarious character than were ever found in any old curiosity shop, unceasingly about me. But tastes differ.

One of the most novel and brilliant effects I ever saw

on the stage was due to the invention of the costumer. It represented—by dresses worn by a number of young men and women—a whole *pack of cards*; with the four queens, the four kings, the jacks, all the different suits, spades, clubs, diamonds, and finally the large spade *ace*. It was very curious; the costumes being peculiarly quaint. The effect was heightened by these people dancing in such a manner as to represent shuffling the whole pack together, then suddenly breaking into groups of all one suit—clubs in one, spades in another, hearts in another, and diamonds in another.

The idea which many people entertain, that the "jewels" worn on the stage are of great value, has led to many unpleasant results for actors. It seems absurd that any one should imagine an actor's costumes and jewels to be of the fabulous value of the 'kings' and queens' who are represented as wearing them; but my father used to tell the story of an attack which was once made upon him, brought on by this delusion.

He was traveling about the country giving theatrical performances in various towns, and journeying of course by stage coach.

A band of highwaymen, seeing his large chests, his numberless trunks, boxes and baskets, conceived the idea that any body traveling with such an amount of baggage must be loaded down with wealth, and the trunks crammed full of silver ware.

So in one of the lonely mountain gorges of Pennsylvania, and just as the night was falling, five ruffians with clubs attacked the coach.

My father and mother were alone, the rest of the company having gone ahead.

The driver seemed inclined to side with the ruffians, hoping of course to share the booty; but my father had no mind that things should take this turn.

Quick as thought he drew a stage sword from its scabbard, and being an admirable fencer, attacked his assailants in earnest.

The old sword was dirty and rusty; but my father's determined air, his dexterity in the handling of what seemed to them a dangerous weapon, soon scattered the vagabonds, and prevented no doubt, robbery if not murder.

It would have been an amusing scene to witness the consternation of the robbers if they had succeeded in capturing the trunks. Instead of finding silver ware or other valuables they would have been amazed at the sight of a lot of musty wardrobe, old stage traps, some faded scenery —the whole utterly valueless except to a party of traveling actors.

Many years ago, while a theatrical company were playing at a State Fair, in a certain town in New York State, the leading actress in the company was awakened at dead of night by the sound of some one breaking into her room.

She awoke and gave the alarm, and two fellows, who confessed their felonious intentions, were captured.

They said they had seen the actress wear a sparkling crown on her head during the performance at the theatre, and believing it to be set with jewels of untold value, they resolved to steal it, and become as rich as princes by its sale.

The crown was made of bits of burnished lead and glass beads, and was worth about half a dollar!

These fellows were as stupid as a brace of robbers whose exploit was the town-talk while I was in London a few years ago.

An English lady of rank, returning from the Continent, had her trunk placed on top of a cab, got inside, and was driven home.

When she arrived there she found the trunk which contained the family jewels had been stolen.

In vain the London detectives searched every jewelry shop, and questioned every jewel merchant, not in England alone but in all Europe—the missing valuables were not to be found.

At length, one day, jewels which corresponded to the description, were found at an old clo' shop in one of the most miserable streets in London.

They were seized, and the thieves detected and brought to justice—a man and a woman. They confessed to have stolen the trunk, and said they had sold the "jewelry" for *a pound*—five dollars—to the old clothes dealer aforesaid.

When asked how they could have been so foolish as to sell nearly a hundred thousand dollars' worth of diamonds for five dollars—they opened their eyes in sorrowful wonder.

"Why, yer honor," answered the man, "we never thought for a minute as how they were *real* jewels; just thought the lady was some play actor woman, and that the whole lot wasn't worth but a few shillings."

Strange to say the old clo' man never suspected his good fortune either, but bought and offered for sale some of the most celebrated jewels in Europe, under the belief that they were "play actors' trash."

When I was fulfilling a round of theatrical engagements in the Southwest, during the war, I was compelled by "military necessity" to pack up my jewels and send them to Cincinnati.

Of course there were a number of stage trinkets in the bag, as well as some little jewelry of real value, but as it happened a fabulous idea had got afloat of the value of my little trinkets, and I was offered large sums for the carpet sack "just as it stood," after I had packed it to send it to Cincinnati.

"I'll give you ten thousand dollars for it without opening it," said one gentleman. "I want those ear-rings for my wife."

"No," I answered, "no; those things were given me in France, and I shouldn't like to part with them."

"Are the ear-rings in here?"

"Yes," I answered.

"And the bracelet?"

"Yes."

"Fifteen thousand—will you?"

"No, no," I answered; and the matter ended. I couldn't help laughing, for truly I might have made a sharp bargain if I had wished. Somebody would have been sold, and that somebody not myself.

I returned to Cincinnati after my trip to Nashville, and there found my effects awaiting me, in good order. One day, in the Burnet House, I was accosted by a pleasant-looking gentleman, who informed me that he had taken charge of the bag from Louisville to Cincinnati.

"Did not Mr. —— send it by express?" I asked.

"No. I was coming up, and he thought it best to entrust it to me."

"I am very much obliged to you," I said.

"Indeed, you have cause to be," he replied good-naturedly. "I give you my word, it's the last time I'll have on my mind the charge of fifty thousand dollars' worth of diamonds."

I thought of the story of the three black crows. How many crows was this?

CHAPTER IX.

Making up the Face.—Ristori's Skill in this Subtle Art.—Painting Age and Youth on the Same Face.—Easier to Paint Old than to Paint Young.—Tracing the Lines of Sorrow, Suffering and Despair.—Daubing with Chalk and Rouge.—A Lover's Disappointment.—How the Artist Rothermel Changed Me from a Young Woman into an Old One in Five Minutes.—Instructions in the art of Making Up.—Coloring for Indians, Negroes, etc.—Magic Effects of Actors by Removing Color while Playing a Part.—Making Up the Figure.—Old-fashioned Ideas on the Subject.—The Modern Triumphs of the Padmaker.—How Bandy Legs are Made Shapely, Thin Legs Plump, and Ugly Forms Beautiful.

To "make up the face" is one of the subtlest arts of the actor.

Who that has witnessed the acting of Ristori in *Queen Elizabeth*, but will remember how from act to act she visibly grew older and older before our eyes! Not only by voice and manner and gait was this change effected; but her face, bright and joyous at the beginning of the play, became gradually wrinkled, pale and careworn; her hair grew grayer and grayer; until, at last, as she lay on the couch representing the dying Queen, she seemed reduced to a skeleton, and livid as a corpse.

This was brought about solely by her perfect knowledge of how to make up the face.

I was behind the scenes of the French Theatre in New York one night when Ristori was playing *Elizabeth*, and when I came to look closely at her face it seemed a meaningless mass of white and black marks, with deep dashes of red under the eyes; but at one step off the effect was wonderful.

It is easier to make up the face to look old than to look young; nevertheless a careful mingling of pink for the cheek, white for the forehead, black for the eyebrows, and carmine for the lips, will go a great way toward making an old and homely woman look like a young and handsome one.

I must say, though, that I always detested the painting up one's face to befool people into thinking you pretty. When I was an actress I had a sort of artistic satisfaction in painting a face to represent age or sorrow, and in the artistic sense, of course, one was truly no worse than the other. But while the careworn lining adds expression to the features, the mere covering it with white and red I have always found to take away expression, and render the features silly and commonplace.

As the practice is very general in society now, readers of this book who do not go to the theatre can easily see the effect for themselves by walking up and down Chestnut street or Broadway of a fine day.

"She isn't all that my fancy painted her," bitterly exclaimed a rejected lover; "and, worse than that, she isn't what she paints herself."

One of the most admirable effects I ever saw of the magic change which a few skilfully drawn lines will make in a face, was made in a picture by one of Philadelphia's most distinguished painters—Rothermel.

It was in Paris, some years ago. Mr. Rothermel had received an order from a wealthy family in Philadelphia to furnish them a picture of some episode in the life of Coriolanus.

He chose the moment when the wife and mother of the warrior, leading a band of matrons, came to entreat Coriolanus to return to Rome.

Mr. Rothermel was in great want of some faces, "with mind in them," as he expressed it, to serve as models for the Roman women. He could not endure the thought of copying the namby-pamby faces of French professional models; and so his own wife and some of her lady friends lent him their faces "for this occasion only."

The wife of Coriolanus was represented by Mrs. Greenough, wife of the sculptor; the mother of Coriolanus by Mrs. Rothermel; and a distressed young lady in the left foreground by myself.

The likenesses were perfect; I would have given five hundred dollars to cut out the figure of myself, and send it to my mother in America; but of course that was not to be thought of.

On subsequent study Mr. Rothermel discovered the fact that there were no young women 'along' on this occasion; they were all matrons.

"Easily fixed," said he—like a true American, applying the word "fixed" even to art.

With a few touches of the brush he transformed my face from a perfect likeness of what it was to a perfect picture of what it *will* be when I am fifty.

The picture belongs, I think, to the Van Sickle estate, and is a triumph of art.

An old work, published in London nearly fifty years ago, contains many interesting particulars with regard to painting the face, etc., which are still further curious as showing how little difference there is between "then and now" in this matter of "making up."

"There can be little doubt that all paint is injurious to the skin, and the object should be, therefore, to neutralize its pernicious qualities as much as possible. Chinese vermilion boiled in milk, and then suffered to dry, and afterward mixed with about half the quantity of carmine, is decidedly the best color an actor can use; it is said to be too powerful for a female face, but this I am inclined to consider an error, especially as the late introduction of gas into our theaters has rendered a more powerful coloring than that formerly used decidedly necessary. Rouge is an ineffective color and seldom lies well on the face; previous to painting it is best to pass a napkin with a little pomatum on it over the part intended to receive the color, then touch the cheek with a little hair powder, which will set the color, and then lay on the vermilion and carmine. A rabbit's foot is better than anything for distributing the paint equally. Performers should bear in mind that it is better to have too little color than too much; but they would also do well to remember that, when heated, color will sink, and it may be well in the course of a long part, to retouch the countenance. Ladies have generally sufficient knowledge of the arts of decking the human face divine, therefore the few remarks I have yet to offer on this subject will be confined to the other sex. It is a common, though slovenly habit, to make mustaches and whiskers by means of a burnt cork; an idle, filthy mode—involving, too, the danger of transferring your lip ornaments to the cheek of a lady, if it be necessary in the scene to salute her. A camel's hair pencil and Indian ink will, with very little trouble, give a more correct imitation of nature; and if the brush be wet in gum water, there can be little danger of the ink running, either from the effect of heat or otherwise. What is termed lining the face, is the marking it, so as to represent the wrinkles of age; this art, for it is one, is little understood upon the English Stage—our Parisian neighbors are adepts. It is impossible to give instructions for it upon paper; the best instrument to perform it with, is a piece of round wire, like a black hair-pin; this held in the smoke of a candle, communicates a finer and more distinct line than can be made by dipping it in Indian ink. * * * *Othello* used not in former days to sport a colored countenance, but wore the same sables as *Mungo* in "The Padlock;" but this, as being destructive of the effect of the face, and preventing the possibility of the

6

expression being observable, has become an obsolete custom. A tawny tinge is now the color used for the gallant Moor, for *Bajazet* and *Zauga;* Spanish brown is the best preparation for this purpose. Previous to using it, the whole face should be rubbed with pomatum, or the color will not adhere. Some persons mix the color with carmine, and, wetting it, apply it to the face, but I never saw this plan answer. *Sade*, *Bulcazin*, *Muley*, *Rolla*, &c., should be colored with Spanish brown, though it is common, especially for comic performers, to use only an extraordinary quantity of vermilion or carmine spread over the whole of the face. To produce the black necessary for the negro face of *Hassan*, *Wouski*, *Mungo*, or *Sambo*, the performer should cover the face and neck with a thin coat of pomatum, or, what is better though more disagreeable, of lard; then burn a cork to powder, and apply it with a hare's foot, or cloth, the hands wet with beer, which will fix the coloring matter. Wearing black gloves is unnatural, for the color is too intense to represent the skin, and negroes invariably cover themselves with light clothing. Arms of black silk, often worn in *Hassan*, have a very bad effect; armings dyed with a strong infusion of Spanish annatto look much more natural; for a negro's arms, it will be observed, are generally lighter than his countenance. A strong coloring of carmine should be laid upon the face after the black, as otherwise the expression of countenance and eye will be destroyed. All persons have witnessed the great effect produced by suddenly removing the color in any scene of fright or surprise; to do this cleverly requires some expertness. In the scene in the 'Iron Chest,' where *Wilford* kneels to inspect the chest, it is easily done by means of a greased napkin, whilst his face is averted from the audience. In *Richard the Third*, a celebrated tragedian of the present day always removes his color in the dreaming scene, and applies pomatum to his countenance, and then drops water upon his forehead; and this he effects while tossing and tumbling in the assumed throes of mental agony. In *Carlos* ('Isabella'), last scene, where, at the sudden discovery of his guilt, he might naturally be supposed to turn pale, I have seen performers try strange expedients; some, having removed the color previous to coming on, have played the scene till the point of discovery, with their backs to the audience, an offensive mode, which has also the disadvantage of preparing the auditors for the trick. The thing can be generally sufficiently executed by oiling the inside of your glove, and burying your face in your hands at the moment of accusation; color adheres to oil immediately, and without the appearance of error the color will be removed. It would be tedious to enumerate the many tricks of this nature that may be practised. Legitimate acting wants little aid of this sort, and nothing but experience can point out when any *ruse de theatre* can be properly attempted. For such situations as those of *Colonel Regolio* ('Broken Sword'), at the table, with the lights burning before him, it is usual to whiten the face, and blacken beneath the eyes, which gives them a hollow and sunken appearance. In *Macbeth's* return with the daggers, the same expedient is resorted to. In 'Bertram' and 'De Montford,' the torches of the monks are sometimes impregnated with a chemical preparation, which throws a ghastly hue upon the hero's countenance when it is held before them, a hue resembling that communicated to the face by the mixture displayed in the windows of druggists."

In the same old work is an amusing paragraph which shows in the strongest light the progress of this enlightened age in the lofty "fine art" of padding. Says the author:

"I have known many actors who look very well on the

stage, except when compelled to exhibit their legs, either in silk stockings or pantaloons. Now, where it happens the leg is what is termed bandy or buck-shinned, no method can be devised for totally concealing the defect, although I have heard that there are means of decreasing even this eyesore; but it requires an ingenuity beyond any that has ever fallen under my observation. When the leg is straight and thin, the most approved method is to use the feet and legs of as many pair of old silk stockings as may produce the required increase of size, carefully leaving a little less on each succeeding stocking, both at the top and bottom; and having thus made the leg perfectly shapely, lastly put on the stocking that is to face the audience, unmindful of the shabby scoundrels that it covers."

In these days of the triumph of human inventive genius, such shifts are no longer needed. In the grand march of progress, the mowing machine and the sewing machine have been invented; the Atlantic ocean has been spanned with the telegraphic cable, and—padding has come to the rescue of bandy-legged and buck-shinned mortals.

One of those high-toned and polished gentlemen who edit newspapers which defend the indecencies of the leg-business, lately broke forth in this brilliant strain: "One thing is sure," he wrote, "when a woman has bad pins, when she is either bandy or knock-kneed, a well-shaped woman on the stage, 'in ten-inch satin breeches,' as Miss Olive Logan says, excites her most virtuous horror; but, when she happens to be one of the 'bending statues' who can enchant the world by furtive glimpses of a well-turned ankle, she not only takes pity on the world, but has a complete charity for her professional sisters behind the footlights."

This would be a crushing sarcasm but for the fact that it is ridiculous to suppose there are any women nowadays who are "bandy or knock-kneed."

The woman—or the man either—who cannot exhibit a shapely figure on the stage, has certainly not learned the way to the shop of the padmaker.

There are quite a number of these "professors of symmetry" in this country, but they are most numerous in Philadelphia. They advertise quite freely in the theatrical journals, and no one need be in ignorance of their whereabouts. They do not boldly advertise the unpleasant word "padding," of course—the popular term for padding is "Symmetrical Goods."

Much need not here be said with regard to the *modus operandi* of the padmaker. The science lies in weaving leggings, or "tights," as they are called in theatrical parlance, in such a way that they shall increase the thickness of the calf, the thigh, etc., add woven silk or cotton in the place where flesh is wanted, and thus conceal leanness or deformity.

Thus a tragedian with lower limbs like pipe-stems, can pull on his "tights," and stand before an admiring audience with the sturdy legs of an athlete.

No such means of concealing an undue development of fatty matter have yet been devised—and the probability is that none ever will be, in spite of the prayers of many a jolly waddler that this "too, too solid flesh would melt."

CHAPTER X.

How Salaries are Paid.—The Etiquette of Actors regarding Salaries.—Exaggerated Ideas of the Pay of Actors.—The Truth in the Matter.—Salaries of Leading Performers, Walking People, Old People, Utility People and Supernumeraries.—Why the Pay of Actors seems Larger than it Really is.—Their Expenses for Dress.—The Cost of Running a Theatre.—The Pay of Stars.—Salaries in Old Times.—An Actor who Regulated his Acting by his Salary.

"Salary-day" is an interesting point in the actor's weekly life, as may easily be imagined; and in view of the exaggerated ideas which prevail, regarding the pay of actors, it may be well to furnish some reliable information on this head.

The salaries of actors, scene-painters, stage-hands, and all the hundred employees of a theatre, are paid by the treasurer of the house, who has a large book in which every member of the company registers his or her name as a weekly receipt. The amount of salary, neatly done up in a sealed envelope, with the name inscribed outside, is then handed over to each person as he passes. These envelopes are all prepared before "salary-day" arrives; and in this manner each member of the company is ignorant of the amount of all salaries but his own. And it is a point of etiquette among these people always to remain in such ignorance.

Unless the recipient of a salary chooses to say what he is paid for his services, it would be quite possible for two or more people to dress in the same room and be cast in the same plays for ten years in the same theatre, and yet none ever know the amount of each other's salary.

"What do you get a week?" would be considered a

very rude question indeed, and one which, with all my experience, I never yet heard asked.

It is this fact which has caused so many wild rumors to fly about relative to the extent of this or that actor or actress's salary. For the most part these reports are grossly exaggerated; and though, of course, there are no absolutely fixed rates for the different players in a theatre, there is an estimate to be made by one who knows the routine thoroughly, which will be found pretty nearly accurate.

The salary of a leading actor or actress ranges from $40 to $60 a week. But I know one leading actress in New York who gets $100 a week, and two who get $75 each.

These, however, are peculiar cases; all three being actresses specially attractive for youth, beauty and talent.

"Walking gentleman" or lady will get from $20 to $35 a week; "old man" or "old woman" from $25 to $40; while other players of a lower grade of talent than these will get all the way from $25 down to $10 a week. I should say there would be no lower salary than $10 a week in a theatre for any one who appears on the stage, even for members of the ballet or "supes," though it is true that sometimes extra men are engaged from the streets for some special purpose, who receive no more than $3 or $4 a week.

I know the above figures will seem large to persons of intellect, culture and talent who work hard all day for perhaps one tenth of the sum gained, let us say, by a leading actress. But even setting aside the fact that special talent brings special reward, and that the stage has always been a fine lucrative field for woman's employment (and this fact is my chief reason for wishing to keep it as pure as possible), there are many other causes why an actress should receive a large weekly salary. The principal of these is that an actress's outlay for dress *must* be very large.

I say it must be, for if it be not she cannot keep her position.

In the "good old days" (which everybody on the stage and off seems to unite in lamenting), a black velvet dress (as often as not cotton velvet), a white satin dress (as often as not a soiled, second-hand article), and a sweet-simplicity white muslin were considered quite a sufficient basis for an actress to do what is called "lead the business" in—that is, to play *Juliet* and *Lady Macbeth*, *Julia*, in the "Hunchback," and any other standard parts which she might be called upon to play.

But *nous avons change tout cela.* A leading actress now-a-days in a large city, must lead the fashions, as well as the "business;" with every new play she must come out in a number of elegant new dresses; and I have more than once heard the remark: "Let's go to the theatre this evening to see what Mrs. —— wears."

This being the case, an actress seldom manages to save much of her salary for the proverbial rainy day which comes to all.

The dress question also affects the male players. The modern comedies now so generally played require a bewildering quantity of elegant morning suits, dress suits, overcoats, shooting-jackets, hats, gloves, canes and boots. These must all be purchased by the actor; and when they go out of fashion, must be discarded.

Stage-carpenters and scene-shifters are pretty well paid, from $10 to $50, according to their abilities. Their work is hard, and their hours of labor long. They are at the theatre at about nine in the morning, and must be there till the performance is over at night—generally not far from midnight. They are paid by the week like the actors, and also, like them, when a play is on for a run, they have quite easy times. That is, easy so far as hard labor is concerned—they must always be around the scenes—never absent.

Ballet girls get from $8 to $15 a week; the prompter, $25 to $30; the call-boy, $15; the property man's salary ranges from $15 to $30. Then there are men up in the rigging loft who attend to the flies and the curtain wheel, and various assistants, at salaries of $20 and $10. There are from two to three scene painters at a salary of from $60 to $100. The back door keeper has $10, and two women to clean the theatre every day at $6 each. The orchestra consists of the leader at $100, and from twelve to sixteen musicians, whose salaries range from $30 to $18 a week. The gas man and fireman get $6 to $25 a week; costumer or wardrobe-keeper, $20 to $40; dressers, $5 or $6; ushers, $4 to $6; doorkeepers, $12; policemen, $5; treasurer, $25 to $40.

The pay of "stars" is a very different matter. Usually these ladies and gentlemen play for a share in the receipts at the door; and when they do this, of course their pay is regulated almost wholly by their "drawing" power.

Sometimes, however, the most celebrated actors and actresses in the land have engaged themselves for a fixed salary per week or per night. In the case of very popular players this sum is sometimes almost fabulously large.

The largest salary that has ever been paid to a star in this country is that which was paid to Joseph Jefferson, at Booth's theatre, in August and September, 1869, namely, $500 per night.

Even at this price he proved an immensely profitable star, drawing an average of $1,200 every night throughout the season.

By the "sharing" system stars often reap immense profits. Any popular star who could not make $1,000 a week for his or her own share, at a metropolitan theatre, would feel very much dissatisfied.

I have myself made that sum per week while starring in the West.

A London journal says: It is curious to mark the difference in the salaries paid to dramatic performers during the last hundred years. If we look into Garrick's theatre, we find the Roscius himself at the head, with a stipend of £2 15s. 6d. per night; Barry and his wife, £3 6s. 8d.; John Palmer and his wife, £2; King, the unrivaled *Sir Peter Teazle* and *Lord Ogleby*, £1 6s. 8d.; Parsons, £1 6s. 8d.; Mrs. Pritchard, £2 6s. 8d; Mrs. Cibber, £2 10s.; Miss Pope, 13s. 4d.; and Signor Guestinelli, the principal singer, £1 13s. 4d. Succeeding the days of Garrick came a host of distinguished performers, including Lewis, Quick, Bannister, Munden, Mrs. Jordan, Miss Farren, *cum multis aliis*, not one of whom ever received "star" salaries. John Kemble, as actor and manager, was content with £55 14s. per week; George Frederick Cooke received £25; and Mrs. Jordan, in her zenith, an average of £31 10s. Drury Lane, in seasons 1812-13, boasted of an excellent company, including John Johnstone, who was retained at £15 per week, and Dowton, who received £16. Covent Garden, at the same period, numbered among its members Emery (whose highest salary during his career was £14 per week), Mathews, Fawcett, Blanchard, Liston and Simmons, and their united receipts from the treasury were less than has since been paid to one actor at a metropolitan minor theatre. Edmund Kean's first engagement at Drury Lane, in 1814, was for three years, ranging from £8 to £10 per week. This was subsequently converted into a contract at £50 per week. Eight years prior to this great change in the fortunes of Kean—in the year 1806—he was playing at the Haymarket, unnoticed and unknown, his salary at that time being £2 per week. Twenty years later, when wrung in heart and fame, physically and mentally weak, he received at the same house £50 per night. As a contrast to the sums paid during the past century, we may state that at Drury Lane, when under the management of the late Stephen Price, the nightly salary of Edmund Kean was £60, and that of Madame Vestris and Liston £25 each; whilst Farren received £35 weekly, Jones £35, James Wallack £35, and Harley £30. In 1838, Tyrone Power was receiving £96 weekly, from the Adelphi, and Farren £40 from the Olympic. It was once remarked, in reference to the enormous sums lavished upon "stars," that the President of America was not so highly paid as Ellen Tree; whilst the Premier of Great Britain had a less salary than Mr. Macready. Madame Malibran was said by the same writer to draw five times as much money as the Colonial Secretary, and Mr. Farren nearly twice as much as the representative of the Home Office.

A story is told of a little thin actor of the name of Hamilton, connected with the theatre in Crow street, Dublin, when under the management of Mr. Barry.

To this performer the chieftain one morning remarked—"Hamilton, you might have thrown a little more spirit into your part last night." "To be sure I might sir, and could," replied Hamilton; "but with my salary of forty shillings per week, do you think I ought to act with a bit more spirit or a bit better? Your Mr. Woodward there has a matter of a thousand a year for his acting. Give me half a thousand, and see how I'll act; but for a salary of two pounds a week, Mr. Barry, I cannot afford to give you my best acting, and I will not."

CHAPTER XI.

The Noble Army of "Supes."—Custom of Laughing at these People.—Rough Treatment by Managers.—A Frightened "Savage."—Utility People.—Fallen Fortunes.—Ups and Downs of Actors.—Making the Most of One's Opportunities.—Attention to Trifles.—How the Celebrated Comedian Robson made his First Hit.—"Villikins and His Dinah."—The Story of a Utility Man.—Green Ibid.—The Summons of Death.

When, in the course of theatrical events, it becomes necessary for a manager to represent upon his stage the British army or the cohorts of the late Confederacy; when a large quantity of sturdy throats are wanted, to bawl "Long live the King!" or to cry "We will! we will!" or to clamor, "Down with the tyrant!" then doth the stage-manager depute his customary instrument to go into the streets and engage a lot of supernumeraries.

The individual who has this duty to discharge is called the captain of the supernumeraries, and he knows where to find the individuals he wants. It is related of a London functionary of this sort, that he had an ingenious mode of proceeding in these circumstances. Having sought out an individual in an advanced stage of starvation, he addressed him in some such terms as the following: "Look here, my man, if you want employment I'll let you have it at five bob a week. If you like the job say so, if you don't I can find somebody else who will. Of course six is what the management offers, but I can't be bothering myself for nothing, and as I do you a favor you mustn't grumble at the per centage." Generally the man didn't make any "fuss" about it.

Whether the same custom is in vogue in this country I don't know. But it is beyond doubt that the lot of a supernumerary is far from being an enviable one.

It is the custom to laugh at these people, to cover them with contumely, to hail them (from the galleries) with the cry of "Soup! Soup!" and otherwise make their lives miserable.

This is quite unnecessary. The "supe" generally has a hard enough time of it behind the scenes. He mustn't mind being sworn at, or, if need be, shaken. If attentive and industrious, he may gradually rise to a position of authority, but in nineteen cases out of twenty the man who has begun as a "super" concludes his theatrical experience in the same capacity.

An amusing anecdote, illustrative of the terrible reality of Mr. Forrest's acting, was told me the other day by a veteran actor.

Forrest was playing the character of *Metamora* at the Holliday Street Theatre, in Baltimore, when he was in the prime of vigorous manhood. As the play developes, five or six ruffians (generally "supers") are in pursuit of his wife Nahmeokee. Just as the head villain has laid hands on her, the "chief of the Wampanoags" (Forrest) rushes in, rescues his squaw, and, leveling his musket along the line of the eyes of the six "savages," shouts, "*Which* of you has lived too long?"

The fearful earnestness with which this line was given nearly frightened one of the "supes" out of his wits—leaving no doubt in the mind of the trembling coward that he was to be dispatched on the spot. With an expression of the utmost terror, he yelled out:

"Not me! not me! the supe with a tin tomahawk!"

Mr. Forrest dropped his piece, and took occasion to embrace his wife during the convulsions of the audience.

It is customary among the careless to confound the "supes" with the "utilities." But the utility people are a step higher on the ladder. They are, in fact, actors, and though their parts are usually light, they *are* parts, and as soon as a "supe" has mounted to the dignity of "lines" he is a "supe" no longer. Though he may have nothing more to say than "Me lord, a letter for your lordship," yet is he an actor.

He shares, however, the custom of being laughed at, with the rabble just below him in dignity. "Why is it," asks a facetious writer, "that these people must always be shabby in costume and stuttering in speech? Why is it that they are always so inexcusably deficient in respect of calves? Why does the theatre keep no Taliacotus to plump out those neglected extremities? Why is a deputation of two from an army which we have just seen victoriously valiant, always sent before the curtains to tack down or take up the green carpet? or, watering-pot in hand, to moisten the stage for the feet of Mademoiselle de la Aplomb? and to let us know that she is putting the last smear of red upon her old cheeks, and the finishing touch of white lead to her lean and scraggy neck, or practising her most fascinating grin by the little dressing-room looking-glass, and will soon present herself to our enraptured gaze, in all the glory of gauze, and spangles, and pink fleshings, which are called so because they do not look at all like the flesh? How can a warrior, no matter how valiant he may be at the real game, muster courage, in the presence of his critical fellow-creatures, to address half a score of bandy-legged varlets, shivering in second-hand shirts, behind their pasteboard shields, as an embattled host? He knows that Smith and Tompkins have no bravery independent of beer; how can he howl to them understandingly as 'Men of England! or 'Men of France!' and, if the slaughter is sufficiently great and indiscriminate, what does the neutral nationality of the pit care whether victory smiles upon the meteor flag of Albion or the five-pointed oriflamme of France? There is a particular warrior in the French ranks—you may know him by the ill fit of the skin about the patella—who has been our fate during the whole season. It was he who caused the great American tragedian to swear so fearfully at the blundering way in which he murdered the fine part of the First Murderer, leaving all manner of 'rubs and botches in the work'; and who, when he should have said, 'My lord, his throat is cut, that I did for him,' actually cried, 'I cut his throat, my lord, and did for him.' We might be pleased to see this blockhead, who cannot understand that a part is a part, whether it be of two words or twenty 'lengths,' deposed from his place of confidential murderer to the Majesty of Scotland, and degraded to the ranks; but we know very well that he will to-morrow night be sent on with a letter, which, should he happen to hand it to the proper character, he will deliver with the awkwardness of a clown, and the air of an emperor, according to his muddled conception of what an imperial air should be. We do not blame the galleries. They are quite right, those Jovian critics, in sarcastically shouting, 'Supe! Supe!' whenever this miserable person makes his appearance; they are quite right in calling, 'Coat! Coat!' at the sight of a garment with which they have a sickening familarity; they are quite right in laughing at him longly and loudly, when, with his fishy eyes, he glances at them defiantly. 'Tis their only consolation. They know that they must put up with him."

It sometimes happens that an actor who aspires to very respectable business in some little strolling company—and who loves his art well enough to stay in the country, if he could get enough to eat—has sometimes been forced by his fallen fortunes to engage in a metropolitan theatre in the smallest of "utility" capacities.

A London writer tells of a poor wretch, who used to haunt Covent Garden during the opera season, and at other periods of the year discharge the heavy business in small provincial theatres, appearing as the *Doge of Venice*, the merciless landlord, or the tyrannical proprietor of an imaginary chateau. "His boots were ever in an advanced state of decay. They might have had heels once, but it is impossible to say when, and from between the soles and upper leathers their proprietor's excuse for socks generally peeped forth with much slyness. The poor man's coat, or rather jacket, was small, threadbare, and curiously pinched in at the waist, his trousers six or eight inches too long; and his hat, soiled and papery, was always pressed rather than placed with an air of sham jauntiness on one side of his head, and so as to display a jet black curl elaborately pomatumed. Whilst waiting for rehearsal he would strut to and fro on the stage, blind to the derision of the company, and perhaps in his 'mind's eye' representing *Hamlet* or the worthy *Thane of Cawdor*. He lived in a state of chronic indigence, and the last time we saw him, appeared, if possible, more dilapidated than ever. On being stopped, he grasped our hand in speechless ecstacy, and when asked if he would 'take anything,' of course did not refuse. We proceeded to a neighboring bar, and engaged him in conversation. 'How was he? What was he doing?' 'Oh, still at the Garden, though lately he had been playing the principal parts at the Theatre Royal, Blankstairs. But he had thrown up his engagement on account of the dishonorable conduct of the proprietor. Not that there had been any remissness on his own side. Oh dear, no! Engaged to play the *Demon King* in a pantomime, and a lover in a comedy on the same night; he had reached the town in the morning, attended rehearsal, and by evening was letter perfect, and brought the house down.' We inquired why, as he was always a 'star' in the country, though unsuccessful in town, he didn't adhere to provincial business: but he shook his head ominously, and endeavored to turn the conversation. He wished to inform us that through the kindness of his friends, he was to be started afresh in life with the proceeds of a benefit performance to be held in a tavern at Hoxton. 'There'll be no end of pros. there, my boy, and I shall be glad if you'll take some tickets.' We did as requested, and supposed that payment would be made at the door. In this we were mistaken. Ready money was solicited, and we deposited coin at the rate of two pence a ticket, to be presently expended in drink. Poor wretch! What could have been his idea of a new start in life? Grant that the performance took place, and that a couple of hundred visitors paid for admission—and this, by the bye, is granting almost a miracle—what a satisfactory sum is one pound thirteen and fourpence, wherewith to commence an entirely new phase of existence!"

A small or insignificant part is a thing which all vain actors unite in dreading. It is natural that a man whose chief object in playing is to cut a figure in the eyes of the public, should endeavor to make that figure as conspicuous as possible. It is related of a utility man, that one night, a certain great tragedian being engaged, the poor actor, enacting the character of a servant, had to repeat these words: "My lord, the coach is waiting." This was all he had to say; but, turning to the gallery part of the audience, he added, with stentorian voice: "And permit me further to observe, that the man who raises his hand against a woman, save in the way of kindness, is unworthy the name of an American!"

Shouts of applause followed. The poor fellow had clearly made a hit; but he paid for it the next morning by being discharged from the company.

It is a great mistake, however, to suppose that a small part cannot be made important. The fact is that *any* part can be lifted into a work of art in the hands of a true artist—while it is equally true that the best part ever written can be murdered by a man who is no artist.

Attention to trifles is one of the surest indications of the true artistic sense and appreciation—as in the case of the utility man who played a prim merchant who has very little to say—when he received a letter, instead of breaking the seal, he took forth his pocket-scissors and cut the paper round it; this was characteristic of the regular and careful habits of the man he assumed to be.

A notable instance of success in a trifling character, is furnished in the history of the English comedian Frederick Robson. When he was still almost unknown and unnoticed in London, he was engaged for a small part at the New Olympic theatre, in that city. "An old, and not a very clever farce, by one of the Brothers Mayhew, entitled 'The Wandering Minstrel,' had been revived. In this farce, Robson was cast for the part of *Jem Baggs*, an itinerant vocalist and flageolet-player, who, in tattered attire, roams about from town to town, making the air hideous with his performances. The part was a paltry one, and Robson, who had been engaged mainly at the instance of the manager's wife, a very shrewd and appreciative lady, who persisted in declaring that the ex-low-comedian of the Grecian had 'something in him,' eked it out by singing an absurd ditty called 'Vilikins and his Dinah.' The words and the air of 'Vilikins' were, if not literally as old as the hills, considerably older than the age of Queen Elizabeth. The story told in the ballad, of a father's cruelty, a daughter's anguish, a sweetheart's despair, and the ultimate suicide of both the lovers, is, albeit couched in uncouth and grotesque language, as pathetic as the tragedy of 'Romeo and Juliet'. Robson gave every stanza a nonsensical refrain of, 'Right tooral lol looral, right tooral lol lay.' At times, when his audience was convulsed with merriment, he would come to a halt, and gravely observe, 'This is not a comic song;' but London was soon unanimous that such exquisite comicality had not been heard for many a long year. 'Vilikins and his Dinah' created a *furore.* Englishmen and English women all agreed to go crazy about 'Vilikins.'—'Right tooral lol looral' was on every lip. Robson's portrait as *Jem Baggs* was in every shop-window. A newspaper began an editorial with the first line of 'Vilikins':

''It's of a liquor merchant who in London did dwell.'

A judge of assize, absolutely fined the high sheriff of a county one hundred pounds for the mingled contempt shown in neglecting to provide him with an escort of javelin-men, and introducing the irrepressible 'Right tooral lol looral' into a speech delivered at the opening of circuit. Nor was the song all that was wonderful in *Jem Baggs.* His make-up was superb. The comic genius of Robson asserted itself in an inimitable lagging gait, an unequaled snivel, a coat and pantaloons, every patch on and every rent in which were artistic, and a hat inconceivably battered, crunched, and bulged out of normal, and into preternatural shape."

An inferior actor would have "slurred" this part; but Robson was a genius, and he made the part one of the most popular low-comedy pictures ever rendered on the stage. The story contains its own lesson for utility people.

But utility people are seldom gifted with the genius of Robson, and it sometimes happens that with the very best intentions in the world, a man may fail—as was the case with Mr. Spriggs, an English utility man, whose story is told in his own words.

"Yes, sir, a General Utility, and nothing more all my life now, till I get too old. It's hard lines, too, I can tell you—not much pull got out of five-and-twenty or so a week, when you've got to find your own shoes, tights, swords and wig. Are the dresses a trouble to us? Ain't they rather? I wonder how *you'd* like it? But it's always my luck, drat it. Never comes a cutting, cold, beastly winter, but I've got to do a Roman citizen in Roman costume, fit to freeze your calves off—short sort o' thing—is it a toga? No—it ain't. It's a skirt not half so long, nor half as warm. With the wind blowing about your heels as if you was a windmill—only you ain't half so good at the price. See us utility men in our dressing-room, waiting to go on; say it's winter time and we've got a star down, Charles Kean, say, or Phelps, or some Yankee leading man for ten nights. Say it's 'Virginius' we're playing. Precious fine game for 'responsible utility man' when *he* has to go on—servant's speech—announcing the company—every cussed Roman name ending in '*us*,' p'raps, and you knowing no more how to sound 'em than a cat knows about the Greek Testament. Then p'raps you'll have a blazing midsummer night—a regular 'greaser'—when the house in front feels as hot as a brick-kiln, and you're togged up in furs and rabbit skins doing a wicked Russian nobleman or an oppressed Polish serf, and you melting all the while you're rubbing your hands and trying to look shivering at the cardboard pine trees all over snow, you know. That's been my luck, too, before now! Have I never had it worse than that? Haven't I cussed a bit when I had to study a little bit of French in such a piece as 'Belphegor, the Mountebank,' or 'The Wandering Jew?' I *never* got a good part—not likely a G. U. at a minor theatre should—unless he makes it himself—but I'm blest if I wouldn't rather study every line of 'Susan Hopley' than one of them crack-jaw bits that seem to me to have only been put in to lick us G. U.'s! If we don't know, why don't we ask somebody? Oh! yes, and let everybody laugh at you as an ignorant image not fit for the profession, and all that—them that laugh not knowing a bit better themselves besides, of course. I remember the first time I got a 'bob' a night extra, for coming on and saying, 'My lord, Sir Henry awaits your greeting in the council chamber!' and so forth—and off again. Wasn't I proud of it! Ah! but I remember the time, too—'Julius Cæsar'—years after, when we had a beast of a *Brutus*—an out-an-outer, too good for everybody—thought so much of himself that I believe, if he could, he'd have liked to have taken everybody's business in the piece away from 'em. I was the servant that comes on—you know, Act iii, scene 1, 'Julius Cæsar'—at our shop that's very responsible utility—and says fifteen lines slick off in the middle of the stage to *Brutus*. I did well enough till I got to the fifth line—and then I funked and knew it was all up with me. Yet I'd studied it well. But the twisting about licked me—all coming together. This is it:

"*Servant.*—Thus, Brutus, did my master bid me kneel;
Thus did Mark Antony bid me fall down;
And being prostrate, thus he bade me say,
Brutus is noble, wise, valiant and honest;
Cæsar was mighty, bold, royal and loving;
Say I love Brutus, and I honor him;
Say I feared Cæsar, honored him and loved him,
&c., &c.

"It was no go. I couldn't hear the prompter, and *Brutus* looked at me as sour as verjuice. I felt my head swimming—couldn't help making a fool of myself. It's my luck. This is how I mulled it:

"Brutus is noble, valiant, wise and loving,
Say—I—feared—Brutus—and—I—honored—him,
But, *but if you please, sir*, I do—honor—Cæsar.

"It was just awful! The 'gods' yelled; one of 'em hit me on the head with an onion; another shouted

'Bravo Spriggs! try back, old man!' and then I rushed off in a cold sweat, leaving *Brutus* with his arms folded, fit to eat his boots.

"Ever hear the story of Green Ibid? That's the nickname a fellow utility of mine goes by, ever since he—but I'll tell you all about it. You know the directions for dressing a piece? So and So, green court suit, silver lace, paste buckles, court sword, white bag court wig; Somebody Else, green court *ibid*—that means, 'the same,' you know—lace, buckles, sword, wig *ibid*, and so on. Well, this young chap he rushes in late—nobody in the dressing-room—all going on. Call-boy hollering away '*Mr. Montmorenci* called twice.' No go. I was first courtier, and I had got to go on in green velvet coat—and was close to the wings when I could hear poor *Montmorenci* saying to somebody, 'My gracious!—I have got no wig—only an old man's here, and direction says second courtier, green ibid—and I can't find a green ibid anywhere. What *is* a green ibid? Hasn't anybody got a green ibid? There isn't one in the house, I do believe."

"You never heard me talk so much before, did you? Well, I don't often talk. I'm so sick of everything now. Life seems to me little else than so much general utility, buttoning and unbuttoning, dressing and changing—so much, or so little, eating and drinking, going to bed and getting up again. All 'flat, stale and unprofitable,' till the exit comes—and I don't care much how soon, blest if I do! I was not always what I am now. Time was when these eyes, now dim with tears, were—no, hang it, I'm not 'on' now. My father kept a large public house in Kent, and he had a pretty barmaid. I was nineteen and she was past twenty—and we fell in love with each other. An aunt had left her £150, and I hadn't a shilling. We were engaged to be married. I had a cousin in business for himself in the borough. He agreed to take me, and I came to London, Mary stopping down with my people for a bit. I fell in with some actors in one way or another—and at last, after several amateur successes at private theatricals, I got wild, threw up my berth, and, two months afterwards, one of my actor friends got me a pound a week at the old Cobourg Theatre. Mary, in a year and a half or so, came up to London after me, and took a little tobacco shop over the water—and on my salary and the little shop we got married—and were happy enough till a little Spriggs was likely very soon to stop the way. I had got on pretty well, for me, by that time. Well, I was to have a benefit one night—not before the time, for a vagabond boy had robbed the till at home and cut his lucky—and Mary was hourly expected to be a mother. I was to play a favorite part of mine—and I'd sold a good many tickets, for I was pretty popular. When the curtain rose, the house looked healthy enough. At nine o'clock it was pretty chock full. I'd been thinking a deal about Mary all night, and somehow I couldn't get her poor dear old pale face out of my sight. The manager slaps me on the back, and says—and he wasn't too fond of that sort of thing—'Hang it, Spriggs, you *are* a doosid clever fellow, and I con-grat-ulate you, that's flat.'

"I felt as if I was first cousin to Baron Rothschild after that—and all the hands I got clapping me. I suppose I must have been deuced funny then. I've never felt so since. Well, it was about a quarter of an hour before the curtain would fall. I was standing handy to go on at the O. P. side, when I thought I heard one of the carpenter's whisper 'Poor fellow!' in such a right down earnest way that it staggered me—thinking, as I had been, about my little missis. But that passed off. When the curtain fell I was called before it, and never felt prouder in my life. As I came behind, the manager came up to me with a grave look, and taking me aside, says very feelingly,

'Spriggs, my boy, I'm afraid I've just had bad news for you. Your poor wife's just confined, and they've sent for you, as they think it will go hard with her.' With that and the 'poor fellow' I'd just heard, you might have knocked me down with a feather. How I ran home round the corner I never knew. The shop was shut, and no sooner had I put the latch key in the door, with my hand all a tremble, than one of the neighbors, a kind old soul, stepped down the stairs and pulling me by the arm into the little back parlor, where my Mary and I used to sit so happy of a night when I came home to supper after the theatre, shut the door and says, 'Mr. Spriggs, that's a dear man, you *must* bear it; poor Mrs. Spriggs is gone. She said she hoped she'd live to see you, but it wasn't to be. There, there, don't take on so, sir; she's better off now.' I went up stairs and saw the poor dear lying dead—she and her baby. That's all—that's all—all, all, my life! I left the Cobourg. That's years ago. Some of 'em that don't know me call me 'Dismal Tommy.' But they don't know what first spoilt 'a rising low comedian,' and made him a G. U. Never mind. It's all gone away now."

CHAPTER XII.

"Sticks" Behind the Scenes. — Bad Acting. — Murdering Parts.—The Woman who went Insane in a Theatre.—A "Scholarly" Fool Plays *Paris.*—A "Gentlemanly" Style of Dying on the Stage.—The Man who Died into the Orchestra.—A Lady's Hand throws an Actor into a Perspiration of Bewilderment.—"*What will I do with It?*"—Lack of Noble Incentives to the Stage Life.—Mountebanks *vs.* Artists.

It is not too much to say, as regards the "common run" of actors and actresses, that not one in ten of those who adopt the stage as a profession, have any real conception of the artistic requirements of an actor.

They are not actuated by those high aspirations which lead the artist to seek to embody his conceptions in outward form—whether by painting, sculpture or dramatism.

They are not *artists*, though every one of them claims the name; they belong to the order of "stage struck barbers."

The "sticks" of the stage are both masculine and feminine—mostly young people—who have no idea of character, but whose vanity is great enough to take the place of everything else.

If it were a penal offense to "murder" a part, what a tumbling off of heads there would be—and what a "weeding out" the stage would undergo!

A woman in Saginaw, Michigan, was some months ago taken insane while witnessing a play, and carried out of the theatre to a lunatic asylum. A wag suggested that the reason she went mad was because the acting was so bad.

Neither the possession of a fine voice, an exquisite elocution, a captivating fancy, a commanding person, classical taste and education, a handsome face, nor all combined, are sufficient to make an actress of the first rank.

There must be the power of individualization. An actress who is a true artiste sinks the private woman in the part she plays. She *is Lady Macbeth*, walking at night beneath the shadow of a guilty conscience; she is *Meg Merrilles*, the weird creation of Sir Walter Scott, masculine, superstitious, hideous and gaunt; she is the *Duchess of Malfi*, queenly, lovely, accepting death with mingled horror and exultation.

Your ordinary representatives of these characters will walk through the greater part of the play in their own petty little individuality, and perhaps burst out upon you in a passion torn to tatters in the more striking passages. Not so a great actress. She assumes the part in its minutest details, and never forgets to *act*, even in situations when ordinary actors would suppose there was nothing to be done. The very fingers of her hands express rage, terror, despair or delight.

And from such a player as this, one can follow a long line of gradations in quality, step by step down the ladder of excellence, and at the bottom of it find the dry, hard, soulless "stick," with the action of a wooden image.

Mrs. Mowatt tells the story of a "scholarly" stick who was on one occasion entrusted with the part of *Paris*, in "Romeo and Juliet." "He delivered the language with scholarly precision, and might have passed for an actor until he came to the fighting scene with *Romeo*. *Romeo* disarmed him with a facility which did great credit to the good nature of *Paris*, for whom life had, of course, lost its charms with *Juliet*. It then became the duty of *Paris*, who is mortally wounded, *to die*. The *Paris* on this occasion took his death blow very kindly. His dying preparations were made with praiseworthy deliberation. First he looked over one shoulder, and then over the other, to find a soft place where he might fall—it was evidently his intention to yield up his existence as comfortably as possible. Having satisfied himself in the selection of an advantageous spot, he dropped down gently, breaking his descent in a manner not altogether describable. As he softly laid himself back, he informed *Romeo* of the calamity that had befallen him by ejaculating—

"O, I am slain!

The audience hissed their rebellion at such an easy death.

"If thou art merciful,

continued *Paris*; the audience hissed more loudly still, as though calling upon *Romeo* to show no mercy to a man who died so luxuriously.

"Open the tomb, and—

faltered *Paris*—but what disposition he preferred to be made of the mortal mould upon which he had bestowed such care, no *Romeo* could have heard; for the redoubled hisses of the audience drowned all other sounds, and admonished *Paris* to precipitate his departure to the other world. The next day, the young aspirant for dramatic distinction was summoned by the manager, and asked what he meant by dying in such a manner on the night previous. 'Why, I thought that I did the thing in the most gentlemanly style,' replied the discomfited Thespian. 'How came you to look behind you, sir, before you fell?' angrily inquired the manager. 'Surely you wouldn't have had me drop down without looking to see what I was going to strike against?' 'Do you suppose a man, when he is killed in reality, looks behind him for a convenient spot before he falls, sir?' 'But I wasn't killed in reality, and I was afraid of dislocating my shoulder!' pleaded *Paris*. 'Afraid of dislocating your shoulder! If you are afraid of breaking your leg, or your neck either, when you are acting,' said the stern manager, 'you're not fit for this profession. Your instinct of self-preservation is too large for an actor's economy. You're dismissed, sir; there's no employment here for persons of your cautious temperament.'"

This young man might have taken a lesson or two in recklessness of consequences, from a Thespian whom Sol Smith used to tell of. This gentleman played the hero's part on the stage, and led the orchestra between the acts besides, playing the first violin. On one occasion he accomplished the brilliant feat of dying into the orchestra. Having fallen, in his character of the murdered hero, dead upon the stage, he quietly rolled over into the orchestra, took up his fiddle and played "solemn music" while the curtain slowly fell. The effect is said to have been very moving—to the risibles.

One night during my starring tour in the West, we were playing "Romeo and Juliet," and the greenest goose I ever saw was cast for *Paris.*

At rehearsal I had fully instructed *Paris* to take my hand at a given "cue," for the purpose of giving proper and indeed necessary coloring to *Romeo's* lines:

> "'Cousin Benvolio, dost thou mark that lady,
> *Which doth enrich the hand of yonder gentleman?*'
> 'I do.'
> 'Oh, she doth teach the torches to burn bright!
> Her beauty hangs upon the cheek of night
> Like a rich jewel in an Ethiop's ear.'

I said that I had fully instructed my *Paris* to take my hand in a tender manner at the proper moment, and he swore on his honor as a gentleman that he would not forget it.

Imagine my dismay, then, at night when I found my "County," my "man of wax," my "flower, a very flower," smilingly oblivious of all instructions and ignoring "father, mother, *Tybalt*, *Romeo*, *Juliet*, and all," and my hand into the bargain. Knowing that *Romeo* was just on the point of speaking his lines, I could stand it no longer, but whispered to *Paris*,

"Take my hand."

"What say?" he retorted, looking as if the occasion were one of the most commonplace.

"Take my hand," I repeated, perhaps a little testily.

He looked at me in what I suppose he considered a very arch manner, and then began to smile knowingly. He had evidently forgotten every earthly thing I had told him in the morning.

But *Romeo* began:

"Cousin Benvolio, dost thou———"

In an agony of despair I leaned over, and stage-whispering, but determinedly, I said: "Take my hand."

He seized it frantically, and then, looking quite affrighted, answered:

"*What will I do with it?*"

Everybody on the stage heard it, and there was a suppressed laugh, which was indulged in fully at the fall of the curtain. I could not help joining in the laugh myself, and have often wondered, but never learned, what in the world he supposed I wanted him to do with it.

Now, why do such men, who have not wit enough for literary pursuits, intelligence enough for mereantile avocations, education enough for professorships, nor brains enough for anything, espouse a profession which requires all these qualifications and personal advantages into the bargain?

Alas, I fear the question is unanswerable!

Public sentiment is such—the common creed of "respectability" is such—that usually, with men and women of genius, and culture, and pure love of dramatic art, it is a very rash step to "go upon the stage."

This fact affords the real occasion of such a woful lack of high merit on the stage.

Look over the list of our best actors and actresses, and you find that most of them were the children of actors and actresses—bred to the stage from birth—and who, therefore, had no gauntlet of horrified relatives to run in adopting that profession.

This state of public sentiment is what renders clowns, and sticks, and loafers, tolerable in a profession whose members *should* take rank with painters and sculptors. That they should, is proved by the fact that the names of such artist's as Rachel, the elder Kean, Booth, Garrick, Siddons, Macklin, Kemble, and many others that might be named, glow as proudly on the historic page as those of Raphael, Rubens, Titian, Vandyke, and the like.

Tom, Dick and Harry have no more right to be classed among dramatic artists, than the veriest daubs and cobblers have in the ranks of painting and sculpture.

There are hundreds of mouthing, grimacing dunces, "periwig-pated fellows," who call themselves actors, who are entitled to no better name than that of mountebanks.

CHAPTER XIII.

The Property Man and his Curious Duties.—His Singular Surroundings. The Abode of a Lunatic.—An Actress Drinks a Bottle of Ink by Mistake.—Amusing Inventory of "Properties."—Quaint Picture of the Property Man and his Powers.

The "property man" of a theatre is a person who occupies a middle ground between the carpenter and the costumer.

It is he who makes and furnishes those numberless little things used by the players in the course of a performance, such as fairy wands, rings, sceptres and crowns, purses, pocket-books, rings, walking-sticks, garlands of flowers, bank notes, handcuffs for felons, packages of letters, gilt inkstands, goblets, pasteboard hams, chickens and rounds of beef.

A visit to the room where this individual holds state reveals a glimpse of what the imagination might easily convert into the den of a lunatic—so diverse are the objects collected there, so closely are they cramped on shelves, so seemingly without order in their arrangement.

If a player has occasion to use a purse, or a roll of bills, or any other "property," in the course of a play, it is the duty of the prompter to write that fact out on a slip of paper, give it to the call-boy, who every evening proceeds to the property man, gets the article, and then hands it to the player.

But between prompter and call-boy this is often neglected, in which case the player must go in person and get it of the property man; for, if it were Ristori herself, no property man is obliged to carry a "property" to her. He might do so out of courtesy, however.

In the "Autobiography of an Actress" this amusing incident is related: "One evening, the property man—so the individual who has the charge of potions, amulets, caskets of jewels, purses filled with any quantity of golden coin, and other theatrical treasures, designated as stage properties, is styled—forgot the bottle containing *Juliet's* sleeping potion. The omission was only discovered at the moment the vial was needed. Some bottle must be furnished to the *Friar*, or he cannot utter the solemn charge with which he confides the drug to the perplexed scion of the Capulets. The property man, confused at the discovery of his own neglect, and fearful of the fine to which it would subject him, caught up the first small bottle at hand, and gave it to the *Friar*. The vial was the prompter's, and contained *ink*. When *Juliet* snatched the fatal potion from the *Friar's* hand, he whispered something in an undertone. I caught the words, 'take care,' but was too absorbed in my part to comprehend the warning. *Juliet* returns home, meets her parents, retires to her chamber, dismisses her nurse, and, finally, drinks the potion. At the words,—

"'Romeo! this do I drink to thee!'

I placed the bottle to my lips, and unsuspiciously swallowed the inky draught! The dark stain upon my hands and lips might have been mistaken for the quick workings of the poison, for the audience remained ignorant of the mishap, which I only half comprehended. When the scene closed, the prompter rushed up to me, exclaiming, 'Good gracious! you have been drinking from my bottle of ink!' I could not resist the temptation of quoting the remark of the dying wit, under similar circumstances: 'Let me swallow a sheet of blotting paper!' The frightened prompter, however, did not understand the joke."

An amusing inventory of theatrical properties was recently furnished to the new lessee of the Drury Lane Theatre, on his taking possession. It was as follows: "Spirits of wine, for flames and apparitions, £12 2s.; 3½ bottles of lightning, £1; 1 snowstorm, of finest French paper, 3s.; 2 snowstorms, of common French paper, 2s.; complete sea, with 12 long waves, slightly damaged, £1 10s.; 18 clouds, with black edges, in good order, 12s. 6d.; rainbow, slightly faded, 2s.; an assortment of French clouds, flashes of lightning and thunderbolts, 15s.; a new moon, slightly tarnished, 15s.; imperial mantle, made for Cyrus, and subsequently worn by Julius Cæsar and Henry VIII, 10s.; Othello's handkerchief, 6d.; 6 arm-chairs and 6 flower-pots, which dance country dances, £2."

Three shillings for a snowstorm! A rainbow for two shillings! Fifteen shillings for a new moon!

These things are certainly enough to stagger credulity. But such is mimic life, and such are the curious standards of value in "property," as it exists behind the scenes.

When the old Chatham Theatre, in New York, came within the talons of the law, and Chancellor Kent was called upon to appoint receivers for its effects, he was astonished that there should be a "property man," when the Sheriff's return of property was, "*non inventus*"!

The property man "has charge of all the movables, and has to exercise great ingenuity in getting them up, and keeping them up. His province is to preserve the canvas water from getting wet, keep the sun's disc clear, and the moon from getting torn; he manufactures thunder on sheet iron, or from parchment stretched, drum-like, on a frame; he prepares boxes of dried peas for rain and wind, and huge watchman's rattles for the crash of falling towers. He has under his charge demijohns, for the fall of concealed china in cupboards; speaking trumpets, to imitate the growl of ferocious wild beasts; penny whistles, for the 'Cricket on the Hearth'; powdered rosin, for lightning flashes, where gas is not used; rose pink, for the blood of patriots; money, cut out of tin; finely cut bits of paper, for fatal snowstorms; ten-pin balls, for the distant mutterings of a storm; bags of gold, containing broken glass and pebbles, to imitate the musical ring of coin; balls of cotton wadding, for apple dumplings; links of sausages, made of painted flannel; sumptuous banquets of papier mache; block-tin rings, with painted beads puttied in, for royal signets; crowns, of Dutch gilding, lined with red ferret; broomstick handles, cut up for truncheons for command; brooms themselves, for witches to ride; branches of cedar, for Birnam Wood; dredging boxes of flour, for the fate-desponding lovers; vermilion, to tip the noses of jolly landlords; pieces of rattan, silvered over, for fairy wands; leaden watches, for gold repeaters; dog-chains, for the necks of knighthood, and tin spurs for its heels; armor made of leather, and shields of wood; fans, for ladies to coquet behind; quizzing-glasses, for exquisites to ogle with; legs of mutton, hams, loaves of bread, and plum puddings, all cut from canvas, and stuffed with sawdust; together with all the pride, pomp and circumstance of a dramatic display. Such is a Property Man of a theatre. He bears his honors meekly; he mixes molasses and water for wine, and darkens it a little shade deeper with the former for brandy, is always busy behind the scenes, but is seldom seen, unless it is to clear the stage, and then what a shower of yells and hisses does he receive from the galleries! The thoughtless gods cry, 'Supe! supe!' which, if intended as an abbreviation of superior or super-fine, may be apposite, but in no other view of the case. What would a theatre be without a Property Man? A world without a sun; an army without a general; a body without a head; a Union without a President; a clock without hands; kings would be truncheonless and crownless; brigands without spoils; old men without canes and powder; Harlequin without his hat; Macduff without his leafy screen; theatres would

close—there would be no tragedy, no comedy, no farce without him. Jove in his chair was never more potent than he. An actor might, and often does, get along without the words of his part, but not without the properties. What strange quandaries have we seen the Garricks and Siddonses of our stage get into, when the Property Man lapsed in his duty! We have seen *Romeo* distracted beneath the bottle of poison not to be found; *Virginius* tear his hair because the butcher's knife was not ready on the shambles; *Baillie Nicol Jarvie* nonplussed because there was no red-hot poker to singe the tartan pladdie with; *Macbeth* frowning because the Eighth Apparition did not bear a glass to show him any more; *William Tell* in agony because there was no small apple for *Gesler* to pick; the *First Murderer* in distress because there was no blood for his face ready; *Hecate* fuming like a hell-cat because her car did not mount easily; *Richard the Third* grinding his teeth because the clink of hammers closing rivets up was forgotten; *Hamlet* brought up all standing because there was no goblet to drink the poison from, and *Othello* stabbing *Iago* with a candlestick because he had not another sword of Spain, the Ebro's temper, to do the deed with. So the property man is no insignificant personage—he is the mainspring which sets all the work in motion; and an actor had better have a bad epitaph when dead than his ill will while living."

CHAPTER XIV.

The Scenic Artist.—His Strange Workshop in the Clouds.—Up in the Flies.—Magic Transformations.—Streets turn into Open Fields—Rivers into Dry Land.—The Stage Manager and his Duties.—Curious Letters between two Old Managers.—Borrowing Assassins.—Lending Shepherds.—A Cupid who had to Find his own Wings.—The Prompter and his Duties.

In these days when such an extraordinary amount of money and care is lavished on the scenery of plays, scenic artists are extremely well paid.

Of course in no department does talent make a more marked difference than in this; fine artists being paid large salaries, and daubers getting no more than if they were painting signs instead of scenes.

There are several artists in New York who get as high as $100 a week; and there is *one* scenic artist who has a theatre of his own. It is one of the finest in Broadway, and the scenery is always beautiful.

The paint-room of a theatre is always situated in the "flies" or clouds above the stage; and it is curious to see the artists with their great brushes changing a street view into a landscape, or "the sea, the sea, the open sea!" into mountains, rivulets or railroad tracks.

Of course, being situated in such an airy region as the "flies," the painter's room has not always a very snug flooring; and many an actress has got a good dress covered with drippings of paint which have dropped from above her during rehearsal. However, scene painters generally use water colors, so there's not much harm done. The spots are easily rubbed off.

The stage manager is a person altogether distinct from the manager. While the manager, assisted by his treasurer, ticket-sellers and door-keepers, and bill-posters, scrubbers, cleaners and upholsterers, is devoting his time and attention to what is called the "front of the house" (*i. e.* the auditorium), the stage manager, surrounded by his actors, actresses, scene-painters, stage carpenters, wardrobe-makers, property men, gas men, scene-shifters and the rest, is preparing the pageant which those who sit before the footlights are to see.

The stage manager may or may not be an actor; he generally is; but he is never an outsider, as the manager so often is.

He is a man who has been reared to the theatrical life through long years of training; he knows how everybody's part should be played, even if he be not able to play it himself—even as many a musician is thoroughly qualified to teach others by dint of scientific knowledge, though his own execution may be poor.

The duties of the stage manager are several. First, the casting of parts. This involves very careful study of the different qualifications of the actors. Next, the "mounting" of plays. This requires study of the date in which the piece is written; for instance, a play the scene of which was laid in France, in the time of Louis XIV. must not have furniture, scenery or costumes which were worn subsequent to that epoch.

Thirdly, the direction of plays at rehearsal. For, though the prompter generally holds the MS., or book of the play, to see that the players do not stray from the text, it is the duty of the stage manager to watch the movements of the players, and direct them if they are guilty of any ungraceful or ill-timed movement; to instruct them when to sit and when to rise; when to stand; in short to act the part of drill master to an awkward squad.

I recently saw copies of some curious letters which passed between two ancient stage-managers, in the old times, when the functions of the prompter were discharged also by the manager. These letters follow:

DRURY LANE, Nov. 9.

DEAR WILD—For pity's sake lend me a couple of conspirators for to-night. Recollect you have borrowed one of ours for a singing Druid, and another of our best is Doge of Venice, on Packer's resignation.

Entirely and devotedly yours,

HOPKINS.

COVENT GARDEN, Nov. 9.

I have ordered to look out two of our genteelest assassins, and I'll take care they shall go shaved and sober. Pray tell Farren he must play our Archbishop to-morrow; will cut the part, that he may dress time enough afterwards for your General in the Camp.

Yours, perpetually,

WILD.

P. S.—If you have a full moon to spare, I wish you'd lend it to us for Thursday. I send you some lightning I can recommend.

COVENT GARDEN, Nov. 11.

DEAR HOPKINS—Pray, how shall we manage without Smith to-morrow? I depended on your lending him us for Harry the Fifth; but I now see you have put him up for Charles Surface. Couldn't you let him come to us, and play two acts of Harry, as you don't want him in Charles till your third, and then Hull shall read the rest, with an apology for Smith's being suddenly hoarse, sprained his ankle, etc.

Cordially, yours,

WILD.

P. S.—My vestal virgin gets so very stout, I wish you'd lend us Mrs. Robinson for a night.

DRURY LANE, Nov. 11.

DEAR WILD—By particular desire, our vestal is not transferable; but we have a spare Venus, and duplicate Junos; so send your hackney coach for whichever suits you. The scheme for Smith won't do; but change your play to anything; for we'll tack *The Lamp* to the School for Scandal, to secure you an overflow.

Thoroughly, yours,

HOPKINS.

COVENT GARDEN, Nov. 12.

MY DEAR FELLOW—Here's the devil to pay about our Tuesday's pantomime—the blacksmith can't repair our great serpent till Friday, and the old camel that we thought quite sound, has broken down at rehearsal; so pray send us your elephant by the bearer, and a small tiger with the longest tail you can pick out. I must trouble you, too, for a dozen of your best dancing shepherds for that night, for, though I see you'll want them for highwaymen, in the Beggar's Opera, they'll be quite in time for us afterwards.

Forever completely yours,

WILD.

DRURY LANE, Nov. 12.

DEAR WILD—I just write a line while the beasts are packing up, to beg you'll not be out of spirits, as you may depend on the shepherds, and any other animal you have occasion for. I have orders to acquaint you, too, that as we don't use Henderson, for Falstaff, on Friday, you may have him for Richard, with a dozen and a half of *our* soldiers, for Bosworth Field, only begging you'll return 'em us in time for Cox-heath.

Truly, yours,

HOPKINS.

P. S.—Send me a Cupid—mine has got the measles.

COVENT GARDEN, Nov. 12.

DEAR HOPKINS—Thank you for Henderson and the soldiers—so let them bring their helmets, for ours are tinning. The bearer is our Cupid, at a shilling a night, finding his own wings.

Generously, yours,

WILD.

The prompter is another attaché of a theatre who may or may not be an actor. He is poorly paid, and pretty hardly worked.

His chief duty is to never for one moment, either at rehearsal or during a performance, lay down the MS. or printed book of the play in course of progress; but to keep his eyes fixed on it as constantly as is possible with his other duties, in the event that any one of the players should forget his words, when, of course, he would have to be prompted.

The prompter also rings the curtain up and down, turns the gas jets up or down, rings for the music to play, and whistles for change of scene.

Added to this, he is frequently called upon to play a part in case any one is taken sick, and if he is able to speak on the stage at all, he will be considered very disobliging if he refuses.

The prompter's seat—or as it is technically termed—the "prompt-place," is a little flap of a table with a chair behind it, placed at the right hand wing, *i. e.* the first scene directly behind the footlights, and situated at the right hand of the actors.

In all foreign theatres—and in operatic performances in this country—the prompter is placed in a little circular box which rises out of the stage just back of the footlights. By this arrangement the prompter is confined exclusively to the book, and some one else attends to the curtain, etc.

CHAPTER XV.

About Managers.—The Top of the Theatrical Heap.—New York Managers.—Speculators, Merchants and others as Theatre-Owners.—Actors and Dramatists as Managers.—How Expenses are Cut Down.—What Managers Should Be, and What, alas! They Are.—Swindling "Agents" Turned Managers.—The Sharks of the Profession.

It will be evident to all who have read the preceding chapters, that behind the scenes there is a world—a world with its aristocracy, its wits, its beauties, its rich, its poor, its artists and artisans, much as there is in the outer world.

At the "top of the heap" is the person who owns the theatre. This is most frequently some capitalist, who rents out his theatre just as he does his other property, and has nothing to do with it except to receive quarterly payments for its use. This, I say, is most generally the case; though in New York there are two theatres owned by a wealthy railroad manager, who it is said also busies himself with the actual management of the theatres he owns. At any rate, he causes his name, as "proprietor," to be placed at the head of the theatre bills. This is Mr. James Fisk, Jr.

Another theatre is owned by a successful actor—Mr. Edwin Booth.

Wood's Museum is owned by Banvard, known throughout the country by his Panorama of the Holy Land.

Niblo's Garden and the New York Theatre are owned by Mr. A. T. Stewart, the dry goods king, who busies himself very little with them, except to see that his rents are collected.

All the other theatres in New York, according to the best of my knowledge, are owned either by stockholders or private individuals, who let them out to theatre managers.

A theatre manager may or may not be an actor. In former days the theatre manager was invariably an actor; but in New York at the present time there are only two permanent first-class theatres which are managed by actors—one is "Wallack's," managed by Mr. Lester Wallack; the other is "Booth's," managed by Edwin Booth.

Theatres—like newspapers, for the most part—are either immensely lucrative or very disastrous affairs; and the first part of this fact has induced numberless men—outsiders in every sense—to invest their money in theatrical stock as if it were live stock—hogs or cattle.

It is these people who have been chiefly instrumental in bringing upon the stage that hideous disgrace known as the "nude drama," which took its rise with the flimsy absurdity called the "Black Crook," and who have continued it by importing "painted Jezebels," known as "English burlesque blondes," to throw still further obloquy on the drama proper, by their shameless can-can dancing, and their perversion of simple nursery rhymes into indecent songs.

No actor-manager could have inaugurated this disgrace; for the simple reason that he would be too much in sympathy with his actors to force them to lower their talents to the level of English burlesque; but, of course, once the thing became a pronounced success, it flew all over the country, and many actor-managers found themselves obliged to admit it into their theatres, or be ruined pecuniarily.

It would be a happy day for the drama if these gross speculators could be driven from the management of theatres, and men with true regard for the histrionic *art*—actors like Edwin Booth and Lester Wallack—could everywhere take their places.

In those cases where successful dramatic authors have turned managers, the rule which governs the actor-manager generally holds good. Such managers usually have some realizing sense of the importance of dramatic art; and, though they may not rise to the very highest conceptions of this, yet it is rare indeed for them to seek success through indecent burlesques or leg-displaying spectacles.

One curious fact is noticeable with regard to managers as a class, and that is that whenever it becomes necessary to cut down their expenses, their first attack is made on the salary list. This is often very severe upon the members of the company, but they usually have no option but to accept the reduction, or make room for some one who will.

John Hollingshead, a London critic, lately remarked:

"A manager is entitled to praise if he produces a good drama, and deserves strong blame if he produces a bad one. It is a lame excuse for him to urge, or have urged for him, that he engaged the reputed best author in the market at a fair market price, and 'left it to him.' This is not the act of a manager, but of a fool; of a man whose greatest successes must necessarily be 'flukes.' It is true that most so-called managers are men of this stamp, who hold scarce properties at the sides of our principal London thoroughfares, and whose whole art of management is to wait for 'something to turn up.' The critics, most of them, know this, but they never say it."

"There was a time in the story of the drama," says another critic,—"its most illustrious time,—when men like Sheridan and Byron were at the head of theatres. In this country, too, we have had managers of cultivated taste, and can still point to names of men which carry to the office the feelings of gentlemen and scholars. But of what material are most of our modern managers composed? The spawn of some concert cellar, or taking their degrees among the diggings, tied to the tusks of some dramatic rhinoceros, and sent round between the acts to gather half-pence, they possess neither cultivation nor refinement, and would sacrifice at any moment for a dollar the dignity of their art."

Low down on the ladder of repute which all actors seek to climb—or at least pretend they do—is a class of soulless, conscienceless, speculating swindlers, who, from having followed the business of theatrical agents, have learned something of the inner life of theatricals, and who aspire to be managers.

These disgraceful persons will have the audacity to gather a company of players together under false pretences, promising them good salaries, and set out to give performances in country towns, trusting wholly to "luck" to carry them through.

If they chance to have good houses, very well; then their baseness lies concealed; but if the first three or four nights of their "season" should fail to bring in money, these swindling "managers" are forced to disband their companies,—for they have not a cent in their pockets.

The evils growing out of this disgraceful conduct are often deplorable, and serve to cast unmerited reproach on the profession—the "poor players" being sometimes left penniless in a strange town, with hotel-bills to pay, and landlords clamorous.

Adventurers of this stamp, who assume the grave responsibilities of management, knowing well their own inability to cope for a single week with what is technically termed "poor business," are worthy of execration by all honorable people; and it will be a good day for the theatrical profession when it shall have combined to resist the rascalities of penniless "agents" turned managers.

In a large city, and among the best class of players, it is, of course, impossible for such persons to practice their "little game." Those who suffer most from them are performers who have achieved neither reputation nor fortune, and with whom an "engagement" means simply their daily bread.

CHAPTER XVI.

My Return to the Stage in Womanhood.—The Dictate of Necessity.—An Unwelcome Duty.—Getting Acquainted with Life Behind the Scenes after a Long Absence.—My Debut at Wallack's.—Following the Advice of Friends.—The Eventful Night.—How it Went off.—The Morning After.—The Interesting Character of Debuts.—Reminiscences of the American Debuts of Ole Bull, Jenny Lind, Alboni, Rachel, etc., by an Old Theatre-Goer.—The Story of Leopoldine, a French Debutante.—Exciting Time in the Theatre.—The Fickleness of a French Audience.—Bravery of the Actress.—Her Scornful Treatment of her Fickle Admirers.—The Result.

For myself, I am free to confess that I never liked the life of an actress. My mature judgment rebels against it, *for me*, as much now as it did when I was led on, against my infantile wishes, to personate *Cora's* child in the play of "Pizarro."

I know that this is equal to an acknowledgment to actors that I had not the sacred fire for dramatic art; and I candidly believe I never had.

It was necessity which drove me to it in the first place, necessity which at different intervals in my life sent me back to it; and I trust such necessity will never come upon me again.

This is not because I am willing to concede that the theatre, *per se*, is an abode of sin, any more than, in itself a grocery store is, or a senate chamber; but simply because the life is distasteful to me—for reasons "too numerous to mention."

After having been for some eight years severed from the stage, I found myself, in womanhood, compelled to return to it, and my re-appearance on the dramatic scene was a debut of such importance (to *me*, you know) that its sensations and vicissitudes are not likely ever to be forgotten.

Stern Fate, and the fluctuations of gold were the cause, and a bad headache and a total dissatisfaction with self the next morning, was the effect. However I determined to make the effort—and did it. I swam the Hellespont and was not drowned, although I confess that I was submerged on several occasions. When, I knew as well or better than any critic could tell me—but let that pass.

I will not linger on the painful details of preliminary events; dresses too small and dresses too large, boots too high-heeled and boots not heeled at all, the dreadful "to be or not to be" of crinoline or no crinoline, the multitudinous varieties of *coiffures*, the equally puzzling choice of colors; and other bewildering questions which I alone was called upon to solve, may be passed over without mention.

They were of fearful moment in their way, but nothing compared to the all absorbing idea—the acting of the part.

The role was a difficult one for me to portray, presenting scenes of light and shadow into which my life picture has never been, and I trust never will be placed.

I never was a governess, nor yet a lady's lady companion, and have little or no idea of the exact conventional bearing of that genus; again, I never was starved, never fell in love with a lord, never made an immense fortune, and never played *Lady Macbeth.*

These you will confess were disadvantages, but why then did I write the play?—(taking it for granted that I did write it, which has been doubted by some, entirely disbelieved by others, and plainly and publicly contradicted by three "well informed persons.") Simply this—before I had any idea of committing such a hideous offence, I went to two managers—told them who I was—explained that I wished to make a *rentree* on the stage—said that I had made a special study of what is known as the legitimate drama, and wished to appear in parts of that stamp.

The first manager had his time positively engaged with stars from now till never.

The second was extremely sorry, but—. In fact how did he know that I was capable of playing parts which Fanny Kemble and a host of others had made famous, unless he saw me in them? And I, how could I prove to him that I was, or was not (much more likely), unless somebody gave me an opportunity of letting him see me?

All, however, were unanimous on one point: the legitimate did not draw now. The sensational was the only wear. The public cried for it, as children do for paregoric and sugar; both are deleterious, but both are nice.

So, the die was cast. I went home, and at once the manager pro tem of the first theatre in the land gave me an opening.

Don't blame him for favoring the sensational—don't blame the actors; blame the public, sweet public—it likes starvation when not experienced by itself, revels in suicides, goes wild with delight over arson and elopements.

Well, the play was written and accepted and the fatal day fixed for my reading it to the artists. This was a dreadful ordeal, but it had to be passed.

I will leave to your imagination the state of my feelings as I opened the MS. on a very dark day, seated as I was on a very uncomfortable chair, leaning as I was on an even more uncomfortable table, the whole placed on Wallack's stage—dull, rusty, unpoetical, ungaslit, silent, *morning* stage—with the eyes of ten people looking at me, and the ears of ten people listening to me—listening to me trying to throw life and character into each different character in the piece; looking at me trying to play every "line of business" known, from the heroine and lover down to the dustman.

Ten people! How did I know they were kind people,

nice people, good sympathising noble hearts, ready to accept me as one of them, without spite or rancor then and there? I imagined they looked upon me as an interloper, as a person of mettle true, but that metal brass, as an effrontèe, as a piece of walking impudence, as a would-be authoress and can't-be actress, as a silly novice, in point of fact.

Nothing of the kind. They understood my position, applauded my resolution, and spoke encouragingly not alone to me but of me to others.

But I did not know this then, and suffered quite as much as if the case had been exactly the reverse.

Show me members of any other craft who will be so magnanimous to a new aspirant for fame and fortune, perhaps a rival, certainly a competitor, and I will show you a surprised and gratified person—myself.

The reading was got over and the piece put into rehearsal. I at once began to study my part. I learned it so well that I soon knew every word of it backwards, and nearly everything else in the piece forwards. Still I had a vague idea that I was not "perfect," (alas! who is in this wicked world?) and my whole time was passed in gentle assurance to the contrary, addressed to my unbelieving self.

When nightmares visited my uneasy couch, they generally took the form of "sticking" heroines and "stage waits" of interminable length. But sober, waking thought confirmed me in the knowledge that I was thoroughly "up."

Then I began to practice the effects, the stage walks, the managing of the voice, the general bearing of the person, the making of "points," the attaining of "climax," the changing of countenance, the gesticulation, the broken tones of grief, the traditional stage laugh of mirth (in contradistinction to the laugh of revenge, or the ha! ha!

of triumph) and the few other trifling details necessary to be observed.

Naturally I sought aid and comfort not from the enemy, but from friends. I solicited hints of all kinds, for I had truly need of them.

You will be surprised to learn that these hints were of the most contradictory character. What was lauded by one was condemned by another. A point that by dint of hard study I had learned from A., I was advised by B. to drop at once if I ever hoped for success.

Modulations of voice which I had practiced carefully by the suggestion of a well known person, universally conceded to be a delightful elocutionist, were denounced afterward as defective and the result of "faulty instruction!"

My gestures were deemed too startling by one, too inexpressive by another, and quite the thing by a third.

My arms were pulled and pinched, my shoulders squeezed, my back thrown in, my chest thrown out, causing me an amount of pain which those who inflicted it would have shielded me from with the ferocity of tigers, had the suffering come from any other source.

But as far as testing the quality and strength of my voice was concerned, by practicing the speeches *viva voce*, that was utterly impracticable. How could I disturb the quiet inmates of Mrs. Biggin's highly respectable mansion (reference given and required), by imploring *Clifford* to leave me, or by peremptorily bidding *Master Walter* to "do it" nor leave the act to me? The thing was not to be thought of, and so my home rehearsals were always given in a whisper. Low as it was, still it was overheard, and the impression went forth at Biggin's that I was mad.

Soon this impression was confirmed, and then all at Biggin's looked aghast.

I was going on the stage—oh, this was more than madness—it was impropriety: it was touching pitch and running great risk of being defiled, it was atrocious, it was unheard of; and there was weeping, and wailing, and gnashing of teeth, particularly when all were assembled at Biggin's festive board.

But time flew, and the eventful night arrived. I was dressed too soon—ready, but alas! not eager for the fray.

It had been raining all day, and Faust kept declaring, in his funny way of thinking French and speaking English, that he didn't believe there would be four cats (quatre chats) in the house.

I didn't either, and ardently hoped that even those four would be engaged in the pursuit of other mice than Eveleen.

Suddenly Faust arrived, almost simultaneously with a huge basket of flowers, and announced that cats were crowding in in large numbers, quite regardless of expense, in the shape of ruined hats and bonnets, and all unmindful of the inclement weather.

I almost wished the rain had drowned, as it must have drenched them.

I really felt very ill.

Mother said it was the odor of the flowers, but I knew it wasn't. I left the dressing-room and went up stairs, for the play had begun and I knew I must soon go on.

They asked me if I was nervous, and I said no, which was true. I was not nervous; I was, as it were, dead to all feeling. My arms were leaden weights, my hands two dumb-bells, cut in a queer human fashion, with four fingers and a thumb.

I felt like a lamb being led to the sacrifice, and yet not like, for a lamb has a happy ignorance of whither he goeth, and I had a vivid, painful consciousness of where I was going.

I was going on the stage, and that almost immediately too—oh dear, dear!

I had discarded the use of rouge when dressing, knowing that generally in excitement I have more need of white than red, and just now I caught a glimpse of myself in the glass.

I was pale to a degree that can only be equalled, not by the blue-veined vivacity of marble, not by the light transparency of biscuit, but by the dull soggen pallor of plaster of Paris.

But hark! My cue! The cue I know so well—a kind but peremptory movement from the prompter, a gasp, a momentary closing of the eyes, and a leap.

Not a leap in the dark, but a leap into the light—into the gaslight, the streaming, gleaming, all-revealing gaslight. It was but five steps from the wing on to the stage, but those five steps brought me into another world—changed me at once, as Fairy Goodgift does Clown and Harlequin with one stroke of the magic wand, from a *femme du mond* into an actress.

I was nervous now—my chest heaved, my breath came thick and fast—for all of Adam's children were condensed into one man and that man was at Wallack's theatre. All humanity had but one great eye, and that eye was glaring terribly at me!

I haven't the remotest idea how it all went off. I only remember that my problematical idea of sticking was on several occasions about to become a positive reality, but happily did not; that I overacted; that I underacted; that I did everything I should not, and nothing that I should.

However, it was over. I had made my debut.

The worst was yet to come—the next morning's criticisms.

Lord Byron hated the friends, who, at news of a disaster, always reminded him that they had "told him so."

I read with dismay the corroboration of my own unfavorable opinions of myself.

Still, the criticisms, like the hints, were very contradictory. Eveleen was pronounced superlatively good, comparatively indifferent, and positively bad. I was received as a bright accession to the galaxy of stars by one critic; as not good enough for the stock by another. Figaro, witty, pungent Figaro, said my acting was too emotional, and he was right. It was all emotional.

Every emotion of my heart and body, particularly every painful one, was awakened, and no doubt improperly betrayed. I felt like crying in the merry scenes and laughing hysterically in the pathetic ones.

Another critic said the beggar's dress was unbecoming to a great degree, and he was right. I wanted Faust to get me for that very scene a *moire antique*, at a hundred dollars the dress pattern, but he, dull man, would not C it.

Figaro said that I did not exhibit the "gross ignorance—"

Gross ignorance! "Why, good gracious, thought I in bewilderment, how does this tally with the remark made only a couple of years ago by Somebody, who, if he is not somebody himself (opinions again divided), is undoubtedly the Nephew of an Uncle who was Somebody (opinions not divided), to the effect that the same person who did not exhibit 'gross ignorance' was unquestionably and decidedly an *esprit fort?* And that in Europe, too, in Paris, too, where *esprit forts* are not lacking! Ah, Figaro, Figaro, tell me who your Suzanne is, and I'll bid her flirt outrageously both with Cherubino and the Count, just to pay you off for that, you naughty, saucy barber!"

En somme, I was pretty thoroughly bewildered by the controversy I have mentioned which arose among the critics, and which at length waxed so warm that the original cause of it—my offending self—was well nigh forgotten.

The interesting nature of first appearances, generally, is well known. The most genial gossiper of our day is fond of referring to this ever-fascinating source of pleasant memories, telling us how "the gossips, as they grow old, renew their youth as they tell the story of the first nights they have seen. A first appearance in Europe is an experiment. Even if it be Jenny Lind or Rachel, the beginning is necessarily without previous reputation, except the warm rumor of the rehearsal and of private admiration. But when Jenny Lind came to us, it was as the recognized queen of song; and when the spectral *Camille* glided from the side-scene in 'les Horaces,' and that low, weird, wonderful voice smote the ear and heart of the listener, we knew that Rachel was, without a rival, the greatest living actress. So, also, with Alboni and Ole Bull. Their fame was made for them when they came. As we write the names, what scenes arise, so freshly remembered, so utterly passed! The very buildings are gone, except Castle Garden, where Jenny Lind first sang, and which is wholly changed. It was in the Metropolitan Theatre that Rachel appeared. It was in Tripler Hall that Alboni sang; and in the old Park Theatre, on a memorable Saturday evening, Ole Bull strode out, with a leopard-like swing, upon the stage, his coat buttoned across his magnificent breast, his fair, frank face smooth and romantic as a boy's, as he bent over his violin during the introduction by the orchestra, and fondly listened, to be sure that it was as sensitively responsive as he required it to be. And, if the buildings are gone, where are the magicians? Rachel is dead. Jenny Lind's voice has flown. And Alboni and Ole Bull—where are they? * * * * Yet these were all first appearances, that were suggestive of each other. If Rachel came, there were those whose pride it was to remember Edmund Kean and G. Cooke. If Jenny Lind sang, your neighbor, who had evidently come down from the generation of George the Fourth, murmured, in the intervals, of Malibran; and you, of a later day, retorted feebly with Miss Shirreff, and with more animation recalled Cinti Damoreau and Caradori Allan. If Ole Bull stood towering and swaying in the spell of his own music, there was some old-fashioned lover of concord, who thought music died with the Hermann brothers or the Boston Brigade Band. The charm of the evening was half in its association, in the tender, regretful memories of other fames and other days. It was the musing, tearful romance of the wanderer who shall hear no more

> "'The bells of Shandon
> That sound so grand on
> The pleasant waters of the river Lee.'"

One of the most interesting debuts I ever heard of was that of a young French girl in Paris, whom poverty had driven to the stage.

On the night of her first appearance the theatre was crowded to excess. Two electric currents seemed on the point of meeting. The first was fed by the partisans of the young girl, at the head of whom was a curious old fellow, named Barentin, who sat in a box with a friend named Gibeau; the second current drew its fire from a certain set of discontented, would-be critics, who are never so happy as when they have set the word "failure" on either a new play or a new player.

Behind the scenes, the stage manager was stalking up and down, in a dreadful state of agitation. At length the *debutante*, whose name was Leopoldine, entered the green-room.

The manager started at sight of her unpretending appearance.

"Why, my child," said he, "your dress is very plain—very plain indeed."

Now Leopoldine was a girl of spirit. She had accepted this stage life as a disagreeable necessity, and had made up her mind that her path would be a thorny one, and had also determined to trip over the thorns as lightly as possible. She scarcely expected, however, that her first rebuff would come from the manager.

"Why, sir," she answered, "I am to represent the 'Orphan of the Bridge of Notre Dame'; it would not be in character to be dressed like a duchess."

"To be sure," answered the anxious manager, "that's true enough. Still—this black de laine dress, with its high neck and tight long sleeves, this plain smooth hair, brushed tight to your head—honestly, you don't look pretty at all."

"I have dressed myself according to my conception of the character," said Leopoldine, firmly. "In the third act, when I am supposed to have fallen into a splendid fortune, they will see me in a handsome dress. Perhaps the contrast will be all the more effective."

"And, in the meantime, the first impression will be poor; and if there is, as I have been told, a body of people in the audience who are determined to prevent you succeeding, they will have it all their own way at the beginning."

"Then I must try to have it all my way before ending."

"Clear the stage!" cried the prompter. "The curtain is going up."

The first act of the Orphan of Notre Dame was rather dull. The audience bore it silently, awaiting with impatience the appearance of the new Star, the dramatic comet who was to draw all hearts in its luminous course.

She appeared.

Everybody was disappointed, it seemed.

A murmur of disapprobation ran through the theatre at

sight of this insignificant-looking girl, poorly dressed, and who seemed to have exerted herself to extinguish whatever natural advantages she might possess.

Even her friends were shocked at the poor figure she cut. Gibeau whispered to old Barentin:

"How strange that she should not make a more imposing appearance. She is naturally pretty; but she looks now as if she had lost every friend in the world, and gone into mourning for them in a shabby black dress."

"I did think, certainly, that she would show to better advantage," responded the other; "but no matter, she is still the sweetest woman in the world. What eyes! what a mouth!"

"Yes," answered the friend; "but she does not show her teeth, and she keeps her eyes constantly on the ground."

"Well, would you have her personate innocence with a bold manner?"

"I tell you what it is—on the stage, even innocence ought to have self-possession. Do you hear? They are beginning to laugh!"

The scene represented a noble marquis, who was trying to make love to the orphan. The conversation ran somewhat thus:

"Lovely girl, why do you withdraw your hand? whence comes this distrust of me?"

"Ah, marquis, you are noble and rich; I, poor and lowly."

"What of that! These distinctions do not affect the heart. I love you, dearest. Your striking beauty (*murmurs in the audience*), your wondrous grace (*laughs*), the irresistible charm which you exert over all who see you." (*cries of* "Enough! enough!")

Here the two friends of the poor girl looked despairingly at each other.

"You hear! They are beginning to express their disapprobation in good earnest."

"I wish I had them in my back-garden, two at a time," growled the other, furiously angry that they should so ill-treat his favorite, "I'd knock their heads together."

On the stage, the girl continued to repeat the set words of her part:

"No, marquis, do not tell me I am handsome. My mirror has too often told me the contrary."

A voice from the audience: "I am of the opinion of the mirror."

Another: "So am I."

Here the actor who played the marquis, whispered in the ear of the debutante: "Do not let this break you down, my poor girl."

"No," answered she, "I am determined to make a success, one way or another."

Then she continued: "Ah, marquis, if it were true that, by a bitter irony, Heaven *had* endowed me with these exterior advantages—"

A voice—"Don't disturb yourself. He has endowed you with nothing at all."

Another voice—from the gallery—"Say, you marquis, what sort of taste have you got, making love to an *umbrella?*"

At this, Barentin sprang to his feet, with rage, and, leaning out of the private box where he was sitting, he cried out: "Beasts! hounds! will you be quiet?"

This disrespectful speech set fire to the powder. The pit rose with one accord, and in an instant two hundred fists were shaken up at the old commander Barentin. The old fellow, who, like a true French soldier, knew only one way of settling quarrels—the duello—indignantly scattered a whole card-case full of cards down upon the astonished crowd.

"There!" cried he, at the top of his voice; "there's my card—one for each of you. I'll fight you all!"

"Hush, Barentin!" said Gibeau; "be quiet, or they'll charge up here, and take us by assault."

"They, the rascals, the scoundrels!" shouted the old man, more and more angry. "Come on, all of you! You dare not, cowards, hounds, idiots, fools!"

The row now became general, and it was in vain that two or three policemen tried to restore order. Their voices were unheard in the tumult. The two men in the boxes, and the crowd in the pit, continued to launch invectives at each other, and already some one had torn up part of a bench, and flung it up at the energetic Barentin, whom it struck violently in the breast.

The fury of the old man knew no bounds. In his rage, he siezed hold of his neighbor, Gibeau, and tried to throw him over bodily, as a missile; but the human projectile absolutely refused to let himself be discharged.

Suddenly, silence was restored as if by enchantment. Every eye was fixed on the stage. The debutante advanced to the footlights, and motioned that she desired to speak to the public. Every one seemed willing to hear what the orphan of the bridge of Notre Dame would have to say in her own defence.

Strange metamorphosis! Her face seemed transformed. Her great black eyes flashed with lightning-like sparkle; a smile of disdain exposed her pearl-like teeth, which seemed as if they were ready to bite; her pink nostrils dilated; and her blonde hair, through which she had run her feverish fingers, formed a splendid crown around the head of the irritated girl. She looked like a triumphant Venus, entering a cage of howling and furious lions.

"There, look how beautiful she is!" yelled out Barentin, still furiously angry.

"Silence! silence!" cried the audience.

The girl stood like a statue until the last sound had died away. Then, in a deep, low voice, she said:

"Gentlemen, the singular reception that you have seen fit to give me, forces me to retire from the stage, and let the remainder of my part be taken by some one else."

"Don't you do it!" yelled Barentin, furiously.

"I should never forgive myself," said she, still in the same quiet voice, "if I were to interfere with the pleasure of this audience, by imposing upon it the further annoyance of my presence. I only desire, before I take my leave, to express my profound regret that my zeal and my ambition were not sufficient to make up for what I lack, alas! in talent and beauty."

The apparent humility of these words were completely nullified by the defiant expression of the transformed face of the debutante, and the public sat like so many deaf-mutes, staring at the features that a moment before it had been stupid enough to pronounce homely. The pit seemed at a loss what to do; one moment more, and it would have risen as one man, and apologized to her. After having enjoyed her triumph a few seconds, and astonished the audience still further by the fiery glances of her star-like eyes, the girl made a slight bow, and walked towards the back part of the stage.

At sight of this movement, the audience cried out, with one voice:

"No, no. Stay—continue your part!"

The young actress paid no attention to this request, but stalked, majestically, off the stage.

And now there arose another tumult, but one of a different kind. It was like nothing but a capricious child crying for the plaything that an instant before it broke into a thousand splinters.

The stage manager was obliged to appear. He announced that Miss Leopoldine, completely prostrated by so much emotion, found herself unable to continue her performance.

At this distressing news, the pit blushed for its cruelty, and the gallery-gods burst into an abashed perspiration at having shown themselves so extremely un-angelic.

At last, after many goings backward and forward, behind the scenes and before the footlights, the stage manager makes the announcement that the debutante will continue her part.

"Hurrah!" Transports, enthusiasm, general emotion, and hand-shaking!

The old Frenchman was in the seventh heaven of delight.

"Gibeau, Gibeau!" cried he, "I am prouder than I was when we took the Malakoff."

The curtain, which had been lowered, was now again "rung up." By a skilful bit of management (suggested by Leopoldine), they had cut out the end of the second act, which remained unplayed, and had begun with the third. The debutante had now put on her handsome costume, of which she had spoken to the manager before the piece commenced.

When she stepped out upon the stage, the astonishment of the spectators knew no bounds. The orphan, now married to the marquis, has become a star in the highest society, and her dress is in keeping with her elevated position. It consisted of a trailing robe of the most delicate satin, cut to fit perfectly her faultless form. About her white neck hung a string of what appeared to be priceless pearls. Her blonde hair now rippled down her back in a profusion of graceful ringlets, and it was a question which to admire most—the beauty of her form, or that of her face.

"Bravo! bravo!" echoed from boxes, balcony and pit. The enthusiasm of old Barentin had infected the whole audience; and, at this moment, if any man had been rash enough to cast any reflections upon the appearance or manners of the debutante, he certainly would have met with uncomfortable treatment.

Tears of joy and pride stood in the eyes of the old commander. He pressed the hand of his friend, and said:

"Gibeau, did you ever see a lovelier divinity than she is, in Olympus?"

"I go there so rarely," answered Gibeau.

The conversation on the stage began. The marquis enters, and looks with astonishment on his wife.

"Ah!" he says, "'tis you! What a change!"

"Indeed, marquis!"

"Yes; you never before looked so lovely!"

Here, the commander shouted out:

"That's true!"

"Silence!" groaned the pit.

Upon which the orphan replies:

"It is very late for you to make the discovery of my charms."

"Yes, indeed, I should think it was—very late!" shouted the commander.

"Silence!" bellowed the pit, again.

"Silence, yourself!" retorted old Barentin.

Gibeau whispered in the old man's ear—

"Do be quiet, commander?"

"Then why do they worry me?"

"Ah, my dear wife," continues the marquis; "let me hope that you will forget the fault I committed—"

"Never!" shouts old Barentin, thinking of the public—not of the actor.

Marquis: "Who would have believed that the orphan of the bridge of Notre Dame was so lovely?"

"I would!" shouts old Barentin.

Here the pit cried out indignantly, "Will he never shut up, that old idiot?"

Barentin roared in response, shaking his fist at them again—"Never, never!"

Another slight tumult, and hisses, during which Gibeau expostulated with Barentin.

"If you *will* talk, talk low."

"It is for you I'm talking, Gibeau," haughtily replied the ludicrous old man, "for these ruffians do not deserve the honor of my remarks. There! They are throwing boquets to her like rain. Good! She don't pick them up. Bravo!"

As he stated, the proud girl now showed her disdain of the homage of her converted insulters. She even pushed away with her foot a bunch of flowers which lay in her path.

Astonishment in the audience, and some signs of displeasure.

Whereupon the marquis resumed speaking: "Ah, cruel one, why disdain the homage of a heart devoted to you through life and death!" Then in a whisper, he said, "My dear young lady, what you are doing is very dangerous. Better pick up the bouquets."

"Marquis," said the girl, aloud, without answering his whispered remark; "marquis, *I treat you as you treated me. The game is now equal!*"

"Bravo, bravo!" shouted the old commander.

Here one of the gallery-gods—those *enfant terribles* of the theatre—cried out,

"Why don't she pick up the flowers? It's insulting!"

"Yes," roared the pit, "the bouquets! the bouquets!"

The girl stopped her acting, and again stood impassable and disdainful before the anger which her conduct had excited.

"You pick them up, marquis," cried a voice from the gallery, which belonged to a small boy with a dirty shirt.

"Yes, yes!" cried the pit.

The actor did as he was bid. Lifting the flowers from the stage, he offered them to the girl with his most gallant bow.

Leopoldine took them—but only for the purpose of throwing them one after another behind the scenes.

This singular stroke of policy awakened a loud murmur. Leopoldine folded her arms and threw upon the public a glance so full of anger, that the astonished spectators, completely taken aback by her unusual conduct, hardly knew whether to hiss or to applaud.

The silence was broken by the old commander leaning out of his box once more, and vociferating—

"Well, suppose she don't want your flowers—will you force them on her? You are free to hiss her; she has the right to despise your cabbage-heads."

"Commander, commander," whispered Gibeau, nervously, "they are camelias."

"I don't care."

Oh, magic power of beauty! Leopoldine had sat down to wait the resumption of quiet. Her cheek leaning on hand, her roguish smile more and more disdainful, she seemed to say to the public:

"Don't hurry yourself, my friends, the theatre isn't rented."

The monster audience was vanquished by her beauty and her audacity. It felt that she was stronger than it, and at length resolved to frantically applaud what in reality it should have hissed.

The play was soon over, and the curtain fell amidst wild cries for the reappearance of the "orphan."

The debutante obstinately refused to again show herself.

The stage manager almost went on his knees to her. How success changes some people's views!

"Please bestow one parting look on them," plead the stage manager.

"No; they are too rude."

"But they are tearing up the seats!"

"Why did they insult me when I was doing my best?"

"But to oblige me—"

"Very well, so be it. Raise your curtain!"

Silence fell like enchantment over the hitherto noisy audience.

The doors at back of the stage were flung open for the entrance of the debutante.

She appeared.

A tempest of applause greeted her.

Leopoldine advanced slowly down the stage, and instead of making a courtesy to the assembled spectators, she wheeled directly in front of the box where Barentin and Gibeau sat, and made to them, and to them alone, three profound curtsies, after which she quickly turned her back on the audience and walked off the stage.

Everything she did was right now. The public applauded her to the echo.

And after that night she became the talk of the town. Crowds rushed to see her every night, and her fortune was made.

10

CHAPTER XVII.

The Story of Carrie Lee, an American Debutante.—Driven to the Stage for a Livelihood.—Secures an Engagement.—Horror of her Friends.—Cast for a Boy's Part.—The Recreant Lover.—The Eventful Night.—"Charlie."—"Will you put out Mine Eyes?"—The Denouement.

There is a young lady now upon the stage—whether in New York or some other city, I think I shall not say, for I do not wish to call unpleasant attention to her—whom I once knew as one of the noble army of suffering, struggling womanhood.

Her name, though public property now, it would not be right in me to give in connection with the story I am about to tell of her; so I will call her Carrie Lee.

Being suddenly left fatherless, motherless and penniless, Carrie Lee was made painfully conscious of the fact that landladies, whatever their sympathies, do not keep boarders for nothing; and that the only irresistible music in this world is the jingle of a well-filled purse.

Knowing then that she must do something for a livelihood, Carrie Lee investigated the subject of women's employment.

But what could she do? Alas! here was the trouble. Carrie Lee had received a good boarding-school education, such as young ladies of the present day commonly receive—a smattering of French, a smattering of algebra, a smattering of drawing, a smattering of music and a smattering of various other genteel accomplishments—all of which were of very small use to her now. They would not, or so it seemed, bring her in five cents a day.

In fact, Carrie had never been taught anything useful in the world—there is not one girl in a thousand who ever *is* taught anything useful, or anything which she could turn to practical account if she were obliged to earn her livelihood.

What *should* she do? Coloring photographs, dressmaking, plain sewing, all these things require time and instruction before a livelihood can be made from them; and in the case of Carrie Lee the material wants were immediate, and must be immediately supplied.

Carrie had always had a taste for the stage; and while she did not think that by going upon the stage she should at once set the town in raptures over her, it was not extraordinary, perhaps, that now in her dire strait the thought of earning a livelihood thus should occur to her; so without a word to any one she set out in search of employment as an actress.

She made application at the door of one theatre after another, until she found a manager who was willing to try what she could do.

There were not lacking people to raise their hands in holy horror at the course taken by this young girl, to say she had disgraced her family by going upon the stage; but Carrie bravely went her ways, and trusted to nothing but her own consciousness of honor and right.

But the poor girl's courage was soon to be sadly tested. Once enlisted in the ranks of a theatrical company, she found that for rigorous discipline she might as well have entered the army; the managerial fiat must be obeyed. And such a dreadful fiat.

The first part for which Carrie was cast, was that of *Arthur*, in "King John;" a part which never would have been given a novice, but that illness of another member of the company threw it upon her shoulders.

Arthur was a good part in some respects; but alas! it was a boy's part; and Carrie shrunk with uncontrollable pain from the idea of donning male attire.

For this she had not calculated when she resolved to go upon the stage.

The odium she incurred even by making an appearance in any guise, however modest, was sufficient to try her courage to the utmost; but now—to appear in the garb of a boy—how could she do it?

What would Charlie think?

Yes, there was a Charlie. There always is.

Charlie was a well-dressed, good looking young fellow, who was a charming beau in society, danced divinely, and had just about brains enough to carry him safely through the German.

Carrie Lee was in love with this young man (girls will do these things), and they were engaged to be married.

Charlie thought it a noble act of graciousness on his part that he should permit Carrie to support herself by going upon the stage. Of course, now that Carrie was cast for the part of *Arthur*, Charlie must be consulted.

That evening Charlie called, and found her with her Shakespeare before her, busily engaged in putting the words of *Arthur* in her memory.

Well, the pretty young gentleman's feelings when he discovered the dreadful state of affairs, may be imagined.

In vain Carrie tried to represent to him the necessities of the case. Charlie was sulky.

"I tell you I don't like it for you to *be stared at* by a whole houseful of people dressed like that! And I won't have it. There!"

"Do you suppose I like it, Charlie?" said the poor girl, her heart almost ready to break. "It is *necessity* with me. I must do it."

"Now, Carrie," said this nice young man, with the delicate instincts of a brute; "you know that I'm displeased with this whole matter, anyway. People know that I'm engaged to you, and it hurts my position. But now for you to go and play a man's part—why I'm not going to stand it now—that's all there is about it!"

Selfish creature! Is it not a wonder Carrie did not dismiss him then and there? But what will not a woman overlook in the man she loves?

The poor girl, with tears in her eyes, tried to talk over this stubborn fellow, who—however much we may excuse his natural repugnance to seeing his fiancée on the stage in a boy's dress—was actuated so thoroughly by a pitiable selfishness, that he could not see how necessity goaded the young girl he professed to love.

"It hurts me, Charlie, more than you know, to play this part, or even to play any part. Do you think it is pleasant for me to go upon the stage in the most novel and trying position in which a woman can be placed? Ah, do have sympathy for me! Do you, I entreat of you, even if no one else can be moved to pity me!"

For the moment the man seemed to be touched, and he went away leaving a ray of hope in the poor girl's breast that, after all, oh, wondrous boon! she might be able to keep both her lover and her situation at the theatre.

But the pretty-faced, blonde-whiskered fellow was true to his own selfish instincts when he was once removed from the softening influence of the poor girl's tears. No, no, he was not going to allow this sort of thing to go on any longer.

He stayed away from Carrie day after day—he who had been in the habit of calling at least once in every twenty-four hours—and Carrie's heart sank within her as time passed and still he did not come.

At length, on the very evening which was to see her debut in the part of *Arthur*, she received a letter from him. A thrill of joy shot through her breast as she received it; but a film passed across her eyes, when she read:

"I have concluded it will be best to break off our engagement. I think I have made a mistake about you. I have been consulting some of my friends, and they think I'd better not marry—an actress."

The letter fell to the ground. Her hands were pressed for an instant over her burning eyes, and then—it was over. The veil had dropped. She would be strong.

She had loved him—oh, how dearly she had loved him! but now he had shown her his baseness at one glance, and she would forget him, like a brave and self-reliant girl.

He who should have been the staff of her steps, the pillar of her strength, was weaker than the broken reed, and had failed her at the point of her sorest necessity. She would show him that she could live and do her duty without him.

Almost as in a dream—a dream as of one who has wandered far from all delights, she dressed herself for the part of *Arthur*, and walked upon the stage—into the glare of the footlights—into the presence of a thousand eyes—with the dream still on her.

Those who remember how Carrie Lee looked on that night of her debut, will bear me out in the assertion that in spite of her unaccustomed dress, she was wonderfully lovely—with her fair hair curling about her head, her pleading eyes full of sorrow, and her face of a marble whiteness.

A murmur of applause ran through the audience at sight of her; but she was unconscious alike of applause or censure.

Hubert, the chamberlain, is commissioned by *King John* to put out the eyes of *Arthur* with red-hot irons. At the beginning of the fourth act *Hubert* enters, bearing the irons, which he conceals behind him. At the same moment *Arthur* enters.

In a low, musical voice, Carrie spoke:

"Good-morrow, Hubert."
"Good-morrow, little prince."

The scene which followed was played by the fair debutante with a pleasing degree of pathos, and it was evident Carrie was making a good impression on her audience. Still it was not an extraordinary ability which she displayed; until the moment when she was speaking the lines—

"Nay, you may think my love was crafty love—"

When, lifting her sad eyes mechanically, there in the stage box she saw her lover—sitting, a picture of sullen displeasure, with some of the friends who had coaxed him to come and see the debut of the girl he had cast off.

Ah, girlhood is weakness, and love is strong! She thought she could put him away without a struggle. But now, at the sight of him, there came back upon her heart all the memories of her love—all the miseries of her situation.

Oh! This *was* cruel. He might have spared her this. Was it not enough that he had cast her so rudely off—that now he must come to exult in public over her anguish and embarrassment! What had she done that he should use her thus? She had been to him all trust—all faith—all kindness.

And as these bitter thoughts filled her mind, she fixed her eyes on his, and speaking the words of *Arthur* as her memory mechanically retained them, spoke still to her lover, sitting there, unable to turn his eyes away.

But she spoke no longer with the tame pleasingness of a mere pretty maiden uttering her part: the words came forth as if wrung from her soul, and her voice was filled with tears:

"If Heaven be pleased, that you must use me ill,
Why, then, you must:
Will you put out mine eyes?
These eyes that never did, nor never will, so much as frown on you?"

There was a visible sensation in the audience. Here was a fine touch of art.

It was such a touch of *nature* that the recreant lover, thrilled to his selfish heart, drew back in irrepressible agitation, and a moment after left the box.

The chord had been struck, however, to which vibrated in true response the sympathies of her audience, and Carrie Lee's portrayal of the rest of the part was such that her debut was an unheard-of success.

As for the lover who didn't want to marry an actress, it is very well known in his circle that after that debut he did want to marry an actress; and it is equally well known in his circle that the actress told him "no! she would never marry a moral coward!"

CHAPTER XVIII.

Stage-Struck Youths.—The Victim of an Unhappy Fever.—A Pitiable Object.—His General Impecuniosity.—His Vanity and Presumption. False Ideas of the Stage Life.—Sticks and Stage-Drivers.—Worthy Industry.—Democratic Possibilities.—The Stage-Struck Heroes of the Midsummer Night's Dream.—Modern Stage-Struck Youths.—Queer Letters to Managers.—A Girl of "Sixteen Summers, and Some say Good-looking."—Two Smart Girls wish to "Act upon the Stage."—A Stage-Struck Bostonian.—A Pig with Five Legs.—A Stage-Struck Philadelphian.—He Appears under an Assumed Name at the Chestnut Street Theatre.—His Love of the Coulisses.—"The Most Delightful Place in the World."—A Species of Infatuation.—A Discontented Manager.—An Actress who "Married Well."—Her Yearnings for the Old Life.—A Letter and an Epithet.

Flesh is heir to many ills, but there are medicines for most of them—though between ills and pills I never could see much difference, as a matter of comfort.

If it were not for the extra p, any one can see that ills and pills are as like as two p's.

For almost all the ills that flesh is heir to, there are medicaments of some sort, with medical men to inflict them on us; but the unfortunate mortal is beyond the reach of medical skill who is attacked with that fever which is not recognized in the medical dictionaries, but which is known to us all by the term "stage-struck."

In this case physicians are in vain; it is impossible to heal this sick soul; and what boots it to cry *shoo!* to the demon who takes possession of the stage-struck sufferer?

It is very easy to laugh at the distress of the stage-struck youth, but it really is no joke to him. His fever interrupts the ordinary course of existence, in the most unhappy way.

Talk about toothache! Talk about corns! Talk about

dyspepsia, even! The stage-struck youth cannot sleep; he cannot eat; he *can* drink—but let us hope he will not, for no drink that ever was compounded will quench his thirst.

He is, indeed, a very pitiable object, with that histrionic fire burning in his bosom.

This fever generally attacks young men in the lower walks of life—idle apprentices and weak-headed boys, who have no more idea of the artistic requirements of the stage than a Bedouin Arab has of the latest Paris fashions.

The stage-struck youth is generally an impecunious person, and there is united to the fever in his blood a famine in his pocket.

He fancies that the road to fame and fortune is a clear one, by the way of the theatre.

Usually he is a person who has been flattered by his friends into the belief that he is a wonderful mimic or a thrilling orator.

He spoke pieces at school with great success, and his vanity has been so fed by the petty triumphs of that little stage, that he is incapacitated for a studious pursuit of education.

He disdains arithmetic, and grammar is altogether beneath him.

And when he is emancipated from leading-strings, and strikes out in the world for himself, he is thoroughly unfitted for a laborious and conscientious pursuit of any vocation.

He has contracted habits of idleness, and desires nothing now, but to go through life spouting for a living—like the whales—that toil not, neither do they spin.

The first mistake of a stage-struck youth is exactly here. He fancies that the theatre, being a play-house, is not a place for work—a mistake which is more likely to land him in the workhouse, at last, than to make him a rich and famous actor.

I have known, I was almost going to say, a thousand examples of the stage-struck youth in my day, and I can count on my fingers, this hour, all those who, having gone upon the stage, still stay upon it; while the number of those who have perished by the way is legion.

The fact is, as I have already intimated, there is no occupation more laborious than that of acting; and, generally, it is only those who have been bred from childhood to the boards—whose parents were actors before them—who are fit to cope with the toilsome necessities of the stage.

Those who, from the outside world, are stage-struck, are almost invariably very poor sticks indeed, and would make a better figure driving a stage than strutting on one in the borrowed feathers of the actor.

"Stage-driving" is not in itself a disreputable employment, by any means. With the memory of Jehu and Tony Weller to inspire us, we shall not underrate the honors which belong to a race of beings now nearly extinct; but a stage-driver is not generally a scholar, nor imbued with high artistic tastes; and therefore he will do better to keep his seat on the box than to seek the approbation of the boxes.

A shoemaker on his bench is a useful member of society, and, in so far as he cultivates his mind, he is entitled to sit higher; but, so long as he pursues his trade for a livelihood, he had better take the advice of the temperance lecturer, and "stick to his last, cobbler."

Shoemakers, we know, have risen to honor and greatness, and blacksmiths have become learned men, and eloquent divines; and I heard once of a *tanner* who became *President*.

I honor *labor*. I honor all those who work, and work

honestly and well, according to their place, whether with head or hand.

I respect a carpenter at his bench, or a blacksmith at his anvil; but a stage-struck carpenter or blacksmith I can laugh at as heartily as any one in the world.

Shakespeare chose for *his* stage-struck heroes, in the "Midsummer Night's Dream," a half dozen of the "hard-handed men of Athens;" "rude patches," *Puck* calls them, "who worked for bread upon Athenian stalls."

There was *Flute*, the bellows-mender; *Starveling*, the tailor; *Quince*, the carpenter; *Snout*, the tinker; *Snug*, the joiner; and *Nick Bottom*, the weaver.

They were all desperately stage-struck, but Bully Bottom by far the most severely. This unhappy man wanted to play *all* the parts in their piece of "Pyramus and Thisby," and, when they were at rehearsal, made a deal of trouble by clamoring for this part and the other.

He was cast for *Pyramus*; and, "What is Pyramus?" he asks, "a lover or a tyrant?"

"A lover," says *Quince*, "that kills himself, most gallantly, for love."

"That," says *Bottom*, "will ask some tears in the true performing of it. If I do it, let the audience look to their eyes. I will move storms—I will condole in some measure."

But, though so pleased with the lover's part, *Bottom* cannot help wishing it had been a tyrant—"a part to tear a cat in—to make all split."

Then, when *Francis Flute* is cast for the part of *Thisby*, *Bottom* wants to play that; he thinks he could play a woman capitally.

"Let me play Thisby, too," he says; "I'll speak in a monstrous little voice—Thisne, Thisne—Ah, Pyramus, my lover dear; thy Thisby dear; and lady dear!"

When *Snug*, the joiner, is cast for the part of the lion,

he is told that he has nothing to do but roar. Whereupon poor stage-struck *Bottom's* vanity is again aroused.

"Let me play the lion, too," he says; "I will roar that it will do any man's heart good to hear me; I will roar that I will make the duke say, '*Let him roar again—let him roar again.*'"

To this *Quince* objects: "An' you should do it too terribly, you would fright the duchess and the ladies, that they would shriek, and that were enough to hang us all. Ay, that would hang us, every mother's son."

But *Bottom* replies, with a persistency worthy of a better purpose:

"I grant you, friends, if that you should fright the ladies out of their wits, they would have no more discretion but to hang us. But I will aggravate my voice so that I will roar you as gently as any sucking dove. I will roar you an' 'twere any nightingale."

The fun these fine fellows make when they are on the stage, to perform their ridiculous play, is as rich as anything to be found in the language.

Among modern stage-struck youths are representatives of every class in society. A gentleman who recently examined a package of some two hundred letters from stage-struck people, addressed to a Boston manager, relates that one was from a refined and cultivated young lady, who had fallen in love with Edwin Booth; another from an awkward, uneducated, rustic boor, who, having seen a troupe of strolling Thespians in some country town, instantly decided that he was born to histrionic fame. Most of the letters, especially those from the ladies, were very long, with long exordiums and long perorations. The writers first beg pardon for intruding, then explain at great length their feelings and aspirations, then make their request for employment or advice, and wind up with a labored apology. In many cases the fair writers adopt fictitious names, of aristocratic sound, like De Forrest, Montmorency, and the like. Some of them strive to excite the manager's pity; one is a "poor orphan," and pines for sympathy and encouragement; another is fading under the blight of a stepmother's cruelty, &c. One young man, whose early education has evidently been neglected, sends a half-page of scrawl, in which he sets forth his histrionic experience in a local dramatic club, and encloses his tin-type, so that his physical advantage may have due weight with the manager. The picture represents a man of thirty-odd, fully six feet high, and weighing about 190 pounds, his face composed to a meant-to-be-dignified, but actually silly expression, and his right hand extended across his ample breast, clasping a roll of manuscript. All the writers beg for an immediate answer, and not a few seem to assume that the manager will jump at the chance of securing their services. One girl of sixteen sends the following:

DEAR SIR—you Will Pardon the Presumption of an Inexperienced young girl in thus Addressing you But Sir What I Wish to Say to you is this, I have Become Completely Infatuated With the desire to become and Acttress and Sir, thinking your Experiance would give me an Answer I have applyed to you I Would Not Wish to Be Connected with the Ballet troupe, But assume the Charicter at first of Page or some Lover in Connection with Some Comedy or farce. I flatter Myself I am Very well Read and have A Very good Memory Witch I Presume is Requisite, for A New Beginner Now Sir I Shall Expect a Reply to this at the Earleyest opportunity and Direct to

Miss MAGGIE ———, etc.

P. S.—Discription—Highth, four feet five inches light Auburn hair Blue Eyes and Some Say good looking age Sixteen Summers—Answer Soon.

A young gentleman, in Springfield, Massachusets, evidently expects to be engaged at once:

DEAR SIR—Thinking of adopting the Profession of an actor i take this meathord of assertaining if you would wish to receive eney new men i should wish to enter as a walking Gentleman if this meets with your approvel pleas address and oblige

HARRY ———.

P S) pleas state the salery that you give to new Hands and all the partickulars if yoo can reletive to a new beginner.

A girl who is "smart," and knows it, writes from Fitchburg:

I now write to see if you do not wish for two smart girls to act upon the stage. I am A good speker and am not afraid to speeke before ten thousands. I can tell you we are real smart girls and are good looking and we would like to come first rate and can raise ned and keep folks A laughing besides put on A long face that would reach from here to Boston and we could be as sober as noah when he went into the ark in the time of the flood just sey come and tell us where and we will be there and I will now say that our names are ——— and ——— plese write soon and drect it to Fitchburg—good evening.

A young Bostonian expresses his sentiments at length, with various personal remarks, as follows:

SIR—I hope you will please excuse me for thus addressing you in a manner so abrupt and intruding upon common politeness. But Sir the emotions and impulses that prompt me to pen these thoughts to you would consider that any formal rules or services were mere secondary and not primitive in a case like this. (A few introductory remarks if you please Sir before we come to the subject) It should be the aim of every human being (as we are stepping upon the threshold of manhood or womanhood and see before us the great arena of life diversified with hills and mountains of misfortune and adversity and also interspersed with plains and valleys of fortune and prosperity and the many paths some smooth and more rough that lead and tend in different ways) to try and find such a path among the many that we could do honor to. One that would be coincidence with our nature and thought or as we are preparing our ship of human existence to sail over the sea of life, we should go as the inward chart of human nature would guide us if we want to arrive on the bright shore of success. How many of us are nuisances to ourselves and to humanity by not following out our natural feeling we do not know. But undoubtedly there are a good many. Now Sir, I think I was inwardly made for a stage actor. Don't think but know that I was, I have often had it said to me that I had ought to go on the stage, and I am bound to go. I am a young man 17 years old, and am fast verging on to the day when 18 years will have rolled over my head, and it is now time I should commence if ever. I always make a practice of committing to memory a certain amount of poetry or prose, and can commit it very easy. I have an Aunt in the city that keeps three boarding-houses and with her I live. Excuse me, sir, for thus relating to you my pedigree but thought that you would want to know something about me. I have not been from school a great while, and that is the reason I want to commence know, when my mind is active. I take the liberty to write this to you to see if you had any chance at the —— or should have soon when you could afford to pay me fair wages. If Sir you would like to know any more about me I would be happy to give it verbally or through letters, Most any time verbally from 3 to 5. Yours, truly,

---

A man in Haverhill desires to secure a star engagement for a performer evidently fitted by nature to shine in the sensational drama:

SIR—I have got a pig that has got 5 legs I dont think there ever was one like him before I have had old men here to see him that say thay never see such a sight before they advise me to send to you and see if you would like him he waighs about one hundred and 25 pounds I send this by express and if you would like it I should like to have you write as soon as you get this.

In former days I knew a young man, belonging to an excellent pious family in Philadelphia, who had reared their son in the most careful manner, only to see him unhappy, restless, discontented.

What was the matter? It soon came out,—he was stage-struck. Prayers, commands, remonstrances, were alike unavailing. His mind was made up—he would be an actor.

He appeared, under an assumed name, at the Chestnut Street Theatre. He made a favorable impression at once. He was good-looking, well-dressed, and had gentlemanly manners.

These qualifications were quite sufficient to make him entirely successful in the "Dear Fredericks" and "Darling Henrys"—lovers' parts of small calibre—in which he first appeared.

He was soon engaged, at an advanced salary, at the Arch Street Theatre, then under the excellent management of William Wheatley and John Drew, and progressed still further in the good graces of the public. He was in the seventh heaven of delight—he floated on clouds.

One chilly rainy night I went, with a heavy heart, to fill my little part, which I was playing in the same theatre.

As I passed the back-door, the old watchman thrusting his lantern into my face to assure himself that I had a right to enter—one which I would gladly have resigned—the musty, fusty odor of the thousand and one articles used for different purposes behind the scenes, met my revolted nostrils, the paint pots, glue, canvas, gilding, wood, gas, blue fire, old dresses, some smelling of camphor, some of other things less pleasant—the humanity which was wearing them, for instance—the whole mixed up with the damp and muggy odor of a rainy night—well, those who have never smelt it, have but to guess, and those who have, have but to remember.

Whenever I hear that old conundrum, "What smells the worst in a drug store?" and listen to the shouts of merriment which follow the answer, "The clerk," I always feel like saying, behind the scenes of a theatre smells worse than both drug store and clerk together.

I groped my way across the stage, in its sombre recesses, knocking against thrones, and piazzas, and Roman chariots, huddled up any way to get them all out of the way till they were wanted, when suddenly I found myself face to face with the young actor.

"Oh," said I, with a shudder, "isn't this dreadful?"

"What dreadful?" asked he, in surprise.

"Why, behind the scenes of a theatre; isn't it a nasty place?"

"Behind the scenes of a theatre a nasty place! No!"

shouted he, with a fire worthy of Beecher or Gough, "no, it is the most delightful place in the world. I love it! I idolize it! I hope I may pass my whole life here! and be brought here when I am dying!"

This same species of infatuation I have often heard expressed by many actresses and actors—nay, by scene-shifters, property men, call-boys, and, indeed, attachés of every grade in a theatre.

I never could understand it. The theatre always seemed to me the dreariest, saddest, most uncomfortable place in existence. I always recognize the beauty of a well-enacted play, a well-sung opera, or even an amusing pantomime; but the theatre in the day-time—or at night, in any place except on the stage itself—always seemed dreary, and tiresome, and depressing.

On the other hand, I have heard many and many an actor, actress and manager yearn for any other sphere of life, and blame their parents for not having fitted them for other business.

A short time ago, a New York manager, fifty years of age—a man who had been connected with theatres thirty years—said to me, with a dreary sigh, "Oh, I do get so sick of this business, sometimes, that I wish I had been a butcher or a hod-carrier, instead of a theatrical manager."

I do not think—far from it—that this utterance was drawn from him from what some people would call the moral sense; but merely because after all these years of toil, with first overwhelming success and then overwhelming failure, and then, *vice versa*, back and forth through all these long years, he found himself, at fifty years of age, probably without money, and still as much obliged to undergo the ups and downs, the uncertainties of theatrical speculation, as when he first entered the business.

As a set-off to this case, I will relate that of a young woman who, some fifteen years ago, was traveling around this country as a star actress in comedy.

She was pretty and graceful, and had a sweet voice for a song.

In the course of her wanderings she got up to Canada, where she played an engagement at the theatre with her usual success.

Of course, to carry off the hearts (for a time, at least,) of susceptible gentlemen, was no new experience to her. But, during this engagement, she met and captivated a young English officer, who was stationed with his regiment in Canada.

She returned his love, and accepted his offer of marriage.

Shortly after their arrival in England the gentleman's father died, thus leaving him the family title. The actress was now "My lady."

She did not, however, forget her theatrical friends. She wrote frequently to them, telling them of what a superb marriage she had made, in a worldly sense—money, position, title—as also, what was far better, in the sense of honor and love. Her husband was an honest, noble, Christian gentleman—she loved him dearly, "but, oh," she added, "you can't think how I long to be back on the stage!"

Her friends here hoped that in a year or two she would forget all about this idle longing. But, year after year, letters in the same strain poured in from her, always singing the same song.

The last I heard of it was this spring, *fifteen years* since she left Canada to sail for England. On perfumed paper, stamped with the coat-of-arms of her husband, she wrote:

"I idolize my husband and my children. My husband's mother is an angel, if ever there was one. So good, so pure, so true a Christian as she is I never before met. I have rank, fortune, friends, amusements of all sorts—but, oh, Kate! I tell you truly, I would relinquish everything (except my dear ones, of course), rank, fortune, position, all—to be back once more in America, 'starring' around the country—the same poor little actress I was when you last saw me."

I do not know how to comment on this case. We are by the Bible forbidden to call our brother a "fool," but there is no Scriptural law that I know of which forbids us to call our sister a little goose.

CHAPTER XIX.

The True Story of Mr. Alfred Pennyweight.—The Elegant Young Society Beau.—Mr. Pennyweight Demoralized.—He is Stage Struck.—He Wants to Play Macbeth.—Besieging the Managers.—An Engagement Secured.—Cast for the Bleeding Soldier.—Pennyweight Frightened.—Procuring the Costume.—The Wardrobe Keeper.—The Padmaker Visited.—Pennyweight's Legs.—The Fearful First Night.—The Curtain Rings Up, and the Play Opens.—Pennyweight's Debut. Effect on the Galleries.—The Catastrophe.—Good Advice to the Stage-Struck.—The Cure for the Fever.—Ridicule, the Remedy.

A very ludicrous history is that of Mr. Alfred Pennyweight—whom it was my fortune first to meet at Saratoga.

He was a gay young butterfly, and the way he flitted from flower to flower, was delightful to see.

It was a family trait, however, for Old Pennyweight made his money in flour.

Where was there to be found a gallant young gentleman with cheek more blooming or eye more bright than those of Alfred Pennyweight? He was a gorgeous youth in his attire, and he indulged in lavender kids, and diamond pins, and flowered neckties and curling-irons, in reckless extravagance.

He was addicted to saying "By George," when I first met him, it is true; but after only a little mingling with the aristocratic foreigners who condescend to associate with us in society, he could utter "Bah Jove, ye know," like an Englishman to the jovial gentry born.

He was elegantly slim and genteelly tall, and he kept a man to groom him and to pick his vest pockets of his small change.

As I sat in New York one evening in November, a card was brought in. It bore the name of Alfred Pennyweight.

With the gay young Saratoga beau in my mind, my first thought was the dreadful one that I was in my quilted wrapper, and that I should shock this young gentleman's refined feelings by my inelegance of attire.

But I might have been robed in one of his father's flour-sacks, for all my visitor would have cared. He was stage-struck, and had ceased to be a beau—to become a bore.

He entered the room. Was it possible that this neglected creature was Alfred Pennyweight? I gazed on him with amazement.

His beard was a week old—his hair was out of curl—his necktie was dirty, and so were his gloves.

He came in with the air of a man lost to society—his proud form bowed with the weight of many cares, and his clothing soaked with the November rain.

"Why, Mr. Pennyweight, how wet you are! You came out without your umbrella!"

"Umbrella! What are umbrellas when there is a storm within, against which umbrellas are no protection? It is the fire of genius yearning for utterance—it is the histrionic fire. I burn to go upon the stage."

It took me a long time to get Mr. Pennyweight down from the clouds; but when I did accomplish it, I found that his errand to me was a very practical one. He wished to obtain my assistance to get him a situation at one of our leading theatres.

"But why do you desire to go upon the stage, Mr. Pennyweight? You cannot wish thus to earn a livelihood. If you were a woman—or even if you were a poor man, I might understand it. The channels in which women can work are few, and obstructed by numberless toilers; but men have the whole field of labor before them, from Wall street speculation down—or up—to boot-blacking."

But argument was wasted on him. He insisted that he was destined to become a great actor, and that I was the very person to assist him. He was not unreasonable, he said. All he wanted was that I should procure him an engagement at one of our leading theatres, to play Macbeth.

I said that I was absolutely powerless to accomplish such a thing. All I could do would be to introduce him to some of the managers, and he must plead his own case before them.

"When will you do it?"

"Oh, almost any day."

"Why not to-day?"

"Very well. If 'twere done, no doubt 'twere well 'twere done quickly."

And so we walked up to Broadway.

I think I never was so talked at in my life as I was by that man on that memorable day. He poured his aspirations into my ears in a perfect flood. He told me how he had steadily refused to enter "trade," but had kept his mind free from the contaminating influences of mere money-getting, to be able at length to proclaim to all the world his devotion to the goddess whom he adored.

"Do you mean Miss Annie Porter?" I asked, abstractedly.

"I mean Melpomone," he replied, in an injured tone.

"Oh, excuse me. I heard a rumor, the other day, that you were engaged to be married to Miss Annie Porter."

"I am—but she can wait till I am gweat."

What a prospect for the poor girl, thought I.

By this time we had arrived at the door of one of our leading theatres.

"Mr. Ryely in?" I asked of the treasurer at the box-office.

"Yes; do you want to see him?"

I gave my card, and that of Mr. Pennyweight, who was now the palest man I ever saw.

The answer was that the manager would see us in a minute.

I think that minute was to poor Pennyweight a period of unspeakable agony. He twitched nervously at the ends of his moustache, twirled his hat in his hands, let his cane fall upon the floor, and thus unkowingly went through the stereotyped funny business of a low comedian in a bashful part.

The manager presently came bustling in—a gentleman endowed with an ample corporosity, and a little hard of hearing—celebrated, by the way, for his success in getting rid of bores with the aid of a formidable ear-trumpet.

He was in a great hurry, and wanted to know of us what we wanted to know of him.

I explained, as succinctly as possible, that this gentleman (designating Mr. Pennyweight), wanted to go upon the stage.

"Yes?" said the manager, who was a very business-like man. "What can he do?"

"His principal ambition," said I, "is to play Macbeth."

"Mac *who?*" roared the manager, as if he were referring to an Irish part.

"Macbeth," said Pennyweight, speaking now for the first time. "You must know Macbeth, you know."

"My good friends," said the manager, looking at us with a strange expression, as if he thought his good friends were two lunatics, "I really must wish you good-day. We rehearse our new ballet at 12. If the gentleman, now, would like to go on in one of the marches—to carry a banner—or, perhaps, he'd like to dance on, and support the danseuses in their poses? No? Well, then, I really don't see what further use my time can be to you. As to the idea of a novice playing Macbeth, and, above all, playing it in this theatre—why, that, you know, is a little too ridiculous."

Ridiculous! Ridiculous is no word for it. It was the sheerest, most incredible stupidity.

So, with an apology for having engrossed the manager's time, we took leave.

I thought it was just possible this would cool down Pennyweight's ardor; but what was my surprise to find that, if anything, he was more stage-struck than ever.

"I assure you," he said, "that the very idea we were in a manager's office, and talking about my appearance, you know, made me burn all over. Oh, I'm sure I shall succeed."

"But you see how poor the chance is for your getting an opening."

"Pshaw! a ballet theatre! What was the use of going there at all?"

"Precisely what I endeavored to show you before we set out, Mr. Pennyweight. There was no use in going there at all; and there will be no use at all in going anywhere else on such an errand. Why can't you put this idea out of your head?"

He replied with an elegant outburst of glittering generalities, and theatrical sound and fury; the essence of which was that he was not going to give it up so, Mrs. Brown, and that, like Shylock, he should hold me to my bond.

So we went from theatre to theatre; but Macbeth was nowhere in demand—at least Macbeth by the pennyweight; and, at length, the whole gauntlet was run.

There were no more theatres to conquer—at least in New York; and I breathed a sigh of relief.

At this juncture, Pennyweight tremulously suggested New Jersey.

"Enough," said I, "I refuse. To New York I am committed, but nothing beyond New York. You see, now, you stand no chance."

"But there was a theatre where they wanted some people."

"Yes—some utility people."

"What are utility people?"

"The utilities are the persons who present a letter—announce that 'my lord, the carriage waits'; and sometimes do the heavy business."

"The—ah—heavy business?"

"Yes—moving chairs, tables, and the like."

Pennyweight shrugged his shoulders with disgust. But he revived.

"There's nothing degrading in doing the heavy—the utility business, is there? I mean in a professional sense."

"Oh, nothing degrading, of course. But would utility business satisfy you?"

"Why, just at first, you know," he replied, very reluctantly, "as it appears I can get nothing else to do."

"Very well, then;" and we returned to the theatre which wanted some utility people.

"My friend would like to engage with you to play utility business," said I to the manager.

"What is the salary?" asked Pennyweight.

"Three dollars a week," answered the manager.

On the way up, Pennyweight had stopped, and bought a pair of fur gloves, which cost seven dollars—more than two weeks' salary.

I thought surely this would be a damper. But, no;

Pennyweight said if the manager would only let him play the parts he wanted, he'd do it without any salary at all.

"Oh, I dare say," answered the manager; "we have plenty of that sort. If I were to listen to all the stage-struck people who make application to me, I should have nothing but green hands in the theatre."

"Stage-struck!" and "green hands!" Pennyweight winced under these expressions. He told me, afterwards, that he wondered professional people would use them. Why didn't they say, "fired with histrionic ardor," instead of "stage-struck," and "unaccustomed to public speaking," instead of "green hands?"

At any rate, it was settled. Pennyweight was now a utility man, at three dollars a week.

"Well, how do you feel now?"

He replied that he felt O. K.

"How will you look your friends in the face?"

"Proudly. 'Tall oaks from little acorns gwow.'"

"But you're not an acorn, Mr. Pennyweight."

"Pshaw! Can't you understand a simile? The best actors have spwung from nothing."

"Oh, you mean if you ever get to be a great actor, *you* will have sprung from nothing?"

But the poor fellow was so elated at the idea that at last—at last! he was to appear on the stage, that he was proof against ridicule.

Mr. Pennyweight now became quite lost to the outer world, ceasing relations with the fashionable set of which, up to this time, he had been such a brilliant ornament, and spending his whole time behind the scenes of the theatre.

What he did there, besides gazing with wonder and amazement on all that was new and strange to him, it is not so easy to say; but certain it is that the earliest comer to the rehearsal and the latest to leave it, testified to the fact that Pennyweight was always earlier and later than they; and the stage-carpenters, prowling about the scenes in the afternoon, said that behind the flats, in some dark, cobwebby corner, Mr. Pennyweight was always to be found; and everybody pronounced him one of the worst cases of stage-struck fever they ever encountered.

One day, as I was going in at the back door of the theatre, I felt my arm held in a vice, as of iron.

It was too dark there, in the gloom behind the scenes, to see any face, but I heard a well-known voice gasp out:

"I am *cast!*"

"By your grip, I should judge you were cast-iron," said I, casting him off.

"No—you don't comprehend. I am cast for a part."

"No?"

"Yes."

"For what part are you cast, Mr. Pennyweight?"

"For the soldier in Macbeth."

There are many soldiers in Macbeth, but I knew at once which one he meant—a part which is usually denominated the "Bleeding Captain" by professional people, though it is not so called by Shakespeare.

"Now, Mr. Pennyweight," said I, "here is a chance for you to distinguish yourself. The part has only three speeches, it is true, but that is quite long enough for a beginner. At the same time the meaning of the words is veiled in some of the most difficult lines Shakespeare ever wrote, and it will require the full force of your intellect, aided by your best elocution, to convey the meaning clearly to your audience."

"Don't say another word about it—I'm frightened almost to death already."

The piece was rehearsed the next day, and I was promptly on hand to see how my protege would get on.

The best description of Pennyweight's appearance on that morning may be found in the words of Ophelia:

> "My lord, as I was sewing in my closet,
> Lord Hamlet, with his doublet all unbraced,
> No hat upon his head, pale as his shirt,
> His knees knocking each other—
> Thus he comes before me."

But it does not require much courage to get through a rehearsal. The speeches are only mumbled over, even by the best actors, and all the novice has to do, is to implicitly obey instructions as to "situation" and "stage business," two technical terms, which signify where he shall stand and what he shall do.

Fortunately for Pennyweight, the soldier in "Macbeth" is, at night, brought in on a litter, being supposed to have been recently wounded, and to be bleeding freely; therefore, as he does not stir, and has nothing to do but lie upon the litter and speak, one of the greatest difficulties of the beginner is overcome.

Pennyweight got through rehearsal so well that he was quite elated; and insisted that I must oversee the preparation of his costume.

"Very well," I said. "Shall we go into the wardrobe room?"

We went into the wardrobe room, and the wardrobe keeper, an excellent woman, with a strong Hibernian accent, asked us what we wanted.

"This gentleman," said I, "is going to play the soldier in Macbeth."

The woman eyed the elegant Pennyweight curiously, and then asked, "if he was wan ov the shupes?"

A supe! Pennyweight, of Fifth Avenue, a supe! He turned green with horror.

"No—oh no. This gentleman is not one of the supes. He is going to play the soldier in Macbeth, and he wants to know what you can give him to wear for it."

She said she could give him "a himlet."

"Thank you," I replied. "But a helmet alone will scarcely be sufficient for him to costume himself in for the part."

She reflected a minute, and then said that "the best ov the kilts wus gon'. She guv wan to Macduff, and wan to Banky, and wan apiece to each ov the shupes, and it's on'y a duzin she hod ov 'em, ony way. But she could give him a himlet."

"Oh, never mind," said Pennyweight, "I shouldn't care to wear the things, even if she had them to give. I say, what a regular old curiosity shop of a place a wardrobe room is, isn't it?"

My attention thus called to it, I looked. It was a curious place indeed, with its piles upon piles of musty garments, from spangled robes to Irish jackets, folded and laid away upon huge shelves, which surrounded the room —with its forest of hats, caps and helmets, of every conceivable pattern, hanging from the ceiling, and its busy Irishwoman, receiving articles which had been worn the night before, and folding them and laying them away, as carefully as if they had really been the property of kings, and lords, and knights.

"Are you going to buy your dress, then?"

"Why, yes, I must have a Scotch dress. I shall want it for Macbeth, some day, you know."

There was no getting that craze out of his head!

As I had promised to see him safely through this business, I went with him to a store, where he bought a very fine article of plaid for his kilt; he then wanted a black velvet jerkin or waist, and bought three yards of black silk velvet, at twelve dollars a yard.

"The next question is," said he," where do I get my pink silk trowsers, you know."

"Your pink silk trowsers? I do not quite understand you, Mr. Pennyweight. What do you mean by your pink silk trowsers? You certainly do not expect to play the Bleeding Captain in trowsers of pink silk, like a burlesque actress?"

"No!—that is—you see—well, I suppose that is not exactly the professional term for 'em. But, you know—those things they wear on the stage in place of trowsers, you know."

"Do you mean your tights? I will show you."

The place was not far off, and while Pennyweight went into an inner room, for consultation, I stayed without; but, the door remaining open, I could hear, though I could not see.

"Mon Dieu!" said a Frenchman's voice, "but you cannot play ze part wiz dat leg!"

"Why not? What's wrong with my legs?" (The voice of Pennyweight, indignant).

"Mais, monsieur, you have ze knock-knee, ze bow-leg, and ze spindle-shank—all tree as one!"

Here was a revelation in regard to the symmetry of the irresistible Pennyweight.

"It shall be necessaire to have ze pair of pad," said the man.

"Pads?"

"Oh, mais oui, monsieur, ze leg is vaire bad."

"And can you really remedy all the defects of—"

"Oh, oui, monsieur. We remedy all of it. We make you -day one leg zat is better zan ze leg of ze nature."

"Why, you're quite an artist, aren't you?"

"Merci, monsieur. It is vair agreeable to meet one Americain dat appreciate. Oh, ze good day have come for ze artiste de pad. Odder day zere was so very little practice; but now—aha!—le Mazeppa, and le Black Crook—we have enough to do."

When Pennyweight returned he blushed guiltily.

Thus padding doth make cowards of us all.

The fearful first night came at last, and poor Pennyweight was in a pitiable plight. The perspiration stood on his forehead, and his lips were white with fright.

"Are you sure you know the lines?"

"Oh, I'm dead-letter perfect. Hear me."

I held the book while he struck an attitude, and re-repeated the lines without a mistake.

"Now be brave—speak out loud, remember."

He said he would remember, and the curtain rang up.

The play of Macbeth opens with a scene by the three witches, beginning with the well-known lines:

"When shall we three meet again,
In thunder, lightning, or in rain?"

with only ten lines more, when the scene opens and discloses a camp where King Duncan, Lenox, Malcolm, Donalbain, and attendants, meet a wounded soldier—none other than my friend Pennyweight.

The first line of this scene is spoken by King Duncan, who says,

"What bloody man is that?"

And here poor Pennyweight suddenly remembered that he had quite forgotten to smutch his face with blood, and so he was *not* a "bloody man" at all.

Malcolm then turns to the soldier, and says—

"Hail, brave friend: Say to the king
Thy knowledge of the broil
As thou didst leave it."

And this was Pennyweight's cue to speak. He began, but in such a low and tremulous voice that immediately wild cries of "*louder, louder,*" issued from the galleries.

Confused beyond measure at this unexpected greeting, poor Pennyweight choked, gasped, and finally—*stuck.*

Here the prompter came to his aid.

The lines were somewhat difficult, running thus:

> "As whence the sun 'gins his reflection,
> Shipwrecking storms, and direful thunders break;
> So from that spring whence comforts seemed to come,
> Discomfort swells."

The prompter, confused at Pennyweight's sticking, and not at all familiar with the lines himself, began prompting wildly thus:

> "As when the sun *jins* his reflection,"

which was uttered in so loud a tone that everybody in the audience heard it, and Pennyweight, taking it up with sense and consiousness all but gone, shouted at the top of his voice,

> "And when the sun *gin slings* reflection—"

No ear could hear more. There broke from the audience a thunder of laughter which echoed and re-echoed from parquet to gallery—from boxes, balcony, and all over the house—so loud and terrible that poor Pennyweight fell back upon his litter as if he had been stunned.

He was borne off the stage by the convulsed litter-bearers, who, as soon as they got behind the scenes, dropped their burthen upon the floor and roared with uncontrollable merriment.

Poor Pennyweight scrambled to his feet, and holding his horrified head between his hands, rushed into the green room, where he sank into an arm-chair, gasping for breath. I followed him and found him there, a picture of despair.

"Oh! oh! oh!" said I.

Lady Macbeth approached him, fan in hand, and gazed upon him in speechless amazement.

12

Pennyweight turned his head away and groaned.

"What will become of you if you go on at this rate, Mr. Pennyweight?" said Lady Macbeth, sternly.

"Don't," he moaned; "for pity's sake, don't! Did you see Augustus Tompkins?"

"Augustus Tompkins?"

"Tompkins! my rival. He had a seat in the front row. I saw him grinning like a monkey at me; and Annie Porter sitting by his side, with her fan up before her face, and laughing all over. Oh, distraction!"

"Well, go home. Change your dress, and go home as soon as you can. Don't be downcast; the worst is over now. I don't think you can do any worse than this. Perhaps you'll do better the next time."

"No! I've had enough of the stage! Oh, how shall I ever look my friends in the face again?"

And he rushed away into his dressing-room.

I have not seen Mr. Pennyweight since; but I am informed he has gone into business, and has now become a useful member of society.

But to this day he is said to be haunted by a horrible spectre which takes the shape of the cruel thing that undid him quite—a "gin-sling."

Old Doctor Franklin, on hearing the remark that what was lost on earth went to the moon, observed that there must be a good deal of good advice accumulated there.

Good advice seems to be lost on the victims of the stage-struck fever; but by the lightest weapons of ridicule a fool is to be laughed from his folly.

Mr. Alfred Pennyweight is a type of the fools who see only the glitter and glory of the stage, and burn to share it, as a boy with a drum burns to be a soldier.

When years and experience have shown the boy that the soldier's life is full of toil and danger, and that the bugles and the drums are not its chief concern, he is very likely to take new views of the desirability of such a life. He finds that merchandise or politics are better suited to his tastes.

But the folly of the stage-struck youth is a graver matter. He is no longer a child; he is old enough at once to enter upon the life which dazzles his fancy and deludes his sense, and he enters upon it.

Thus is the stage cumbered with a load of human rubbish, the like of which is to be found in no other sphere of art.

Men with no true sense of art, actuated solely by vanity, are as numerous as the leaves of Vallambrosa, in that vale which should be bright with intellect, and grace, and culture.

With all the power I possess, I would hold the stage-struck youth up to ridicule. When sober reasoning will fail of its end, ridicule will touch the sore spot as with caustic.

Make a thing ridiculous, and many a young man will recoil from it as if it were a snake.

I have had proof—substantial proof—of the effective work my efforts in this respect have wrought; and *I know* that all the anathemas ever thundered from the divine desk against this thing will not terrify the soul of the victim of stage fever as will a titter from behind a lady's fan.

CHAPTER XX.

My Tour in the West as a Star Actress.—From Paris to Cincinnati.—My Critics.—My First Benefit.—Generals and Poets in the Green-room.—Down the River to Louisville.—An Operatic Company.—My First "Soldier Audience."—Military Necessity.—Southern Refugees.—Queer Gratitude for an Actress's Services.—Trouble in Getting to Nashville.—Cutting Down the Wardrobe.—Soldiers in the Cars.—The Mason.

If there ever was a truism in this world which is a truer truism than other truisms, it is that veracious one which asserts that "everything goes by comparison."

Of course I know I shall not be contradicted in this statement, but for the sake of argument I choose to believe that some disagreeable, mythical personage flatly denies the possibility of a sensible man's having two opinions on the same subject, merely because a certain space of time has elapsed, and other scenes have intervened between his first statement and his last.

Perhaps it may be so—with sensible men. The genus is somewhat limited, and as a rapidly disappearing race, I suppose we must be somewhat lenient with them. But with sensible women I know it is different.

But to resume, and in the conventional style of theatrical story-tellers (I beg pardon, nothing *sous jeu* meant by this play) continue.

It was on a July day, in the second year of our civil war, that I left the sunny coast of France.

It was raining that day on the sunny coast of France.

To use a mild and singularly appropriate metaphor, it was raining cats and dogs that day on the sunny coast of France.

This did not prevent me leaving, however.

I left However, and However saw me depart with the greatest apparent apathy. My gay and lightsome bark sat trimly on the waves, buffeting the billows, and calmly smiling on the raging waters' breast.

Perhaps the mythical personage will urge here that a bark cannot smile; in which case I will but pray him to point out the exact anatomical section so widely known as the "breast" in a river, and I shall then be at no loss to find something to sustain *my* simile.

I thought of poor Mary Stuart in leaving. Her adieux to the heartless vales, her valedictory remarks to the stoical mountains, her watery and tearful tributes to the unheeding rivers, all rose before my mind with extraordinary accuracy.

I tried to be sentimental, but I failed. I could do nothing but gaze with mute astonishment at the wine traffic which was going on about me.

In a word, the wine made me positive, and sentimentalism went—up.

Not that I imbibed any wine. Not that any one about me imbibed any; but it was the evidence of wine, the people of wine, the servants of wine, the caskers of wine, the makers of wine, the growers of wine, the police of wine, the incontrovertible evidence that in France, at least, wine was King. But at length my gay and lightsome bark cut short my reflections, and conveyed me gently dancing o'er the ocean's foam.

She tripped it on the light, fantastic toe.

My bark was very majestic. I was proud of her. Her cabin was magnificent. She could seat two hundred and fifty people at dinner every day; but *she never seated me!*

I paid one hundred and thirty dollars for lodging for ten days.

Board? No.

But that was not the bark's fault, you may say.

Granted. But I declare it was not mine. Give me a choice in the matter, and I never, never *would* be seasick.

At length, the bark accomplished her mission, taking me from France, and landing me in Broadway—I should say, America.

After we landed, I was driven up Broadway. Great Heaven! was this my favorite street? What! Decorated with these floating canvas signs, these grotesque oriflammes, these parodies on banners, these painted attractions.

But it was funny, wasn't it, to see a charger all out of drawing, carrying a rider, whose only really distinguishable article of apparel was a Kossuth hat, the twain accompanied by an unsheathed sabre, dashing frantically from the fourth story of a house in Broadway towards an oligarchic slave-holding foe, lying perdu, it would seem, on an apparently innocent housetop on the opposite side?

Or again, to behold a battalion of ferocious (painted) Zouaves bayonetting nothing with undiminished ardor during the somewhat protracted space of four years, while tender invocations to the patriotism of young male America met the eye at every step. He was conjured to conquer or die, and get $325 either way; he was entreated to join the "finest regiment going," and to "look at this" as well; he was supplicated to "come in out of the draft," and at the same time become possessor of "the biggest bounty yet." These things, most fortunately, have all disappeared. But they were there then, and tended greatly towards diminishing my idea of the beauty of our much vaunted Broadway. They made the street look cheap, and were altogether unpleasant.

After my entrée at Wallack's (whose vicissitudes have been related in a former chapter), I was for seven long months on the wing, or, less poetically and in fact more truthfully, for seven months I was traveling about in those very unpleasant railway conveyances yclept "cars," through the greater portion of our Western and South-western States. As soon as I returned, I was requested by all parties to write, and I yielded to the dulcet supplications of that organ more powerful than even the Boston one, generally known as the Vox Populi.

But in general I hate notes of travel, don't you?

Ah, thank you! These are not notes of travel. I am nothing if not high-toned, so I think I may dub them at once, "*Les Impressions d'une Voyageuse.*"

Often such impressions are very silly affairs. I think to be obliged to read of the exact spot in Switzerland where Maria lost her toothbrush, or to digest the progress of the Joneses on the Rhine, is about the mildest of all amusements. But this is gentle agony compared to the lively torture of wading through Mrs. Magacer's "Ancient Greece" or Lady Bigot's Rome.

While I am on the subject I may say at once that I honestly believe I have read everybody's "Paris" going; read it and sometimes liked it, but I will also make a clean breast of it and openly avow that one man's "Central Asia" is enough for me.

One man's "Central Asia" satisfies the requirements of my inmost soul. How any one can stand promiscuous varieties of Central Asia is a mystery which I have yet to fathom.

Why, look at it in a sensible light! If all men are our brethren, so be it. I am not political; I have not, nor never had any unfriendly animus towards American Africans. Dinah is a splendid washerwoman, and Uncle Joe excels any gentleman of my acquaintance in the accomplishments of whitewashing and carpet shaking. If he is my brother, he is at least an honest, inoffensive man, and an upright creature in every respect. But your Central Asiatic, it appears, can do nothing on earth but stick arrows into unoffending white travelers, pilfer all the Mericans he can lay hands upon, and make himself in many other ways intensely disagreeable. If *he* is my brother, why I can only say, I am not proud of the relationship.

But what under the sun, be it tropical or polar, am I doing in Asia, when I should be among the quiet citizens of the splendid town of Cincinnati, where began my round of Western engagements?

What, indeed!

I must confess I felt rather timorous about appearing in Cincinnati. It had been the stronghold of my family for years, and I had a disagreeable inward conviction that my crudities, inevitable to a novice, would be doubly palpable to a public whose great theatrical deity was my sister; a public who saw no ill with her, no good without her; who scorned any *Evadne* but hers, and figuratively snapped their fingers at anybody else's *Adelgitha*. She had retired from the stage, true; but she still lived in their memories, and with jealous eye and unwilling ear they observed the usurpation of her roles by any new aspirant for public favor. Contrary to my expectation, however, they received me with open arms, crowded my houses, bestowed upon me fifty times the applause I merited, and when, at last, I left their town, they sent me on my way with many a hearty God-speed.

But my great fun in Cincinnati (as it was in all the towns) was reading the criticisms on my acting which appeared in the different papers. Somehow, like that fable of Æsop's which tells of the man and his donkey, I could not please everybody.

One critic said I was as fine a tragedienne as Rachel, whereupon the afternoon paper came out and said I wasn't.

I agreed fully with the afternoon paper.

You will be pained to learn, as I was, that the critic

who compared me to Rachel is now an inmate of the Walnut Hills Insane Asylum—a mild but hopeless lunatic; but I think, from his writings, that his mind was slightly failing him when I was there.

It was at Cincinnati I had my first great benefit, attended by the distinguished officer and commander of the post, Major General Hooker, by the talented author of "Sheridan's Ride," and by that much-talked-of and seemingly ubiquitous body, the *elite* of the city. The theatre was prettily decorated with flags in honor of the event, while a pictured representation of the Father of his Country hung over one proscenium box, having for companion (a worthy companion, too), General Grant as a *vis-a-vis*. Washington looked rather bored and sleepy, I thought, but Grant sat bolt upright, as though he had fully determined to sit it out on that line if the performance took all winter.

Of course the evening could not pass without a speech being called for, and General Hooker made it; modestly disclaiming the honor of being the star of the evening. After the performance I had something like a diminutive levee within the sacred precincts of the green-room, and the show of gold lace and military buttons was very pretty indeed. As they were going, Mr. Buchanan Read remarked:

"Of course you have nothing to say to me, a poor civilian, lost amid all these military heroes?"

Hadn't I anything to say? I should like to see the time when I hadn't anything to say! In the first place, I am a woman, and in the seeond, I have a pretty good store of quotations lying near or on that metaphorical mental repository, the tip of my tongue.

"Oh, yes, I have!"

"Indeed; what is it?"

I replied in something of a Weggian strain, that "beneath the rule of men entirely great (like yourself, for instance), the pen (especially the one with which you wrote 'Sheridan's Ride,' you know) is mightier than the sword (Mr. Read)."

He smiled very pleasantly, and, being an inveterate punster, bade me adieu, saying that after such a compliment there was nothing left him and his friends but to make their boughs and take their leaves.

It seems to be the fashion with travellers in the West to invariably speak in the most laudatory terms of the steamboats which ply on the Ohio and Mississippi rivers. The reckless profuseness in the matter of diet offered the traveler, the richness of the furniture which adorns the "Ladies' Cabin," the white-and-gold decorations of the sleeping berths, are a few of the points brought up to sustain the praises usually bestowed.

I am quite willing to acquiesce most fully in all this. The dinners are wastefully luxurious, the ladies' cabin never without the inevitable grand piano (generally most woefully out of tune), and the sleeping berths always provided with those expensive and uncomfortable spring-bottom beds, which during the night of occupancy impress the sleeper with the vague but cheering idea that he is being jolted about on the cushions of an antiquated stage coach. The illusion is so complete that in the morning one looks about for the horses and the driver, and is surprised to find them missing.

So far as regards the table, I repeat that I humbly concur in its being sinfully extravagant. I wish those steamboat captains, or whoso's duty it is to cater for the steamboat table, would read that useful little book entitled, "What to do with the Cold Mutton," and then, after the mutton has been fully digested, I wish they would read another book, which I am going to write myself, to be called "What to do with the Dinner Gongs."

My hearing is not the acutest of all my organs. If,

therefore, gongs nearly drive me distracted, what must be their effect on persons whose "tympanums" are umblemished, whose "glottises' are above reproach, whose "larynxes" are unimpeachable, and whose "Eustachian tubes" are in that highly satisfactory condition initially known to the world as O K?

I want these gongs to be got rid of at once, and placed where mortal eye can never rest on them again.

What say you to the bed of the Potomac? Or quick-lime?

Some of the steamboats have discarded gongs, and taken up little hand-bells as a means of ringing the traveler in to dinner, or, if you prefer it, dinner into the traveler. But these are as offensive to my sense of dignity as the gongs are to my sense of hearing. Am I a *femme de chambre*, that I am rung after in this manner? Is this gentleman a "Boots" that he is tintinabulated at thus ruthlessly? I always use these hand-bells when I want to summon that liveried servant of mine who invariably Enters R. 2 E., and tells me, in a very weak voice, that "My highness's coach is waiting," or that "My lord's below, and craves admission to my ladyship." Perhaps this is another reason why I don't fancy them. What I do really like is the mode now pretty universally adopted in hotels all over the country, which permits you to stroll in whenever you feel inclined, and dine or sup at any time between certain hours. I thought I would try to inaugurate this system on the steamboat which took me from Cincinnati to Louisville. You shall see how it worked.

After the bell rang, I let the first rush get over, and then I quietly strolled in to get my dinner. Although not more than half an hour had elapsed since the order was given to "fire," scarcely a vestige of food was to be seen. What did remain was so disfigured by bad carving and inartistic cutting, that I could not have eaten a morsel if I had been starving. A more unappetizing looking mess I never beheld. I walked away in disgust. Madame Mère had observed the whole proceeding, and, as she prides herself on being a very matter-of-fact, common-sensical old lady, she saw fit to apostrophize me in this strain:

"Well, you're a sweet young female *Hamlet*, aint you? walking about and letting on that the world is out of joint, oh cursed spite that ever you were born to set it right! I wish you joy in fighting windmills, and trying to innoculate innocent Western steamboats with your fine French notions. Why didn't you come and take your dinner when the rest did?"

And that's all the good I got out of *that*.

The steamboat which took us from Cincinnati to Louisville was called the "General Lytle." This brave young soldier, a Cincinnatian, was killed at the battle of Chickamauga. His body fell into the hands of the enemy, who paid a knightly tribute to the fallen foe, by decking his remains with flowers, and sending them back with the untarnished sword lying on the manly breast, and escorted by a guard of honor composed of ten colonels.

On board the boat we found a large body (seventy-two in number) of really clever artists, the German opera troupe.

It would be difficult for me to tell how delightfully that evening passed away. The cumbrous boat moving heavily down the stream, the faint lights from little villages on the banks reflected dimly in the turbid waters beneath, the occasional stoppages to "wood up," at which time all was bustle and commotion, the low moaning chaunt hummed in unison by the negroes at their work on the boat's machinery below, all made up a scene of picturesque novelty which will not soon be effaced from my mind.

Inside, we were jolly companions, every one. The Germans sang, as only Germans can sing, a lot of choruses, snatches, refrains and what not, without instrumental accompaniment, but with wonderful precision and harmony. Anschutz directed, and told me he had never heard them sing better. A novel feature of the entertainment was the debut of some of the musicians as solo singers. I have forgotten the name of a young man, a trombonist or something of the sort, who dashed off the drinking song from "Marta" with such admirable *verve*, and low, rich basso tones, as made Hermanns prick up his ears and look wildly around after his laurels.

This was followed by dancing, which was kept up till a late hour. All went in with a will. Marguerite and Robert le Diable, Mephistopheles and la Dame Blanche, Marta and Fidelio, Stradella and Mrs. Page in one set, while the fishwomen of Faust and the sprites in the Magic Flute footed it merrily beyond.

During the melée Canissa and I escaped, and made for the "hurricane deck," where we indulged in a brisk walk and brisker conversation. Canissa was a nice child—a Hungarian. She was a lady-like, modest girl, and deserving of all praise. Her mother was with her, and the two buy their daily bread with the notes the daughter issues.

It was in Louisville I had my first taste of the "soldier-audience." I must say I didn't like the taste. I liked the sight better.

It was certainly very picturesque. That mass of army overcoats, filling every nook and corner of the building, a solid background of light blue men, the unity of color finely relieved by the bright glitter of their bayonets' steel.

Bayonets in every imaginable posture, but generally reposing gracefully along the ledges of the tiers, thus pointing directly at the performer.

When I came on the stage the first night in the "Hunchback," it quite took away my breath. I thought perhaps they imagined me to be a disguised deserter, and were going to make a "*charge a la bayonette*" instanter. It was a cheerful feeling—only I wished I was in New York just then.

There were no women to be seen in the whole house, except in the boxes.

A very pleasing peculiarity of the soldier-audience is its amiable tendency to laugh. Tragedy affords more amusement than any other style of play, and is therefore provided more frequently than comedy for the delectation of the mass. I was informed by the leading actor at Louisville, that the mournful tragedy of "Jack Cade," which he had selected for his benefit, and played the night before I came, was received with shouts of mirthful derision, and groans of bitter mockery from beginning to end. He was a good actor, and I felt sorry.

"That's very bad," said I, sympathizingly; "of course it must make you careless, and in the end will ruin your school."

"School! Thunder!" he exclaimed; "it would ruin a university!"

They did not laugh much during my engagement. They had a happy faculty of applauding in the wrong places, and throwing me bouquets just when I was myself dying, or murdering some one else, and expecting me to stop the action and pick them up—but they didn't laugh. I think it was the presence of the excruciating elite which subdued them, for the elite *was* there, led, as it was in the halcyon days of yore, by the yet beautiful Mrs. George D. Prentice. She came to see me act, which I took as a great compliment, as she had never entered a theatre since the death of her son.

"I can't go in my carriage, as I used, to see your sister,

my dear," she remarked, in a melancholy tone. "What do you think they did the other day? They walked into my stables and carried off all my horses for the army!"

"They" were the impressing agents, who were very busy at that time "drafting" horses for our troops.

"Military necessity" may be necessary, but it is not always agreeable.

At Louisville I stumbled unexpectedly over my distinguished cousin, Major General John A. Logan. I think I may call him distinguished without any undue amount of family pride.

General Logan was very undecided whether to go down to Nashville and supersede Thomas, who had just been obliged to fall back before Hood, or return to Washington, or stay where he was severely. I must add that the report of his going to supersede Thomas *was* only a report, and people were intensely curious to find out whether it was true or not. I thought he might tell *me;* but, strange to say, he thought he mightn't.

Opinions differ, you know. He told me no more than if my name had been Jones and his Jenkins.

It positively rained, hailed and snowed refugees while I was in Louisville. The poor wretches came up the river from the South in droves; hungry, shoeless, hatless, and almost garmentless. Some benevolent people (in fact, I think it was government action), took a house for their reception, and clothed, fed, and finally found them employment. I determined to do something towards this charity, and with the aid of the manager of the theatre, gave a matinee for their benefit. The receipts were large, and were handed over to the committee.

But it appears there was refugee and refugee. There were loyal refugees and others. I was astounded the day after the matinee to find my room invaded by two women of the latter class.

"Are you Olive Logan?" asked the elder of the two, impudently.

I was vexed, and yet felt inclined to laugh at her haughty manner, contrasting so strangely with her abject appearance in other respects. I was on the point of jestingly replying that I wasn't anything else, but merely gave an acquiescing nod.

"Well, where's that money you took in for us yesterday at the *mattanee?*"

"Money! Why, in the hands of the committee directing the Refugee House, to be sure," I answered; "I have not seen it."

"The Refugee House, indeed! Do you think we would go to such a horrid hole as that?"

"I suppose you would go there, if you are refugees, and have no other place of shelter. I know *I* would, under those circumstances."

"But do you know they won't let us in, without we take the oath of allegiance?"

"Indeed!" said I. "Well, that is perfectly proper."

"Is it? I'd see them in tarnation before I'd take the oath. I'd cut myself in pieces before I'd do it. I wouldn't take that oath—not for a million of dollars!"

"Would you do it for five?" I asked, having heard such bravado before, and knowing what it was worth.

"What?" ejaculated the woman.

"Would you do it for five?" I repeated, taking a greenback of that denomination from my pocket-book.

They looked at each other a moment, and then the elder said, in a low whisper, throwing a glance around the room, "*Is there anybody here that can swear us in?*"

"No," I replied. "Go, offer your oath to the authorities, if you wish, though what good it would do them I cannot imagine. Such people as you are lost to honor and honesty, and would set no more value on your sacred oath than I do on this bill, which has been contaminated by our colloquy. Oblige me by taking it, and leaving my apartment."

"That's what you get," said Mère, "for howling through a five-act part on a rainy afternoon for such ungrateful people."

I had been pained at the scene, and "howling" sent me off into an immoderate fit of laughter.

Howling was good. Howling, like the mobled queen, was very good. I had a perfect *acces de fou rire.* I recommend the word to critics. It's so expressive.

The "Old Boy," whoever he may be, seemed to be "in it" when I had made up my mind to leave Louisville for Nashville. He wouldn't let me leave. He sent guerrillas to burn the railway bridges, and stop the trains, etc. The "Old Boy" was generally unkind to me. I don't think the young boy would have acted so. I didn't deserve it, I'm sure.

To be somewhat more explicit, intelligence of the most reliable nature was furnished us that communication between Louisville and Nashville had been closed by the burning of an important trestlework bridge on the road, the stopping, and firing the trains, and the countless other acts that usually succeed to those mentioned, such as the robbing of passengers, the driving away of an insufficient force of soldiers, and the general harassment that would materially afflict everybody to the fullest extent, who like me were anxious to *appear* in Nashville.

At the very moment I was announced as positively to appear on "this evening," at Nashville, I was sitting in Louisville, in an agony of despair. I don't like to break my engagements; I have a foolish respect for my word. Therefore, when it was urged that I had better relinquish all idea of filling my nights in Nashville, I received the proposition with coldness and disdain. The manager was telegraphing me to come, and, if I must be candid, I was anxious to see some of the peculiar features of a city, which at this particular time, had the reputation of occasionally giving Vesuvius-like evidences of the smouldering crater of rebellion in its midst. A love of adventure is a part of my nature, and this was too new and too attractive a field for me to relinquish without a struggle. But it seemed for several days as if fortune was going to be unkind to me. No trains were running, the road being under repair, and constant depredations of various kinds made it highly dangerous to proceed with the work of restoration. It is true a steamboat occasionally made the trip to Nashville, and one was on the point of leaving about the time I wished to do so. I was recommended to go on "her."

"How long will she be?" I inquired.

"Oh, it's very uncertain. Sometimes she does it in three days; sometimes she is nine or ten at it."

Nine or ten days longer, added to what I had already lost of the engagement, would have brought it fully to its date of termination! I declined the boat.

At length the road was announced as being ready to receive such passengers as were provided with the necessary military passes, having only so much baggage as could be carried in *the hand.*

This was cheering to an actress with nine trunks, three boxes, and a large wicker basket. Fancy carrying any one of those articles in the hand!

In vain I sought to set aside the harsh decree. There was still a mile or two of railway track which had not been repaired, and every passenger had to transport himself and his baggage over this hiatus in the road. The case seemed desperate, but the game was not yet lost. A brigadier-general, himself bound for Nashville, appeared on the scene. He kindly instituted a series of inquiries on the baggage question, and from him I learned that I might take a trunk or two if I was prepared to fee heavily for its transportation across the "break."

The separation of the indispensable from the superflous articles in a lady's toilette is a matter requiring great discrimination and much forethought. This is doubly the case when the lady in question is called upon to personate a series of characters, each requiring a widely different costume, with manifold accessories in the shape of hats, head-dresses, flowers, feathers, etc.

But at length the selection was made, and several formidable trunks forwarded to Cincinnati, to await the termination of my Nashville engagement.

"I suppose you are fully aware that the train may be attacked again by guerrillas?" said the brigadier. "I wouldn't advise you to take any valuables with you."

"What! not even my watch?" I asked.

"Above all, not your watch. Guerrillas have a weakness for watches. As for those rings, they are an invitation to the most moral guerrilla to begin depredations at once. Better take them off; indeed you had!"

"Why, they wouldn't steal a lady's rings off her fingers, would they?" I asked, indignantly.

"Only temporarily, no doubt," said the general, with sarcasm. "Perhaps they'd send them back to you by Adams' express."

I saw the force of the argument, and yielded, making up a little carpet-sack of jewelry, which followed the trunks to Cincinnati. I knew if the guerrillas had a *penchant* for finger-rings and watches, money would be doubly attractive; so, expressing almost every dollar I had to New York, I found myself in a ludicrously denuded condition, without a ring on my finger, a watch in my pocket, or a penny in my purse. It was a novel situation for me, and one which constantly provoked my mirth.

Perhaps if it had been otherwise than temporary, I should not have found it so amusing.

A dark, dull, drizzling morning saw our departure from Louisville. It "assisted" at the departure—it assisted in wetting my trunks, in drenching my clothes, and in soaking my feet; it could not assist at any damping of my ardor. A short drive brought us to the railway station, and never shall I forget the scene of activity there presented. A painful scene—a scene of misery, of despair, of mental and physical anguish. Poor mothers, who had wounded sons lying low in Nashville; unhappy wives, holding in their hands letters written by their husbands, *dead* before the letters came to hand; white-faced daughters, pleading piteously to be allowed to go down on the train to their wounded fathers—all supplicating, and all refused. These women had no military passes, could not obtain any, and were therefore not permitted to leave Louisville. A hard duty this refusing of tears and prayers! When I saw a military railroad conductor, with clanging sword, and pistols in his belt, it struck me that a man might be almost a hero, and do a good deal of hard service, off the battle-field.

Our passes being *en regle*, we were permitted to enter the car, already nearly full. Not a pleasant place to enter on a murky, damp morning, before the sun was up—a strange, close smell, bespeaking many occupants not over cleanly, and a little ventilation not too well managed. A toppling stove giving out a sickening heat, with the tank for iced water placed in such cheering contiguity to the fire, as certainly must transform it before many minutes into boiling water.

But what impressed me more than all was the vast crowd of men, clad in the omnipresent army overcoats, who were to be our traveling companions. My hopes of seeing the guerrillas vanished. What guerrilla would have the temerity to attack a train so heavily guarded? It gave me a grand idea of the circumstance of war, though, to be truthful, the pomp was lacking. That man is a hero on the battle-field; and reading of his deeds in the letters of army correspondents makes your pulses beat and hot tears rush into your eyes. But sitting in the car next him, you see him in quite a different light. He chews tobacco, and puts his feet up. He brings his musket down on your toes, and swears impossible, impious and stupid oaths. He eats tough-crusted pies, and comments on their similarity to sole leather; he buys the "Knapsack of Fun," and shrieks out the stale jokes to a remote comrade at the other end of the car. He is a hero, and you know it; he is your country's defender and yours, and you respect him; but as a traveling companion he does not fill your soul with glee. You feel this, and so does he, and he glories in your discomfiture.

Our immediate party consisted of Mère and myself, the brigadier, and a gentleman whom I shall call The Mason. I confess to a partiality for Masons.

The Mason was trowelled, and cross-keyed, and compassed, and "G'd" at every available point of his exterior economy. "I am a Mason" was written in a thousand indescribable ways about him. In fact, he labored under a seemingly painful and ever-present consciousness of his Masonic character. I couldn't help remarking it.

"But why such a violently demonstrative Masonic scarf-pin?" I urged, pointing to a neat article, a Maltese cross with a few hieroglyphics in the centre, the whole affair measuring, perhaps, three inches in length by two in breadth. It was chaste, no doubt, but not elegant.

"Oh, you can't tell how it protects a fellow," he answered. "If the guerrillas were to attack the train at this moment, I don't believe they'd take anything from me—that is, not if they were Masons."

"Would a Mason be so horrible a thing as a guerrilla?" I asked.

Ignoring my question, he said:

"If a Confederate Mason finds a Federal Mason on the battle-field, he cares for him, aids him, succors him, brandy-and waters him——"

"But why does a Mason fight a Mason originally?"

It's a vexed question, isn't it, dear reader? I can't solve it yet. If Masons, bound by fraternal ties, were to refuse to fight any except those who were not Masons, and those who were not Masons, knowing this, were to avail themselves of the ——. It makes me Twemlowish. I put my hand to my head hopelessly, and say with my prototype, the great original Weak-Minded: "I must not think of this."

I wish I had the pen of a Bulwer, to describe the peculiarities of that railroad journey.

It is the fashion with writers to wish for this pen whenever they are called upon to describe anything particularly interesting, or strikingly beautiful.

I wish I had it to describe this trip. I wish I had it anyhow, and always. That much-wished-for and rarely-obtained pen would be of considerable pecuniary value to me. Altogether, the possession of that pen would afford me the highest possible inward satisfaction.

But, after all, it was more the knowledge that the guerrillas had been on the road, and were even now, in all probability, lurking behind every tree, and crouching beneath every bush, which gave the trip that singular charm which the zest of danger always lends. You may believe me when I say that they put on a great deal of steam, and ran that train through very fast; also, that their stoppages at "stations" were of the shortest. When these stoppages were made, the displayal of the "All Right" white flag had indeed a signification. Those persons who alighted,

questioned the others with an eager air and somewhat bated breath. The answers, given in the same tone, and with eyes glancing restlessly to see if perchance the guerrillas were not even now somewhere about, were only partially satisfactory. They had attacked, committing fearful depredation, and might attack again at any moment. A grasp of the hand between the parties, a hurried good-by, a spring on the platform, and we were off.

It takes a great deal to check my gayety. Like Mark Tapley, I feel there is really a merit in being jolly sometimes, and at other times I am jolly because it is my nature, and I don't care whether it is meritorious or not. But on this occasion, I confess I was a little subdued. This mysterious journey reminded me of Dante's trip into hell. To be sure, he didn't go there on a railroad car, surrounded by soldiers, and after having paid the exacted fare in greenback currency. But the anxious state of mind, the frightful *prestidigitateur* feeling of now you see yourself alive, and now (perhaps) you don't, the whirling motion of the steam-propelled, shrieking, creaking, madly-rushing car, the *entourage* of soldiers, the sobs of those women who were allowed to go, the clanking of swords, and now—I gasp as I write it—the sharp rattle of musketry.

Who spoke of Dante?

We are attacked by guerrillas! Good-by New York. Hope enters not here.

One word repeated from car to car as the infernal vehicles still dashed wildly on, one word uttered in alternate tones of hope, of fear, of bravado, of resignation, of excitement in all its phases, one word of deep significance:

"A—lert!"

Great Heaven, what a *coup de theatre!* Every soldier sprang to his feet as if by magic, levelling his musket in the direction of the shots. A glorious picture! Where is that man who chewed tobacco a moment ago, who swore stupid oaths, who offended your olfactory nerves, who spat and was altogether offensive, who wondered if the leathern apple-pies were sewn or pegged, who informed the assemblage that at Fort Donelson the Yanks gave the Johnnies promiscuous—Dante—and that himself contributed largely towards that desirable result; where is he? Gone.

In his place stands a demi-god.

Look at the lithe form bending eagerly forward, every muscle strained to the utmost; observe the keen eye peering far into the distance; admire the cool precision with which he tȧkes aim; see the mingled scorn and rage depicted on that curling lip, and then confess that you, with your fashionable reserve, your high-toned touch-me-not-ativeness, are a poor, weak, paltry creature, grovelling miles beneath the high status which this man occupies in his capacity of hero.

On the whole, our guerrilla attack was a very trifling affair. One woman had a bullet put through her bonnet; it was one of those abominable high-fronted things, and deserved no better fate. We had a coroner's inquest, and the verdict was that it served the bonnet right; but the poor little woman was terribly frightened, and *pour cause.*

At the next station some very underboiled potatoes and some very overboiled eggs falsely announced themselves as "refreshments," and were partaken of as such, though under violent protest, by the hungry travelers. For myself, the moment I heard there was the dead body of a guerrilla lying in the "back shed," I felt no inclination for food. A guerrilla! When Du Chaillu first heard of the presence of one of those of his, of different orthography, he could not have become more excited.

This man had been a terrible creature. He had murdered, and pillaged, and burnt. He had invaded the homes of helpless women, and been a thousand times worse than an assassin; but the fearful retribution had come at last.

"Well, did you see the guerrilla?" I asked, as The Mason came rushing wildly out of the "back shed."

"Yes," he answered, gasping, "and I'll be switched if—"

"What?"

"If the confounded scoundrel wasn't a Mason!"

"How do you know?" I asked.

He sighed faintly as he pointed to his scarf-pin, and said, in a hoarse whisper, "The very fac-simile of mine."

Our next stoppage was at the "break." Here the rails had been torn up, and a bridge burnt down. Workmen, protected by soldiery, were busy repairing the damage, and expected to have it "all right" in a few days. Now, it was all wrong. A rapid and deep stream separated us from the opposite bank, and, after reaching that haven, there was nearly a mile to walk through mud and slough. We forded the stream in a wagon, with water over our ankles; the horses got stuck in the mud on the opposite side, and may be there yet for all I know; and then we commenced our dreary walk over the desolate plain of yielding mud before us. No conveyances were to be had, for love or money; if there had been, their owners might have reaped a rich harvest of both commodities.

I am pretty tough in this matter of fatigue, but there is no shame in saying I was too tired to speak (a fearful state of things) when I reached the car. The utter inutility of keeping a dog and barking yourself, has often been commented upon, but it seems to me to be fully equalled by the inadvisability of paying a railroad fare and walking the distance.

CHAPTER XXI.

Nashville Experience.—A Candid Critic.—A Model Hotel ("Over the Left.")—More Military Necessity.—Two St. Clouds.—Hogshead Cheese.—A slippery Actor.—Miss Griggs.—A Bellicose Official.—Mrs. Ackley's Sorrows.—The——"*Nasty*."—Farewell to Nashville.

It was late in the evening when we arrived at Nashville. The second night I had been announced as positively to appear, when I positively did not. But the third night I was on hand, and ready at the proper time to go through the loves and woes of *Juliet.*

It was raining in torrents as I left the theatre that night,—a drenching deluge of rain, which saturated me in stepping only from the door of the building to the door of the carriage. As we were being driven off, we were arrested by a shout of "Stop!" I opened the door to see what was the matter. A man with a slouched hat and military cloak was giving an unfortunate female a shower bath by holding a dripping umbrella over her head, while she, vainly endeavoring to gather up some voluminous skirts from off the wet pavement beneath, was affording the rain full play upon the back of a velvet cloak.

"Ladies," said the man, addressing us in a polite tone, "I can't get a carriage high or low. Will you permit us to drive to our hotel in yours? It's only about a square up this street."

It was rather a cool request, but I reflected that necessity knows no law, and that there were really no carriages about. Besides, I hope I am never churlish, and I begged them to step in at once. They did so. I soon discovered three things from their conversation: That the gentleman was a major; that they had been to the theatre, and that they did not recognize me.

"Well, what did you think of the *Juliet?*" presently asked the major.

"*The worst I ever saw,*" she answered tightly,—I mean tritely.

Now, that was pleasant, wasn't it?

You take two strangers, who may be pickpockets or Mullers, into your carriage; you order the driver to go to their hotel; you submit uncomplainingly to the accession of dampness brought by them; you permit yourself to be crowded for them; you take your traveling bag off the front seat and place it on your knees for them; you put yourself to all sorts of inconvenience for them—and all for what?

To be told you are the worst *Juliet* they ever saw.

I never had such difficulty to restrain my laughter in all my life. I had the greatest mind in the world to disclose myself. But I didn't. It would have been cruel, would it not, under the circumstances? I thought so, and I refrained.

"Oh, Shakespeare's all played out anyhow," responded the major. "What I like to see is Madame Mazeppa in her bareback act."

I was shocked; upon my word I was.

A sudden "pull up" announced our arrival at the major's hotel. The driver assisted the lady to alight, and while they were still standing near the door of the carriage, opening the umbrella, the hackman addressed me with:

"Shall I drive you home now, *Miss Logan?*"

You should have seen the expression of their faces! I know they would have welcomed an untimely but temporary grave with joy; a trap-door would have been dearer to their hearts than an oil well in Pennsylvania. The very umbrella in the major's hand partook of his humiliation, collapsing from its distended proportions, and hanging listlessly by his side. I never saw two people look so thoroughly ashamed of themselves.

In the course of several years of peregrination I have lodged in a somewhat large number of hotels, good, bad, and indifferent. I have sipped café noir at the Grand Hotel du Louvre in Paris, and have partaken of café muddy at what I suppose must be called the Grand Hotel at Cairo, Illinois. I have eaten oranges in Spain, and whitebait at Greenwich; have slept in spotless linen sheets at the Clarendon, in London, and slept without sheets, either spotless or otherwise, at some of the Albergos in Italy; thus I have been in hotels which were something open to censure, but, take it all in all, it is my humble opinion that the palm for utter badness in hotel-keeping must be awarded to those hardy individuals who did set up their local habitations and their names as innkeepers in Nashville during the war.

It was alleged that the "City Hotel" would suit us exactly,—a totally false allegation, and I am now thoroughly convinced that that alligator knew it.

It didn't suit me, and I don't believe it suited anybody. How could it? A large, ricketty, barn-like frame house, built with that entire disregard of comfort which seems to be the special end and aim in some localities.

Tottering verandahs running the length of the house on every floor, of no earthly use except to admit the cold, which was intense during the whole time I stayed in Tennessee. Windows with sashes determined to be hateful—which would not come down when they were up, nor go up when they were down; doors of an equally obstinate frame of mind—which "stuck" with great pertinacity when closed, but generally insisted, being quite innocent of lock or key, on swinging open at all hours of the day and night.

We had telegraphed for rooms in the plural, and the obliging proprietor reserved us a room in the singular. A singular room, too, by the way. You had to get on the bed to shut the door, to stand on the table to look in the glass; the united efforts of three men and a step-ladder were required to get the gas lit; to turn it off before morning's ruddy beam greeted the opening day was a thing not to be thought of for a moment; it had to burn all night, thus depriving you of sleep, for which the proprietor made an extra charge.

Again, the door of the apartment had to be left open in the coldest weather, to give the fire a "draft,"—"blowers," except of the human species, were unknown. I extemporized one with a newspaper. It answered the purpose capitally until it burnt up, by which time the fire was generally alight, as by that tender foresight which tempers the wind to the shorn lamb, the coal in Nashville is of a bituminous character, and easily ignited.

The furniture of the room, too, was rather peculiar. A carpet full of neglected rents, which threw the unwary traveler down many a time and oft; a rocking-chair which seemed to have a speciality for tipping over backwards; a table irremediably "shaky;" a clock with an unwavering partiality for a quarter past two; a flower vase with a brilliant painting representing a sickly peasant girl eating something which may have been an apple, but which looked uncommonly like a diseased tomato, and a pair of greenish brassy candelabra representing nothing with equal fidelity, and the same striking adhesion to truth.

This was the room; with the additional disadvantage of having recently been occupied by an officer of rank whose brother officers insisted on pouncing down on me at particularly inopportune moments, under the impression that the apartment was still the stronghold of their chief, and who required the most minute explanation in regard to his sudden change of base (about which I, of course, knew so very much, never having lain eyes on him), and the cause of my own unlooked-for and no doubt unwelcome appearance.

I think that general must have evacuated the room but a few hours before I took possession of it, and I fancy he left his packing to the care of a servant, for many little remembrances of his were lying about which, like *Ophelia*, I wished to re-deliver. Cigarettes were scattered around in Sardanapalan quantities; evidences of "prime old port" were abundant; Mrs. Woolt—(the rest burnt off for a cigar lighter) would be happy to see him at dinner next Sunday at half-past three precisely; his old friend G. wanted to know how about it for the 17th?—and yours ever D. B. would feel obliged if the general would let him have the precise state of military law on the point of which we were speaking.

A well-regulated hotel would have caused the room to be put in order before I entered; but this foolish custom was more honored in the breach than the observance, in Nashville.

The door proving utterly false to me, I was forced to push the table and two chairs against it before I took my afternoon siesta. I am sure I was not allowed five minutes' oblivion of my grievances before I was ruthlessly awakened by hearing the whole construction tumble to the ground; on arousing myself, what was my surprise at beholding a smart young lieutenant gazing upon me with an expression of astonishment not unmingled with awe.

"Well," I exclaimed, "this is pretty!"

"Just what I was about to remark," he replied.

"What are you doing in my apartment?" I inquired, savagely.

"Golly! that's cool," he retorted, "*What are you doing in the general's bed?*"

I fainted.

Bad as it all was, however, I should have been glad enough to remain there, for I soon learned that it was really the best hotel in the place. Under these circumstances, you may understand my feelings on the second day after my arrival, when I was informed by an unhappy man who served my very cold dinner in my yet colder room, that this was the last meal which was to be provided for me at the City Hotel.

"The very last," he moaned.

"Amen," said I, "and wherefore, pray?"

"They are going to take the house for a military hospital."

"They—who?"

"Military necessity," he replied.

I found that this personage was all potent in Nashville, and indeed everywhere else in the conquered territory. Perhaps he used his power in rather an unjust manner sometimes; others said so, at least, but we have no earnest that themselves would have shown more equity in such matters if the chances of war had permitted them to exercise the hated military necessity over their enemy, instead of being obliged to submit to the reverse.

In a half an hour after the first premonition of our approaching ejection, we found ourselves in the street, bag and baggage, in the midst of another drenching rain, totally ignorant of what steps to take to get another lodging.

As for the City Hotel, I never saw a building transformed into a hospital in a shorter space of time. I can only say I do not envy the patients who are forced to remain there in very cold weather.

From a cabman we learned that the St. Cloud was the next *best* hotel.

"Vogue la galère alors, pour St. Cloud, et vive la joie," said I, with delectable abandon.

He remarked, Hey?

Somewhat quenched, I inquired his fare from our present lodging on the cold ground to our objective point, the celebrated next best.

He said ten dollars.

It appears it is ever thus in Nashville.

It costs five dollars to go a "step," and ten to go "round the corner," with an additional five in case it comes on to rain, which it invariably does, probably for the benefit of cabmen. Grumbling I paid; a good deal of grumbling and a very crisp bill.

Words fail me to describe the misery which was to be purchased at four dollars a day and one extra for fire, making five, at the St. Cloud, in Nashville. Oh, visions of the joyous dinners partaken of at the charming village of that name on the sloping banks of the rippling Seine, within the hospitable walls of the cheerful and well-known hostlery, "*La Tete Noire*," with what bitter mockery ye presented yourselves to my regretful but admiring remembrance! The tempting "carte," handed to me as *Majeste Regnante*, to select whatsoever I pleased, totally irrespective of price, from *potages* down to *pousse cafes!* And did I not? Answer, ye kindred spirits who were there and know, did I not select the dinners totally irrespective of price, but thoroughly respective of good taste, and perfect *savoir diner?*

Tell me how a man dines, and I'll tell you whether he is a vulgarian or not.

But now I think of it, that rule does not always hold good; for if I had been judged by the way I dined in Nashville, I might have been set down as the lowest of all possible *canaille.*

An inhuman and unearthly substance, yclept "hogshead cheese," constituted our breakfast at Nashville; hogshead cheese, with some very weak tea and some very stale crackers, was served at dinner, and some very stale crackers and some very weak tea, without any hogshead cheese, was sent in at supper. We stood this unflinchingly, but on one point we were perhaps unreasonably exacting. We insisted on clean sheets. We were assured that this was a stretch of luxurious *faste* which had never been indulged in, and which the proprietors of the St. Cloud were determined not to tolerate. Sheets were put on for a week, and there they must stay if the heavens fell, or, what was more likely, if half a dozen different lodgers occupied the room.

I tried a *douceur*, and the chambermaid said she would see what could be done.

In half an hour she returned with a couple of sheets neatly folded. They were the very same sheets she had taken off. She vowed they were not, but I knew them at once.

They were indeed my long-lost sheets!

They had a strawberry mark on their left arms. I mean a rectangular tear in their left corners, besides sundry other evidences of railway dust and dirt, which the wash-tub alone could obliterate from memory and view.

"Now, Mère," said I, with desperation, "there is no use in our endeavoring to stand this. Let's try something else."

"What else can we try? This was the 'next best.'"

"Let us put ourselves in the hands of Providence. The ravens are fed from Heaven's garners, and no doubt if clean sheets were a necessary attribute to their happiness, they would get them. Let us see if we are not of more value than sparrows, for verily I say unto you—"

"Hush! hush!" said Mére; "don't be nonsensical—and wicked, too."

Whatever I was, I was determined to find a comfortable lodging, and find one I did—a large, bright, airy room, in one of the whilom fashionable streets of the now much more unfashionable city. The landlady struck me as being a very nice person, evidently quite correct in all things but her grammar; a quiet, mild old lady, somewhat terrified at my impetuous manner. Necessity, I have observed before, knows no law, and hogshead cheese was beginning to have a deleterious effect on my mental organization. Therefore, impetuous.

"What! air you the actor?" she inquired, breathlessly, when I told her my name.

I said I wair.

She looked a little uncomfortable at first, and then asked, in a tremulous manner, if I would have any objection to paying the week's lodging in advance.

I replied that paying the week's lodging in advance would cause me an amount of inward satisfaction which no words could portray. Still I urged, but merely for curiosity's sake, wherefore?

"'Cause," said she, hesitatingly, "there was a man-actor down here some weeks ago—he were a clownd in a suckus, I think—and he ran off and never paid his bill to Miss Griggs, the washerwoman."

So saying, she looked spooney, and I forked.

I ultimately made the acquaintance of Miss Griggs. Miss Griggs tore my laces and committed ravages on my linen which time will but deepen, but she was a poor soul, and an honest widow, with a very large and very willful baby, and a very small and very precious income. She told me who the "clownd" was, and, out of compassion for her, I paid his claim. Though it is doubtless written on high, on the scroll of fame, I never heard the clownd's name, before or since; but he is cautioned that *he is known*, and this means is taken of conveying to him that he had better come forward at once and pay me fifty-three cents, to avoid any unpleasant consequences which might ensue.

Ye who have free souls, and can, without the slightest let or hindrance, take a ride out to Central Park, or continue on to Albany if you are so minded, have little idea of the many forms and ceremonies necessary to be gone through with before one was allowed to emerge from the gates of Nashville. I say gates, because gates is eminently poetical.

But shall I ever get out of Nashville?

Never, apparently.

Three times my loyalty had to be sworn to; three times my name given and registered. I was informed by an official that if I was a spy, and was trying to escape across the country with the information which I had, no doubt, been assiduously picking up in Nashville, I would find it would cost me more than I imagined; to which he added, did I hear that?

I told him I did. My hearing was slightly defective, but I heard that very distinctly.

Then he told me I had better remember it.

And I have done so. The proof is, that after years have elapsed I am now telling it to you, word for word, just as it happened. I hope the official will read these lines, and see how minutely I have obeyed him in all things. He was a pompous official. Spite of his brusqueness I liked him, for he displayed a zeal in the cause which was not observable in all officials whom I met.

The Mason said the official and I reminded him of Beauty and the Beast.

You will forgive my repeating that little compliment, won't you? The truth is, my *Trompette* was slain while making a most brilliantly valorous escape from the enemy at Bull Run, and since that time these onerous duties fall on me, and if I fail to perform them, both myself and they are undone. When I get very rich, I shall erect a monument to my *Trompette.* On one side shall be a basso-relievo of the deceased in the act of blowing, and underneath these striking lines of Shakespeare:

> "*Blow*, blow, (thou winter wind),
> Thou art not half so unkind
> As man's ingratitude."

And Nashville?

Another official said he didn't see what people wanted to go visiting battle-fields for, when the fighting was all over. He observed that when the parties were giving each other thunder, then's when the fun was.

You will forgive my remarking that, to my perverted imagination, then's when the fun isn't.

He said when they fought, he was "in."

Soit! when they fight, I am out.

He told us that if any fighting was to be done, he wanted to be as near the battle-field as possible.

Well, I do not; at that particular moment I desire to be far from the battle-field's gaze. Like a beautiful dream, it might seek me in vain, both by meadow and stream. It would not be likely to find me.

But this official continued in his bellicose strain, and finally gave me my pass in a very warlike manner. I learned from the Mason that he had never been out of that room since his first entering of the army, his duty being entirely among papers, and not bullets. He had been a dry goods clerk, for some years, in a second-class establishment in Nashville, and by reason of his somewhat sudden assumption of shoulder-straps and military airs, he had received from the Southern women, to whom he was especially repugnant, the slightly contemptuous sobriquet of Tadpole.

Tadpole, adieu!

A battle-field! What is it, after all, when the fighting is over, and the wounded carried away, and the dead buried, and the victorious gone off victorious, and the vanquished skulking away vanquished and perhaps pursued? A few rough graves, and a lot of abattis, and some breastworks, and some trenches; a great many canteens and knapsacks, cast off to expedite the flight; here and there a dismounted cannon, *et voila tout!*

Not all. It requires a little study, and you must make it. See the bark of trees all ripped off by bullets; observe how some of them, and those of the finest, too, unfortunately are rent in twain by the heavier balls, and are now dragging their yet green branches, never to bloom again, down to the dusty earth. How close they were upon our boys! A hard struggle this, evidently; but the harder the struggle the more complete the final triumph.

"Oh, dear me!" I exclaimed, "who in the world lived in that house?"

"Why, Mrs. Ackley," responded a man with whom we had scraped up a sort of conversation on the road, through his volunteering a good deal of interesting information about the battle—which he said he had witnessed.

Strange as it may seem it is nevertheless true that I had never heard of Mrs. Ackley until that moment. They told me all about her, though they seemed to think it was rather odd that any one not quite an ignoramus should know absolutely nothing about so celebrated a personage. She was a lady who had owned this valuable property all her life, who had inherited a fortune of three millions of dollars, who was accomplished and talented, who had taken two trips to Europe to furnish this house, who had gone to Italy for the statuary which adorned the garden, who had bought her pictures at Rome, and her porcelaine at Sevres, and beyond peradventure her coals at Newcastle, who was altogether orthodox in the spending of her money, and now what had it all resulted in? In having her English park turned into a bear garden, her serpentine walks into wicked ways, and alack and alas! her tulip beds into soldiers' graves! Poor house, very rich and imposing and comfortless, what a shame to riddle you so! Thomas' broadside broke the cheval glass, and Hood's grape smashed the champagne bottles.

Our informant, in the approved American style, told us precisely what Mrs. Ackley had paid for the decoration of her gardens. I have no doubt that, divided by two, his statement was about correct, but even then, I can only say the money was very injudiciously spent.

Inferior statuary can be obtained in Italy as well as anywhere else, and Mrs. Ackley's giving two hundred and twenty English pounds does not prevent her "stooping Venus" looking exactly like a female who had resorted to that posture for the express but unsuccessful purpose of allaying a sudden attack of cramp.

I was curious to know the politics of a lady, placed like Mrs. Ackley so literally between two fires. I have not yet mentioned the fact of her being a widow.

"What has she done?" I inquired of our informant.

"Why," said he, leaning forward on his horse and hissing out the words harshly, "she has done the——*nasty!*"

I was thunderstruck, and so was the little mare I was riding, for she jumped aside as if the words had been a a missile and struck her full on her pretty forehead. Our informant did not observe my surprise any more than he waited for my reply.

"Perhaps you don't know what that is?"

I replied that I did not indeed.

"Well, then," he answered, "I will tell you. That's what we call people when they are Southerners by birth,

Southerners by heart, by education, by fortune, by the will of God, in fact and yet, who"—and he fairly gnashed his teeth as he spoke—"who, to save that paltry trash they call their property, go and put themselves under the protection of a flag which they hate and abhor, merely because it happens to be the victorious one. And these people, ma'am, are what we call the ——*nasty*."

He was a study for an artist as he spoke. His iron-gray locks, failing to give a look of age, imparted one of great solidity to his scornful face; his quivering lips, white with the excitement of the moment, curved with a purity and force which was far from being mimicked in any of Mrs. Ackley's statues; and his rustic garments, made of some homespun material of the commonest order, gave no look of clownishness to his athletic frame.

I had only a minute's time to make these observations, for so soon almost as he had finished speaking, he turned scornfully and left us.

I have said that I was restricted in the way of wardrobe, having left almost everything in that line in Louisville. I can laugh now at the straits I was put to, to vary my toilettes, but at the time I was really very much inconvenienced. I had in reality only two dresses of the modern school with me; one a pink moire antique, the other a white of the same character. They had both cost in Paris that figurative sum commonly known as "a pretty penny," and were in fact silks of the first *water*. But I must say I agree with the logical Mrs. Malaprop in the observation that "familiarity breeds despisery." The hate I bear those two dresses knows no words. I was obliged to wear them constantly. First I would wear the pink, then the white, then the pink looped over the white, then the white looped over the pink, then the pink trimmed with white, then the white trimmed with pink; in fact, I was a woman in white, with a strong tendency to *couleur de rose.* I have had my revenge on them since, by suffering them to repose calmly in the bottom of my trunks. After Nashville's fitful fever, they sleep well!

I learned in Nashville that it was a matter of the greatest difficulty to visit rebel prisoners of war, which fact greatly enhanced a desire which I had long entertained to see some of the better class of the parties in arms against us. I was gratified in this, but after many struggles; and as the war is over now, I shall not mention in what town I made the visit. It was not in Nashville, but the recital comes in here as well as anywhere else.

CHAPTER XXII.

The "Felon's Daughter."—Actresses' Cartes de Visite.—The Flower Basket Nuisance.—Theatrical Critics in the West.—Dumb Waiters.—Ohio Legislators. — Western Hotels. — Andersonville! — A High Private. — From the Shoe Shop to the Camp. — The Guide Book Nuisance. — Chicago. — Miltonian Tableaux. — Number 99.—On the Cars.— Flirts and Babies en Route.—The Newly Married Couple.—The Gum-Drop Merchants.—The New York *Hurled*.—A Walk in a Graveyard.—A Terrible Gymnast.—Indiana Loafers.—Nomenclature.

"Shall we stay here over night, or shall we go straight on to Cincinnati?" I asked of Mère when we arrived at the Galt House in Louisville.

"Better go on, I think, and spend all the leisure time you have in Cincinnati."

We did so, and that very night the Galt House was burned to the ground, with an immense destruction of property, and loss of life to six people. Mère thanked Providence for our preservation, but I could not do this. Is it not a bitter mockery to those who have met their fate, to offer thanks that you have escaped it? No, it was a settled decree of an inscrutable Providence that we should avoid this horrible calamity, reserved, perhaps, to meet some still more dreadful one. Who knows? There is a divinity which shapes our ends, rough hew them as we may.

In Cincinnati we spent a delightful week, at the house of Monsieur Monfrère. Monfrère is as pleasing a specimen of the fine young American gentleman as can well be found. Of his oratorical talents, and, indeed, all those requisites to make a mark in the legal profession, I do not hesitate to say he stands far ahead of his compeers. His handsome face, his rich voice, his admirable gesticulation (as necessary to the lawyer as they are to the player), and, above all, his clear judgment and scholarly acquirements have gained for him an enviable and an enduring position.

Monfrère is something of a litterateur as well, and kindly said he would give me a little advice about my play of "Eveleen," transformed to suit the growing appetite for the sensational into "The Felon's Daughter." The piece had already been much changed since I first produced it in New York, and was now no more like the original play than that jack-knife was like the original jack-knife which got first a new blade fixed to it, and then a new handle fixed to that.

Monfrère said he thought the effect would be better if I were to enrich the heroine by making her authoress of a few sensation novels, rather than by the hackneyed and quite delusive plan of acquiring a fortune through acting parts.

"That's all very well, Tom," I remarked; but, under existing circumstances, it seems hardly modest in me to make all my characters talk about the wonderful genius of this young lady as an authoress, and her enriching herself by the mere power of her pen."

"Well, my dear," said Monfrère, coolly blowing away his cigar smoke, "it strikes me it's about as broad as it's long. You made your heroine a magnificent actress, which you are not; then, why object to making her a splendid authoress, which, permit me to observe, but without wishing to give offence, you are not, also."

This was quite true, but I had never thought of it before. Indeed, it was painfully true—and truth, you know, is stranger than fiction. I altered the play. Eveleen, no longer Lady Macbeth, is Miss Braddon, Mrs. Henry Wood, George Eliot, George Sand, Mrs. A. B. C. D. E. F. Southworth, Olive Logan, or "what you will."

It was from Monfrère I had a ludicrous account of the

sale of photographic "cartes de visite" in the front of the theatre. I had been told that "stars" realized immense profits from this source. Nevada, Colorado and Arizona paled before the gold which "photographs" yielded. Several castles in the Moorish regions had been built by "stars" in this way, and a railway to Chimeraville was about to be opened to the public, on Photographic rôle-ing stock. Of course, to be orthodox, I must do the same, and the inevitable small boy, with ill-kept nose, came to me in every town, and took away several dozen of cartes de visite.

But pray mark the mode of procedure of the inevitable small boy with ill-kept nose!

In a fiendishly exultant manner, he rushes up to an inoffensive spectator, and, thrusting the picture under the visual organs of the aforesaid, cries out, in a shrill voice:

"Have Olive Logan, sir? Street dress and costume. *Do* take Olive Logan, sir. *Only twenty-five cents!*"

And if the inoffensive spectator remains obdurate to my varied charms at such a very low figure, the inevitable small boy cries:

"What! not Olive Logan, sir? Olive Logan, *the Felon's Daughter—the Robber's Wife!!*"

Is it extraordinary that, under these circumstances, I immediately stopped the sale of My Photographs?

The town of Columbus, the State capital of Ohio, stood next in my line of march, and a pretty wide-awake place it is, too, especially in the legislative session, during which period I happened to be there. I was particularly pleased with the general appearance of Columbus. If I say it reminded me forcibly of an English town, I mean this as a compliment. Beautiful villas, nearly or quite surrounded by wide-spreading trees, by well-kept gardens, full of the rarest flowers, and possessing so many other attributes of the country as might well cause one to believe they were situated miles out of town—while, in reality, they have the very great advantage of being only around the corner from the principal street—are features of which Columbus may well be proud. There is a certain elegance about the shops, too; and, above all, a perfect cleanliness in the streets, which New York itself might emulate with advantage.

It was not because my engagement was a pecuniary success that I liked the theatre-going public of Columbus. It was because in no town did I meet with a more discriminating audience, severe as well as generous. I promise you that in Columbus no such insulting farce would be permitted as that we see enacted every night in New York, at the different theatres, and which, for want of a better name, I may call the bouquet and flower-basket nuisance. Any such attempt to interrupt the progress of a serious play by a few addle-brained admirers of pretty actresses, would be immediately and peremptorily discountenanced. But, if we analyze this thing carefully, we will find that the pretty actresses themselves are in many instances very much to blame in this unpleasant matter.

This reminds me of an anecdote which ran the rounds of Parisian *salons* a few years ago. We all know the fight which was carried on for so long a time between the Piccinists and the Gluckists, but a similar struggle, of a more amusing character, took place in the French capital at the time of the great success of Madame Doche in "La Dame aux Camelias." Mademoiselle Page, who for some reason is always supposed to be the rival of Doche, was playing "La Dame de Monsereau" at the Ambigu.

But behold young Lord Viri Sappi, who has just come of age, and entered into possession of his titles and estates, finds his beloved Mlle. Page all in tears when he pays his afternoon visit.

"Oh—ah," says his lordship, using what may be called the monosyllabic "headers," which the English take before ducking into the French language, "Qu'est-ce que too ah mar chèrie? What is the matter?"

"Ah, milord," says the pretty Page, sobbing convulsively, "that ugly Doche—oh—oh—is going to have a splendid pair of diamond ear-rings presented to her—oh—oh—to-night."

Milord wonders where they were bought.

Mlle. names the jeweller.

Milord asks if he has another pair like them.

Mlle. thinks he has, but is rather in doubt.

Milord makes it no longer a matter of doubt, and Mlle. Page gets the ear-rings similar to Doche's.

Now turn we to Doche's apartment.

The Prince Talloweateroff, the rich Russian, fancies his brilliant Dame aux Camelias is despondent.

"Oh, nothing now, prince," replies Camille; "a bagatelle. But they tell me that presuming little Page is going to be the recipient of a magnificent bracelet, set with pearls, this evening."

The prince would like to know, Sapristi, about what this bracelet cost, because, Pardieu, Doche shall have one three times as valuable, Saperlotte!

Doche gets the bracelet.

Which proves that she has more ruse than the Russe.

And Mlle. Page gets the ear-rings.

And if you think there was collusion between these two pretty actresses, you are a very naughty man, and I shall tell you no more French stories.

In fact, I have no right even to tell you this one, for my business is now with Columbus.

The principal newspapers of the place are very good samples of the general go-ahead-itiveness which is one of the marked characteristics of the West.

I don't know the editors, nor the critics, nor any of the attachés of these papers from Adam—in fact, I would recognize Adam much more easily than I would them, from peculiarities of costume which, I have no doubt, are carefully avoided by the gentlemen in question. Therefore, if there is any value in an honest opinion, you have it in this. And now a line about theatrical critics in the West. A great deal of twaddle has been written in New York about the hopelessness of getting an impartial criticism from a Western editor, about the openness to bribes of Western editors, and a lot more of it. Of course I can only speak from my own experience, and that is not very extensive, as I have had but one season of "starring." But in that season I am willing to give my word, as an honest woman, that I never paid a Western editor a penny —I never invited a Western editor, or an attaché of a newspaper, to dine or sup with me, or to call on me, for the purpose of inveigling myself into his good graces; I never requested editors' favors through any third party, and yet I venture to assert that I was judged as kindly, criticised as impartially, and lauded as highly as I deserved. If it had been unconditional praise I should not say this, for it would appear like egotism; but it was sound, clear-sighted, thoughtful criticism, which was eminently beneficial to me, since it pointed out faults, to acquaint me with which was to enable me to rectify them at once. As far as offering money goes, I should as soon have thought of calling a man a robber, and should have expected the same retort that such an epithet would have been likely to provoke.

I object to a practice, too common in the West, as regards the dramatic critic.

He is called a "reporter," and I resent the appellation; not that there is anything dishonorable, or in the least degree objectionable, in the cognomen, except that it is inappropriate. The man who goes to a fire, and tells how many houses were burnt down, is a "reporter;" he who was in a beer shop at the time of a dreadful row, and gives the names of the participants in the melée is also a "reporter." Shall we, then, bestow the same title on the person who is able to write a clear and exhaustive criticism of a scholarly play, comparing the actor or actress before him with others who in years agone have essayed the same rôles, thus showing that his knowledge is not of to-day or yesterday, but is the careful study of time? Ladies and gentlemen of the West, you may call these gentlemen reporters, or Hottentots if you like, but, with your kind permission, I will call them critics.

The principal hotel in Columbus has marked features like everything else in the West. In the first place, it is scrupulously clean.

During the blissful period I passed at boarding-school, it was predicted I would be an old maid, because I happened to be somewhat neater in my appointments than the majority of the school girls. Why is this prognostication always made in similar circumstances? Must married women of a necessity be untidy? Must old maids perforce have the bump of order largely developed? I know instances, and could name a dozen, where the cases are just reversed.

I admire neatness.

Tidiness is my hobby.

English houses delight my inmost soul on this account; but I have discovered that there is such a thing as carrying cleanliness too far. In its efforts to be next to godliness, it becomes like vaulting ambition—o'erleaps itself and falls on the other side.

Clean floors are very nice, but if they must be scrubbed previous to dinner, thus leaving the guests to sit for at least a half an hour with feet reposing on the dampest of pedestals, I must say I would rather the floors remained dirty.

Clean towels are somewhat essential to happiness, but if they must be brought in as near soaking wet as the washtub and a hasty "mangling" will allow, I prefer letting my face go unwashed—or, washing it, to wipe it on a yesterday's towel, which at least has the merit of being dry.

Silver cream jugs are pretty when very bright and shining, but if the Spanish chalk comes off on my fingers, communicating to them an unpleasant odor of verdigris which remains and is offensive, until I get an opportunity to wash my hands, I confess I would rather see the jugs unpolished. Still, for all these triflng disadvantages, the Neil House is a very nice hotel. Compared to some in which I have stopped, it is the Palace of Aladdin with all the modern improvements.

Apropos of modern improvements, let me say here that I hate them.

The intimacy established between the drawing-room and the kitchen, through the medium of those speaking-tubes or blow-trumpets, or whatever the beastly things are called, is quite appalling.

Miss Amanda, seated with a gentleman friend in the drawing-room, is startled by a stentorian

"Sa-a-y!" shrieked through the tube.

"What is it, Bridget?" asks Miss Amanda, gently.

"Tell yer mar I want her."

"I want her," is pleasing, considering the source from which it comes.

"Mar" answers the call.

"Sa-ay."

"Well?" says mamma.

"Is that *young man* going to stay to dinner? Because if he is, I'll have to put on some more potatoes!"

The dismay occasioned by this requires no comment.

Then, again, that lively innovation of modern architectural art generally known as the "dumb waiter."

Dumb, indeed! Would it were!

Just in the middle of the first course at dinner, a thundering noise is heard issuing from an apparently innocent cupboard, causing one member of the family to start up, rush frantically towards the closet and open the door, thus exposing a very incongruous array of articles!

On the first shelf, perhaps, the week's washing—or, more correctly, ironing.

On the second, sometimes a pair of boots for the third floor, garnished with candles for everybody.

And on the third and last shelf the roast for dinner, with the gravy (very often) spilled over everything, making a charming relish, particularly for the dessert. These are modern improvements!

I was standing in the Fifth Avenue Hotel one day, waiting for the elevator or car to come down and "elevate" me to a friend's room. After we got started, a little boy rushed up and, gazing intently after us as we sailed upon the bosom of the air, he cried out: "Oh, hookey! Sis, come look. Here's a bully dumb waiter!"

I thought the simile was very striking.

Columbus, as I have said, was full of legislators. And O why is it that legislators never vary from that obviously inappropriate costume of black (?) dress coat and black baggy-kneed trowsers? Or if this hideous apparel *must* be worn by some inscrutable legislative decree, why, oh, why, need it always be shabby?

Does it issue shabby from under the soothing influence of the legislative tailor's goose?

I have heard of putting new wine into old bottles, and the likelihood of the bottles bursting under such circumstances; but it seems to me, if I were a new legislator, and were put into old trowsers, I should just be impetuous and indignant enough to do as the bottles did.

It cannot be poverty which induces this state of things, because I have heard that legislators were well paid, and champagne (which to avoid argument, we will concede is Widow Cliquot's, and which costs eight dollars a bottle whether it is or no), is not a favorite beverage with gentlemen who are restricted in income. So the mystery of shabby black clothes still remains unfathomed.

On the whole, the legislator himself is rather an unfathomable party. Why he eats so much, drinks so much, talks so much, and legislates so little, he and he alone can tell.

In fact what is legislation as understood and practiced at State Capitals?

I give it up, Brudder Bones, as the middle man at the minstrels always does the end man's conundrums. It is too profound an enigma for me to solve.

The legislator is condescending, affable, and as polite as his heavy duties will allow. He generally knows everybody, and sometimes permits a favored few to touch the end of his fingers in the friendly "handshake."

It is not very difficult matter to know everybody in a Western hotel. In fact when once you get the run of these hotels, they are as much alike in their boarders as they are in their everlasting French side dishes. Of course I am speaking now of permanent parties.

There is the newly married couple, all blushes and little appetite.

There is the old married couple, very intent on the bill of fare, who try experiments on their digestive organs in a fearfully reckless manner.

There is the sentimental clerk who belongs to the hotel.

And there is the rather scrubby party who don't, but who occasionally purchases one of those precious talismans known as a "Meal Ticket," and thus gets entrance to the festive dining hall with newly-washed floor and rather strong effluvium of yellow soft soap. Besides this he has the inestimable privilege of partaking of those entrées that are announced in a lofty manner, which may be attractive to the general public, but which, sooth to say, are rather bewildering to the French scholar. Can you wonder that when fish is heralded as

"Poison ax finns erbes—"

I decline it verbally and substantially?

Or that

"Harricotte des mouton a la Bony femme" suggests cannibalism in its least appetizing form?

Added to which the proof-reader of these bills of fare often allows to escape his observation sundry cheerful little errors like the following:

Peach Fie. Cabinet Mudding. English Hickory Ruts. French Boffee.

In Columbus I received the card of a young gentleman whom I had known in Paris, where he shone with great brilliancy as a member of the *jeunesse doree.* You may imagine my surprise at finding him dressed in the uniform of a private in our army! Him! who used to be so much of a swell that he was almost a *gandin*, whose "dogcart" was the admiration of all Paris, and whose American "trotteur" sent the Bois de Boulogne into spasms of delight.

"Is this Mr. C.?" I asked, in amazement.

"For the first time in my life I am proud to say it is," he replied.

"But wherefore this apparel so unmistakably shoddy?"

"Why, I belong to the army."

"What? not the rank and file?"

"Yes; that is, a good deal of file and no rank."

"A private?"

"Strictly private, and very confidential."

"And Paris?"

"Alas!"

"And the *bals masques?*"

In a frantic manner he sprang to his feet and executed a "forward two" in true Parisian style, and with such utter abandon that a mild old lady knitting socks with a pair of blue spectacles—I mean, knitting spectacles with a pair of blue socks—well, at all events, evidently under an impression that this soldier was going mad very suddenly, she uttered a terrific shriek and bolted. "Alas!" he said, sinking into a chair quite exhausted; "it's no longer the 'Can-can' with me; it's the 'Can't-can't!'"

"The reason?"

Only one word was the reason; but that was a word which makes the blood run cold, the teeth to chatter, and something very like an anathema to come to the lips. You know the word well.

Andersonville!

Think of a man with a fine income and delicate organization, and pampered and palled tastes, and having enjoyed the most luxurious of all lives, being thrown into that prison-place! This young man had stayed there four months, and the tales of horror he told me have no equal in the annals of crime. I will not repeat them, for I do not wish to cause you pain. He had stayed there till it was believed he was as good as dead; then he was sent back, and, awaiting an exchange which never came, he was prevented from fighting for his country, the very thing for which he had relinquished, with noble self-abnegation, all the tastes and habits of his former life. I asked him what use he found for his income, now that he was taken care of at government expense.

"Why," replied he, with *naivete*, "I don't want much money while I'm in the army, you know; so I've just made over half my annuity to the Sanitary Commission for so long as the war lasts, and the other half will be accumulating for me."

"But why didn't you get a commission as captain, major, or something of the sort? Surely, with your position you might have—"

He didn't let me finish the sentence. In a vehement tone he replied, with what I suppose the French would call by that funny word "explosion"—"Get a commission! Is *that* the way to serve your country?"

He terrified me somewhat; so I replied that I did not know really—which was strictly true.

Then he changed the tone a little, saying with great contemptuousness of tone—

"*That's* not the way to serve your country!"

To which I answered in a semi-interrogative strain, "Isn't it, really?"

He explained why it wasn't really; but though I fully agreed with him on all points, I didn't understand a word of it beyond that there was something particularly glorious in "shouldering a musket," while Grant himself had not enjoyed the privilege of carrying a knapsack stuffed full of unadulterated Fame. I suppose it was all right, and I know I felt much prouder of the acquaintanceship of private C. than I ever did of the friendship of Monsieur C. the Paris swell.

I met another person in Columbus who exemplified in the most striking manner, the American aptitude for throwing off commonplace avocations and becoming heroes as quickly and as easily as if heroism were the natural attribute of all mankind. This gentleman's name was Col. McGroarty. I had known him from my girlhood. It is that very correct writer, Mrs. A. Trollope, who gives the following definition of "girlhood" as placed in contradistinction to "youngladyhood." You must not hold me responsible for it:

Girlhood is the period when the pantalettes are worn longer than the dress.

Youngladyhood is the period when the dress is worn longer than the pantalettes.

I knew Col. McGroarty (not the least bit of a colonel about him then) during the first period.

At that time he was doing nothing, with great pertinacity.

I was engaged in the same useful occupation.

Then I knew him during the second period.

At that time he was keeping a shoe store in the town of Toledo, Ohio.

I rather fancy he was doing nothing then, too.

N. B.—This is not a paradox.

Suddenly the war breaks out, shaking the little shoe-shop in Toledo to its very centre; and presto, my old school friend, the whilom shoe-vender, gets his right arm shot three times, requiring three amputations, and a ball goes through his cheek, and he is known as the Demon Colonel by the Confederates and the fire-eating Irishman by the Federals, and when he goes into the street the boys cheer him, and the men raise their hats to him, and the women smile and kiss their hands to him!

"What will you do when the war is over?" I asked of the hero.

"Sink back again into my boots—and shoes, I suppose," he replied, laughingly.

This adapting oneself to circumstances is a splendid trait in the American character. If boots do not succeed with the colonel, no doubt he will try something else; and, if that doesn't succeed, something else again.

Here I pause to say that I really hope these sketches are not getting to be suggestive of a guide-book; for I think if there is anything on earth which is both useless and disagreeable, it is a guide-book. A guide-book is a literary nuisance, not worth the paper it is printed on.

In the first place, it always gives you wrong information about the starting of trains. Secondly, it insists on telling you how many miles it is from one place to another, which you don't care a fig to know so long as you are certain how much time it takes to get there, which important bit of information is never vouchsafed. Thirdly, it gives maps which are just as inaccurate as they can well be, and flourishes before one numberless time-tables which nobody can decipher. For instance, the following will illustrate my meaning:

GOING NORTH.		GOING SOUTH.	
ARRIVE AT		ARRIVE AT	
Big Licks	2.40	Hullibaloo	6.20
Slap Dash	3 05	Blowtown	7.00
Blowtown	4.00	Slap Dash	8.05
Hullibaloo	4.31½	Big Licks	8.59

Passengers going in a north-easterly direction will here change, and take the cars which will be found waiting for them in the south-western corner of the depot.

Now, this is very clear, no doubt, to anybody who knows in what direction he *is* going, which I never do. I tell you, candidly, if I were asked what was the most difficult task on record, I should reply—not boxing the compass, but understanding it after it is boxed.

Why, I can't get it straight, even in New York, let alone out in the open country. I maintain, however, that this is not my fault—somebody else is to blame. Why on earth the Hudson, washing the poetic shores of Eleventh avenue, is called the North River, while the gushing stream in a diametrically opposite direction, which meanders murmuring love songs to the natives of the First avenue, is called the East River, is an enigma to me. Why is it not South River? Won't somebody tell me something about this? Which is it? How come you so? Do husbands go down South when they fly to the auriferous regions of Wall street? Are we a little way on the road to the North Pole when we drive out to the Park?

In spite of my defects in this respect, I repeat that I feel I am a guide-book, notwithstanding my earnest choosing to be a Daisy. I know I shall be bought in railway cars by bored passengers, who will afterwards begrudge the money, and leave me on the seat. I shall be bound in calf, and printed on foolscap, with cuts by all my literary friends.

Chicago, then—unhappy traveller reading me—is a lively town, of a good many hundred soles, some of whom live in the lake and are caught for breakfast. They are nice with lemons, who go in and are squeezed. Chicago is bounded on the north by the lake, on the south by the prairie, on the east by the Sherman House, on the west by McVicker's Theatre, on the sou'-sou'-west by a hog-packing establishment, and on the nor'-nor'-east by an affirmative, I suppose, as two negatives make it.

An adverse political sentiment evidently reigned in Chicago as long ago as when the streets were named—since Randolph street flourishes, spite of its Virginian origin; and Monroe street runs parallel, but refuses to contaminate itself by traversing its antagonist. The name of Chicago is derived from two French words, indicative, no doubt, of the two classes who flourish there, as they do in other cities, *i. e.*, those who are "*Chic*" and those who speak "*Argot.*" (See Bumfoodle's American History of Nomenclature).

But, joking aside (if you will allow me to use the word in relation to my own effusions), joking aside, Chicago is a delightful place. On the whole, I think it is my town of predilection in the West. Cincinnati, to be sure, like Rome, sits on her seven hills, which are very majestic and excessively hard to climb.

It is certainly a magnificent city.

Which?

Why, either, to be sure—I can't abear questions.

Cincinnati is grand, pompous and imposing, but Chicago is undoubtedly the gamest place in the whole western country.

And then such a nice hotel as the Sherman is! Oh, butter and rolls, what a nice hotel! No French mistakes there on the bill of fare—not exactly. The warmest, cosiest hotel; the nicest rooms, the best table—ah, well, retrospection is painful; I must drop the subject.

Perhaps you think I mean this as a *reclame* for the Sherman House. Well, I may; only it is unintentional on my part, I assure you. If I meant it as a puff, I should say something about the urbane and gentlemanly proprietors. But I won't; though I think they must be urbane and gentlemanly, or else they wouldn't provide such nice rolls and butter for their guests, while the French coffee, and the *cannetons rotis aux petits pois* are, in my opinion, incontrovertible signs of their urbanity and gentlemantility.

The newspapers in Chicago are full of political matter, which I always skipped, confining myself to the perusal of a fracas in an oyster saloon, descent on a gambling Hoyle, and the criticism on Miss L—— as ——. The *Times* newspaper was exciting a great deal of invidious comment when I was there, though I don't exactly know what for. But I condoned the offence, no matter what it was.

> "If to its share some political errors fall,
> Look on those criticisms (of me) and you'll forgive them all."

That is, you will if you are at all kind. Never mind, Mr. Chicago *Times*, you said everything delightful of me, and if ever you make your debut on any stage, you will find a lenient critic.

The "Felon's Daughter" "ran" nearly the whole of my engagement in Chicago; when she "stopped" we played the "legitimate." Taking this term as the adverse case to my heroine, I felt rather pained at its use. However, beggars—I mean authors, must not be choosers.

But in Chicago, opposition met me in a novel form. For many days before his appearance the citizens were enjoined to "look out for Satan;" they were requested to "prepare to meet the original proprietor of Rebellion," and mildly invited to "take a trip to Hell, through Chaos into Paradise." We soon found out what it meant.

Somebody was coming with "a series of great Miltonian tableaux, showing Paradise as *seen* by the great *blind* poet!"

We thought if he could see it in that light, we would too, and so we went.

Oh, Mr. Rossiter, I thought it was impossible to do anything more dreadful in this line than you have done, but I found my mistake. Why, only think of it! You have been surpassed in badness!

We were a small but very rollicking party that rainy afternoon; two larky girls, myself and a bright little child.

Besides seeing Paradise as the blind Milton saw it, the purchaser of a ticket was put in possession of a mystic number which entitled him to a chance in a lottery, or, as it was termed, a Grand Gift Distribution, which was to take place after Paradise had been lost.

I am quite unable to give any description of the Miltonian tableaux. I know I am making a confession which may cause unpleasant remark when I say that I felt the greatest interest in, and the liveliest sympathy for, the great king of evil, Satan. The truth is, I am much influenced through the medium of the eye, and Satan's was the only face with the slightest spark of nobility depicted on it. Both totally inane, we could not tell Adam and Eve apart, until her hair began to grow long, which it did after the interview with the serpent. While our first parents wandered about in the silliest and most lackadaisical manner, Satan, gloriously treading on nothing, and dressed in a red bandanna handkerchief, flew through space in the grandest style. Milton's poem is sublime, undoubtedly, but it is the funniest thing in life to see angels on canvas, dressed in regular orthodox angel costume, firing off cannon and planting howitzers and Dahlgrens.

A pale-faced, weak-voiced youth explained the tableaux to the audience, interlarding his discourse with scraps of the grand poem, and even quotations from Scripture. This would have been well enough if all had been of a piece, and uttered with solemnity and dignity; but only fancy Satan ushered in with the grand lines with which Milton presents him to his readers, while the brilliant pianist strikes up, "Wait for the Wagon!"

Then, again, when the solemn injunction is given, and over the bewildering darkness of chaotic life the orb of morning shows itself, for the first time:

> "And God said, Let there be light; and there was light,"

the sun rose in a jerky manner to the admired tune—something of an anacreonism in this relation, however—widely known as "Johnny comes Marching Home."

We got very tired of the sun rising in Paradise. It rose on four distinct occasions, and it was such an everlasting time about it! Then, there were six moons in the Garden of Eden, and, by a singular astronomical arrangement, only two stars. Perhaps Adam was a brigadier. Who knows? Certainly they had a dreadful rebellion up there. They exiled *some one*, and I must say, to my certain knowledge, he has cut up a lot of naughty capers since that time.

The last we saw of Adam and Eve they were being cast out of the Garden of Eden. The expounder (not the pianist), again quoting, said that they were going down the "Rocky Way," but you can't think how much the rocky way looked like those "runs" they always build at theatres for ladies on bare-backed steeds to take terrific leaps over bounding precipices.

I am sure you will forgive the inaccuracy of "bounding precipices" in a geographical sense for the sake of its novel and startling character as a flight of rhetoric.

"I'm so glad it's over," said the bright little child.

"Oh, there's the Grand Distribution yet."

To be sure; we forgot that. The Grand Distribution was placed on the smallest table I ever saw, and was composed almost exclusively of very small and very German silver hand-bells.

The only thing worth carrying away was a decent sort of photograph album, which was heralded as "the most magnificent article of the kind to be seen in Chicago."

"No. 99 takes this Magnificent Article," said the weak youth.

A frantic examination of numbers takes place among the audience, and the exclamation bursts from the bright child, to whom I bear no other relationship than that which is always engendered by love and sympathy,

"Why, Aunt Olive's got it!"

So I had, but they couldn't induce me to go up and get the album. Why, the conditions were something fearful! You had to promise to come again; that I would never do. Then you had to give your word to send twenty friends. Friends! Why, I wouldn't send twenty enemies there if I had so many, which I trust I have not. I threw the ticket down to end the controversy. An impudent young one, a lad of about fourteen, who had annoyed us the whole afternoon with saucy remarks, picked it up.

"Say, Ma'am," he called out as we were leaving.

"What?"

"Ain't you going to use this?"

"No."

"Then I will."

You should have seen the agile manner in which that delightful specimen of youthful America tumbled over benches, knocked down chairs, trod on gentlemen's toes, and tore ladies' dresses in his insane progress up to the Grand Distribution where the Grand Distributor was still calling for the recalcitrant No. 99.

"Give me the album," said the boy, "here it is."

"Here what is?" asked the Distributor.

"Why, No. 99."

"The doose it is," shouted the other, forgetting his Miltonian character, and getting red in the face: "I tell you what it is, boys have been arrested for less than this."

"Less than what?" asked the lad, beginning to whimper.

"Do you mean to say you don't know this is No. 66?" said the Distributor, turning the ticket upside down.

We were close to the door by this time, and had the full benefit of the scene. If ever I was glad in my life that I had not been hasty, I was so now. Fancy the Grand Distributor telling me that ladies had been arrested for less than this! By the most singular coincidence in the world, a man bearing a strong resemblance to the door-keeper held the lucky ticket, and carried away the photograph album, looking very much as if this were part of his business, and as if he personally were not going to derive the least amount of benefit therefrom.

Chicago raised men for the war, raised money for the men, and raised the uneven streets for her citizens. When she razes a block of unsightly frame buildings in South Clark street, and ejects from its precincts a horrid Jew whose shoe store is in a chronic state of "selling off below cost at prices to suit everybody," but which seem unfortunately to suit nobody, then, and not till then, will be attained a consummation devoutly to be wished.

It would be a very dreadful thing if I were to omit mentioning the large number of railways which come in at Chicago. It is a most unparalleled sign of the great activity of the Universal Yankee Nation, which spreads its Ægis wings over our Manifest Destiny, causing the Monroe Doctrine to appear in all its Force, with the entire Collapse of States' Rights, and the utter Downfall of Secession—only, on the other hand, it's pesky disagreeable when you want to go to Cincinnati to find that by mistake you have taken the train bound for Milwaukee.

It is with pride that I refer to the election of John A. Rice, Esq., to the mayorship of Chicago, which office the whilom actor and manager filled to the entire satisfaction of that generally dissatisfied body—everybody. We others of the profession may well feel pleased at the flattering distinction, for Mr. Rice was elected by a larger majority than was ever before given to any candidate. Truly, we have taken a good many steps forward since the days when actors used to prowl about the country shaving people, pulling their teeth, and bleeding them.

But, now I think of it, I remember it was barbers who used to do that.

Well, what uncomfortable thing was it actors *did* do during that misty Elizabethan era?

As it seems that talented families are the rage now, I may mention that Mr. Rice is closely related to that delightful comedian, Mr. William Warren, and to that very versatile actress and refined lady, Mrs. Anna Marble. Now, since these two persons are clever theatricals, you will at once understand that Mr. Rice, their brother-in-law, must be a good mayor.

At least, that is the modern style of reasoning.

My cousin is a major general.

Therefore,

I am a splendid actress.

Why, it's evident.

I never knew anything evidenter.

Sur ce, I bid Chicago adieu for the present.

A life on the ocean wave may be attractive to many persons, but a life on the cars has its pleasures and amusements as well. I think the peculiar idiosyncracies of the great human family are more noticeable on cars than on steamboats. On the sea everybody is sick as a general thing, and the favored few who are not, are for the most part the ubiquitous commercial traveler, the man who writes his "voyage round the world," and others of an equally uninteresting stamp. But on the cars we see all the world and his wife, and children, too, particularly his marriageable daughters, who wear pork-pie hats and flirt.

Flirt—flirt—flirt! The occupation of their lives! Flirt with anybody or with anything, while mothers look on with utter complacency and the assurance that "there is no harm in it." Perhaps so; but, for my own part, when I wear my heart on my sleeve for daws to peck at, *a l'Americaine*, I shall have marvellously changed my present mode of thinking.

I often wonder why babies travel so much. It seems to me I have met the very same babies several times in the wide range from Maine to Georgia. I never saw anything like it. I think they must make a tour of the States on an average two or three times a year. They always travel under protest; still they travel—till they are babies no longer.

Then they travel more desperately than ever, and, what is worse, write books about it, which makes us wish they had remained babies.

There is always a newly-married couple on board the cars, going out West to try their fortunes. I love to see them! The sweet confidence in each other which beams in every glance of the eye, the entire absence of any such law as *meum* and *tuum*, the beautiful oneness of sentiment, the unselfishness which, fade as it may in after years, exists now in force, make me wish from the bottom of my heart that I too had red hands and was going out there with him to do my own housework.

I know I should not shine in the housework line, laboring as I always do under the greatest uncertainty in regard to whether water is boiling or merely simmering; but love will do a great many things, you know, and might even transform a woman who is a dreamer into a first-class cook.

Of the boys on the cars who have gum-drops for sale, but who never sell any, I will say but a word. How these poor little wretches get a livelihood is a mystery to me; certainly it is not through the activity of their business in the gum-drop line. The sympathy which their impoverished condition might awaken in this breast is quenched by the disgust which the exhibition of their wares always occasions. A roystering four-bottle man, the morning following a bout, could not have a more uncertain state of feeling, lying somewhere between nausea and not nausea, than I always do after a long night's ride in the cars. What, then, do I not suffer when, more than half sick and altogether despondent, an inhuman little wretch thrusts gum-drops upon me at the wee small hour of four o'clock in the morning, and insists on my partaking of them at only ten cents the package done up in glazed paper and emetic-ally sealed?

Then, too, we have the New York *Hurled* at us wheresoever we may be, at prices varying from four cents the copy to fifteen. It is always bought, whatever the price, and seems invariably to awaken invidious comment from one cause or another. But, of course, so long as it *is* bought that is not the question.

I think nostrum vendors should be excluded from the cars. It is enough to meet their advertisements in every newspaper, to find them painted on rocks and plastered on curbstones, to have them thrust under our front doors, and handed to us as we are leaving church, without being obliged to submit to the infliction on the cars, in the shape of a very shabby man who stands up gravely and assures us that the small bottle for sixty cents, two for one dollar, will cure every known and unknown ill under the sun. There should be a police regulation in regard to this, for some misguided people might perchance buy the stuff, and then who knows what might happen? Like the antidote of the Borgias which the lyric *Gennaro* refuses to take, instead of curing the disease this medicine might generate it; which is probably the intention of the "gentleman" who puts up the decoction and gets somebody to give it a high-sounding Greek name.

A character quite peculiar to America is the boy or man who brings around iced water to thirsty travellers. I always welcome him with delight, and see him depart with sorrow; for not only does he furnish me with the clear fluid as a beverage, but he also vouchsafes me enough to perform as many Mussulmanic ablutions as the end of a dampened handkerchief will permit. I think this bounty is not rightly appreciated, and much as saucy chambermaids and impudent waiters are fee'd, I have yet to see the first *douceur* bestowed on the trusty water-carriers of the cars.

Let me enter my feeble protest against the shameful manner in which trunks are tossed about by railway porters. These men are paid and overpaid, and fee'd and bribed, to carry and transport trunks and boxes from one

16

train of cars to another, or from cars to omnibuses, as the case may be, and yet, irrespective of consequences in the shape of breakage, they fling boxes and trunks containing the most fragile articles from off the eminences of baggage-cars into the slough of despond of awaiting depots. I venture to assert that a trunk could go to Europe and back, and even make the "grand tour" up and down the Rhine, and incur far less damage than it would receive in going from New York to St. Louis. A set of stringent rules would remedy this evil, and I trust they may be enforced before my next journey.

The day I arrived in Indianapolis almost the whole military force stationed there was being sent forward to strengthen Sherman, who had just made the much-abused terms of surrender with Johnston. The depletion of the camp was a cheering prospect to me, in a financial point of view, as the theatre depended almost wholly on its soldier-patronage for support, and, unpleasant and inappreciative auditors as these sometimes proved, their entrance fee in greenbacks was as Very Hard Cash as that of the Proudest Peer of England's Isle—if that individual, who figures so largely in ballads, had been in Indianapolis, and had come to the theatre, which, of course, if he had had the slightest taste, he would have done.

A regiment or two drawn up in solid phalanx looks very pretty, even when doing nothing more warlike than standing at ease and listening to a farewell harangue by a local orator. This scene was being enacted as I drove up to the principal hotel in Indianapolis, and, while awaiting the kind attention of the busy clerk, I had an opportunity of listening to an orthodox Yankee "oration." It was not a bad speech, and far from badly delivered; but, as usual, the flights of rhetoric indulged in were of so grandiloquent a character that my feeble comprehension only barely grasped them, which fact no doubt accounted for the indifference with which the remarks were received by the soldiers, composed in great part of German emigrants, Irish "roughs" and Indiana farmers' boys.

Not to speak it profanely, by all that's Greek-y, what do "Indiana 'uns" care about the Spartan Mothers?

Will somebody tell me, also (in this connection), if the Spartan fathers had anything to do with those sons who made it a general practice to come back from battle either bearing their shields or borne on them?

It was noble in them to do that, wasn't it? Though I don't know what else they could have done with their shields, unless they had thrown them away, which would not have been economical.

But really, now, who ever hears of the Spartan fathers? Did such creatures ever exist?

Awaiting the answer, which I trust will come, like the "solution" of the "rebus," "next week," I may say that the orator at Indianapolis was a pleasant, genial-looking, middle-aged person, rather incongruously arrayed in a very military hat, and the most civilian of all suits—a nondescript pepper-and-salt affair, made, no doubt, at the most *chic* establishment at Indianapolis. I ventured to offer him a little compliment when he had finished his "oration," which he took in rather an indifferent manner, wondering, no doubt, what a blonde young woman in a dusty traveling dress knew about speech-making.

Indianapolis was kinder to me than I expected, spite of the absence of the soldiers, and for many causes I conceived a great liking for this little town, though, in point of architectural display, or even natural beauty, it stands far behind Cleveland, Columbus, and other places I might name. There is a bewildering number of railways that *debouchent* here, and for that reason it will always be a sprightly town, though I, myself, am un-American enough to like it better in its deserted quarters than where the gay shops flaunt out their wares and crinolines are sold.

I mind me of a solitary walk I took here, one Sunday, just as the shades of evening were falling over all things, while the chill March air made me draw my cloak more closely around me, and quicken my lagging step. On I went past the railway depot, with its now deserted cars awaiting the morrow's traffic; a great monstrous weird-looking place, fit habitation for ghouls and goblins, whose grinning faces I thought I saw up in the gothic rafters of the roof, menacing me in the uncertain light with skinny arms and noiseless jabbering jaws. Past the ladies' room, now tenantless. Past the ticket office, with its begrimed window shut. Past the place where "refreshments" are sold to men who drink it down, and change Humanity into Deviltry. Past the stand where the baggage is checked, and where two trunks, never to be claimed, the property of a dead man, lie, like their owner, covered with dirt and dust. Past the creaking, rusty gates, whose ponderous bars make me feel like a prisoner and a culprit. Past the blood-red flag of danger, and the dirty-white one of safety, both now unemployed. Past the sunken, indented rails themselves, and then, thank Heaven, with a sigh of relief, into the air again!

A lonely path to the left looked inviting because of its loneliness, and I took it.

"Ah," thought I, "here is peace! Who would be a dweller in the city's busy maze, when tranquillity and quiet joy may be had in such abodes as these?"

For now I had reached some little cottages which lay contiguous to the railway, and were occupied, no doubt, by its employés. Surrounded by trees, which only awaited the warm breath of spring to make them start forth into loveliness and verdure, fronted by a little garden, whose well kept beds showed both care and taste, with bright green shutters and newly painted front, one little cottage in particular attracted my attention. "Oh, for a little home like this!" I sighed; but even as I did so, the sound of angry voices issuing from an inner room reached my ear. A man in rage; a woman in invective. Frightened, I hurried on.

Peace? Mockery!

No Peace where rush the surging waters of the turbid passions of Man. Peace may come when these have subsided in the eternal quiet of the grave.

The Grave! As usual, there are some not far off. A quiet, inviting spot. Thither I bend my steps, and, pushing aside the swinging gate, I enter the churchyard.

The same old story on all the headstones. No wicked people buried here! All "respected for their virtues;" "honored for their benevolence;" "beloved and regretted by all." Faugh on the lying records!

I sink on a mound and think of that grave whose headstone bears, beyond the name and date of birth and death, but one line:

"Our Father which art in Heaven."

No mention of the large mind, the brilliant intellect, the culture of study, or the poetic heart which lie there, now forever hushed. Better so. We who knew and loved him, know all this; and those who knew him not, need not be told.

The cold night wind soughs mournfully through the gaunt trees and chills me; hot tears trickle through my fingers as I cover my face with my ungloved hands, and a few convulsive sobs, which relieve a heart full of melancholy remembrances, fall, where many more such have fallen, reverberating with a hollow echo on the dull churchyard air. Mysterious spot! My flesh creeps as I survey the numberless tenements of the dead, which lie on every side, and old stories that I have not thought of since childhood now force themselves on my brain with horrible distinctness. The rising and the walking of the dead! Their midnight revels; their capture of the living for interment with themselves.

Terrified, I rise to go; but as I do so a sight meets my gaze which to my dying day I shall never forget. A dark, uncertain mass advancing towards me rapidly; irrespective of their sanctity, up and over the graves with a strange and uncouth mode of locomotion; a headless, body, with two unnaturally long arms, borne, now straight upright, now distended wide on either side of the trunk to which they are attached.

To fly or to remain—which?

Flight? Impossible!

What progress can I make against this lithe thing—I, with my trembling limbs stiffened with cold, and my whole body paralyzed with terror?

Remain? For what?

Great Heaven, how do I know? For the doom which mortals meet when they meddle with the immortal—for torture—for agony—for despair! Tremblingly and with averted eyes I await my fate, for It is close upon me! As it nears me it *speaks*—my blood freezes at the voice of Nothing!

"Sa-ay, Ma'am, can't I walk on my hands bully?"

A ragged, saucy brat, offspring, perhaps, of the angry father and the invective mother, walking on his hands across the churchyard on a dark Sunday night for a wager of one cent with a timid chum!

Disgusted, I rise. Disgusted with all things, particularly myself. Annoyed that the phantom was not what I had prayed it might not be, wishing it had been what I was overjoyed to find it was not, humiliated unto blushes, fallen into the ridiculous, myself a laughing-stock to myself, ashamed of my fright, laughing through tears, biting my lips with annoyance while their corners were distended into smiles, I leave the churchyard and walk back to the hotel.

Thus ever;

Behind the cloud, the silver lining; behind Grief, Mirth; behind the sallow, forbidding mask of Tragedy, the grinning, obese cheeks of Momus.

Life and Death, Sorrow and Gladness, Birth and Pain, Love and Hate, Eternity and Futurity, are but other names for that indefinite word—Mystery.

When I get back, the gong is sounding loudly for supper, the gas is flaring and hurts my eyes, that pretty girl is still flirting with the same gentleman in the ladies' parlor, and above all there is a strong odor of baked griddle cakes.

The next day I have a bad cold in my head, and at the end of the week two dozen handkerchiefs in the wash.

This is the end of the episode.

I feel I must say something about Indianapolis. An irregularly built town, not without charm. Two rival hotels, both of which might be better. One only "Square," paradoxically called "The Circle." But the prevailing feature of the town seemed to be the undue amount of that unpleasant specimen *genus homo* known as the "Loafer." Both for quantity and nasty quality in this article, Indianapolis bore off the palm. Loafers everywhere. On the hotel steps, in the streets, and even in the sacred circular square itself.

Shabby wretches who stand for hours picking their teeth —which are, in all probability, quite innocent of dinner. Flashy wretches who wear ponderous watch-chains and loudly pass comment on every female who goes by. Boy wretches trying in vain to master their first cigar, which finally masters them, and sends them skulking off, looking very pale. Old men, leering wretches, standing in the uncomfortable posture of one foot in the grave and the other on the hotel steps in Indianapolis, go to make up a group which, for ugliness and even vice, is worthy of the pencil of a Hogarth.

English writers comment frequently on the inappropriateness of American nomenclature, and, in truth, with some reason. Why "Pea Ridge" should be, and "Sugar Creek," also, we know not. Neither one nor the other has any characteristic of the descriptive adjective, and, in point of accuracy, "Sugar Ridge" and "Pea Creek" would answer every purpose. But there are other peculiarities which puzzle me quite as much, if not more than these. For instance, Indianapolis is invariably pronounced Indian*o*ppolis, Cincinnati converted and perverted into Cincinnatt*a*, while, to do the thing according to rule, you must not call Chicago as that combination of letters would lead you to do, but change it into Chic*aw*go, under pain of being considered either a "prig" or a "muff;" in other words, a pedant or an ignoramus.

True, in support of this singular practice, we have the well-known example of the English, who call their Pall Mall *Pell Mell;* but I do not see that this is in the slightest degree a palliation for error on our parts. For, call the great English thoroughfare either as the letters spell it, or as custom pronounces it, and it is still the most outrageously unmeaning name for a street that could well be found.

They manage these things, as they do so many others, better in France. One reads the history of the country, from the days of Charlemagne down to those of the third Emperor, written up on the houses at corners of streets; from the Rues Agincourt and Rivoli, Otranto and Magenta, we turn to the broad sweep of the Rue de la Paix and the inspiring vastness of the Place de la Concorde. Chieftains figure largely—les Rues de Saxe, Prince Eugene, and Bonaparte. Nor are great men other than

those distinguished in battle, forgotten by the street sponsors. Witness the Rue Richelieu, Rue Mazarin, the Rue Montaigne, and the Rue Lord Byron. I always quarreled with the Boulevard des Italiens because of its inappropriateness, much as I liked the Italiens (?) who were born on that boulevard; but the suggestive and majestic Boulevard de Sebastopol looms up grandly beyond, and silences carping and censure.

As a reverse picture to this comprehensible style, I may mention what I believe is pretty generally known—that there are no less than fifteen "King William" streets in London; while I myself, within a very small radius near Hyde Park, counted *four* entirely distinct and separate "Ebury" streets. Who or what "Ebury" was, or what he, she or it had done to be so distinguished, I never discovered. I had a friend living in London, who told me I must remember she lived on the Ebury street down which the Queen always drove when she went to Parliament. I explained this to the cabman, and the information saved a world of trouble.

CHAPTER XXIII.

Street Entertainments for the Million.—A Procession.—Juvenile Sufferings on Gala Days.—The Prominent Citizen in the Procession.—The Day of Gloom.—Theatricals under the Cloud of Death.—The Theatrical Grandaddy.—Girl Waiters.—Erring Women.—The Death of a Magdalen.—Doffing the Sock and Buskin—Homeward Bound—Travelers' Miseries—Funny Western Actors—The Balladist of the Parlor.

A heavy cold—contracted through a pleasant habit which railway firemen have of filling the car stove to repletion with wood and then allowing the fire to die completely out, leaving the passengers in Arctic regions (generally over night), forced me to reliquish my engagements and return to Cincinnati, seeking the house of Monfrère for the express but rather gloomy purpose of being ill therein. This plan I carried out *con amore*, and by attending to it faithfully I managed to become quite a sick person at the end of a couple of weeks. At the beginning of the third, however, by good professional treatment, kind nursing, and a determination to avoid poor Mrs. Dombey's example, and to "make an effort," I had so far recovered my health as to be able to witness, from one of the windows of Wood's Theatre, the "grand civic and military procession" which took place on the 14th of April, in honor of the surrender of Lee and his army. Of course, to New Yorkers, who have the best of everything, this would have seemed but a trifling affair; but I had been so long an exile that I was quite charmed by the display of banners, flags, mottoes, etc., and somewhat amused at the satirical allusions everywhere apparent along the line.

The military part of the procession was good, nor could it well have been otherwise with General Hooker and staff leading off, preceded by the Mayor of the city and his subordinates. In appearance Hooker is certainly the very impersonification of a soldier and a general; the erect form, the breadth of shoulder, the close-cropped, slightly grizzled hair, the clear blue eye, the firmly set, handsome mouth, and, above all, that easy seat on a horse which indicates unmistakably the experienced rider, are all "sights and sounds" which are great points in his favor. What may be his real talent as a strategist, or a tactician, or a "handler of troops," I know not. By a singular accident I did not "assist" at the battle of Fredericksburg, and therefore cannot say who is responsible for that catastrophe.

Of course the Fenians were represented in the Cincinnati procession, and very nice they looked with their green sashes and their boughs, as they trod gaily along keeping step (sometimes) to the merry national air of "The Sprig of Shillelah," and the sad though martial one of "The Harp that once through Tara's Halls."

If a few of the brethren *were* a little unsteady on their pins, it must be borne in mind that it was quite late in the afternoon, that they had trudged many miles (with divers stoppages) and that the day was intensely warm; besides, was it not a brotherly duty to lift the sportive cup very frequently for the purpose of drinking "Down with England" and "Ireland for the Irish?"

Much firmer in their step, spite of lager, came the Germans, apparently quite satisfied with themselves as citizens and Cincinnati as a place of residence, and never bothering themselves about "Germany for the Germans," or "down with" anything—but lager.

After these there was rather a promiscuous display; "hose companies," "hook-and-ladder companies," and, I suppose, "bucket companies," closely followed by "Odd Fellows" and "Masons," tricked out in all their funny finery.

A procession in the West would not be complete without the presence of the inevitable public school children, who seem to think that because they attend a public school they must make themselves as public as possible. You can't imagine what torturing things they force these children to do on gala days.

They choose a girl whose nose has a speciality for getting blue, and whose teeth chatter habitually, and they tell her she is the Goddess of Liberty. The poor child, laboring under a heavy sense of her own importance, lies awake the whole night before the "great day" unable to sleep through the combined influence of agitation and curl papers. The next day it rains and the curls fall out, but as goddesses *must* have ringlets, she compromises the matter by letting her wet locks fall in a sodden mass down her dampened and eventually rheumatic back. This done, she envelopes herself in a very soiled American Flag, and showing a great deal too much of a figure whose angularities may be filled up by maturity, but which does not now recommend itself to the critical eye, she considers herself a living and beautiful embodiment of the fabled guardian spirit of our land.

Nor is this taste for the allegorical confined to the softer sex. There is always a male somebody with a large nose, who personates Washington, representing the Father of his Country as very dirty in the neckcloth, and very groggy in the legs. His Continental suit does not fit him, and his powdered wig is not at all powdered.

The two generally mount into a Chariot of Triumph, which belongs to the ice-man, but is now covered with pink muslin, and bears evergreen boughs. They grasp hands spasmodically, and the band plays "Columbia's the Gem of the Ocean," which being written for Britannia, and used by her from time immemorial, is highly appropriate in every respect.

Towards the close of the day, the shaking of the ice-cart, together with the unpleasant peculiarities of Washington's character, which lead him to twit Liberty on her sharp elbows, to ask her how much her hoop cost, and if she intends finally to devote it to the interest of hens, in the shape of a coop, quite wear out the temper of the tired school-girl, who takes off her Liberty cap, and, sitting down on the dirty floor of the Triumphal Chariot, cries to be home, saying that her head aches and that supper would not be unacceptable, as she has eaten nothing since early morning; the light but pleasurable breakfast of excited and delighted anticipation.

Alas, poor Liberty! as she lays her weary head on her pillow that night, she reflects with sadness on her career as a goddess, and tastes—perhaps for the first time, for she is young yet—the fruit of that bitter tree, disappointment.

Washington may not have *his* headache till the next morning. When attempting to get up, he becomes fully impressed with the idea that his stomach is going over to Europe in stormy weather, and that his head has suddenly changed into one of the cannon balls used at Yorktown.

These personages were not lacking in the procession at Cincinnati. In fact, there were schoolchildren there *pardessus la tete.* A Bunker Hill monument on wheels, appropriately surrounded by little sailors, shouting, "We are marching along," which, I believe, is the very thing sailors do *not* do, unless a ship's course can be called "marching," was followed by a carload of little girls, representing nothing in particular, but singing in as many different keys as there were children, that very popular air—that then, alas! *too* popular air—of "Johnny's Come

Marching Home!" Rejoicing at this, we can only regret that the schoolchildren do not at once imitate such a laudable example, and "march" to the very place where "Johnny" did—*i. e.*, home.

The next feature in the entertainment was the following of the procession by a mounted body of "prominent citizens." I think if there is anything excruciatingly funny, it is your "Prominent Citizen" on horseback. There is a Pickwickian richness in it which words fail to convey. In all probability he never was on a horse before, and his attempt to be at ease, to look as if he were so, to frown severely at the boys who laugh at him, and who predict that that "hoss will go to praying next"—a mild allusion to a weakness in the knees of the Prominent Citizen's animal—is ludicrous in the extreme. As he turns the corner of the street where Arabella lives, he determines he will look the perfect horseman, and, as he catches a glimpse of her bright eyes behind the window-curtain, he steadies himself in his saddle, and grasping the reins in a loose and *degage* manner, he tries to appear smilingly oblivious of all around, while he flatters himself inwardly that Popkins (as a rival) is now completely done for.

But just at that moment the weak-kneed animal becomes aware of the close proximity of a donkey-cart, and as donkeys are a species to her especially repugnant, she determines to revenge herself for the appearance of this one on the unoffending Prominent Citizen. She kicks and she shies; she rears and she neighs; then she performs a circus-feat—standing on her two front ones.

In vain does the innocent P. C. clutch madly at the reins so close to the animal's neck as almost to strangle her; by a skillful manœuvre she throws her head up, loosening his hold; then, giving one frantic rear in the air, she casts the much-abused P. C. down into the slimy mud with such a thump that the poor man gets knocked on the head, and becomes insensible.

When he recovers consciousness he finds himself in Arabella's house, and sees the hated Popkins stuffing his handkerchief down his throat that the P. C. may not observe his choking fit of laughter, in which Arabella has been joining. Humiliated and crushed, the P. C. calls a carriage and goes home, and that night, however separate in body, in spirit he joins the Liberty Goddess in eating the bitter fruit of disappointment.

But the hours roll on and bring us the next morning. Alas! alas! I find my occupation as a fun-maker gone now. How shall I describe the fearful panic, the overwhelming stroke of grief which crushed the People's heart at the news of President Lincoln's assassination? For several hours it was disbelieved, and then, when disbelief was no longer possible, the scene which must have been enacted in every loyal city took place in Cincinnati. Weeping, wailing women; hollow-eyed, silent men, wandering listlessly up and down the almost deserted streets. Hushed the prattle of childhood, stopped the traffic of business, *dead* lay the great, common heart in the coffin of its martyred chief. Where, now, the merry-making crowd of yesterday? Where, now, the exulting participants in the procession? Even the groggy Washington has sobered up, and by his deep-drawn sighs shows he has a soul, spite of his dirty necktie, while the Goddess of Liberty, through a flood of tears, sews a border of crape around her American flag.

The fearful spirit of revenge which was everywhere manifested against the assassin, was greatly aggravated by the presence of one of the Booth brothers, then fulfilling a professional engagement at Cincinnati. According to the usual custom, the name was posted at every available spot all over the city, and turn where one might,

"BOOTH" met the eye. The subdued sadness of the early morning seemed to disappear at view of this fearful reminder of the author of such a heinous wrong, and men, even those most noted for their mildness, became possessed as of a demon. The bills were torn down, divided into infinitesimal fragments, and then crushed, with maledictions appalling to hear, under the grinding heels. The excited mob threatened to tear down the theatre in which Mr. Booth was performing, and were only appeased by the assurance that he should not appear again. The gentleman was visited by an officer at his hotel, who demanded the immediate surrender of all papers or letters in Mr. Booth's possession. This, I believe, was refused, and I heard a great many people denounce the proceeding as one utterly uncalled for and altogether unjustifiable. The following Sunday, sermons were preached not more violent in their character than the outraged and insulted auditors looked for and desired. But one feeling was rife. Revenge! To catch the assassin, to torture him, to make him suffer a thousand-fold what he had caused the pure-minded Lincoln to suffer; to draw him, to quarter him, to hang him by the neck till he was dead—dead—dead.

Oh, thank God, those days of fierce excitement, of mad desire for blood, are past! Men quoted Scripture, "an eye for an eye, a tooth for a tooth," *a life for a life;* Shakespeare, too:

> "Accursed be the air on which he rides,
> And damned all those that trust him."

There was something very touching in the mourning of the negroes for their "Father," as they called Mr. Lincoln. I think there are very few affluent negroes in Cincinnati, and the sacrifice by poor people of a few shillings earned by hard labor to buy a bit of crape or a villainous "likeness" of the President, had so much of beauty in it that it lifted this much-despised race quite up into the regions of poetry. Our washerwoman, who wept so unrestrainedly that she actually dampened my clean linen, otherwise unexceptionably "done up;" and "Nigger Jim," the wood-sawyer, were objects of general interest. The hope of the negroes was gone. They did not now understand at all that they as a race were unchangeably emancipated, but believed that Freedom was Lincoln, and Lincoln Freedom, and that when one was dead the other died with it. For this reason their grief was doubly keen. Their friend, emancipator, defender, originator of the American citizen of African descent, President, *god*, struck down at one fell blow. No wonder the little blacks huddled together on the door-steps, with woful faces, which, had they been white, would have shown the dirty traces of tears, and that the elder people neglected to go out for work, at the risk of creeping supperless to bed!

But "inconstant as the wind," to the general public, full of oil and railroad stocks, the death of the noble Lincoln became every day more a thing of the past, and the newspapers, from containing daily eulogies on the character and life of the President, began to squabble about what cities the funeral cortege should pass through as it conveyed the remains of the great Dead to their final place of interment.

The time arrived for me to resume my journeyings, so donning my shell-decked pelerine and grasping my staff, I make me ready for my pilgrimage. There are the children to be kissed, and *mon frere* also, and the neighbors' hands to be shaken, and Tray, Blanche and Sweetheart, our canine friends, to be patted, and Mére to be ensconced safely in the carriage, and then I look out of the window with a doleful smile, which I try hard to make cheerful, but there are tears in my voice, though I manage to keep them out of my eyes, as I gaze back fondly and utter that hateful word GOOD-BY.

A dreary ride of a day took us from Cincinnati to Cleveland, which latter place we found making mournful preparations for the reception of the President's remains, which were to pass through that city on their way to Springfield. Funeral arches were being erected at various points, and mourning drapery was displayed in even greater profusion than at Cincinnati.

I think that to no "business," "trade" or "profession" was given a greater shock by the death of the President, than to theatricals.

The public mind was not bent on amusement, and I can answer for it that the actor's mind was no more bent on furnishing it; but the tearful clown cries "houp-la!" while his baby is lying dead at home, and the hungry actor feasts on wooden pheasants and drinks from golden goblets at the "royal banquet," while, in point of fact, those much abused edibles of the South, called "hog and hominy," would be as Sardanapalan viands to his famished vitals.

By which, I trust, it will not be understood that I was very hungry, when I add that I played two dreary nights in Cleveland to about the worst houses I ever saw. I only wondered why anybody came. I know I shouldn't have gone to the theatre if I had had my choice. Not only was there a beggarly account of empty boxes, but the dress circle and parquet presented an absolute deficit.

Of course, like everything sad, there was a *cote ridicule* to this spectacle. I burst out laughing in a tragic part when I entered and took a look at my auditorium.

It was the queerest auditorium you can well imagine. One solitary enthusiast in a private box, who cried "Bray-vo!" and clapped his hands, when the action of the piece demanded absolute silence; two misguided infants in the dress circle, one of whom squalled and the other had the whooping-cough; a sprinkling of severe dead-heads, determined to be sternly critical, and refusing to be pleased with us, do what we might; my chambermaid at the hotel, to whom I had given an "order," weeping piteously at our fictitious woes, and blowing her nose with cheerful persistency; half a dozen "supes," who were to be noble Romans in the last act (and who had already got their "tights" on) but who consented in the interim to grace the "pit" with their presence and carry on a conversation (totally irrelevant to time and place) with a b'hoy who run wid der mashine, had a black eye, and was now lodged temporarily in the upper gallery. It will be well understood from this that my share (after expenses) in the gross receipts was absolutely *nil*, and I have the proud consciousness of knowing that whatever I may have been in other cities, in Cleveland, at least, I was a "pearl—without money and without price!"

But mark the change. The next day the city began to fill with strangers, flocking in in droves to see the remains of the President, expected to arrive the day following. The consequence was that that night our house was filled to overflowing, and two or three pleasing fights for seats took place by way of a prologue to our play. This latter was received with bursts of applause, and in a little comic piece which followed, the shouts of laughter, the general hilarity, and the incontrovertible signs of the amusement of the audience served, indeed, as a strange precursor to the solemnities of the morrow.

We are very apt to blame the French for insincerity, for heartlessness, for *insouciance;* but tell me, if you can, anything more—well, more French—than stopping at a theatre on the road to a burial!

Heaven knows it is not my province nor desire, my

profit nor interest, to deprecate the seeking of amusement.

I hold that diversion of a high order is as beneficial to the mind, especially to one overtaxed by business cares or mental anxiety, as the administering of certain apt drugs is to the diseased body. But there are times and places for all things. If the funeral of Lincoln was a "show," like the carrying of a Princely Nonentity to his ancestral grave, why, then, I have nothing to say. *Vive la galere!* Out on a holiday, be jolly and amuse yourselves to the top of your bent, dear public! But if it was to be the signal for the bursting out afresh of the deep wound which had rent every breast at Lincoln's death, why, then I take it, it would have been more consistent with propriety to avoid theatres as well as every other species of amusement, at least till the ceremonies were over.

If this had been done, the writer of these lines would have had a few dollars less in her pocket, and a better feeling towards her fellow-creatures in her heart.

I don't mean to say that the grief for the President was other than very deep and very sincere; but that it was more a great shock than a great sorrow is proved by the fact that the subscriptions to the Lincoln monument, very active at first, quickly dwindled down into mere nothingness; that if Mrs. Lincoln is not starving, it is not due to her having received any aid from the government or the public; and that a mocking pedestal, more hollow and meaningless than our stage trickery, stood for weeks, till it became weather-stained and time-faded, on the left side of Union Square, in New York, and then, I think, was taken down without any explanation.

In passing the coffin of the simple-minded but illustrious Lincoln, men uncovered their heads, and women shed tears; but when these people were edged on by other curiosity-seekers, the men put on their hats and the women dried their eyes, and the first began to speculate on what "Andy's" policy would be, and the latter to wonder what the chenille cost a yard. I know it will be urged that this is human nature; but, if it is so, I wish somebody would inform me what on earth *in*human nature is supposed to be. *My* opinion is that it is inquiring the price per yard of the white chenille which decked the interior of the Martyr's coffin.

The catafalque at Cleveland was very beautiful, and the police arrangements (that any should be required!) were so complete that nobody's eyes were knocked out, and nobody's skull knocked in. Happy consummation! The true patriots at Cleveland were those ladies of wealth and refinement who spent whole nights in making garlands, festoons, nosegays, &c., to deck the bier on which the coffin was to repose but for a few short hours. Through a drenching rain they adjusted their handiwork, which was doubly beautiful for being prepared by such dainty fingers. It may be there was a little spirit of emulation shown; a little desire that their catafalque should be more beautiful than that of some other town; but, if there was, it was a noble pride, and must not occasion a word of censure.

I must add that the theatre was closed the night on which the President's remains lay in the town.

I have a tender fear of becoming a nuisance in attempting to describe Cleveland. I feel that I might as well attempt to describe "around the corner." Everybody knows Cleveland. Everybody has been there. You can't get anywhere without passing through there. This being the case, I think the proprietor of that restaurant in the depot would enhance his claims to public gratitude and heighten his character for equity if he would give us a better breakfast for One Dollar. Ham and eggs are not objectionable once in a way; but ham stretching out like the line of Kings in Macbeth, till the crack of doom, at which period the eggs are apt to become stale, must be rebelled against even by a non-epicure like myself.

The Fifth Avenue, The Belgravia, the Faubourg St. Germain of Cleveland, is a very beautiful avenue, wide and imposing, called Euclid street. On either side are truly majestic residences, but happiness is no more an inmate of palaces than it is of cottages, and if they have only a small share of it and health, I can assure the young ladies of Euclid street that they have cast their (hair) nets into pleasant places.

The pretty public square of Cleveland is graced by a creditable statue of Commodore Perry, standing in a position usually unknown to public-square statues; that is, one which a man in life and the enjoyment of his reason might really have assumed. I am not very certain what madmen do in lunatic asylums, but I have always imagined they must stand as defunct bronze horses are made to stand, and have that questionable seat on horseback which the departed marble equestrian invariably affects. 'Tis quite true that Perry is represented in this statue as ordering a vigorous broadside into nothing, and frowning ominously, as Mr. Toots' dog barked, at an imaginary foe; but the likeness of the naval hero is, I believe, good, the adjuncts of rope coil, spars, anchors, &c., go far toward heightening the effect, and the whole *ensemble* is very pleasing.

The Academy of Music was a pretty theatre; the most thorough artist of the troupe being the manager as well. I will not tell you his name, because my moral principles forbid my puffing any one except myself; but I will say that he is one of the few lacrymose "fathers" who commands my respect and can make me feel any "pity" for the "sorrows of a poor old man."

Perhaps I am more hardhearted than befits one of my

sex, but when the Heavy Old Parent comes on, white as to wig, shaky as to legs, paralytic as to all the members, with much handkerchief and little voice, and begins his inevitable long story about something very stupid and very unfortunate which happened

"Some tew-wenty years ago,"

you can't tell how much I'd give to be home!

I was told there were some beautiful drives about Cleveland, but no drive is beautiful to me when I am blinded by the dust and can see nothing ahead but the driver's a-back.

From Cleveland I proceeded to Milwaukee, to fill a short engagement at that beautiful and healthful place. Clean, regular, well laid out, with the purest air and the serenest of skies, I do not wonder the residents are proud of their town. Milwaukee is everywhere famous for the fine quality of brick made there, and such fame is well deserved. I could not help thinking how capital an effect might be made by a talented architect with this delicate, lemon-tinged brick, relieved by red, black or brown, according to taste. A feudal mansion, for instance, of alternate red and yellow brick, with a chateau roof of brown or black, would be very striking.

(Mére says she thinks that would be Harlequin's House, but never you mind her. She is a dreadful old fogy, is mamma.)

How people made of flesh and blood can stand such a rigorous climate as that of Milwaukee is a mystery to me. I was there in May, and I do not think I ever experienced such bitter cold in all my life. The wind howled round the corners in such a terrible manner that it fairly froze my young blood, and made each particular hair to stand on end like quills upon the fretful porcupine. If the shorn lamb is really of any avail, and had come along just then, he would have been as dear to my heart as the scenes of my childhood when fond recollection presents them to view.

There are lots of "big Injuns" in Milwaukee. There is the unapproachable or Bull-dog Indian, who wears the aboriginal dress and is generally intensely disagreeable. These they call the "pure Indians. Then there is another class, who are, I suppose, "impure," as their faces are whiter and they laugh sometimes. These wear a pleasing variety of old clo', and look as if they had made a promiscuous haul in the sanctum sanctorum of a theatrical costumer.

The men, if dirty and tattered, have a certain ferocity about them which is not devoid of dignity; but the women, always fond of gewgaws, now affect the hoop-skirt, which looks "real sweet" worn under the scantiness of a Mackinac blanket.

The principal hotel in Milwaukee served to remind me again that Western hotel service is often very defective. However useful at private houses, and at other houses which are not private, the "waiter girl" in a hotel is a nuisance. Their hoops are in the way; themselves are in the way. They chatter and giggle and make mistakes and a noise. They lean familiarly over the back of your chair, and ask you if you "wish" some beefsteak, when in truth, the only thing you do "wish" is that they would be gone at once and not trouble you any more.

In an humble way, I have done something to push forward the great project of female emancipation, by labor, from the slavery of waiting to be married merely to have one's board and lodging paid.

It is the essence of my creed, regarding woman's rights, that a woman should be able to feel when she lies down at night that she is really thanking her Maker, and not her husband, for having given her this day her daily bread.

Some years ago, in a beautiful city beyond the sea, I

belonged to two societies formed and carried on by ladies of my acquaintance. One was for the Employment of Females—the other was for the Redemption of Erring Women. One hinged on the other, and both did a vast deal of good. But we obtained no situations as "waiter girls" for our *protegees*. We found that where poverty and frailty were thrown in contact with wealth and vice, weak nature fell, and was, alas! as tinsel against bullion in the balance scales.

One girl died on our hands. She was only eighteen, but oh Heaven! what a career of vice hers had been! Her repentance was complete, and no one can ever persuade me that Divine forgiveness did not hover around her lowly bedside. Her death was calm as an infant's, and as her spirit took its flight she murmured a little French prayer, in substance much the same as that expressed in Byron's beautiful lines:

"Father of light! to Thee I call;
My soul is dark within;
Thou, who canst mark the sparrow's fall,
Avert the death of Sin.
Thou, who canst guide the wandering star,
Who calm'st the elemental war,
Whose mantle is yon boundless sky,
My thoughts, my words, my crimes forgive;
And, since I soon must cease to live,
Instruct me how to die."

My list of engagements being completed, I was now free to doff the sock and buskin, and set my foot once more upon my native heath. With a joyful heart I "assisted" at the packing of my trunks—if that means looking on and not doing anything—while visions of joyful faces, mine perhaps the cheeriest of all, filled my waking and my slumbering dreams. I bought a happy railway ticket and gleefully made haste to be gone.

It must not be inferred from this desire on my part to

leave the beautiful country which sees the last gleams of the setting sun that I had other than the greatest fondness for the West and for the Western people.

At the risk of uttering truisms and being altogether a platitudinal truist, I may mention that it requires a pretty strong organic construction to stand the ravages of an eight months' tour in the land of fast eaters. The way food is bolted at those Western hotels is enough to make the mildest-tempered and the best-intentioned liver stand on end: if that is the way in which livers express dissatisfaction. I utterly abandoned catching meals at railway "stations," and made up my mind to daily starving on board the cars. Sometimes I was rewarded with a delicious dinner in the town for which I was bound, and sometimes, I may observe, I was not.

There is generally a pleasing diversity of opinion on the cars in regard to whether the windows shall be shut or open. The strongest party of course wins, but when the yeas and nays are equally divided, it is often a very pretty struggle. The conductor is sometimes called in to cut this Gordian knot, and, so long as he remains, peace is generally maintained; but when he goes, as he must sooner or later, the strife begins again, and continues *ad infinitum.* It is amusing to hear the different reasons assigned for espousing either side. This man is of a plethoric habit and requires air; the next one consumptive, and can't sit in a temperature lower than 75°. This woman has fainting-fits, the other the rheumatism; baby has a stiff neck, and Billy rush of blood to the head. It is the old story of the clerk of the weather inquiring whether he should send rain or no; opinion was so antagonistic, the reasons pro and con so conclusive, that the poor caterer for public happiness, quite at a loss to please everybody—or, indeed, anybody—now pleases himself, and there's an end on't.

Who is the architect of cars? And if so, why does he always put the ice-water tank almost on top of the red-hot stove? Why, also, is wood invariably used as fuel on railway cars? Because it makes a tearing, roaring, ferocious, unbearable fire? Because it goes out quickly and completely, leaving a poor lot of freezing, sneezing, wheezing unfortunates lost in the mazes of cold in the head?

These are only a few of the miseries the traveler must endure. I thought they were unparalleled until an elderly gentleman once kindly related to me some of the discomforts experienced in the olden time when stage coaches formed the only means of transit across the vast prairies of the West. I execrate the railway, but I now understand that to take up stage-coaching would only be going from Scylla to Charybdis.

With regard to the Western actors with whom I came in contact on the stage, I can speak, as a rule, in terms of the highest respect. Still the Western actor is sometimes very funny; I suppose I am so too when I don't want to be, and the reverse when I do. But I know you will forgive my smiling at the pomposity of "my lord" who comes to a ball dressed in brown trowsers, a "frock" coat (than which no more hideous garment was ever devised or imagined), and a pair of darkly, deeply, beautifully *green* gloves, which with Some hands inside, he lays, now on his "breaking" heart, now on my "perjured" arm, whose "alabaster whiteness" he tells me, "rivals the lily;" and no wonder, since it is covered with Lily-white. He swears by the "ble-ue" heaven above him that he is contaminated by me touch, and casting me down in a fainting state he only waits for the curtain to fall on the tableau to gallantly falsify his words and rush to assist me to arise; which I forthwith do, stumbling over my train and wiping away the black traces of his painted whisker off my perjured cheek. I don't know why "my lord" always talks so much about his "le-ady mother;" except it is because real lords are never known to use that form of phrase. In fact it is both tautological and unnecessary; for himself being a peer of the realm, if the lady is his mother, his mother must be a lady, as you will at once admit. But regardless of this fact, he goes harping on his le-ady mother worse than *Polonius* did on his le-ady daughter, until I get to such a pitch of nervousness that, as Mrs. Gamp aptly describes it, "fiddlestrings is weakness to expredge my feelinx."

CHAPTER XXIV.

About Audiences.—A Sketch of a New York Audience.—Specimens from the Audience.—The Rights of Audiences.—The Right to Hiss.—Carrying Dissent very Far.—An Ungrateful Pit.—A Furious Canadian Audience.—Row in French Theatre.—Restoring Good Humor.—An Actor who was Hissed to Death.—The Right of Free Applause.—The Claqueur Nuisance.—Putting Down an Honest Hiss.—The Bouquet Nuisance.—Curious Swindlers.—The Encore Nuisance.—Coming Before the Curtain.—Bad Habits of Audiences.—Curious Anecdotes.—The Audience that Had to be Told to Go.—A California Specimen.—"Won't you Light that Gas-burner?"—An Unbiassed Witness.—Jenny Lind and the Hoosier.—Mrs. Partington at the Play.

To the general play-goer, it is presumed that the most interesting part of a theatre is behind the scenes.

To actors and actresses, naturally enough, the chief interest lies with the audience—Before the Footlights.

At least, it has always been and is so with me.

I am never tired of studying that many-headed animal—the Audience. I love to take it up in its different elements, and ponder it—looking out from a cozy corner in a stage-box, myself unobserved.

The doors are thrown open, and now comes in the promiscuous crowd—that sea of human nothings which makes up a "good house" at the theatre. Kitty and her beau, who don't care a pin for the play, but have only come for a long conversation, in which they indulge during the entire evening, much to the annoyance of their immediate neighbors, who, strange to say, prefer listening to the comedy to overhearing Kitty's love confessions, and sometimes even intimate as much to young Larkins, who rudely heeds them not.

There is the school-girl of fifteen, who worships the

walking gentleman, and refuses to believe that his moustache is painted.

There is the adolescent, who robs himself of sugar-plums to buy flowers, which he throws at the feet of the danseuse.

There is the habitual theatre-goer, who remembers seeing this piece, or something very like it, at least thirty years ago, and according to whose statements theatricals, theatres and stage appointments of the present day are in a complete state of degeneracy.

There is the ex-artiste, of fifty well-told winters, who wonders why managers will let that chit of a girl play *Juliet*, when herself could play it a thousand times better.

There is the man who laughs at everything.

There is the universal fault-finder.

Ah, that is you, isit, Mrs. N.? You are coming in on a free ticket. Your sack is not of this year's make, dear; it looks old-fashioned. Never mind; you are honest. Your ideas of astronomy consist in the belief that the sun rises in the east of your husband's well-worn coat, and sets in his western boot-leg. You are naïve to insipidity, but you are as good as you are soft; so *ma foi*, I harm you not. Bless you—bless you!

Not so with you, Mrs. R. Your husband is a clerk in a commercial house, on a salary of fifteen hundred a year. How do you manage to pay $60 for your new but ugly little Empire bonnet? How do such trifles as cashmere shawls, diamond rings, and threadlace flounces find themselves in the wardrobe which your husband looks at admiringly, but ignorantly, too? He sometimes thinks that your various "aunts," who send you so many presents are very generous creatures, and often wonders why they never call at the house except when he is from home.

Why, Miss S., I hardly expected to see you here! Are your preparations for flight all made? Going to Europe, eh, with that dear fellow who may be seen and is seen every day picking his white teeth in front of the St. Nicholas? Well, he is handsome, I admit. Owns an estate in the South, does he? Well, perhaps so. I never was very bright about boxing the compass, and a faro-bank in — street may be down South or up North for all I know. Only, why don't he ask you to marry him first?

Among the late comers is Mr. J. He doesn't enjoy the piece much, but twists uneasily in his chair, and starts suddenly and looks at the door. Compose yourself, J. Your employers don't know it, yet.

Four times the curtain comes down, and four times there is gossip, and flirting, and scandal, and hypocrisy of all sorts.

Mrs. X comments on her neighbor, and calls her a "horrid creature." They kiss, nevertheless, each time they meet, and have a joint pew at Dr. Nobby's church.

Mr. ——, who, having neglected to call on Miss I, now crosses over to her, and says a few pleasant words; then bowing low, as he leaves her side, he congratulates himself that that bore is over. Miss I. smiles at him, and looks very archly through her long lashes, but she inwardly hates the ground he walks upon, as if the ground were personally to blame for receiving his weight. This she tells her mother, who, knowing that he is rich, is anxious for her daughter to entrap him.

But at last the curtain comes down for good, or bad perhaps, and Kitty gets her dress trod upon, and young Larkins loses his umbrella, and Pa leaves his overcoat on the seat, and a sweet-scented billet-doux passes from a small neatly gloved hand into one which is larger and not gloved, and P. lights a cigar, and Mrs. P. says the smoke makes her sick, and the swells take carriages, and the mediocrity take the omnibuses, and the plebeians walk, and the gas is turned off, and there is a damp smell in the theatre, and in an hour or two, critics, and criticised, swells, mediocrities, plebeians and artistes are in that happy sleepy land where criticism comes not, and newspapers are unknown.

A witty writer points out some of the peculiarities of theatre-attenders in this style: "There is the hypercritical man, a fool who amuses himself painfully. No convict condemned to shoemaking in a State prison suffers the pangs of disagreeable labor half as severely as a hypercritical individual when he attempts to enjoy himself in a theatre. Around him are people who have left dull care outside the entrance-wicket, who have bid melancholy a temporary farewell, and who have invoked all the gayety and joyousness of their natures for an hour of salubriousness. Relaxed features, unfurrowed brows, smiling faces, are about him, and there he sits beside, but not of, the general hilarity—morose, bilious, critical, watching, like an evil accusing spirit, for the occurrence of errors, of omission or commission. He retires from the theatre to look up the authorized version of the play, then sits down and writes an article on the decadence of the art of acting, which he sends to a theatrical paper, whose critic laughs at the strictures as absurdly severe, and dooms the essay to the oblivion of the waste-basket. There is the stupid theatre-attender, who is generally an individual who has 'nowhere to go' and no desire to go anywhere, who has little social feeling and less intellectuality, and who goes to the theatre merely to pass the time between supper and bed. To him, the theatre is not a temple of the drama, but merely a sort of waiting-room for bedtime, a room well lit up, bustling, noisy, spectacular, where one can do, in a quiet way, as one pleases—listen, look, or nod, and, above all, go out at regular intervals to 'liquor up.' When there happens to be a large number of these people in the house they act like a wet blanket on the spirits of the actors, for there is neither sign of approbation nor disapprobation, and the dullness that fills the house before the footlights seems magnetically to oppress the spirits of the people on the stage, and makes them look on a good hearty electrifying hiss as a change for the better. But the style of theatre-goer most delightful to the player is the unsophisticated young woman who believes it all. She knows not, and if she were told would not believe, that the youthful *Juliet* who makes her love, laugh, weep and hate, by turns, is the mother of grown-up children, and that the stern *Capulet* is a far more tender and a much younger man than the romantic *Romeo*, who has played the part for a quarter of a century. She is innocent, too, of all knowledge of machinery, and make-up, and all the very disagreeable resorts and devices of the stage. What would the knowing ones, who yawn and fume, and worry through a performance, not give if they could exchange their foolish wisdom for her blissful ignorance?—to think that the heroine has not studied every classic pose, winning expression, and thrilling accent: that the funny man is not sweating and toiling with heart-aching eagerness for the sake of a family nest built in a distant garret; that the hero is not suffering excruciating pangs of envy, and from unmerited neglect; that all the people beyond the footlights are enjoying themselves, and are merely acting, instead of working!"

In these days of battle for "equal rights," it seems to me that something ought to be said in behalf of the rights of audiences.

Among these, unquestionably, is the right to hiss. It is difficult to say just where the limits of this right are to be drawn; but that an audience has a right to express disapprobation is a thing which must be freely conceded.

I would urge all audiences to be generous in the exercise of this right, however. I would have them lenient toward the poor player who does his best, and does it honestly, however poor that best may be. But I would have every audience hiss, and vigorously hiss, exhibitions of vulgarity, indecency and drunkenness in actors—for these are insults to an audience, and it ought to resent them promptly.

Among the humorous anecdotes of audiences which have expressed disapprobation in a rather marked manner, is that of an individual who undertook to give a concert all alone by himself, in a New England town, and thus related his experience:

"After the performance a large number of the audience crowded on the platform to congratulate me, while another party started around the town in search of something appropriate to present to me. It being late, all the jewellers' stores and book establishments were closed. The only house that they could find open was a family grocery. Determined not to be balked in their efforts to show their appreciation of my vocal powers they bought up a basket of eggs to present to me on the stage. When they arrived at the hall the crowd was so great around me that the deputation could not reach me. They accordingly threw the eggs one by one over the heads of the audience, and, strange to say, by the time the eggs reached me they were rotten."

M. Baron, once celebrated throughout France, and beyond doubt one of the greatest actors of his time, found that when he grew old the cruel French audiences of the period, forgetting his past greatness, began to insult him, and, as he was one night playing Nero, they even hissed him! The aged monarch of the stage folded his arms, walked sternly down to the footlights, and exclaimed, "Ungrateful pit! 'twas I who taught you!" It was a slip of the tongue, he used to say; but he was nettled that they who had been made by him judges of good acting should have turned their knowledge against their instructor.

An exciting scene occurred in a Montreal (Canada) thetre two or three years ago. It appears that a French company had advertised with the pretensions of a troupe from a first-class theatre in New York, and the house was crammed from the family-circle to the pit—the latter being particularly crowded—to witness the performance of a beautiful French drama as the opening piece. "The curtain rose, and the performance went on. A very ugly actress acted in a still more ugly manner, and a very young man attempted to act the part of an old man, with an immense quantity of flour on his head and smeared over his face. To crown all, another actress made her appearance, rattled off a few words in bad French, and seemed to have the one desire to get off the stage as quickly as possible. The drop-scene fell amid a chilling silence, and the second act began by the audience gradually realizing that they had been completely 'sold.' A 'hiss' was quickly followed by others, and yells and hisses were then given with might and main. The performers looked terrified, but still went on; but the crowning act was accomplished. An actress fell on her knees, and, in execrable French, cried out to the young man with the flour on his head. The audience were furious. Yells and hoots filled the air. Bouquets made from the shockingly printed programmes were thrown by dozens at the players. This was quickly followed by a lobster thrown in the same direction, and cabbages, pieces of sticks and cloth were vigorously hurled upon the stage. The performers, in a terrified manner, flew from the stage, and, amid a storm of yells, imprecations and hisses, the drop fell. A man attempted to apologize for the acting, but was forced to retire. The whole pit then indulged in a free fight, while from the family-circle some two or three seats were torn up and came crashing on the stage. The house was in an uproar, and the ladies were quickly leaving, in terror for their safety. The pit then sung a song, and indulged in another free fight. At length the green curtain fell, and such a storm arose as would be hard to describe. It was well the performers did not make their appearance again, for the rage of the audience was thirsting for a victim, and the first that came would surely have been first served. At last the house was cleared, and the stage was left ornamented with the lobster and cabbages, sticks and broken seats thrown on it." The scene was a thoroughly disgraceful one, and as extraordinary as disgraceful.

French audiences are, however, notoriously given to strong expressions of disapprobation when excited, and are also notoriously excitable. On the evening of January 1, 1868, a disturbance took place at the theatre of the Porte St. Martin, Paris, on the occasion of the first representation of the review, entitled "1867, ou si tu n'es pas content, demandes autre chose." Mlle. Silly was on the stage, imitating the intonations and gestures of Mlle. Schneider in the "Grand Duchesse." As the imitation was well hit off, the audience were evidently amused, and loud applause arose from every side. Several persons were crying out loudly for an *encore*, when suddenly a hiss, or rather *whistle*, was heard from the first row of the gallery. The applause was then redoubled, but the same whistling sound from the pipe of a key was repeated. The claque then shouted out against the perpetrator of the obnoxious noise, and the next moment the whole house had risen and were regarding the man in the gallery. A police agent was then seen to approach the spectator in question (who was respectably dressed in black), and apparently to ask him to quit the place, the other shaking his head in refusal. Cries of "*Sortira! Sortira pas!*" ["He shall go! He shall not go!"] were heard in all directions, when at last the police agent withdrew. All this had lasted seven or eight minutes, and the performance was just recom-

mencing, when two gendarmes and two sergeants de ville appeared and proceeded to drag the offending whistler from his place. He resisted manfully, held firmly to the wood-work in front, and, although his cravat was torn off, still kept his place. At last, amid indignant cries of protest from the whole house, the agents carried the man bodily off, but still making the most violent opposition. The exclamations and noise then became quite furious, and shouts of "*Rendez-le! Qu'il revienne!*" ["Give him up! He must come back!"] continued to be heard for several minutes. The stage manager came forward, but the audience refused to hear him. The curtain was let fall, but the spectators continued their cries for the liberation of the man, declaring that he had a right to hiss or whistle as he pleased, since he had paid his money to applaud or the contrary, as he thought fit. The ladies in the boxes had by this time been seized with the general emotion, and stood up, waving their handkerchiefs. At last, when the audience were in the greatest exasperation, and apparently on the point of tearing up the benches, an exclamation was heard of "*Le Voila! Le Voila!*" and the next moment the man appeared in his former place, and was received with the loudest applause, a triple salvo of bravos greeting his entrance. The performance was then resumed, and went on quietly to the end. The hero of the evening was named Langlois, his position in life being that of clerk in a commercial house.

A manager in a Western theatre adopted a much more sensible plan of quelling expressions of displeasure. During the performance of "Hamlet," the actor who should have played the "Ghost" was prevented by illness from making his appearance. An ambitious supernumerary volunteered his services, which were gladly accepted. His execrable performance aroused the ire of the audience, who hissed him from the stage. The disapproval being marked by further acts of violence, the manager came forward and said: "Ladies and gentlemen, Mr. Smith has given up the 'Ghost.'" This sally diverted the popular indignation, and the play continued.

As an example of the power an audience has, for good or evil, in exercising its right to hiss, I give the history of the Fullerton case. Fullerton was an actor in a Philadelphia theatre, many years ago. A cabal was formed, it seemed, for the purpose of driving him from the stage. It began early in the season, and the disturbance increased nightly, until at length, some eight or ten different disturbers, distributed through the house, contrived to confuse and distract the performer who happened to appear in the same scenes with Fullerton. "Every effort possible was made to ascertain the cause of this continued persecution, but in vain. A nervous man at all times, poor Fullerton became nearly incapable of all effort. His terror and agony on entering the stage were truly pitiable. At length his little courage gave way, and repeated shocks brought him to the very edge of insanity. He became melancholy and morose, frequently hinting that the death either of his enemies or himself should end his sufferings. After an attempt at suicide, which Francis' sudden appearance prevented, he affected a calmness which could ill conceal his misery. On the evening of the 29th of January, after acting the *Abbe del Epee*, with less exhibition than usual of outrage from his persecutors, he left the theatre, in apparently good spirits, for his lodgings, as he stated. Not having arrived there, search was made, after some hours, but no tidings could be heard. On the following morning his body was found floating near one of the wharves on the Delaware." His persecutors had hissed him to death.

Another of the inalienable rights of an audience is the right of free applause. This right has usually been vouchsafed to American audiences without reserve; but of late that abominable institution the *claque* has been introduced into this country.

The *claqueurs* as they exist in French theatres are terrible fellows. No needy gazetteer or Scotch freebooter ever levied heavier black-mail than these chartered applauders. No one connected with the opera is exempt from their begging-box. The most brilliant "star" of the lyrical and terpsichorean horizon never rises without assuring them of the tenacity of her memory by some valuable consideration. No trembling candidate for choreographic or musical honors ventures on the maiden "pas" or quaver without propitiating their kind favor by a roll of bank-notes, thickening according to a well-established sliding-scale with the new-comer's ambition. No actor whose talents linger painfully near the verge of mediocrity, ever sees the end of his engagement at hand, without appealing to their good taste by arguments as irresistible and as weighty as he can rake and scrape together from old stockings, savings-banks and usurers, to give him those zealous, hearty, repeated rounds of applause which managers mistake for fame. The authors of new works,—the Scribes, Rossinis and Meyerbeers—themselves paid tribute to these gods of success. And the great opera bends before their oaken staves and resonant hands, and respectfully places pit-tickets in their begging-box as peace-offerings, and these tickets they sell, for they have no need of tickets for their own use.

These *claqueurs* are admitted by the stage door before the theatre opens. Fanny Elssler, we are told, always gave fifty francs a night for their services. A well known American performer tells a story of his having once appeared in gay Paris, and though he really did not stand in need of hired applause, when about to leave the city, a demand was made upon him by the *claqueurs* for six hundred francs, much to his astonishment; but, being assured that it was "regular," he paid the little bill.

The most celebrated of these vicarious trumpeters of fame, was a fellow named Auguste, who, after having "procured the success" of Guillaume Tell, Robert le Diable, Les Huguenots, and several other celebrated and forgotten pieces, has retired full of years, honor and wealth to a suburban villa, where, after marrying his daughters well and setting up his sons, he fights over old battles and tells of the feats of prowess "he," Meyerbeer and Rossini accomplished. How contemptuously he speaks of the "claqueurs" of the other theatres, who have, he says, nothing in the world to do, as plays are easily "carried," for they require nothing but hearty laughers, and the public is never angry with a laugher, while applauders are frequently menaced with "the door." These discounters of the public applause weigh rather heavily upon the manager, it being the custom to give them a hundred pit-tickets the night of first performances, forty or fifty when the opera has obtained slight success, and twenty when the most popular opera is performed—no small usury, for the price of pit-tickets is never less than a dollar. They are well organized into ten divisions, each commanded by a lieutenant, who sees that the signals given by the chief are faithfully obeyed. The chief, of course, has the lion's share of the profits, which generally range from six to eight thousand dollars a year. Indeed, he is the only person the manager knows, and the subalterns hold their seats entirely at his good pleasure.

In this country, the *claqueur* system is by no means so extensive, nor so thoroughly organized; but that it exists, any experienced theatre-goer will at once discover on visiting Niblo's Garden. The difference between genuine applause and the regular clap-clap of the hired men around the outer aisles is easily distinguishable by the cultivated ear.

In writing, not long since, of indecency in theatres, I remarked that when the "Black Crook" first presented its nude women to the gaze of a crowded auditory, a death-like silence fell upon the house, and men actually grew pale at the boldness of the thing.

This statement was denied by an unsophisticated editor in these words: "Our recollection of that notable night is that when the performers in the foremost skirtless ballet—afterward celebrated as the 'Demon dance at 9:30'—had executed their initiatory *pas*, and assumed their introductory *pose*, there burst forth such a spontaneous, unanimous and overwhelming storm of applause as was like to bring the dome about our ears."

The innocence of this is amusing. The "demon dance" was witnessed in silence. At its close the *claque* began to applaud; and the amiable audience, aroused from its astonishment by these mercenary palms, good-naturedly followed suit—for they wanted to see it over again.

The critic of the New York *World*, of August 6, 1869, gives an example of the way in which the *claque* of this theatre outrages the public will. After commenting on other actors in the play of "Arrah Na Pogue," the critic says: "Both these two actors, and the principals themselves, were badgered beyond endurance on Tuesday evening by the actor who played *Colonel Bagenal O'Grady*. The *O'Grady*, to put it plainly, was very much the worse for liquor, and insisted on staggering about and muttering his part in an incomprehensible manner, to the annoyance of all on the stage. The inclination of the audience was to hiss him from the boards at once, but a tolerant claque insisted on his support, and quenched the corrective and honest outbreak with cries of 'Order,' and much banging of boot heels. There seems to be a growing opinion among the warm personal friends of actors that only those noises will hereafter be permitted in theatres which are indicative of unqualified approval."

It would be a blessed thing for the drama if every actor who insults his audience by appearing before it intoxicated, should be hissed at once from the stage.

In another theatre—which I do not name because it has since mended its ways—the claque was placed in the front row of orchestra chairs.

A gentleman of my acquaintance found himself one night last winter, placed by some mistake in this noisy row, with two vociferous claqueurs on each side of him. Not knowing their character, my friend was astonished and annoyed by the persistent stupidity they exhibited in applauding certain players—who had paid for the privilege. At length, unable to keep silence any longer, my friend turned to the man at his right and said,

"Why *do* you applaud such bad acting so loudly? Surely you don't admire it."

To which the man responded gruffly:

"You mind your business and I'll mind mine."

The tone of the response opened my friend's eyes.

"Oh," he said, "you are paid to applaud, perhaps."

"Well, what if I am?"

"Oh, certainly—if you earn your money that way—"

Here a very noisy round of applause drowned my friend's voice, and at the same moment his neighbor stooped over and drew from under his chair a huge bouquet, which he hurled on the stage.

It presently appeared that every chair in that row was provided with a bouquet—and one by one they were drawn out by the *claqueurs* and thrown upon the stage.

These same bouquets did duty at that theatre every night till no longer presentable.

The bouquet nuisance has been touched upon in a previous chapter. It is not always *claqueurs* who do the bouquet-tossing, however. Addle-pated young men, who would have to beg for a living if they had no more money than brains, are much given to buying bouquets and throwing them to actresses.

A trio of curious swindlers were up in the Tombs Police Court during the "Black Crook" fever, charged by a Broadway florist with having purchased from him $192 worth of bouquets which they had not paid for. These young sports represented themselves as having rich "parients" who could liquidate the amount. The florist charged them with fraudulent intentions, and that their representations regarding wealth and business connections were all false. These bouquets were thrown upon the stage at Niblo's to the "Black Crookites." The young noodles, not having the money to pay for their bouquets, had to go to jail.

Another nuisance, to which also I have before reverted, is that of excessive and repeated *encores*. A critic remarks: "We have frequently seen artists called out to repeat a dance when they have been so exhausted that they could scarcely stand. It is only a few weeks since that Miss Adelaide Nixon, while performing with Chiarini's Circus, in Cuba, was *encored* three times. She finally so overtaxed her energies that she was obliged to sit down in a chair for rest. She was immediately stricken with paralysis, and it is thought she will never fully recover. We have frequently seen dancers, both solo and coryphees, after having been compelled to repeat a dance on a warm evening, come off the stage so tired that they have fainted and fallen to the floor, while others have resorted to drinking freely of ice water, which has thrown them into fits. This is no fancy sketch, but truthful. Some will say that it is their own fault. But would such things occur if the public, instead of compelling them to repeat, would be satisfied with their answering the call with a bow? Brignoli made it a rule a year ago never to answer a call by repeating a song, because he found that it was taxing him too much. What was the consequence for doing so in Boston? Why they actually hissed him off the stage the next time he did appear."

For many years past it has been the custom when an actor or actress was "called out," as the phrase is, that they should come out before the curtain; the great wooden roller having to be dragged out of their way, while they crushed out through the narrow pathway thus afforded them.

Charlotte Cushman was the first person in this country to change this foolish custom. She ordered the curtain to be raised, in response to prolonged applause, and appeared upon the stage surrounded by all the players who had assisted her. The habit got to be general immediately. But some actors are not willing to share the honors with those about them. These then made a further innovation by having the curtain raised and stalking on the stage all alone, bowing their acknowledgments and retiring.

The practice of calling performers before the curtain began with the appearance in this country of the elder Kean; and a Philadelphia manager under whom Kean played an engagement thus refers to the practice: "The absurdity of dragging out before the curtain a deceased *Hamlet*, *Macbeth* or *Richard* in an exhausted state, merely to make a bow, or to attempt an asthmatic address in defiance of all good taste, and solely for the gratification of a few unthinking partisans, or a few lovers of noise and tumult, is one which we date with us from this time. It has always been a matter of wonder with me that the better part of the audience should tolerate these fooleries.

Can anything be more ridiculous, than that an actor, after laboring through an arduous character — a protracted combat, and the whole series of simulated, expiring agonies, should instantly revive, and appear panting before the curtain to look and feel like a fool, and to destroy the little illusion he has been endeavoring to create? 'The time has been that when the brains were out, the man would die, and there an end; but now they rise again with forty mortal murders on their heads.' This custom, reprehensible as it has ever appeared, even in rare cases of superior talent, becomes absolutely insufferable when seeking to gratify the vain aspirations of commonplace powers. To such an extent has it of late years obtained, that on some occasions nearly the whole characters of a play have been paraded to receive the applause of their partisans; as they certainly must have done the derision of the more numerous and sensible portion of the houses. We are all aware that this custom was borrowed from the French stage, and was doubtless a part of the system employed by the *claqueurs*, or acknowledged hired applauders. Not the least offensive feature is the establishing of a personal communication between the audience and the performers; a practice equally indelicate and unwise. The invidious feelings among performers from supposed injurious preferences may be easily imagined. A minor branch of this stage quackery is exhibited constantly in the liberal bestowal of wreaths, bouquets (with or without rings enclosed) upon insignificant as well as upon distinguished stage artists. These in most cases are openly prepared and paid for by the 'grateful, recipients' of their own purchases. Even in the case of Fanny Ellsler (who certainly stood in no need of such aid) the baskets of bouquets, etc., formed an unconcealed part of the dressing apparatus for the evening. It is well known to me that in the career of other performers, these marks of a grateful and admiring public were made use of on several different nights, when the ambition of the performer outran his means, and not only so, but that the identical vases, goblets and cups, have traveled with the performer from theatre to theatre, and been presented and accepted at every place with new 'emotions of the deepest sensibility.' It is time that such foolery and imposture should cease."

Among the bad habits of audiences may be enumerated the habit of chewing tobacco and expectoration; the habit of profane and vulgar talk; the fashionably vulgar habit of going late to the theatre or concert, after things are in progress, and thus disturbing that part of the audience which is in season; the habit of creating an uproar by rushing for the door at the effective closing parts of the performance; the habit of stamping for applause and raising a shocking and choking dust, while the hands should be sufficient for the polite expression of approbation.

Some of these habits are far too common, and I hope all good people who read this will resolve to discountenance them.

Many curious anecdotes of audiences might be told. On one occasion the play of "Oliver Twist" was given in Lowell, Mass. When the curtain fell, the audience retained their seats for several minutes, but at length the stage manager appeared before the curtain and said: "Ladies and gentlemen, I wish to inform you that the play has terminated. As all the principal characters are dead, it cannot, of course, go on." The hall was soon cleared.

A California rustic, who was not accustomed to villainous saltpetre and cold iron, as used on the stage, went one night to see "The Robbers." When the shooting commenced, he threw himself, at two movements, under a bench, and kept his place till the smoke cleared away.

Quiet restored, he crept softly up to his place, and sat till the stabbing scene in the last act. As *Charles de Moor* stabbed poor *Amelia*, our rustic patron of the drama was wrought up to an agony which worked his countenance into horrible shape. He uttered one unearthly shriek, and made a break for the door—over the heads of everybody in his way—knocking down a doorkeeper, and vanished, howling, into the night.

At a Washington theatre, not long since, considerable amusement was caused during the performance of the "Heir at Law" by a nervous individual in the dress circle, who happened to notice that a gas jet near him was not lighted, rising in his seat and asking, in a loud tone of voice, if the usher "*wouldn't light that gas-burner?*" It so happened that the actress who was playing *Cicely Homespun* had occasion to repeat the words, "Oh, no, I cannot," making it sound very much as though she was replying to the interrogator in the dress circle. The effect may easily be imagined.

The play of the "Long Strike" was being enacted at a theatre in Harrisburg, Pa., and, during the court scene, while the audience were deeply interested, and the Judge asked the question, Guilty or not guilty? a well-dressed, intelligent-looking man left his seat in the audience and pushed through the crowd to the front of the stage, and very calmly called out, "Stop!" The manager of the theatre, who was personating the part of *Moneypenny*, thinking the man intoxicated, came to the footlights, and the following dialogue ensued: "Will you oblige me by taking your seat, sir?" said the manager. The man replied, "I want to give my evidence in this case. It was not that man" (pointing to the actor who represented the character of *Jem Starkie*) "who killed him. I saw who did it. I saw the man shoot him from behind the hedge." At this point a roar of laughter from the audience brought this unbiassed witness suddenly to his senses, and he took his seat in confusion.

A lady in whom I have the fullest confidence relates, as an actual fact, the story of Jenny Lind and the Hoosier. She tells me that during her march of triumph through this country, and after her visit to Cincinnati, where she captivated all hearts, Jenny Lind found herself one evening in the (then) small town of Madison, Indiana. Mr. Barnum had made an arrangement with the captain of the mail steamer which plies between Cincinnati and Louisville, to have the boat lie by on the Indiana shore long enough for the divine Jenny to give a concert at Madison.

The largest building in town having been prepared for her reception, an auction of the tickets took place in the hall on the morning of her arrival. The capacity of the building was fully tested by the anxious Madisonites.

"Comin' thro' the Rye" was given first. This was followed by "Home, Sweet Home;" and who can describe the marvellous effect of that song, as rendered by Jenny Lind? The famous "Bird Song" was then the popular air of the country, and it was given as a concluding piece on the evening in question. The last line of the song runs thus, "I know not, I know not why I am singing," and Jenny gave it with her full power. At this moment, a genuine Hoosier, indigenous to the soil, rose up in the auditorium, and thus delivered himself:

"You don't know why you are singin', eh? Gosh! I know if you don't! You're singin' to the tune of five dollars a head, and I reckon dad's hogs will have to suffer for my ticket!"

In an old number of the Boston *Post* I find an account of Mrs. Partington's visit to the play, to see my sister, Eliza Logan, in the character of *Juliet*, and never was there a queerer specimen of an auditor than that old lady was (she must be about 130 years old now, by the way,) if the *Post's* account can be relied on. "It was our fortune," says the editor, "to sit behind Mrs. Partington during the entire performance, and we were much interested at the effect of the play upon her unsophisticated mind. It was to her an all-absorbing reality. The characters were real characters, and *Mercutio* and *Tybalt* were as sensibly killed as though she had felt for their pulse and found it not. She criticised *Juliet's* haste to get married, and said they didn't do so when she was young, and didn't believe so beautiful a young lady would have gone unmarried, if *Romeo* wouldn't have had her, and gracious knows he seemed to love her terribly, though hot love she knew was soon cold. But it was at the scene where *Romeo* bought the 'pizen' that she became most excited. 'It's agin the law to sell it to him,' said she, half aloud, and turned to see if Patterson was anywhere within hailing distance. But even that functionary looked calmly on, nor raised a finger to stay the fatal draught. She saw through the whole plot, and knew that *Juliet* had taken nothing but a sleeping potion, and wasn't dead. 'Won't somebody go down and tell the poor young man she isn't dead?' said she, wringing her hands, and dropping a tear on the bill in her lap—'the dear young man will do something harmonious to himself if somebody doesn't stop him.' The scene shifted, and the tomb of all the Capulets was revealed, with the grief of the noble Count *Paris* and the violence of *Romeo* in killing him, and when the latter drank the poison she uttered the faint ejaculation, 'I told you so,' and bowed her head forward to shut out the scene which she knew must follow, by so doing chafing the neck of a young man in the front seat with her bonnet, while Ike sat wondering what they did with all the dead folks that they killed at the theatres. When Mrs. Partington raised her eyes the green curtain was down, and the bodies of *Romeo* and *Juliet* were bowing their thanks to the audience for a complimentary call."

CHAPTER XXV.

About Menageries and their Tenants.—How the Animals are Obtained.—Dealers in Wild Beasts. — Prices of Hippopotami, Leopards, Tigers, Hyenas, etc. — Curious Freaks of Caged Animals. — The Trade in Snakes.—Cost of Boa Constrictors and Rattlesnakes.—The Trade in Rare Birds. — Pheasants, Parrots and Cockatoos for Sale. — How Monkeys are Caught.—Fright at a Wild Beast Show.—"The Animals are Loose!"—Fire breaks out in the Winter Quarters of a Menagerie.—Terror of the Animals.—They escape into the Streets.—How they Behaved.—Wild Beasts' Frightened by a Storm.—Chloroforming a Tiger —Elephant Stories. — Cracking a Cocoa Nut. — Protecting a Friend.—Afraid to Cross a Bridge.—Debarking an Elephant at the New York Wharf.—A Leopard attacks an Elephant and gets the worst of it.—An Elephant Attacks a Locomotive and gets the worst of it.—A Lion Loose in a Village in Mississippi.—He Eats a Horse and Escapes into the Open Country.—His Ultimate Fate.

For menageries I have great respect, as a rule. As an interesting and instructive branch of the "show business," free from objectionable features, these exhibitions of the animal kingdom are worthy of support.

It is true, the animals are not usually, in their cages, very ferociously wild; but they serve to show the children—who are always the most delighted visitors to the menagerie—how wonderful are the creatures of other lands, even in the subdued condition of captives.

Animals are obtained for menageries through a few regular dealers in wild beasts. These dealers are generally Germans—both in this country and in Europe. Two brothers of this nationality, whose place of business is in Chatham street, New York, are the principal American dealers in such interesting goods as lions, tigers, elephants, and the like; though there are numberless small dealers, scattered all over the country, in the large towns, who deal in birds, and various creatures of the smaller sort, which go to make up menageries.

A New York paper furnishes the information that "a man, to succeed as a wild-beast dealer, must have a thorough knowledge of natural history (theoretical), and be acquainted with its specimens practically. He must be able to judge at once of the strong points and the weak ones of any beast presented to him; he must be able to tell at once its health and physical condition; he must know what species are most in demand; he must know the proper mode of feeding and of the medical treatment of each animal, with a hundred other matters. He must also have a good deal of personal courage, and a peculiar love for his peculiar profession, together with any amount of patience and perseverance. The wild-beast business fluctuates, just like the dry goods, and has its spring and fall trade. The winter season is comparatively busy, and the summer comparatively dull. The wild-beast traders employ agents in Asia and Africa, and sometimes elsewhere, to hunt up rare and valuable animals. Thus a New York house has kept a man in Africa for two years seeking for a peculiarly rare and immensely valuable species of hippopotamus; but, as a general rule, the agents of the traders are persons who reside permanently in some wild-beast-frequented portion of this habitable globe, and who are commissioned to buy any valuable specimens they may come across. Having procured their animal, the agents generally depend upon some captain of some vessel whom they know, and who may chance to leave for a European port, to bring it across the sea, the said captain charging the house to which the animal is consigned a heavy tariff for freight, more than twice the amount charged for ordinary material of the same weight and bulk, besides the expenses of the 'keep' of the beast, which latter are large. Having arrived at its destination, a truck adapted for the purpose is sent to convey the beast to its temporary home, where it is re-caged, and fed and cleaned, etc., until it is finally disposed of. Thus it will readily be seen that the expenses in the wild-beast trade are considerable, as well as the risks. The beast has first to be bought from its original captors; then the agent who buys it must be allowed his commission; then there are the freight expenses by sea, the transportation expenses by land, the cost of the feed, the wages and expenses of the man who takes the charge of the animal *en route*, etc., besides the risk of the animal being lost at sea or dying from disease at any time; all of which items, however, are duly remembered in the little bill, and come out of the pocket of the final purchaser. The scale of prices of wild beasts is regulated by their rarity, size, quality of species, and the expense attendant upon their capture and their keep. Among the rarest animals are the hippopotamus and the gnu, or horned horse. A first-class hippopotamus is worth five or six thousand dollars, a lion brings from one to two thousand dollars, an elephant from three to six thousand dollars, a giraffe is worth about three thousand dollars, a Bengal tiger or tigress will bring two thousand dollars, leopards vary from six to nine hundred dollars, a hyena is worth, at current rates, five hnndred dollars, while an ostrich rates at three hundred dollars. The price-list shows that, although expenses may be heavy, receipts are proportionately large, and that it does not require many large beasts to make a good business for one trader. A New York house in the last three years has sold twenty lions, twelve elephants, six giraffes, four Bengal tigers, eight leopards, eight hyenas, twelve ostriches, and two hippopotami; being a total business of about $112,000 in three years, or over $37,000 per annum, in the line of larger beasts alone, exclusive of the smaller show-beasts, such as monkeys, and exclusive also of birds, which latter items more than double the above amount. Gnus, or horned horses, have become lately in demand, both from their oddity and rarity, and are valued at seventeen hundred or eighteen hundred dollars apiece; one firm has now two of these curious creatures on consignment—one of them recently took it into his horned head to die, without giving any previous sign, and accordingly one day eighteen hundred dollars was found lying dead in its pen. An elephant is always in demand, and sells whether it be male or female, large or small, 'trick' or otherwise. Some months ago, the smallest elephant on record was sold by a New York house to a traveling circus for an enormous price. He was only eighteen months old, and not over twenty-four inches in height. This animal when bought cost hugely, and ate up his own bulk of hay, at the rate of a bale per diem, in a very short time. Ostriches, however, though heavy eaters, are not very expensive, as they have cast-iron stomachs, and digest stones, glass, iron, or almost anything else that one chooses to give them, though they are judges of good meat when they get hold of it. There are two species of ostriches known to the trade, the black and grey; both are very strong, fleet, and practically untamable. Lions, tigers and leopards form constituent attractions of almost all menageries, and are too familiar to need description. It may be here remarked, however, that, as a rule, people who deal with these creatures find that there is comparatively little danger to themselves to be dreaded from either lions or lionesses. These animals never attack any human being save when excessively hungry; and when enraged from any cause, always show such visible signs as put their keepers on their guard; whereas the opposite of these statements is true in regard to tigers and leopards—the latter especially, which are considered by those in the trade as the most dangerous, cruel and treacherous of all the beasts with which they are brought in contact. American lions or jaguars, and American or Brazilian tigers, have of late come into fashion. These animals are very fierce, untamable and strong, though inferior in size to the lion or tiger proper. The Brazilian tiger is spotted like a leopard, has fearfully lurid, bright, wild eyes, and is worth, in currency, anywhere from six hundred to one thousand dollars. The hunting leopard is a peculiar species lately introduced to the show-trade. These animals are long and narrow-bodied, and especially long-backed, combining great speed with elasticity and compactness, as well as strength. They are comparatively gentle in their instincts, have much less dangerous claws and general qualities than the rest of their kind, and can be readily trained for hunting purposes, for which ends they are highly in demand in the East. They can outstrip the ostrich, and are worth a thousand dollars apiece. Of monkeys and baboons little need be said, as everybody knows almost everything that can be said about them. There are some one hundred and fifty species of these creatures, the most intelligent of which is the ring-tailed monkey, and the most stupid that variety which is known as the lion-monkey, from its being gifted, instead of brains, with a long mane. The varieties of deer and antelope are numerous, and always find ready purchasers. The genuine antelope is comparatively scarce, and brings in the market about three hundred dollars; so that it is 'a deer (dear) gazelle,' indeed. A show of wild animals is one thing, and a very good thing sometimes; but the same number of wild beasts when not on show, but merely on hand waiting a sale, presents a very different, and, sometimes, a curious spectacle. Thus, in a certain back-yard in the city of New York, and a small yard at that, near the commencement of the Bowery, as singular a sight is presented to the lover of animal life as is afforded probably in the range of the whole world. You enter by a low doorway, and at first glance you see only a number of boxes, with iron bars in front—amateur cages in fact—and arranged alongside of each other, or on top of each other, just as the case may be, without the slightest order or general arrangement. If you look a second time at these boxes, you will be made aware of the fact that they are inhabited by certain animal movables, or moving animals; for pairs of bright eyes will gleam out upon you from the boxes in all directions, and occasional switchings of some beastly tails against the sides of the cages will become audible, as will every now and then a deep-mouthed roar. Inspecting the box-cages, or cage-boxes, more closely, you will see further that one of them contains a three-year-old lion, just getting his young mustache, or what answers the same purpose to a lion—his mane. Next box to this you will find a lioness, about the same age as her mate, a fine specimen of an African female, who seems very much attached to a dog, who shares her cage with her in perfect harmony; at least so far as the lioness is concerned, for she does all she can to live at peace with the dog, yielding to his wishes in all particulars, giving up her meat whenever he takes a fancy to it, and getting out of his way whenever he wishes to walk about; although doggy does not seem to be a very amiable partner, and every now and then gives the lioness a bit of his mind by biting her in the ear. A little beyond this strange couple lie two more boxes—the upper one containing a pair of young hunting leopards, as playful as young kittens, which spend their time in calling to the cats of the neighborhood, the lower one being the scene of the imprisonment of a full-grown, very handsome, very cross leopardess, who is always snarling and seeking whom she may devour. This latter beast has a special antipathy to a young lad who has charge of her, and tries half-a-dozen times a day to make mincemeat of him, though she has never yet succeeded in this laudable design. On the opposite side of this thirty by twenty-five foot back-yard are a number of boxes, containing monkeys of various species, and baboons. One of these monkeys is a jovial female, christened Victoria, who is one of the most expert pickpockets in New York, and that is saying a great deal. Vic can relieve a visitor of his watch or chain or pocket-book in a manner most refreshing to a monkey-moralist to witness; and, although as ugly as sin, is as quick as lightning. Next door to this kleptomaniac ape is a happy family of monkeys—father, mother and baby—who live together lively as clams at the turn of tide. On the ground, at a little distance, lies another box, which contains a monster baboon, larger than the one which was recently exhibited as a gorilla, but which, like that, is only a big ape. This fellow is called Jonas, and is, without exception, the ugliest individual in existence to which the Almighty has ever given a shape—such as it is. It is utterly impossible for anybody to state in sufficiently strong language how ugly the fellow is, and yet he is as strong as a giant, and as gentle as a lamb, and smart, too, and can be taught tricks like a dog; he is grateful, also, has a memory for favors much better than most politicians; is fond of tobacco, and is worth eight hundred dollars in his own right—that is, he will fetch that money any day. In the rear portion of the yard is a sort of inclosure, stretching some ten feet further back, in which three or four horned horses or ponies, called gnus, are digesting their rations; next to these is a case in which is confined a fretful porcupine, who shows his bristles on the least provocation, and sometimes when there is no insult meant at all; he is over-sensitive, poor fellow; but doubtless confinement for life has told upon his spirits. The catalogue of cages or boxes is completed by that in which is held in duress a Brazilian tiger of the fiercest possible description, who does nothing but glare upon you, and want to eat you. A little boy was brought into this menagerie in a back yard, and immediately all the animal instincts of the beast were developed in the most pleasing degree. Every wild animal, however tame before, as soon as he or she scented the young and tender meat, sniffed the air hungrily, and growled so expressively as to lead the boy's mother to withdraw him and start away from such dangerous proximity. Order was, however, finally restored, amid the introduction of a few lighted lucifer matches, seeing the flame of which the animals at once slunk away in their boxes in terror. As a rule, the majority of wild beasts, even those which are not and cannot be tamed, become readily attached, for the time being, to the party who takes care of and feeds them; and, within certain limits, will allow him familiarities on the outside of their cages which they would not permit to any one else, or even to him on the inside. Especially does a wild beast become attached to those who attend to its wants in the time of sickness. Luckily for the traders, however, the diseases of beasts are comparatively few and simple, and all that is done for them is to put sugar in their water, or pepper or soothing-powder upon their meat. Great care has, however, to be constantly exercised in regard to the diet of the beasts. Nature takes care of them well enough in their original state of freedom; but in the artificial state of confinement, rule and system come into play. The meat-eaters are fed only once a day—at noon,—and cost about a dollar per day to feed; the grass-eaters, like the elephant, eat all the time as fancy prompts; while the vegetarians, like the monkeys, take their three square meals a day. As a rule, all animals enjoy a better average of health than man, because they have no acquired tastes or dissipated habits. The elephant lives for centuries, the parrot is a centenarian, while the lion lives but twenty years or so. On the whole, the average life of man is greater than that of the majority of so-called beasts, though their average of health exceeds his. Two singular varieties of wild animals have lately been introduced to the notice of the trade. One is the wild ass, a beast much spoken of in the Scriptures. He is a 'kickist,' and a decidedly unpleasant companion for any respectable and civilized quadruped, and is worth eleven hundred dollars in gold. Another rare beast is the white tiger, which has no spots or stripes, though in other respects it resembles the Bengal variety, exceeding it in ferocity and strength. This animal is very difficult to catch, and is worth some three thousand dollars in currency when caught. Dwarf horses are also becoming valuable articles. There is a demand for snakes; and the supply does not equal, strange to say, the demand. Common snakes, it is true, are readily procured in quantities; but then common snakes are not the kind of snakes which people want. Boa-constrictors are much prized, and boa-constrictors are not to be found beneath every bush. The fact of the matter seems to be, that snakes that are harmless to man are not valued by man in the least. A snake which can poison you at a touch, like the rattlesnake, is of considerable worth,— say seventy-five dollars. A boa-constrictor, which can crush you at a hug, is valued at two hundred and fifty dollars; while a few snakes which can crush you and poison you both are worth any money that can be asked for them. There are about fifty different species of snakes known in the trade, besides various kinds of blacksnakes, some of which are worth forty dollars and upward. A full-size African boa-constrictor, with a small head, has been sold for three hundred and fifty dollars. One great advantage to the trade in keeping snakes is the fact that they do not cost much to keep. The larger ones are fed only weekly or monthly, and swallow their birds or rats without any cooking. The catching and selling of birds is a branch of the animal business which has more followers than any other, but is in itself of comparatively little interest. It is pursued to a great extent, and is a branch which has amateurs and connoisseurs innumerable. Many rare birds have been recently imported, and find ready purchasers. What is called the love-bird, from its affectionate disposition, and the fact that it can only live when praised, is of a bluish brown, the male having a variegated head. African birds of the smallest possible sizes, with bills as red as sealing-wax, and brown bodies, known as wax-bills; African canaries; American nonpareils, little birds with all the colors of the rainbow; yellow bishops; red-bodied, black-headed Napoleons; large Mexican parrots, in green and gold; noisy African paroquets, brown, ugly, and smart; pure white cockatoos, of large size; Cuban parrots, greenish, striped with yellow, some of which are very smart, and one of which has recently been taught to sing a Spanish song in pretty good style; hump or heap paroquets, who live together all in a heap, clinging to each other and to the sides of their cages; young parrots, susceptible of training; golden and silver pheasants—these are the birds most prized by traders and the public. Of these, the most valuable are the golden pheasant, which is estimated at fifty dollars gold; the talking African parrots, which are sold at fifty dollars; the cockatoos, which range from twenty-five to seventy-five dollars; and the Mexican parrots, which range at about thirty dollars."

Monkeys are such cunning creatures, that one would suppose them much more difficult to catch than other wild animals. Pitfalls will take a lion, and the famished monarch of the forest will, after a few days' starvation, dart into a cage containing food, and thus be secured. But how are monkeys caught? The ape family resemble man. Their vices are human. They love liquor, and fall.

In Darfour and Sennaar the natives make fermented beer, of which the monkeys are passionately fond. Aware of this, the natives go to the parts of the forests frequented by the monkeys, and set on the ground calabashes full of the enticing liquor. As soon as a monkey sees and tastes it, he utters loud cries of joy, that soon attract his comrades. Then an orgie begins, and in a short time the beasts show all degrees of intoxication. Then the negroes appear. The drinkers are too far gone to distrust them, but apparently take them for larger species of their own genus. The negroes take some up, and these immediately begin to weep and cover them with maudlin kisses. When a negro takes one by the hand to lead him off, the nearest monkey will cling to the one who thus finds a support, and endeavor to go off also. Another will grasp at him, and so on, till the negro leads a staggering line of ten or a dozen tipsy monkeys. When finally brought to the village, they are securely caged, and gradually sober down; but, for two or three days, a gradually diminishing supply of liquor is given them, so as to reconcile them by degrees to their state of captivity.

Many incidents are given of the wild beasts in menageries getting loose; and sometimes panics have taken place in menageries, causing considerable injury to the people, under false alarms of the animals being loose.

One afternoon while a menagerie was exhibiting in Dayton, Ohio, there came very suddenly a furious gale of wind, followed by a heavy shower of rain, which, for a short time, seemed as though it would scatter everything before it. The performance was about half over, when, all at once, the guy-poles inside were lifted from the ground, and considerable squeaking was heard through the entire canvas, which spread great consternation among the vast number of people gathered under the pavilion. It was evident that the pavilion would instantly fall unless great force was applied outside to hold on to the ropes. Some fifty men took hold of the ropes on the south side, and attempted to hold it from blowing over, but it was utterly impossible. In another instant the ropes snapped, the centre pole came unfastened, and, with a terrible crash, the large pavilion was dashed to the ground, upsetting, at the same time, two of the wagons containing wild animals. At this point several voices cried out,—"The animals are loose!" This terrific alarm, added to the intense excitement caused by the falling of the canvas and breaking of the seats and screaming of women and children, made confusion worse confounded, and the scene one of the wildest disorder. The people were terrified, and fled everywhere in the wildest confusion. Amid the screams of at least a thousand people, who were trying to extricate themselves from beneath the broken benches, and crawling out from under the canvas, mothers and fathers seized their children and frantically rushed their way out as best they could. Many of the children were pressed down in the excitement, and trampled in the dirt; some were very much bruised. Many men and women fled to adjacent houses, and closed the doors behind, to escape from being overtaken by the wild animals, which they imagined were in pursuit of them. But two persons were seriously injured, a man, who was flung across a bench while attempting to support a guy, and a little girl, who had her arm broken and received a severe wound on the head.

A fire broke out one November night, not long ago, in a building in Philadelphia, used as the winter quarters of a menagerie. In the yard were quartered the cages containing lions, leopards, tigers, bears, and monkeys. These were saved, the cages being run out before the fire reached them. The scene during the hauling out of the cages was terrific, as the animals, frightened at the flames, were darting backward and forward in their cages, uttering fearful cries. In the excitement some of the dens were overturned, and in two instances the bars were so displaced that two leopards and a lion made their appearance on the street. One of the leopards took shelter in a neighboring stable, where he was soon secured, and the other ran along Jefferson Street to Twenty-third Street, and then passed in at an open doorway of a dwelling, through the entry, into the yard, where he was captured. On his way through the hall he passed several members of the family, and their condition can be better imagined than described. The lion, in his frantic efforts to release himself, succeeded in removing a bar, but as he jumped from the cage, a daring fellow threw a packing box over him, and he was housed until after the fire was extinguished, when he was placed in safe quarters. Thousands of people were on the grounds, and rumors were numerous. One minute you heard that a lion had escaped, in another two lions, in another a tiger was added, and in another the entire stock of animals had escaped and were prowling around. The consternation was very great, but nobody was hurt. Had the animals been very wild, there would have been several casualties to announce, most probably.

A menagerie exhibiting at Muscatine, Iowa, not long since, struck its tents at eleven o'clock at night, and started for Davenport. Before a dozen miles had been traversed, a fierce storm let loose its lightning, thunder, and water. The lightning was blinding in its brilliancy, the thunder was terrific, and the rain, violently driven by the wind, came down in sheets. A panic seized the whole cavalcade—men, horses, and animals seemed terror-stricken. Eight of the drivers deserted their teams, and it was not long before wagons and horses were in inextricable confusion—a jammed up mass of floundering animals and overturned vehicles. The darkness, save when lightning illuminated the scene, was impenetrable. The caged lions, tigers, leopards, wolves, and other beasts became frightened, and bounded from side to side of their prisons, and roared and growled and shrieked in very terror. The elephants laid down in the road and refused to move. Three of the horses were struck by lightning, and killed. It was a wonder that no human lives were lost. The show reached Davenport at a late hour in the day, men and teams well-nigh exhausted by the terrible night's work and the hard journey which followed it.

It seems curious to think of applying chloroform to a wild animal, but I heard of a tiger which was placed under the influence of chloroform at Tiffin, Ohio, one Sunday, when "the menagerie" was there, and a leg, which had been badly mangled in a little unpleasantness with a panther, was successfully amputated.

No animal furnishes more curious and interesting stories than the elephant. It is well known that this ponderous creature is given to return injuries or insults in kind. In Madagascar an elephant's cornac, happening to have a cocoa-nut in his hand, thought fit, out of bravado, to break it on the animal's head. The elephant made no protest at the time; but next day, passing a fruit stall, he took a cocoa-nut in his trunk, and returned the cornac's compliment so vigorously on *his* head, that he killed him on the spot.

But if vindictive, the elephant is also grateful. At Pondicherry, a soldier, who treated an elephant to a dram of arrack every time he received his pay, found himself the worse for liquor. When the guard were about to carry him off to prison he took refuge under the elephant, and fell asleep. His protector would allow no one to approach, and watched him carefully all night. In the morning, after caressing with his trunk, he dismissed him to settle with the authorities as best he could. Both revenge and gratitude imply intelligence ; still more does the application of an unforseen expedient. A train of artillery going to Seringapatam, had to cross the shingly bed of a river. A man who was sitting on a gun-carriage fell ; in another second the wheel would have passed over his body. An elephant walking by the side of the carriage saw the danger, and instantly, without any order from his keeper, lifted the wheel from the ground, leaving the fallen man uninjured.

These anecdotes, however, it must be borne in mind, are exceptional in their character ; and I would advise anybody who thinks of throwing himself down in the elephant's track to be picked up, when the menagerie procession is passing through the streets, to think a long time before doing it.

Elephants generally seem to have an extreme development of caution with regard to bridges. An elephant belonging to a menagerie which was exhibiting in Vermont, while traveling from Waterbury, in that State, to Northfield, in crossing a bridge over a creek, crushed the floor with his enormous weight, and fell partly through, his fore quarters only remaining on the bridge. By this accident he was lamed for several days, but not sufficiently to prevent him from traveling. When he was brought to the Long Bridge over the Richelieu river, at St. John's, he evidently retained a vivid recollection of this mishap, and neither coaxing, threats, persuasion, nor force, could induce him to budge an inch on the, to him, perilous structure. Nor does it appear that his apprehensions were unfounded, for the proprietors of the bridge notified the menagerie managers that they were dubious of the capacity of the bridge to bear the weight of the elephant, and that if they crossed him they must do so at their own risk. The morning was rather chilly, and as they did not

wish to risk his health by swimming, they concluded to make the venture. The band chariot and den of lions were started on ahead of him, in order to give him confidence, and when he saw that they went safely over, he was induced to follow, which he did very slowly, testing each plank and timber with his fore feet and trunk as he progressed. Whenever he discovered any of the timbers to be defective, he would cross over the division to the opposite roadway, and would so progress until he came to another doubtful place, when he would cross back again. He worked along in this way until he had come more than half way over, when he became suspicious that neither road was safe, and started rapidly back, driving back the long den of cages that were following, and clearing the bridge for a space of ten or more rods. At this juncture a flock of sheep came running past him, and he vented his spleen by picking them up, one by one, with his trunk, and throwing them into the river, until he had disposed of seven in this way. He was finally induced to go on, and after having been more than two hours in crossing, arrived safely over.

The elephant Empress, the property of the City of New York, and the distinguished guest of the Central Park, is said to be the largest tame elephant in the world. She was formerly the property of the Emperor Alexander, of Russia. She is about twenty years old, and stands twelve feet and a half high. On the morning of her arrival from Europe, the Hamburg steamer dock at Hoboken was crowded with an eager throng, who waited patiently for the enormous animal to come forth. At last came the Empress, slowly and deliberately; turning sharp at the gang-plank, she suddenly gave a snort and a roar that sounded like distant thunder, and seemed disposed to make trouble. The keeper sprang ahead, and, in the most endearing manner, persuaded her highness to descend. The ship almost careened as she advanced a little more to the side, and one huge foot, like the pillar of the Custom-house, rested on the gang-plank. There was something absolutely touching in the way the gigantic beast would reach forth her trunk and put it around her keeper, who would pat it and again invite the Empress to come on and not be afraid. The huge animal slowly descended, the crowd parting silently as she advanced. When she reached the dock the people cheered loudly, and the keeper put his arms around her trunk, and kissed it with delight. As for Her Highness, she trumpeted out her pleasure in a series of whistles and screams. Then advancing stately up the wharf, and reaching *terra firma* once again, she expressed her satisfaction by taking dirt in her trunk, and tossing it up on her back. On reaching the stable provided for her, the Empress appeared delighted with her quarters, and pranced and whistled, and seemed well pleased with everybody.

A leopard escaped from his cage in a menagerie which was exhibiting in Cincinnati. The first intimation the keepers had of his escape was his leaping upon a dog and killing him. His appetite for blood being roused but not sated by this, he attacked and disposed of another dog, and then leaped upon the back of an elephant. The keepers had fled in terror. The elephant, however, seized the leopard with his trunk, and hurled him about a dozen yards against the lions' cage. There was a great hubbub for a few moments among the animals. The lions roared, and the noise he had created, added to the effects of his unexpected reception by the elephant, so cowed the leopard, that he retreated, thoroughly subdued, into a corner, when, the assistants taking courage and returning, he was easily captured and returned to his cage.

A thrilling series of events occurred in the town of Forest, Mississippi, last summer, all growing out of a foolish man's trick in giving tobacco to an angry elephant. Inside the menagerie tent the huge elephant Hercules was chained to a stake; and by way of caution to those entering the canvas, John Alston, his keeper, stated that he had for several days manifested a disposition of insubordination, and begged that no one would approach sufficiently near to receive a blow from his trunk. A man named Mark Kite, coming in after the keeper's admonition, thoughtlessly handed the elephant a piece of tobacco, which so enraged him that he struck at him with such violence as to dislocate his shoulder, although it was a glancing blow. He then plunged with such force that he broke his chain, and although his keeper used every effort to subdue him, he was entirely uncontrollable, and would strike and kick at every object near him. By this time the scene was beyond description. The vast crowd flew for life. He then turned on his keeper, and pursued him under the canvas. The eleven o'clock freight train being behind time, and not having any freight for Forest, and the engineer not intending to stop, came rushing along at the rate of twenty miles an hour. When it had approached within two hundred yards, the elephant looked up the road, and seemed doubly enraged. He immediately ran toward it with great speed, and met it with such a shock that he broke one of his tusks and was immediately killed.

The engine was detached from the train by the shock, and thrown from the track, and the engineer having failed to shut off the steam, it unfortunately ran into the canvas and smashed the lion's cage, killing the lioness and releasing the lion.

The lion, finding himself uninjured and at liberty, and

being frightened by the steam and whistle of the engine, started at full speed down the Homewood road, roaring terrifically. He had gone but a short distance when he met a man named Sheppard, and gave chase. Mr. Sheppard, finding that the beast was gaining on him rapidly, and that he would certainly be overtaken, attempted to climb a sapling. The lion struck at him with his paw as he ascended, but fortunately did no other damage than to tear off his coat tail and carry away a part of his trousers. Mr. John Smith, a resident of Raleigh, who was riding to Forest with his little son behind him, on horseback, met the lion on the road. As soon as the horse saw him he neighed, when the lion rushed at him, seized him by the throat, and threw him to the ground. Mr. Smith, with his little son, escaped to the woods, and made their way to Forest on foot. While the beast was devouring Mr. Smith's horse, Mr. James J. Rich, who was on his way to Forest with a load of chickens, drove up. As soon as the lion saw him he reared on his hind feet, lashed the ground with his tail, and sprang at him. Mr. Rich eluded him by jumping from the wagon, when he mounted and began tearing open the boxes containing the chickens, and turned them out. He then seemed to lose sight of everything in his efforts to catch them. When the excitement in town abated, about twenty mounted men, well armed, started in pursuit, with all the dogs belonging in town, as well as many that had followed their owners. Mr. Reynolds, the owner of the lion, begged them not to kill him, and sent several men with the crowd, with instructions to capture him if possible; but a long chase failed to discover the escaped animal, and the citizens returned to the town.

About two weeks later, in Monroe county, Mississippi,

the lion turned up again,—many miles from the place where he broke loose.

A young man named Coleman was informed by a servant girl that she had just seen a "bear as big as a cow in the edge of the woods," a short distance from Mr. Coleman's place. Her excited manner at once roused his curiosity, and arming himself with his Spencer rifle, loaded with twelve balls, (a piece that he had used in the late war,) he started out in search of the monster. He was accompanied by a servant and a large and very fierce bulldog. Arrived at the spot, a brief survey soon discovered to him the object of his search, in the shape of a genuine lion. The beast, at the sight of the men, sprang into the branches of a dead tree, and there waited further developments. Mr. Coleman, who is described as very cool and daring, did not allow him to wait long, for, elevating his rifle, he at once discharged several loads at him, which caused the beast to spring from his position on his foe. Mr. Coleman continued firing till he had exhausted all his charges, the second shot, as he afterward discovered, passing clean through the body of the beast, without disabling him. And now came the tug of war. The lion, infuriated with his wound, and with glaring eyes, reached the ground near Mr. Coleman at the first leap, and made a second spring a moment afterward. Nothing but the courage of his dog saved Mr. Coleman from instant destruction. The noble animal threw himself on the king of beasts ere he reached his victim, and seizing him by the nose, though knocked about as a feather, fought him so tenaciously that the lion abandoned his purpose, and, by a single bound, seated himself on the lower limb of a tree, about twelve feet from the ground. At this moment Mr. Coleman's servant handed him a double-barreled gun, which he had brought along; he advanced almost immediately under the beast, took an aim that was to seal his own fate for life or death, fired both barrels, and brought the lion dying to the ground. On measurement, the lion was found to be nearly nine feet in length, and to weigh one hundred and eighty pounds.

CHAPTER XXVI.

About Jugglers and Gymnasts —Hazlitt and the Italian Juggler.—The Mountebanks of Paris. — Lively Scenes on the Champs Elysees. — Queer Juggling Tricks. — Pompous Street Spouters. — The Seven Indian Brothers.—Chinese Street Jugglers.—Arab Miracles.—Conjurors' Perils.—Japanese Jugglers and Acrobats.—A Western Acrobat's Feat.—A Gymnast's Account of his Sensations in Falling from the Trapeze.

Hazlitt relates that when he was a boy he went once to a theatre. The tragedy of Hamlet was performed—a play full of the noblest thoughts, the subtlest morality that exists upon the stage. The audience listened with attention, with admiration, with applause. But now an Indian juggler appeared upon the stage—a man of extraordinary personal strength and sleight of hand. He performed a variety of juggling tricks, and distorted his body into a thousand surprising and unnatural postures. The audience were transported beyond themselves; if they had felt delight in Hamlet, they glowed with rapture at the juggler. They had listened with attention to the lofty thought, but they were snatched from themselves by the marvel of the strange posture. "Enough," said Hazlitt; "where is the glory of ruling men's mind and commanding their admiration, when a greater enthusiasm is excited by mere bodily display than was kindled by the wonderful emanations of a genius a little less than divine?"

This incident is curious as illustrating a sort of thing which no longer degrades the stage, to wit, the supplementing of a classic play with the tricks of a juggler. In former days it was quite common for theatres to present these hybrid entertainments, but the fashion, I am glad to say, has now gone out.

Nowadays, our confessed mountebanks confine their trickery to their proper sphere, and when mountebanks are seen in theatres, they are not theatres where legitimate plays are enacted.

I have never seen anything in this country to compare with the street mountebank exhibitions of foreign countries. Particularly in Paris is the scene they sometimes present a most picturesque and exciting one. A writer says: "Le Grand Carré des Fêtes, an open space in the Champs Elysées, is, three times a year, the resort of all the mountebanks in France. The enumeration of these nomadic shows is, I take it, unnecessary; every one knows it by heart. Their *modus operandi*, however, is unique, and deserves more than a passing word. They invariably commence by attracting a crowd before their tents or stalls. This is done in a great many ways, and very often the performance outside is much more amusing than that which is enacted inside. In front of each tent or wagon is erected a sort of piazza or scaffolding. Upon this the whole company—father, mother, and all the children—get together, and lay themselves out to rivet the attention of the passers-by. They are all dressed in gay colors and gaudy ribbons. They execute a polka, perhaps to the music of a keyless bugle, or some one of the troupe dresses up as a very little man with an enormously large head, and dances till he becomes red in the face, only this the spectators cannot see; or else a fellow on stilts pretends to be drunk, and tumbles about as if he were going to fall from his dizzy eminence into the midst of the crowd below. Or perhaps a juggler, robed in a long black gown covered with hieroglyphics, like an eastern magus, plays off a trick or two upon some one dressed as a clown, who pretends to be very silly and to believe that the juggler really pulled a potato from his nose. These means generally succeed in getting a pretty good concourse of people together. The manager then comes forward, and announces, at considerable length, the programme of entertainment which will be spread before the delighted audience. He goes through with it two or three times, and assures you that the exhibition has been patronized by the first society in all the cities he has visited. He generally uses very stately language, and you are sometimes lost in doubt as to whether it is possible that this flowery speech really can refer to a two-penny show. The conclusion of his address sets you right in a moment. 'Now, ladies and gentlemen, let me endeavor to induce you, in the interest of the Fine Arts, to lend your countenance to this entertaining and refining exhibition. Walk in and sit down, while our performers go through with their exercises before you, and if you are not satisfied, your money shall be refunded. The price of admission has been diminished, for this occasion only; it has usually been six sous, and everybody has been astonished that so varied an entertainment could be afforded at so moderate a sum. To-day, however, being a day intimately connected with the glory of our beloved country, and it having been suggested by several influential persons that a reduction of price would be attended with beneficial results, the slight compensation of two sous only will be asked from those who favor us with a call. Two sous! Two sous, only! So that every one may be able to amuse and instruct himself almost for nothing. Two sous! Who hasn't got two sous!' Now follows a scene impossible to describe, The manager seizes a trumpet and shouts, 'Two sous! two sous!' till he ought to be hoarse. Then the children and the clown cry, 'Two sous! only two sous!' till they are ready to faint from fatigue. Then the manager holds up two fingers in the air, keeping down the others with his thumb. The children and clown do the same, 'Two sous! two sous!' Then they begin to dance again, the stilt man reappears, more drunk than ever, the music strikes up afresh, and a frightful din ensues, in the midst of which you hear a voice rising above the turmoil, shouting, 'Two sous! two sous!' Then the manager opens the gate, and a rush commences up the steps. Two sous! Up they go! nurses with children in their arms, men with little boys, soldiers, and families of six! Two sous! The manager stands near the gate, helping the old women up the stairs and piling them in at the door, all the time yelling, 'Two sous!' and holding up his two fingers. Such is the noise and confusion, that people lose their senses, and do very strange things. Sober citizens, who only came out to breathe the air, are seized with a sudden panic, and go rushing up the steps in a most incongruous manner. An orange seller is separated from his basket, and, being caught by the tide, is whirled into the tent and disappears. We go in with the rest, and get a seat upon a bare board which, in the florid speech of the director—two sous!—was covered with damask; but what can one expect for two sous? When the rush ceases, we look around us and find about fifty persons in the tent, which is little more than half full. A silence ensues, and the manager looks in at the door, and then goes away again. This is disheartening, and everybody turns wistful glances at the curtain. Suddenly the bugle commences again on the outside, and the scaffolding begins to shake as if somebody were dancing upon it. The sun, which shines full upon the cotton front of the tent, daguerreotypes upon it the shadow of a very large head, which seems to be carrying on in a very singular way. A fellow on stilts is evidently counterfeiting intoxication for the amusement of the bystanders. In short, the sickening conviction comes over everybody that they are doing it all over again. The explanation, the trumpet, the fingers, the two sous, the rush, all follow in the same order as before, and with pretty nearly the same numerical results, for the second fills the benches. This method of catching audiences is practised by all these exhibitions, and the description of one will suffice for the whole. The performances commence speedily, for it is now the object of the manager to get rid of this audience as soon as possible, and to set about inveigling another. The exhibition sometimes is very poor and uninteresting, and sometimes more extraordinary and inexplicable than anything to be seen in the more pretentious fifty-cent museums. I remember that once having got into a place where a very fat woman was to appear in conjunction with an African nondescript, it was announced that the lady was sick, but that the nondescript would be exhibited. This was nothing more than a sickly armadillo, about a foot long, who was obliged to do duty for himself and his colleague. The exhibitress played all sorts of pranks with him, poking him with her finger in tender places to make him squirm, and tossing him up in the air and catching him again like a pancake. No doubt he wished that the big lady would soon get well again. As we went down the steps, the manager was again holding forth upon the numerous attractions of his exhibition, giving a slight biographical sketch of the fat woman, and an anecdotical history of the armadillo. The next show was a very different affair. The tricks of necromancy were like all other tricks of the sort, but what followed was worth walking a mile to see. A girl, perhaps the juggler's sister, seated herself in a chair in front of the spectators, though at some distance from them. She was then blindfolded. The juggler came among the audience and asked the people to lend him any small articles they might have, and the girl would tell what they were. He soon had his hands full of purses, rings, pencils, snuffboxes, handkerchiefs, etc. Then, taking one from the rest, and holding it in such a way as that it would be impossible for the girl to see, even if she were not blindfolded, he went on somewhat in this way. 'What do I hold in my hand?' She answered, without a moment's hesitation, 'A pocket-book.' 'What's it made of?' 'Morocco, with a steel clasp.' 'What is there in it?' 'Money.' 'How many pieces?' 'Three.' 'What are they?' 'A five franc piece, a one franc piece and a sou.' 'What's the date on the sou?' '1828.' 'On the one franc piece?' '1847.' 'What do I hold in my hand, now?' 'A ring.' 'What is it made of?' 'Gold, with six turquoises in it.' 'Is there any lettering on it?' 'Yes.' 'Read it.' 'Charles to Marie.' A very pretty young lady is seen to blush violently in the corner, and when the ring is handed back to her, everybody tries to get a sight of her face through her closely-drawn veil. 'I wouldn't mind being Charles, myself,' remarks a laughing gentleman at the left. 'I hope Charles is well,' says the juggler, and then proceeds. I handed him my watch, which had a cover over its face. Without opening it, he asked the girl what time it was by the watch he held in his hand. 'Ten minutes to nine,' she replied. As it was about two in the afternoon, this seemed guessing pretty wide of the mark, and the people began to titter. But the necromancer quietly displayed the dial of the watch, and there it was, sure enough, ten minutes to nine! 'You put it back on purpose to catch us, didn't you?' said the magus, with a triumphant air. 'Yes,' said I; feeling very much as if I had been caught robbing a hen-roost. 'Well, I've a great mind to keep your watch, as a lesson to you; but you may go this time.' So saying, he magnanimously handed it back. In this way he went on for nearly half an hour, never making a mistake, and puzzling all the wise-heads who undertook to discover his secret. For one, I could make nothing of it, and was content to consider it very miraculous, without attempting a solution. On the piazza of the next tent in order, was a man playing on the violin in a very droll way. First he played as everybody does, then he took a bow in his left hand, and scraped away just as easily as before. Then he put the fiddle over his head, and behind his back, without incommoding himself in the least. The tune kept on as merrily as ever. Then he put the violin under his left leg, and over his right leg, playing away all the while. One would have thought that there would have been a break in the sound at the moment when the bow and fiddle separated, but if there was an interval, it was quite imperceptible. All this he did with perfect ease, interlarding his music with humorous observations. When he had thus collected a good-sized crowd, he left the stage to another man, and retired to a distance to eat some bread and cheese. The other man then began a speech, the sum and substance of which was as follows:—Within the tent, he said, was perhaps one of the greatest novelties to be seen in or out of France. This was no less than one of the former wives of Abd-el-Kader, the great Algerian trooper. The way this distinguished foreigner came to be exhibiting herself at two sous a head, was briefly this:—A French officer, being on service in Africa, was one day in danger of being surprised by a troop of Arab horsemen, who were lying in ambush for some third party unknown. From this awkward position he was in some way or other released by the fair Algerian. The officer, finding no better way of repaying the debt of gratitude he owed her, bought her of Abd-el-Kader, and sent her to France, where she of course became free, and her own missis. 'She speaks Arabic, French, and English,' continued the showman, 'and all will be permitted to address her in any of these languages. Her education,' he went on, growing warm and eloquent, 'has been in all respects such as befits the bride of a chieftain of the desert.' A crowd of us went in, and after a breathless suspense of some moments, the lady made her appearance. She was quite dark, with wooly hair and a flat nose; very wide nostrils, a large mouth and thick lips. Her teeth shone as the teeth of people of her complexion always do. She had on a white muslin gown, very low in the neck, and reaching but little below the knees. Her arms, which were bare, were fat and chubby, and the palms of her hands were almost white, as if they had been used to washing dishes and scrubbing floors. Around her neck was a string of imitated pearls, and in her hair was a festoon of artificial flowers. She came forth and stood still till every one had gazed his full. The audience, who were mostly French, almost quailed before the eagle-glances of the free roamer of the desert, and their thoughts wandered to her far-off home among the oasis of Sahara. As for myself, a dim recollection of things I had left behind, was beginning to come over me like a southern sea-breeze. The showman now begged the audience to address to her some question in French or English. A military man, with a moustache, bowed politely to the lady, and made some trivial inquiry in French, which she answered after various breakings down. It was now my turn, being the only representative of the English language present. The choice of an appropriate question was rather difficult, and I thought of several without deciding on anything satisfactory. At last, for want of something better, I said, 'How is your mother?' 'I hab not heerd ob her health since de last time dat I hab dat honor.' Visions of banjos and melodies on the banks of the Roanoke, coupled with memoirs of home, rose before me. I said, nothing, but waited for further developments. 'Now,' said the showman, 'she'll sing you a song in her native Arabic. Pay attention to this, I beg you, as it may be the last time you'll ever hear that beautiful language. The words depict the scouring of a troop of horsemen across the desert.' The fair Algerian took an attitude harmonizing with the spirit of her song, and commenced in vigorous style—

'Clar de kitchen, old folks, young folks;
Clar de kitchen, old folks, young folks;
Clar de kitchen, old folks, young folks;
Old Virginny neber tire!'

If this be expressive of the way the Arabs 'go it' in the desert, I have been wandering in a maze all my life, laboring under a benighted idea that I was speaking and writing English. In plain Arabic, then, Abd-el-Kadir's wife was no other than some Lucy Long, or Coal-black Rose from Virginia, who had left her sunny home in her youth, and by some strange mutation of fortune had fallen in with a company of strollers, and turned her dark complexion to account in the manner described. Some of the out-of-door exhibitions are as amusing as those that take place under cover. Just outside the American's tent, was a man with a table before him, who was explaining the properties of various glass tubes and vessels. In these tubes were liquids of several colors. Some red, like water tinted with checkerberry candy, and some green, like asparagus juice. These were for different scientific purposes. One was to blow in, to see to what height the liquid could be raised by the force of the breath. Another, and the most extraordinary, was an instrument for telling the character. This was an upright tube, three-fourths filled with a fluid of no particular color, or rather of all sorts of colors, as if a child's paint-box had been dissolved in it. At the bottom it came to a point, forming a sort of handle. This handle had a thin bore running through it, containing a small portion of the liquid. According to the explanation of the exhibitor, this liquid, being highly impressionable, would be differently acted upon by the hands of different individuals. Persons of great nervous energy, strong minds, etc., would affect it much more powerfully than others of weak character. To illustrate this by experiment, any one might have his disposition told for two sous. It was rather a dangerous risk to run—thus exhibiting your inmost self to a holiday crowd; but there was no lack of adventurers. First came a baker's boy, with lazy gait and listless air, and a cotton turban on his head. He took the glass in hand. The top of the liquid seemed to be slightly ruffled, and something appeared to be trying to break forth. A bubble rose slowly upon its surface, and after a moment's hesitation, burst. The agitated waters subsided, and all was still. 'There,' said the showman, 'there is probably the most insignificant character that has ever, during a long career in the most populous cities in France, been presented to my observation. That young man will never set the Seine on fire, though he might his bedclothes. Look at him, gentlemen, and then tell me if my glass has not been singularly accurate in its indications? Don't get run over, my friend, in going home.' Then came another applicant. He seized the glass and held it tightly. The liquid immediately began to boil and bubble as if it meant to break its bonds and give the spectators a sprinkling. A continuous stream rose from the body of the fluid, and dashed itself in spray against the top of the tube. Really, the contents of the glass were as much agitated as the fountain in the park. 'There's a contrast for you,' exultingly exclaimed the exhibitor. 'Let go the glass, young man. A minute more and you'd have it in splinters. There's a fellow I shouldn't like to have a tussle with. I only hope he won't come to harm, with such a temper as he's got. Look at him, ladies and gentlemen, and judge for yourselves!' The man's glass was right again, this time; the young fellow would have been a severe customer in a fight. He was pale and ragged, but had a determined bearing, and a bold, unquivering eye. Such is the Grand Carreé in fête time. A tremendous, though confused din of music, drums, shouts, vociferations, applause and laughter, bursts upon the ear. On three sides of the square is arranged, in long array, the army of menageries. They all face the square, presenting their fair side to the audience. Behind are the broken-down horses that drag the tents and wagons from place to place, taking their morning's meal in silence and sadness. At every ten steps is a rude sort of kitchen, hurriedly built of stones, in the open air; an odor of fried potatoes, and the hissing of a row of griddles, tell that even jugglers must eat, and that necromancers, like other mortals, are susceptible of creature comforts. Occasionally a gaily-dressed harlequin, whose term of service has expired for the morning, and who has an hour to himself, leaving his jests and his antics behind him, throws himself upon the ground, where the sun is warm and the earth dry, and, huddling up his body into a ball, goes quietly to sleep. The strolling mountebank, whether juggler, clown, or tumbler, has but one dress, which serves him for all the purposes to which dress can be applied. His gay holiday attire, his red and yellow velvet; his silk and feathers, are his everyday costume. He travels in it, sleeps in it, jumps in it. His closely-fitting tights are his only trousers, his spangled jacket is his only coat, and very often he can claim no other head-dress than his cap and bells. Anywhere on the road that they may stop to take an hour's rest, he is always ready with his jingling brass and bright colors, to give a taste of his quality to the peasants and villagers. His meals are never so hearty as to prevent him from turning somersets the next minute. His sleep is so light that he will wake at a moment's call, dance a Highland fling, put the lighted end of a segar in his mouth, stand on his head, walk on his hands, while anybody else would be rubbing his eyes, and composing himself to slumber again. I notice a very palpable progress in the art of exhibiting puppets or *marionnettes* in Paris. There are five of these exhibitions in the open air, upon the Champs Elysées, besides two stationary theatres devoted to that specialty, on the Boulevard du Temple. I do not see that the latter are at all superior to the former. There are two kinds of puppets, those managed from underneath—the exhibitor's arm being run up into the garments composing their body, and his fingers forming their arms—and those managed from overhead, by means of very visible wires, which sustain their weight, and strings which communicate the necessary movements to their legs and the appropriate gestures to their arms. The former—puppets proper—have no legs, of course; they must be supposed to touch ground three or four inches below the spectators' line of vision. They have great strength in their arms; and their principal duty is to carry heavy objects from place to place, and their principal pleasure, to whack each other with clubs. The latter—*marionnettes* proper—have but little force in their upper limbs, but can give a very plump and well-directed kick, if desired. The conversation is of course carried on by the exhibitor in two or more voices. If the number of *dramatis personæ* require it, his wife lends him the assistance of her vocal organs, sustaining, naturally, that part of the dialogue which falls to the more shrill-voiced of the characters. On Sundays these out-of-door exhibitors perform to audiences varying from thirty to fifty persons, seated on straw-bottomed chairs within the ropes. Fifty persons, at two sous a piece, make a dollar, and fifteen performances may be given easily from three o'clock to nine. On other days, however fair the weather may be, the receipt is barely one-third as large. The lady who takes the money, and who seats the audience, often gives the choice of the play to the visitors—

naming over a dozen or so of the best pieces of her husband's repertory. I remember that once it fell to me to select the entertainment, and I chose, without any particular reason for so doing, a farce in one act, entitled 'The Change of Lodgings.' I have never ceased to regret, to this day, this most unlucky selection. We had an audience equal in point of elegance and toilet to any I have seen of late at the Italian Opera, but the farce was barely decent in its character, summoning blushes untold to many a mortified cheek. It was calculated to offend the fastidious in a supreme degree. In no other country than France, probably, would an elegantly-dressed lady sit with her children at a puppet-show in the open air, not twenty feet from the most fashionable promenade in the city, where, perhaps, her carriage and servants attend her."

Some time ago a French juggler, who had for a whole week entertained the inhabitants of a small German town, and had astonished the natives with his amazing and numberless sleights, was at once, as it seemed, completely discountenanced and beat down by an announcement which was circulated through the town, to the effect that seven Indian brothers would exhibit the following feats:—The youngest, with a lighted candle in each hand, would jump down the throat of his senior brother, who, also armed with two candles, would jump down the throat of the next, and so on till there was only one left; and this was to make an end of all by jumping into his own throat! The performance was to take place at the usual hour, at the same hotel, and in the same hall in which the French juggler had, with so much success, exhibited his own feats; and he himself came in as a common spectator, openly confessing that the announced tour de force was entirely beyond his power of conception, and he was curious to witness it, to see whether he could make out the artifice of it. The price of the places had been raised to double the usual figure, but the hall was early crowded. The spectators had been waiting a long time, and were growing impatient, when it was announced that the seven Indians had disappeared. Whether they had swallowed one another, no one could say; but they were no where to be found, and the money received had disappeared with them. The disappointment was great and general, as may easily be imagined, but soon gave place to a different feeling. The disappointed crowd, who had swallowed the hoax, seemed determined to vent their spleen on the benches and furniture, when the French conjuror, who was among them, kindly offered to entertain them gratis for that evening, to thank them for their former favors. The offer was gratefully accepted. The evening was spent agreeably, and the disappointment almost forgotten. The French conjuror went away the next morning, and it was only when he was gone that the good people were informed, through him, that he had reserved them his very best trick for the last. It was he himself who had devised the hoax of the Seven Indian Brothers, and he who reaped the profit.

Street jugglers abound in China. Says a correspondent: "Sword swallowing and stone-eating appear to be the commonest feats, and operators of this description can be seen in almost every street. One fellow, however, performed a number of feats in front of our hotel, which demand from me more than a passing notice. He stationed himself in the centre of the street, and having blown a blast upon a bugle to give warning that he was about to begin his entertainment, he took a small lemon or orange tree, which was covered with fruit, and balanced it upon his head. He then blew a sort of chirruping whistle, when immediately a number of rice birds came from every direction, and settled upon the boughs of the bush he balanced or fluttered about his head. He then took a cup in his hand, and began to rattle some seeds in it, when the birds disappeared. Taking a small bamboo tube, he next took the seeds, and putting one in it, blew it at one of the fruit, when it opened, and out flew one of the birds, which fluttered about the circle surrounding the performer. He continued to shoot his seeds at the oranges until nearly a dozen birds were released. He then removed the tree from his forehead, and setting it down, took up a dish, which he held above his head, when all the birds flew into it, then covered it over with a cover, and giving it a whirl or two about his head, opened it and displayed a quantity of eggs, the shells of which he broke with a little stick, releasing a bird from each shell. The trick was neatly performed, and defied detection from my eyes. The next trick was equally clever and difficult of detection. Borrowing a handkerchief from one of his spectators, he took an orange, cut a small hole in it, then squeezed all the juice out, and crammed the handkerchief into it. Giving the handkerchief to a bystander to hold, he caught up a tea-pot and began to pour a cup of tea from it, when the spout became clogged. Looking into the pot, apparently for the purpose of detecting what was the matter, he pulled out the handkerchief and returned it to the owner. He next took the orange from the bystander, and cut it open, when it was found to be full of rice."

A number of interesting explanations of Arab miracles are given by Robert Houdin, the celebrated French conjuror. The Arabs eat pounded glass. Houdin powdered some for himself and ate it, and he avers that his appetite for dinner was improved by the dose. They walk on red-hot iron with bare feet, and pass their tongues over a white-hot plate of iron. Prof. Sementrici discovered that by rubbing into the skin a solution of alum evaporated to a spongy state, it was rendered insensible to the action of red-hot iron. He rubbed himself with soap, and found that then, even, the hair did not burn. He rubbed the alum into his tongue, and lapped the glowing metallic surface without pain. Houdin himself tried passing his hand, slightly dampened, through a stream of melted iron, and found, as others have done, that it left no scar on him. An English conjuror used to thrust a sword through his body, shove a knife up either nostril to the handle, and, thus spitted, sing a song. Houdin bought the secret of the invulnerable, and now divulges it. The performer was very thin. With a waist-belt he strapped his tender paunch tight down upon the vertebral column, substituted a card-board stomach for the suppressed part, covered all with flesh-colored tights, between the true and false abdomen fastened a scabbard, covered the apertures on the sides with rosettes, placed a sponge filled with red liquid in the scabbard, and there thrust his sword, which came out covered with bogus blood, of course. The pug-nosed mountebank enjoyed a physical conformation which permitted the delicate and delightful performance.

Houdin used to say that if the public knew what passes through the mind of a conjuror when he sees the barrel of a pistol turned towards him in the course of a "fire-arm trick," they would perhaps give him credit for as much nerve and courage as the bravest soldier shows in battle. An omission in some trifling point, the breaking off of a small part of the false ramrod or of the real bullet as it is being withdrawn, may make the discharge fatal. Often, too, the trick is a new one, and some miscalculation may make the plan a failure, where failure may mean death. An event which took place in the Cirque Napoleon strikingly illustrates Houdin's words. Dr. Epstein, the conjuror, had offered a gun to a spectator, with directions to take good aim at the doctor, who was to receive the discharge on the point of a sword. The man refused, but another fired off the gun as directed. The moment after, the doctor staggered and fell to the ground, exclaiming: "I am a dead man!" Several persons hastened to his assistance, and, a surgeon being sent for, the unfortunate performer was removed at once to his own residence. Naturally, a great sensation was excited among the spectators, although few were aware of the full extent of the injury done. It appears that the slight piece of wood used in ramming down the charge, had broken in the barrel, and that a piece of it had traversed Dr. Epstein's body, inflicting a painful, though not very dangerous wound.

Everybody remembers the *furore* which was created in this country by the first troupe of Japanese acrobats and jugglers which came here. The history of this troupe, of which little "All Right" was the bright particular star, was a rather doleful one. In October, 1866, two Americans, then residing in Yokohama, Japan, entered into an agreement with several Japanese acrobats and jugglers to give performances in the United States and Great Britain. By the laws and customs of Japan no native is allowed to leave the country without the permission of the Tycoon. The two Americans obtained authority to take the company and receive their services for one year from October 20, 1866. The penalty imposed upon the jugglers by the Tycoon for noncompliance with the terms of this agreement was death—provided he could catch them. Twelve performers were selected. The principal ones were Foo-kee-matz, who acted as leader; String-kee-chee, Ling-kee-chee, and Ring-kee-chee, his son of nine years; with Zoo-shee-kee, Chee-shau-kee, La-as-kee, Chee-zah-chau, Ai-noo-schee, Foo-choo-chee, and I-as-kee as assistants. They were of one family, and servants of the house of Yoo-ku-chu, a Japanese prince. No sooner had they arrived in this country than they got entangled in all sorts of law-suits and other troubles, which kept them in constant distress, and their great desire was to go back to Japan. But between the prospect of death, at the order of the Tycoon, and their overwhelming home-sickness, they found it difficult to decide what course to take; and, though remaining in the country, they became the prey to gloomy feelings, until finally one of them committed hari-kari—running himself through with a sword. The acrobatic feats of these people were very extraordinary.

A western acrobat performed the astonishing feat, two or three years ago, of riding a circus horse from the bottom to the top of the circular stairs leading to the dome on the Court House at Chicago. The dome is one hundred feet from the landing. The stairs are winding, and not more than four feet wide, and the banisters not more than three feet high. The daring performance attracted a large crowd.

A gymnast who fell from a trapeze, in New Orleans, gave the following account of his sensations: "Amid the sea of faces before me I looked for a familiar one, but in vain, and, turning, I stepped back to the rope by which we ascended to the trapeze, and going up, hand over hand, was soon seated in my swinging perch. As I looked down I caught sight of a face in one of the boxes that at once attracted my attention. It was that of a beautiful girl, with sweet blue eyes, and golden hair falling unconfined over her shoulders in heavy waving masses. Her beautiful eyes, turned toward me, expressed only terror at the seeming danger of the performer, and for the moment I longed to assure her of my perfect safety, but my brother was by my side, and we began our performance. In the pauses for breath, I could see that sweet face, now pale as death, and the blue eyes staring wide open with fear, and I dreaded the effect of our finish, which—being the drop act—gives the uninitiated the impression that both performers are about to be dashed headlong to the stage.

Having completed the double performance, I ascended to the upper bar, and, casting off the connect, we began our combination feats. While hanging by my feet in the upper trapeze, my brother being suspended from my hands (the lower bar being drawn back by a super.), I felt a slight shock, and the rope began slowly to slip past my foot. My heart gave a great jump, and then seemed to stop, as I realized our awful situation. The seizing which held the rope had parted, the rope was gliding round the bar, and in another moment we should be lying senseless on the stage. I shouted 'under' to the terrified 'super.,' who instantly swung the bar back to its place, and I dropped my brother on it as the last strand snapped, and I plunged downward. I saw the lower bar darting toward me, as it seemed, and I made a desperate grasp at it, for it was my last chance. I missed it! Down through the air I fell, striking heavily on the stage. The blow rendered me senseless, and my collar-bone was broken. I was hurried behind the scenes, and soon came to my senses. My first thought was that I must go back and go through my performance at once, and I actually made a dash for the stage—but I was restrained, and it was many weeks before I was able to perform again."

CHAPTER XXVII.

Accidents to So-called "Lion Tamers."—An Amateur Tamer torn to Pieces.—A Lion attacks its Keeper in Wisconsin.—Narrow Escape of an English Keeper.—Almost a Tragedy at Barnum's.—A Lion Tamer's Story.—The Killing of Lucas, the Paris Lion Tamer.—What it Costs to get up a Menagerie.—The Headless Rooster.—The Gorilla which had a Tail.—How the Happy Family is kept Happy.—A Dog that wouldn't be Put on Exhibition.

The valorous "lion-tamers" (as they are called), who enter the cages of wild beasts and cuff them about in a style startling to the unsophisticated mind, do not always come off entirely unharmed from their little amusements.

An amateur lion-tamer was killed a short time since, at Ballein, in Belgium. The regular lion-tamer of the show was ill, and the director proposed to exhibit in place of him. He entered the cage, and succeeded for a time in making the lions go through their performance; but when it came to the close, which consists of giving the animals raw meat, the director lost courage, and instead of keeping a firm eye on the animals, he trembled and made for the door of the cage. This sealed his doom. A large lioness pounced upon him, and in a few minutes the rash, unfortunate man was torn to pieces.

An animal performer in Madison, Wisconsin, had on one occasion nearly completed his usual performance in the lion's cage, and was in the act of firing off his pistol as the *finale*, when one of the lionesses sprang furiously at him, and tore the flesh in shreds from his arms and legs. The unfortunate man's bones snapped under the terrible violence, and all the spectators were stricken with fear, expecting to see him killed outright. The employées of the menagerie, however, quickly realized the peril of the situation, and made a furious attack on the lioness with spears and lances. They succeeded, with some difficulty, in beating her off, and in rescuing their comrade, who was immediately placed under treatment, and his wounds dressed. The crowd of spectators were thrown into great confusion during the affair, and many, fearing for their lives, fled from the scene, but fortunately none were injured.

At Bradford, England, last Summer, a fair was being held, among whose attractions was a menagerie of wild beasts, which included a Barbary lioness and a good-sized male puma. At intervals these animals were put through a performance by one of the keepers, named Joseph Pearce. While the latter was in the cage with the animals on Friday evening, the lioness suddenly seized him by the arm, threw him down on the floor of the cage, and held him by the throat in its grip. The spectators became greatly alarmed, and while some, in the hope of rendering assistance, began to tear out the boards near the cages, others began to retreat by the passages. In a moment of the greatest apprehension, the puma fortunately struck the lioness a blow with its paw, and thus diverted from its keeper, the brute turned savagely upon the puma, and the pair engaged in a fierce fight. The keeper, apparently little injured, immediately regained his control over the beasts, and persisted in finishing the performance.

A similar scene took place at Barnum's old museum, in New York, during a performance of a drama callled "The Christian Martyrs." In the fourth act, *Sebastian* (represented by the keeper of the animals at Barnum's) is cast into a cave full of "wild animals." The keeper had been in the den but a few moments, when he noticed an unusual glare in the eyes of the leopard. He had forgotten to take his whip in with him, and told an attendant to pass it to him. This done, he administered a smart stroke on the leopard's nose, and then laid the whip aside, when almost instantaneously, the treacherous beast sprang upon him, and a fearful interval ensued. The keeper, however, adroitly contrived to extricate himself, but not before he had received several severe injuries, namely: a deep wound of two or three inches on one of his hips, a long, deep wound on both thighs, and another commencing below the knee-cap down to the ankle, laying the bone open. The sufferer speedily recovered.

Herr Lengel, a Philadelphian by birth, and a lion-tamer by profession, tells the following story of his own experiences. After stating that lion-taming was a gift of nature with him, he continues: "I have no fear of them. People tell me every time I get a wound, that it ought to be a warning to me, and should make me fear to go into the cage again. But it does not. When I am away from the lions I get homesick, and when I can go where they are and my wounds prevent me from going into the cage, I get more homesick still. I never met any lions I could not tame. Three years ago I tamed five, in New York, which, while in Europe, had killed one man and badly mangled another, who attempted to tame them. In three weeks after they were put in my charge, they were as tame as I wished, though they were before considered untamable. I very seldom use force in taming them, but sometimes it becomes neceesary,—kindness is my usual plan; I am always careful to keep my eye upon them. Every one who has seen 'the lion-tamer' leaving the cage after his feat of lying down among the lions, putting his feet on their heads, feeding them, and firing off pistols, has doubtless noticed how careful he was,—stepping out backwards very deliberately, and watching closely the beasts, which always advanced upon him. If

I did not keep my eye upon them they would jump at me. They have sense enough to know that I am retreating from them, and they gain courage; there is more danger to me at this time than at any other. If the lions were at liberty, I would fear to go near them. Some people think that a lion born in America is more docile, partaking less of the savage nature of the brute than one born in Africa or Asia. Not so. I would rather have to tame a litter born in either of the last two mentioned places than a litter born in this country—the latter are more dangerous and less easily tamed. I have been bitten a number of times by lions, lionesses I should have said, for the males have never done so; the lionesses are more treacherous and deceitful than the lions. I have been slightly scratched an almost innumerable number of times, but never had to lay up but twice from wounds. The first wound was a bite in the left leg, in Western Pennsylvania, while with Barnum's. The second was received while with S. B. Howe & Co., in Augusta, Georgia, being severely bitten in the left hand. The wound caused me to lose the use of my middle finger. The third was inflicted at Little Rock, Arkansas, by a lioness in Howe & Castello's collection. This time two fingers of the right hand were mangled. I have full use of them now. The fourth was received in Madison, Indiana, last Summer. The lioness seized me by the right leg, driving her teeth into the calf of my leg until they nearly met. The fifth was received last April in New Orleans. The animal seized me by the left leg, inserted one tooth of the lower jaw an inch and a half into the calf, and a tooth of the upper jaw the same depth into the upper side of the knee joint. I was confined to my bed awhile, but when the show moved I came along, and gave two exhibitions, one in Augusta, and one in Savannah. I do not think I was bitten but once intentionally. The lionesses, when together, never meet, but they snap and snarl at each other —two of them never live peaceably in the same cage—it is my opinion that, with the exception mentioned, when I aggravated one beyond endurance, I was in the way, and was bitten for one of the lionesses. I have the teeth and claws of the lioness which I think bit me purposely. The teeth are an inch and a half long, with a root about two and a half inches in length. If the teeth were driven in flesh up to the gums, a large-sized peach stone could be planted in the hole. The claws, which the animal, like the cat, keeps unexposed till wanted, are formidable looking objects. I do not now doubt, as I once did, the assertions of travelers, that one blow from a lion's paw would kill a man, or tear out great masses of flesh. I fear their claws more than their teeth—they generally strike before they bite."

Lucas, the celebrated lion-tamer of the Paris Hippodrome, was killed a short time ago by his animals. He was paid at the rate of five hundred francs per month, or about three dollars for each time that he risked his life in a cage containing four or five wild beasts. He went into the cage, at the Hippodrome, where there were two lions and two lionesses, with only a whip in his hand, instead of the heavy cudgel which he generally carried. A lioness, presuming upon his being unarmed, sprung at him and seized him by the nape of the neck. A cry of horror arose from the spectators. Many women fainted, and others rushed out of the theatre. The other lions, attracted by blood, rushed upon Lucas and bit and scratched him severely. In a few moments he would have been killed had not one of his assistants, who was not in the habit of entering the cage, come forward and knocked the lion about the head with an iron bar. Lucas said to him "Go away, leave me to die alone." The man dragged him away from the lions. The doctors discovered no less than thirty-one wounds. M. Arnaud, the manager of the Hippodrome, had the presence of mind to close the door of the cage after the faithful servant got Mr. Lucas out of it, otherwise the lions might have made a raid upon the audience. Lucas died soon after.

If any of my readers have a spare $100,000 in greenbacks, about them, they can get up a very respectable menagerie on that capital. Here is an estimate of prices (in gold) for a very tolerable show, to make a beginning with:—

One elephant	$16,000
Lion and lioness, with cage	9,000
Sea cow, a rare animal	8,000
Pair of very large leopards, and two smaller ditto	5,000
Australian kangaroo	2,000
Australian wambut	2,000
Ostrich	1,000
Royal tiger	4,000
Sacred camel	2,000
Rare birds, monkeys, and lesser animals, including those of American nativity	20,000
Total	$60,000

With gold at a premium of say forty per cent., this relieves you of all but $3400 of your greenbacks.

You may get some idea of your other expenses by referring to the chapter treating of circuses.

And, to cheer you on, I would casually remark, that about one menagerie in ten makes money. The other nine—don't.

As a general rule, in this branch of the show business, a little humbug goes a great way, and saves a pretty penny of expense.

Not long since a man created a great sensation by exhibiting what he termed a headless rooster.

Crowds thronged to see this extraordinary freak of nature. To all appearance it was a rooster without a head, which walked about quite comfortably.

Some one detected the "sell" one day. The rooster was found to have a head, which the unfeeling wretch of a showman had concealed by cramming it out of sight, and sewing a dead rooster's decapitated neck and breast-feathers over the living head of the unfortunate fowl.

The fellow was arrested and punished.

The humbugs of Barnum are celebrated, but I think this showman was never guilty of such cruelty as this. It is even stated that he refused to cut off a monkey's tail once—though he was exhibiting the monkey as a gorilla, and gorillas have no tails.

Many people who have looked on in amazement at the "happy family" of dogs, cats, birds, monkeys, mice, etc., sometimes exhibited in the same cage in museums, wonder how these creatures, of such antagonistic natures, are kept "happy."

Their "happy" state is similar to that of a man who has stupefied himself with liquor. They are stupefied with morphine, with some exceptions. The monkeys are generally left in possession of their faculties, and sometimes a dog may be found of a sufficiently benign disposition to be trusted.

Apropos of dogs, an amusing story is told of a sagacious canine in England. The dog's owner resolved that it should be sent to the Birmingham Show. The coachman, who had known the dog for years, was thereupon instructed to get the animal into condition. Thomas began his work with tender care, dressing the dog's coat, and looking after him with unusual attention. Nelson (the dog's name) grew dull and moody under the treatment, and at last, when he was put into a new collar, and saw himself dragging a spotless chain, he refused to notice his master or any one else. The dog evidently felt that he was the object of some wretched design. By and by the time for his removal arrived. Thomas patted and coaxed him, but Nelson resisted all friendly appeals, though he permitted Thomas and a couple of other servants to lift him into an open light cart. The coachman chained his companion to the seat, and away they started for the show. When just on the borders of the family estate, Nelson suddenly leaped upon the coachman, pulled him down upon his back, and seized the reins in his mouth. The horse, a quiet, steady beast, continued the even tenor of his way, and Thomas, in a wholesome fright, dared not interfere with the dog, which continued to exhibit ugly signs of desperation. Failing to stop the horse by means of the reins, Nelson, plunging to the full length of his chain, seized the horse's tail, and by this time Thomas, coming to the front, turned the horse and drove home, unmolested by Nelson, who, however, regarded him with a watchful and threatening eye. "I knew he'd never go, sir," said Thomas, "he never meant to go," and he did not go.

CHAPTER XXVIII.

About Circuses and Pantomimes.—Children as Acrobats.—Barbarous Treatment of a Little Girl by her Trainer.—Cruelty of a Father to his Two Performing Children.—Excitement in a Philadelphia Variety Hall.—How Children are Driven to their Tasks in Circuses.—Death in the Ring.—The Clown's Dying Wife.—Leaping through a Hoop into Matrimony.—The Cost of a Circus.—Behind the Scenes in the Circus.—How Engagements are Made.—Circus Clowns and Stage Clowns.—Pantomime.—An Evening of English Pantomime.

I am no admirer of the circus; but especially do I abhor seeing *children* in the ring.

I have said that the sight of a child-actor on the stage excites my deepest sympathies—because it does not seem to me as if any child could naturally like the life.

This feeling is intensified in the case of child-acrobats and circus-performers; for, if it is unnatural to see a child go through a part on the stage, how much more unnatural it is to see a child performing the perilous feats of the acrobat!

I know that boys who go to circuses are apt to be fired with the desire to convert the limbs of trees into horizontal bars, and to make a trapeze out of an old rope in the barn; but the frolics of an active child, imitating that which tickles its little fancy, are a very different thing from the making such performances a daily labor.

No schoolboy, driven unwillingly to school, ever hated his books as the child-acrobat hates his toilsome and dangerous feats; and, to their shame be it said, those who train children for the circus and the variety hall are often guilty of the most brutal and cruel treatment of their little protegees.

I remember a case of this sort which took place in Cincinnati, and was made the theme of indignant comment by some of the newspapers. A circus owned and managed by a celebrated clown was exhibiting there. The clown-proprietor introduced a little girl to the audience, saying that she would exhibit her skill in riding. He stated that the horse was somewhat unused to the ring, and if it should happen that the rider should fall, no one need entertain any apprehension of serious accident, for the arena was soft, and injury would be impossible. It was surely an unhappy introduction for the child, and calculated to fill her with fear and doubt. The child whirled rapidly round the ring two or three times, using neither rein nor binding strap. She stood on one foot, then changed to the other. After this, she was called upon to jump stretchers. Had her horse been well trained, the feat would have been no very difficult one. But she became entangled in the cloth, and fell to the ground under the horse's feet. She was placed again on the back of the horse, and compelled once more to try the feat. Her fall had not given her new confidence, and she fell a second time. Evidently much against her inclination, and in spite of her trembling and her tears, nature's protest against barbarity, she was tossed again to her place. But her nerve had gone. She was utterly demoralized. Judgment of distance, and faith in herself were lost. Again she attempted to execute the leap. Again she fell to the ground, this time striking heavily upon her head. She rolled directly under the horse's feet, and only by a sheer chance escaped a terrible death. The audience—more merciful than those within the ring—by this time had become thoroughly aroused and indignant. Cries and shouts were heard from all quarters: "Shame! shame!" "That'll do!" "Take her out! take her out!" came up from every side. It would not answer to disregard such commands, and with a smile the ringmaster went to the child, raised her from the dust where she lay, and led her, crying and sobbing, to the dressing tent.

This disgraceful scene was bad enough; but when the trainer of a child chances to be its father, and exhibits such brutality, there are no words to express one's indignation. The New York *Clipper*, which is a kind of organ for "show" people, and is of course disposed to be very lenient with the shortcomings of the class on which it depends for patronage, recently furnished this testimony: "It is pretty well known to the profession that many of those connected with the circus business who take apprentices to teach them to ride and do circus business generally, resort to considerable lashing of said apprentices in order to make them proficient. We have been eye witnesses where the tutor has given some poor apprentices a good cutting with a knotted rope, raising huge lumps upon their bodies, and otherwise maltreating them. No matter how hard the apprentices strive to do what they are bid, if they make the slightest balk, away goes the lash of a whip or a rope's end at their fragile limbs. About two years ago we were obliged, owing to his brutal treatment, to give a certain popular performer a sharp talking to for abusing his children. He is a powerfully built man, with two children—his own—whom he postures. He opened an engagement at the New Theatre Comique with his boys, who are very smart and exceedingly hard working children, about fourteen and sixteen years respectively. During their posturing, one of the boys happened to make a slight mistake, and, notwithstanding the performance was enthusiastically applauded and the children called out, the father actually kicked one of the boys as he was leaving the ring, which was noticed by many of the audience. Not satisfied with this, he beat him so outrageously in the dressing room that blood oozed from his nose and mouth, saturating his clothes, and the screams of the child brought to his rescue several of the company, who threatened the brute of a father with bodily injury if he dared to punish them again in such a manner in their hearing. We ventilated the affair at the time, and it had the effect of staying his ill treatment for the time being only; for we learn from members of the circus com-company with whom he has traveled this season, that on several occasions he has abused them in a shameful manner. He has reappeared in this city, and has again resumed his inhuman punishment, such as putting their heads in a bucket of water, and holding them there untii they can scarcely breathe, and then kicking them with his big feet, and actually picking them up and throwing them against the side of the room, and otherwise ill treating them. It seems almost incredible to believe that any so-called man, and he a father, could descend so low as to so abuse his children; but what we have stated is true, and not in the least colored."

On another occasion the same paper spoke as follows, referring to a performance in a New York variety hall: "After having executed some very clever feats, without a mishap, for which they were heartily and deservedly applauded, a stand about twelve feet high was brought forward, and the father ascended with his two boys, and after forming a pyramid descended, accompanied by his youngest son, leaving his oldest son, about twelve years old, to throw a number of flip-flaps from the top of this stand, and alighting on the same. When we inform our readers that the top of this stand is scarcely as large as the top of a flour barrel, they can readily see what a feat it is to accomplish. While turning these flip-flaps, the father kept hurrying him up, and all at once he missed his footing, and down he came to the stage, striking very heavily upon his head and shoulders. Knowing, probably, what he would catch if he dared to show to the public any signs of pain, he jumped up, turned a couple of flip-flaps, and, while leaving the stage, and before he was out of sight of the audience, his father gave him such a blow on the back that sent a chill through the audience, and was the cause of many leaving the house in disgust, bestowing upon him anything but table talk language. It was a disgraceful as well as inhuman act. The profession is talked about enough already as to the abuse inflicted by members of the equestrian profession upon their apprentices and those they are bringing up to the business, without any one making a public exhibition of it."

Considerable excitement was caused in a Philadelphia variety hall, one night last summer, through the efforts which were made to drive a child to the performance of perilous feats, for which she was unfitted by nervousness and fright. The little girl had been performing on the trapeze with an older person, and, as she was descending from the dizzy height, the man whose duty it was to catch her failed to do so, and the poor child fell to the platform placed over the orchestra, a distance of several feet, and struck her head and otherwise injured herself. The child was picked up, when she immediately placed her hands to her head, and it was apparent that she was seriously hurt. Notwithstanding this she was brutally ordered to remount the platform in the gallery and repeat the feat. The child obeyed, but such conduct on the part of those having charge of the exhibition was too much for the audience to stand, and there was a unanimous cry of "No, no!" "Shame, shame!" "Take her back, take her back!" etc. In the meantime the child mounted the platform, and then stood ready to repeat the feat, but the audience rose, *en masse*, to their great credit, and prevented the ropes from being handed to her. Unable to combat such a display of public indignation and disapproval, the child was ordered to retire, which she did amid the most tumultuous applause. After she had retired, the stage manager advanced and stated that she desired to perform another feat, and that she was not injured, and the consent of the audience was asked. There was a general cry of "No, no," and considerable hissing; but, taking advantage of a few cries of "Go on," from the boys in the gallery, the child again appeared, and, mounting the platform, took hold of the rings and swung herself off for the purpose of catching the hanging trapeze with her feet, and then making a sommersault while descending into an outstretched net. As the audience felt would be the case, the child essayed the feat, but failed to catch the trapeze, owing to her nervous state, which was natural, under the circumstances, but she was saved from injury by her commendable presence of mind in not letting go of the ropes. The consequence was that she swung backwards and forwards amid a scene of much excitement, and was relieved from her perilous position by persons in the audience, who caught her and carried her to the stage.

The editor of the Galveston (Texas) *Bulletin*, who speaks from personal knowledge of the way children are driven to their tasks in circuses, says: "It is altogether useless to tell us that these athletic children take to these feats naturally as does a duck to the water. They are unwillingly forced to them. It is not in the nature of things for them to look down from their giddy altitude without fear. Those children that ride rapid horses are driven thereto by the lash, and beneath their spangled petticoats are to be found the blue welts of the rawhide. It is useless to tell those who know better that these children love the sports of the arena."

The accidents which are continually happening to the people who follow the perilous profession of circus performers do not seem to have the effect of driving away the candidates for gymnastic glory. In Illinois, not long since, a circus performer broke his back while performing, and the strange scene ensued of a clergyman performing the last offices of religion by the side of a dying man in tights and spangles, stretched on the sawdust of the ring.

The incongruities of the hilarious painted clown in the ring and the plain man with a family out of it, are sometimes painfully illustrated. On one occasion, in Chicago, the clown at Yankee Robinson's Circus, was notified while in the ring of the sudden change for the worse of his wife's health, and was transferred from the show a moment after he had set the audience in a roar of laughter at some taking joke of his, to the bedside of his dying wife. Truly, in the "midst of life we are in death."

As a contrast, there is a story of a circus performer—a woman—who leaped through a hoop into matrimony. An old marquis near Paris went to the Rue Montmartre to see M'lle Paquita dance a cachuca on four flying steeds and jump through a hoop. Just as she was doing the act, she missed her foothold and fell plump in his bosom. Both were carried out insensible, and the result was that henceforth the dancer occupied the best portion of the old fellow's chateau, and bore his title.

In former days the circus and the menagerie were separate institutions—the circus being "a foe to its zoological rival, but like it struggling onward in the race for popularity and importance. The advertiser who now travels with a carriage and pair, followed by a couple of dashing two-horse wagons, with a *paste brigade* and the pictorial bills, was then represented by a 'solitary horseman' and a bag which held both the bills and the wardrobe of the rider, or, as often as otherwise, the latter made his 'stands' on the spot. Step by step, both these branches have advanced to their present combined proportions; for at this time a traveling expedition is not considered perfect, especially in the rural districts, without the amalgamation of circus and menagerie. An estimate of the cost in organizing and perfecting a first-class "show," with the requisite proportion of horses, ponies, carriages, wardrobe, trappings, paraphernalia, tent, show-bills, etc., was made by a Western reporter, showing the following figures:

The polyhymnia, a mammoth and elaborate musical instrument	$9,000
Golden dragon buggy, made in Chicago	2,800
The "Undine throne" car	4,000
Twenty-four wagons and vehicles, at $800 each	19,200
Sixteen animal cages, cost $200 each	19,200
Harness	10,000
Thirty-four performing and ring horses at $500 each	17,000
One hundred and seventy-eight baggage horses at $150 each	23,700
Trappings, wardrobe and properties	18,000
Engravings for pictorial bills (the drawing of one cost $1,000)	20,000
Stock of illuminated bills to start with	12,000
Tent, poles, ropes and seats	6,000
Zoological panorama, dividing the circus from the menagerie	2,000
Total	$162,900

The organ of the circus people, already referred to, gives many curious details of circus-life behind the scenes, and "on the road." In the circus dressing-room "they are preparing for the 'grand *entree*.' Helmets are lying around loose, and wardrobes appear to be in a state of great confusion. Cheap velvet gaily bespangled is quite plentiful. It looks best at a distance. Quantities of white chalk are brought into use, each man's face being highly powdered, his eyebrows blackened, etc. The dressing-room is small, and there is apparently great confusion while the performers are donning their respective costumes. But each knows what his duty is, and does it accordingly, without really interfering with any one else. Close beside is the 'ladies' room;' into this we are not permitted to cast our profane peepers, but we know from exterior knowledge that paint and powder, short dresses and flesh tights, are rapidly converting ordinary women into *equestrienne* angels. Outside of the dressing-rooms are the horses, ranged in regular order. At a given signal the riders appear, mount and enter the ring. As they are dashing about in apparent recklessness, let us look more closely at them. They all look young and fresh, but there are old men in the party who for twenty-five or thirty years have figured in the sawdust ring. Chalk hides their wrinkles, dye-stuff their gray hairs, and skull caps their baldness. Yonder lady, who sits her steed gracefully, and who looks as blooming as a rose on a June morning, is not only a mother, but a grandmother. And there is George, who was engaged last winter 'to do nothing,' you know. He finds his duties embrace riding, leaping, tumbling, object-holding, and occasionally in 'short' times driving a team on the road. There is one rider who was formerly a manager himself. He had a big fortune once, but a few bad seasons swamped it, and he is now glad to take his place as a performer on a moderate salary. Returning to the dressing-room after the *entree* we find the clown engaged in putting the finishing touches to his costume. We must look closely to recognize him. He does not really seem to be the same fellow that we met at the breakfast-table, in stylish clothes and a shirt-front ornamented with a California diamond. He has given himself an impossible moustache, with charcoal, and has painted bright red spots on his powdered cheeks. You think him a mere boy as he springs into the ring, but he has been a 'mere boy' for many a long year, and his bones are getting stiff and his joints ache in spite of his assumed agility. The 'gags' that he repeats and the songs which make you laugh are not funny to him, for he has repeated them in precisely the same tone and with exactly the same inflection for an indefinite number of nights. He comes out to play for the 'principal act' of horsemanship. Meantime, in the dressing-room, the acrobats, if the air is chilly, are wrapping themselves in blankets or moving about to keep warm. When the 'bare-back rider' returns from the ring, he usually disrobes, takes a bath, and dons his ordinary attire; but the less important performers must keep themselves in readiness to render any assistance which they may be called upon to perform. There is but little repose for the weary circus people during a season. Frequently they stay but one day in a place, and the next town is fifteen or twenty miles distant. All the properties must be packed up, the helmets and cheap velvet, the tights and the tunics must be stowed away, and the journey made by night. It is morning when they reach their destination and ere long they have to go through with the 'grand procession;' then comes dinner; then the afternoon performance; the brief interval; supper; the evening exhibition, and then another night's travel. It isn't safe to bet on more than five hours sleep out of the twenty-four, and the 'talent' musn't be over nice as to where and when he takes his uncertain snoozes. In view of the hard work and the frequent exposures to the elements it is a noticeable fact that the average health of the circus people is very good. The season over, the company disperses, most of the members lavishly spending their hard-earned salaries, and 'touching bottom' before the winter fairly sets in. By January you will find many of them back at their favorite hotel, anxiously awaiting a fresh engagement for the next season.

"In the month of January the 'talent' for the forthcoming summer season is usually engaged by the circus managers, written contracts are duly entered into, and are properly signed, sealed and delivered—provided, of course, that the 'talent' can write. *Entre nous*—I have noticed that students, clergymen and men of sedentary habits generally, were particularly fond of displaying their physical ability. And so the circus folk, on the other hand, pride themselves on mental culture. If one of their number can write a passable song—no carping criticisms are made on troublesome *iambics* and *trochaics*—he is greatly admired, and is held up as a paragon of intellectual excellence. The man who can turn all imaginable 'flip flaps' and who rides with exceeding grace, would much prefer that you should praise his penmanship than his horsemanship. The circus people usually congregate during the winter at some well-kept, moderate-priced hotel. If the landlord be a thoughtful, good-hearted man, his reputation slowly but surely spreads through the country, and his tavern eventually becomes a sort of headquarters for the profession. To such a place come with me on a winter morning, and we shall see what we shall see. We enter a room fifty feet long by twenty wide, which answers for the office and bar of the circus hotel. This room is well filled; in fact, crowded. And of this assemblage six are managers and seventy-five are 'talent.' The talent awaits engagement, and the managers have come to fill up their lists for the tenting season. We approach a round-faced jolly-looking man who evidently has stamps in his pocket. He is talking to a big fellow, a manager like himself, whom he calls 'Doctor.' He seems to be in a confidential humor, for he says: 'Well, Doc, I had the poorest show on the road last season, but I made stacks of money, and all by advertising. I had one little sick elephant, about as big as a horse; and the bills used to say that there was a herd of elephants, including several trained animals and a few wild ones. I also had the names of all the best talent in the country on my bills, though in point of fact my company consisted of only five persons, and they were no great shakes.

My 'celebrated five-pole tent' had left four of its poles somewhere and leaked pretty bad in rainy weather. 'But,' adds the complacent manager, 'I'm going to have a bully show this year.' The doctor chuckles, and arm-in-arm they walk deeper into the room where riders, acrobats, gymnasts and clowns are waiting for something to turn up. Contracts are made something in this style: 'Holloa, George,' says the manager, 'have you got an engagement for the next season?' 'No, not yet.' 'What's your price?' 'A hundred dollars a week.' 'One hundred dollars for doing what?' 'The double somersault, the two horse act and leaping.' 'Oh, we don't want that. We've got too many riders and leapers already; all that we care for is your name; that's worth something, of course; but no such figure as you mention. You'll have nothing to do except the double somersault.' And so after plenty of haggling, the price is fixed upon and the engagement made. The clown, who has quite ceased to be a funny fellow, holds out with great pertinacity for an extra ten dollars, while the 'Brothers,' who are very seldom brothers, refuse to come down in price or to take any new brothers into the family excepting on liberal terms. As soon as a performer is engaged he subsides into the nearest seat and leaves the coast clear for those whose future is not yet settled. The work occupies the greater part of the day, but usually before night the available talent of that hotel is booked for the tenting season, which, as is generally known, covers a space of twenty-six weeks. As I have said all this occurs in January. Between that time and April, when the show starts out, the circus actors are frequently short of funds and are sometimes broke. Then it is that the landlord's good nature and kindness are tested. First, he must sift the 'beats' from their more worthy brethren. With the former class he deals sternly, showing them no mercy.

But those whom he has trusted before and who have come honorably to him when they received their salaries, and liquidated their bills, he treats with great consideration, not only trusting them, but occasionally supplying them with small sums of money. He seldom loses by thus casting his bread upon the waters, but receives gratitude and greenbacks as his just reward. In comparative idleness the winter passes with the circus people, but in April comes an excitement, a bustling, a general packing up. The 'properties' are brought forth, the horses are trotted out, the freshly painted band chariot is exposed to view and things generally are arranged for the tramp."

The circus clown and the stage clown of pantomime are two very different creatures. The one talks—and usually his wit is coarse, his humor vulgar, his jokes old and stupid. I never could understand what people found to laugh at in the stale stupidities of the poor old circus clown.

The pantomime clown seldom talks; and when he does he is usually as stupid as the circus clown; but he has a wealth of laughter-provoking power in his whitened face.

Pantomime, as a means of expressing ideas, may be one of the most beautiful of arts, in the hands of a man or woman of genuine artistic ability.

The origin of pantomime was no doubt synonymous with the linguistic troubles which developed themselves at the tower of Babel.

There is as good warrant for pantomime on the stage as for any other representation in the way of "holding the mirror up to nature." Richardson relates that there is a dialect of hands, arms and features in common vogue between white men and Indians. "A trapper meets a dozen savages all of different tribes, and though no two have ten articulate words in common, they converse for hours in dumb show, comprehending each other perfectly, and often relating incidents which cause uproarious laughter, or excite the sterner passions. To a novice, these signs are no more intelligible than so many vagaries of St. Vitus' dance; but like all mysteries, they are simple and significant—after one comprehends them. All Indian languages are so imperfect that even when two members of the same tribe converse, half the intercourse is carried on by signs. Mountain men become so accustomed to this, that when talking in their mother tongue upon the most abstract subjects, their arms and bodies will participate in the conversation. Like the Kanakas of the Sandwich Islands, they are unable to talk with their hands tied. Thus the Greeks carry on long dialogues in silence; and the Italians, when in fear of being overheard, often stop in the middle of a sentence to finish it in pantomime. It is even related that a great conspiracy on the Mediterranean was organized not only without vocal utterance, but by facial signs, without employing the hands at all. How much more expressive than spoken words is a shrug of the shoulders, a scowl, or the turning up of the nose! The supple tongue may deceive, but few can discipline the expression of the face into a persistent falsehood; and no man can tell a lie—an absolute, unmitigated lie—with his eyes. If closely and steadily watched, they will reveal the truth, be it love, or hate, or indifference."

An evening of English pantomime is a scene of great juvenile hilarity. There is nothing the bold Briton so dotes upon—in his youth, at any rate. The great pantomime occasion of the year is Boxing Night—which is the night of the twenty-sixth of December. "The turkeys have been carved, the plum-puddings have been eaten, and the mince-pies disposed of. Bills are pouring in upon paterfamilias; crossing-sweepers, with sprigs of holly in their brooms, are doubly assiduous in wishing pedestrians the compliments of the season; crowds of holiday-makers throng the streets, and block up shop-windows, and Messrs. Tacks, Hammer and Bradawl are slaving away for the honor of the Theatres Royal, to which they are attached, to complete the preparations for the first representation of the 'Grand and original Christmas pantomime of Harlequin King Canute, or, The fourteen Princesses of Pearldom.' The good-natured father, taking dress-circle tickets at the box-office, thinks nothing of the hurrying to and fro, of the hammering, painting and polishing going on within the dingy brick walls; the languid gentleman who has agreed to be present in a private box at the first representation of the pantomime, does not trouble his head about the labor and talent employed in producing the grand scene of the Princess Peewit's Palace of Pearls; and the students of the many-colored posters stuck upon the boardings of the metropolis care nothing respecting the means by which the Demon Discord's dismal dungeon is to be transformed into the realms of dazzling light. Messrs. Tacks, Hammer and Bradawl slave, without ceasing, surrounded by glue, beer-cans, shavings and tools, while fairies in dingy skirts practice their poses under the direction of a blustering ballet-master. But what have the public to do with this, provided the curtain rises at the proper time on the opening scene of the grand new pantomime of 'Harlequin King Canute?' Ting-a-ring-a-ting sounds the prompter's bell, and the orchestra strikes up an overture of popular airs, to the great delight of the gallery, who recognize their favorite tunes and keep time with their feet, and to the still greater pleasure of the junior members of a numerous family of children, who crowd one another against the edge of a private box, standing literally on the tiptoe of expectation, and peer and peep and gaze in wonder, first on the brilliantly lighted, crowded house and then on the dull green baize which shuts out fairyland. Hark! the prompter's bell a second time, and the curtain rolls slowly up and discovers the abode of the Demon Discord. There is Mr. Sittyman, smiling good naturedly, and holding his youngest in his arms, quieting her fears of the Demon Discord with acidulated drops, and pointing out the beauties of the Bower of Everlasting Peas with a fat, stubby finger. Mr. Sittyman is a hard-working merchant, who goes home by the six o'clock omnibus to Peckham with the regularity of clockwork, and whose only dissipation in the year is this one visit to the theatre with his children on Boxing Night. What a day this twenty-sixth of December has been to Mrs. Sittyman at Peckham, preparing for the annual festivity! What ironing of muslin frocks, sewing on of buttons to tiny garments, and finally, what bustle and confusion, packing the entire family into a cab to set off to meet papa in St. Alphage Lane! It was a severe trial, doubtless, for Mr. Adolphus Sittyman, aged seventeen, to enter the theatre with a laughing sister of eight clinging to him, and asking absurd questions in a terribly loud voice, while a juvenile brother clutched his coat-tails—the tails of that sacred thing, a first dress-coat—and shrieked with laughter at some joke of papa's. A severe trial for Mr. Adolphus, who last pantomime season had only been Master Dolly in a jacket and lay-down collars, home from school for the Christmas holidays, but who is now a man of business, glib in City quotations, cognisant of Mincing Lane matters, and interested in the rise and fall of stock. Next to Mr. Adolphus in order of seniority is Miss Adelgitha, a blooming damsel of ten, who has, with Sittyman precocity, already attained the 'first sweetheart' stage of life, has interchanged sugarsticks with the object of her affections, and has danced with him an entire evening at Mrs. Mincing's ball. Alas, for the fickleness of the female heart! Miss Adelgitha, this twenty-sixth of December, is enslaved anew by the prince in the pantomime, and that her Arthur Henry, in tunic and knickerbockers, is already forgotten for the velvet-caped, silk-stockinged scion of a regal house, who puns, sings, and dances with mock hilarity before a sham castle on the boards of the Theatre Royal. Miss Rosalind Sittyman is there, too, with large dark wide-open eyes, drinking in eagerly the wonderful sight before her, and Master Horace lounges in front of her, dividing his attention between a cake and the antics of the Demon Discord. See, my good friend, the grand transformation scene is about to commence. The dismal dungeon of the demon parts in the centre, and the realms of dazzling light are disclosed, glittering and sparkling with the greatest attainable theatrical brilliancy. Every moment fresh beauties are disclosed to the open-eyed children, who clap their tiny hands together and vie with each other in exclamatory 'oh my's,' till the culminating point is reached and Clown, welcomed with a shout of delight, comes bounding on the stage followed by Pantaloon, while Harlequin and Columbine pose themselves in graceful attitudes in the full glare of the colored fire. * * * But through the chinks of this interesting scene, before which Harlequin and Columbine are dancing with so much animation, I can see the gleams of light for the finale, which tell me the grand Christmas pantomime of 'Harlequin King Canute' is drawing to an end. The final chord is played in the orchestra, the green baize has fallen on the last scene, the box-keepers are tying Holland pinafores over the ormolu, and the vast audience is pushing and rushing and fighting its way out into the cold, slushy streets, setting us an example which we, my patient companion, had better follow, unless you choose to remain here through the night, to picture to yourself the different occupants those boxes into which we have been gazing may have had since the first opening of the theatre."

CHAPTER XXIX.

American and Foreign Theatres Contrasted.—Scenic Superiority in this Country.—Full Dress in London Theatres.—Curiosities of Accent.—The Pit and the Pea Nut.—The Dress of English and American Actresses.—Behind the Scenes.—Stage Banquets.—The Vanishing Green-room.—The New York Stage as seen by English Eyes.—Decorous Audiences.—Persistent Play-goers.—The Star System.—Poor Encouragement to Dramatists.—The English and French Stage Compared.—"The Cross of my Mother."—Decline of the British Stage.—The Dramatist's Power.—London Theatres.—The Most Celebrated Playhouses of Europe.—Theatres in Germany.

Until late years, the stage decorations of American theatres have been of so poor a description that my first entrance into a prominent London theatre, about ten years ago, struck me with speechless astonishment at the beauty of the *mise en scene*, which was far above anything I had ever seen in America—of whose theatres I had been a *habitue*, both "in front" and "behind the scenes," since my earliest childhood.

The play, I remember, was one in which Miss Amy Sedgwick appeared, and the whole performance was so good that it was to me like a revelation in histrionic art.

Passing my time about equally between Paris and London for the six years following this event, I was able to form a pretty correct idea of theatrical matters in these two centres of civilization, and to compare their theatres with those of America when I returned to my native country in '62.

Then I found that American managers had discovered the great fact that comfortable seats in the auditorium, plenty of chandeliers, and the tabooing of babies in arms, were not all that was required to make a play attractive, and had consequently begun to adopt the European plan of "mounting" every piece which they thought destined for a "run."

This needed reform soon bore its fruits; and now it is not too much to say that New York can safely compete in almost every respect with any London theatre, whatever its grade.

I dare not extend the boastful comparison to the theatres of Paris, for the trail of the Gymnase is over me still, and the halo of the Comedie Francaise is as bright a nimbus in memory's heaven as though half a dozen years, headed by a rebellion, punctured with a war, closed with a peace, had not passed since I sat in that classic temple and listened to "Britannicus."

Many pieces which have been brought out in London and considered well mounted there, have been transferred to New York and placed upon the stage in such a way as quite to throw their original decking into the shade. As an instance, I may cite the comedy of "Ours," which an English officer who had seen the piece in London and had taken a great interest in it on account of having served in the Crimean war, told me was placed on the stage at Wallack's Theatre so much better than in London as almost to be unrecognizable. This was not due, however, to the superiority of the scenic artists—for in this direction the Americans were not to be compared to the English —but to the extreme care bestowed upon other details by the management: the reckless extravagance in furniture, pianos, paintings, etc., of whose richness I can give no better idea than by saying they looked as though transplanted from a Fifth avenue drawing-room.

It seemed to me during my different visits to London, and in course of conversation about theatres with English people, that an idea prevailed that, in American theatres, were invariably presented entertainments of a low order, and that American audiences were composed in great part of Pike's Peak miners sitting in the best boxes in their shirt-sleeves, and with their legs up.

To visit one of those American theatres, and to observe the elegance of the ladies' toilets, the "stunning" get-up of the *jeunesse* greenbacked of New York, the wild extravagance of outlay in both sexes, is to correct this idea at once.

As for the entertainment itself, it is usually as near the European model as three times the money expended on it there can make it.

In England, I found prevailing a rather stupid rule, that a lady must be in "full dress" to go to the best seats in any theatre; and I well remember with what annoyance I removed my bonnet, in obedience to a peremptory command to that effect from the ticket-seller at Astley's. To enter that sacred abode of horsey art, I was told, I must be in full dress. To go in full dress to a circus seemed a very stupid thing to do.

Besides, did the mere removal of the obnoxious bonnet constitute "full dress" in England? My own American idea of full dress meant a diamond necklace and as little else as possible. Then, again, the gentlemen of our party had thick shoes on, and, if I am not mistaken, these were rather muddy from walking about London streets all day engaged in sight-seeing. *Their* dress, however, was not objected to; and, my bonnet removed, the whole party was immediately in that "full dress" which the high-toned entertainment presented at Astley's rendered indispensable!

This same full dress so generally prevailing in England is frequently so shabby that the appearance of an English theatre compares most unfavorably with that of the same species of entertainment in America. I do not now speak of the toilets of those English ladies who can afford any Parisian luxuries their taste may dictate, but rather of that middle class of gentlewomen who, compelled to be in full dress, compromise the matter by appearing in old-fashioned and unbecoming opera cloaks, with faded artificial roses in their hair, and not infrequently soiled gloves. Perhaps these same ladies have bonnets or round hats and neatly fitting velvet or silk jackets at home, in which —if they were allowed to wear them at theatres—they would look as well dressed as the American ladies.

That the American custom is an agreeable and convenient one is very evident from the fact that English ladies visiting Paris theatres, where it is also in vogue, quickly and gladly adopt it. Nor can it be urged that there is anything inelegant about it; for bonnets and street-jackets, as all continental travelers know, are not pronounced *mauvais ton* even at the Italiens in Paris.

In regard to the comparative excellence of the acting at American and foreign theatres, I may quote Mr. Boucicault, who says it is better here than in England; and in the better class of our theatres I think it is. The only branch in which we are distanced is in the field of burlesque, which American actors and actresses as a class are incapable of portraying.

Where American histrionic talent shines most brightly is in fine sentiment or tragedy, and were it not that the American accent is so distasteful to English ears, I think such an actress as Mrs. Chanfrau, and one or two other beautiful and sympathetic young women now charming American audiences, would scarcely have the meed of praise withheld from them by that London public which every player holds in such high esteem.

It is rather curious that the American accent should be so unpleasant to English audiences, while the English accent is received without comment by the American public. "It is as far from your house to my house, as it is from my house to your house." If the Yankee twang is objected to by London audiences, I see no reason why dropped and inserted "h's" and the like should not be rebelled against by Americans.

For it must be remembered that while a few bright particular stars of England consent to shine in the American horizon, that same horizon is densely clouded with the very refuse of the British stage; the tramps of circuit actors; such "barn-door" mouthers as lived and traveled even in *Hamlet's* time. These are the people who, in receipt of salaries such as the leading professionals in England do not obtain, are constantly grumbling at and abusing this country, and threatening to return to H'England —a menace they always fail to carry out.

The French accent appears to be rather an advantage than otherwise in London, when we remember the success of Mr. Fechter and Mlle. Stella Colas. In New York, however, we carry the cosmopolitan spirit still further, as was shown one winter by our supporting a French theatre, two German theatres, two Italian troupes, one lyric and one dramatic, and a French opera—to say nothing of wandering Japanese, Chinese and Arabs! Their polyglot performances were not, as one might suppose, sustained solely by the foreign-born citizens who speak the foreign tongue in which they were given; but, with an absurdity which words fail to express, they were listened to by vast crowds of Americans, who would sit for from three to six mortal hours listening to a play whose language they did not understand.

I am very certain in no other country in the world would Madame Ristori have been able to make in one short season the great sum of one hundred and fifty thousand dollars for her own "share."

The "pit," which is so common in London, has for years had in American theatres no existence, except in the sole instance of the Old Bowery Theatre, where, until very recently, the odoriferous peanut was munched and the critical newsboy took his nightly sup of histrionic horrors.

The peanut is a production of Southern soil, and I believe is unknown in England—thrice happy in the ignorance; and as in German music halls "c-a-k-e-s—p-r-e-t-z-e-l-s" are hawked with sleepy perseverance, so in the Old Bowery Theatre an odious little ragamuffin carried about a ricketty basket containing apples, oranges and "candy," while, above and before all, *bonne-bouche* intended for dirty *bouches*, "p-e-a-n-u-t-s" made vocal all the air. The "Bowery boy" might be jacketless, hatless and barefooted, but he purchased largely of the crisp-coated nut, and thereupon rose on the atmosphere a strange earthy odor, which no one who has once smelled it can ever forget.

In all the numberless theatres which America can boast of or blush for, there is now no instance to record where the ginger beer, so disagreeably frequent in English pits, is allowed to be popped; there are no apples, oranges, nor other edibles; in fact, there is no pit at all.

The dress of American actresses is more luxurious than any one who has not seen it would believe; as far above that of English actresses as a pound is above a dollar; so extravagant, indeed, that, in spite of the large salaries given, American actresses are almost invariably required to do so much in the way of toilet, that it is no unusual thing for them to be largely in debt at the box-office; the yearly benefit only sets them "square" again with the world, leaving them iu the unpleasant predicament of having worked the whole season for nothing but a livelihood. Nor can they ever be said to reach that point where what is technically known as a "wardrobe" has been purchased, and will now serve them the rest of their days. The American actress must vary her dress with

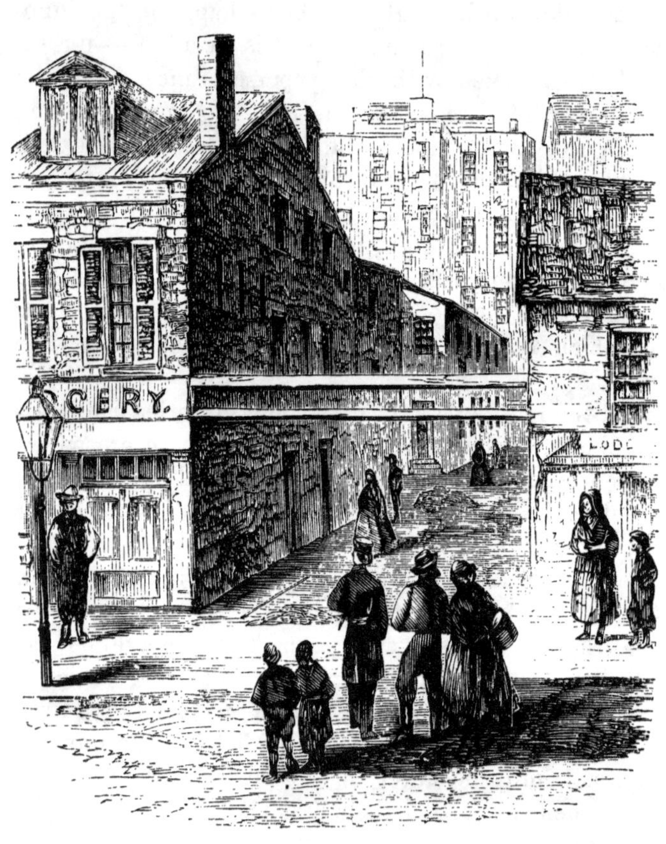
CERY.
LODG

every varying fashion. Modern comedies require modern toilets, and that these are expensive, every married man can testify.

It is related of Miss Madeline Henriques, leading lady of Wallack's, that she once said her salary was not much more than sufficient to keep her in boots and gloves. Her father being a successful merchant, and her benefit receipts being always enormous, enabled her to hold the position with *eclat.*

This extravagant system of stage toilet was "inaugurated" by a leading actress known to every visitor of New York theatres during the last dozen years—Mrs. John Hoey, a fortunate lady who made one of those splendid matrimonial *partis* which actresses are reputed to be in the habit of making so frequently.

This lady, whose husband unselfishly permitted her to remain on the stage merely because she was fond of it had a merchant-princely income at her disposal and spent it in a regally artistic manner of habiting herself.

Lady Teazle— who would "rather be out of the world than out of the fashion"—was less elegantly attired than her American impersonator.

Julia in the "Hunchback," was going to have "not brooches, rings and ear-rings only, but whole necklaces and stomachers of gems." Mrs. Hoey, who played the part, had all these. *Julia* says, "then will I show you lace a foot deep, can I purchase it." Mrs. Hoey had purchased it long ago.

Nor has this extravagant system gone out with the retirement of Mrs. Hoey. It is true other actresses cannot boast of such diamonds and laces as hers; but for silks, velvets, satins, *moires*, and the countless paraphernalia of a fashionable woman's toilet, those who succeed her dare not be far behind.

An item copied from Paris papers informs us that Adelina Patti recently wore a dress that cost two thousand francs. I do not know why American newspapers should copy this as an extraordinary bit of information, for it was a frequent thing to see Mrs. Hoey on the stage with a dress which cost twice that amount; and even now it is quite a common matter for actresses to wear dresses which cost two and even three hundred dollars.

English actresses coming to America and bringing the thin satins and well-worn velvets which have served them for years, are frequently surprised to see subordinates of the company walk on the stage so finely dressed as quite to overshadow themselves.

Strolling behind the scenes, we find pretty much the same set of rules in vogue in American theatres as in those of England. We have no national anthem to be sung, which necessitates the assistance of every member of the company; the dirge in "Romeo and Juliet" is now "cut out," and the masquerade scene of the same piece is generally filled up by supernumerary aid, or not filled up at all; but the choruses of "Macbeth" and "Pizarro" still call for the grumbling lyrical efforts of every individual, from the leading lady down to the call-boy, in American as in English theatres.

The halcyon days of comfort for players, both in England and America, are over, it appears. No longer are succulent viands prepared for stage eating; no longer are bottles of porter provided for stage drinking; indeed, nothing is provided for stage drinking nowadays, and actors sigh as they drink it out of golden pasteboard goblets and solid wooden jugs.

Perhaps this is the reason why the festive bowl is so often drained by professionals in private.

Except in a few theatres which cling to the old customs, the luxury of a call-boy has been dispensed with, and players are now obliged to hang wearily around the wings till the cue is given and they may "go on." Formerly, they were permitted to remain in the green-room until within about five minutes of their appearance, and thus much fatigue was saved. Now, in many cases, the green-room itself has been dispensed with, and the call-boy's occupation is, like *Othello's*, gone.

The disappearance of the green-room was caused by the new fashion of building "stores," warehouses and the like, on the ground story of theatres, which reduced the temples of histrionism to the smallest possible space, scarcely providing for dressing-rooms, much less for the luxury of the green-room.

This system prevails principally in the West, for in New York, Boston and Philadelphia theatres are conducted with more liberality than anywhere else in the United States.

Mr. John Hollingshead, the dramatic critic of the London *Times*, was in this country some two years ago, "takin' notes," and when he returned to London he did "prent 'em." As a singular illustration of the mixture of stuff and sense which so many foreigners write after a week or two of observation in this country, this gentleman's article is here quoted from at length. "With the exception of the Bowery," he says, "the New York theatres, considered as edifices, furnish models which the London architect would do well to imitate, as they are light, commodious, and so arranged as to allow nearly the whole of the audience a good view of the stage. The theatres in London that most resemble them are Astley's, in its present condition, and the small house at Highbury Barn. But a far better imitation—one, indeed, that exceeds the originals—is the Alexandria Theatre, Liverpool, in which the lightness of the American house is qualified by gorgeous 'appointments' scarcely to be matched anywhere. The New York audiences are, for the most part, extremely sedate and decorous, and, save at the Bowery, seem devoid of the decidedly plebeian element. This deficiency, which, perhaps, more than any other peculiarity, renders an American audience remarkable to an English visitor, may be attributed partly to the architectural arrangement by which the gallery, with its low-priced seats, is kept out of sight, partly to a disposition among the operative classes to make as good a figure as their fellow-citizens. It is is quite probable that a workingman may be among the aristocrats of the house, a contingency which is scarcely possible at a fashionable London theatre. The sedateness of the New York public may, however, be suddenly broken up when a change seems least to be expected, and an assembly that has apparently been composed of stern judges will at once be tickled with a straw. Of this we had one instance in the enthusiastic delight created by Lotta, in the 'Pet of the Petticoats.' Nor does the Puritanical element of the population at all control the moral tone of the theatre as it does in England. It keeps several people away altogether, and confines them to 'museums' and concerts; but those who have once passed the Rubicon that separates the playhouse from the rest of the world will endure grazes on propriety that would scarcely be tolerated in London. The people of New York are, as a rule, resolute playgoers, like the people of Paris. The formal and decorous are quite as steady in the patronage of the drama as those who make noisy demonstrations of delight, and the theatre is a necessary social institution in America, to a degree which can scarcely be conceived by the ordinary Londoner. The merchant of the British capital, who retreats from the neighborhood of the Exchange to his handsome suburban villa, and there

"'——otium et oppidi,
Laudat rura sui,'

has quitted the theatrical world altogether, and, if he speaks of the stage at all, refers to his early patronage of it as to one of the venial sins of his youth. The commercial grandee of Wall street, on the other hand, who performs an analogous operation by moving from New York to the adjacent city of Brooklyn when the hours of business are over, finds two theatres in his vicinity. Fancy two big play-houses at Clapham, or Tottenham, or Holloway, sufficiently patronized to permit the engagement of the first actors of the country! With all their ardent love for theatrical amusement, I have no hesitation in saying that the Americans care much more for the actors than for the merits of the play itself. This predilection is consistently accompanied by a regard less to a perfect *ensemble* than to the excellency of the 'star' of the evening; and granted the almost impossible case of a theatrical critic devoting the whole of his notices to the exclusive exaltation of one particular artist at the expense of every other member of the profession, New York would offer a fine field for his exertions, with, however, this drawback— that he would be answered by literary opponents in a plain, 'show up' kind of style, totally unlike anything in the old country. Youth and personal appearance have much to do with the success of a female artist, and, I fear, are allowed to overbalance the proper estimation of talent. At the present day, no performer who is regarded as *passe* in London, should look for success in America, unless backed by a reputation sufficiently large to awaken universal curiosity. As a consequence of this fact, I would, however, mention another, which is of high importance to the English public, and that is that the 'star system' prevails in America to an extent elsewhere unknown. Wallack's regular company stands, indeed, apart from the rest, but an actor at any other theatre, who has only appeared as one of the 'stock,' never as a 'star,' has obtained no testimonial whatever of the estimation in which he is held by the American public. * * * * Those who imagine that New York is a convenient place for carting off any old rubbish that is useless in Europe, are egregiously mistaken. The Americans can appreciate histrionic excellence, and they have appetite for novelty, but for anything that is neither new nor good, they have no relish whatever. And let me emphatically repeat an assertion which I made on a former occasion, that there is nothing vulgarizing in their influence. Like all other people, they may be tickled by an oddity, but they are perfectly capable of appreciating the utmost refinement in acting. To prove this assertion, I need only refer to the crowds who have thronged to witness Mr. Jefferson's representations of 'Rip Van Winkle.' To the dramatist, save under certain exceptional circumstances, New York offers, in my opinion, but slight encouragement. In the first place there is the international law, or, rather lack of law, which permits the manager of the American theatre to use the whole of the London repertory gratis; in the second, a piece that has already received applause in the old country, will be preferred to one that has already passed no ordeal whatever. But a great scene painter would, I think, find it worth his while to cross the Atlantic. He would find a people endued with an almost morbid appetite for scenic decoration, and no artist at hand at all to supply the demand. The grand scenes are now purchased in England, to be taken to America after they have answered pantomimic purposes at home; but there is plenty of money to pay for them if they were shown at New York, in the first instance, and they do not come like a celebrated piece on the strength of their English reputation. The lack of scenic art cannot be better expressed than by the assertion that, whereas in London even the humblest theatres can boast of a well-executed drop-curtain, such a luxury is rare at New York. If, however, some undaunted genius should aspire to write original plays for New York, in spite of all judicious warnings to the contrary, I would advise him to try his hand at a class of composition which, without the assistance of a manager filled with the spirit of Mr. Charles Kean, would not gain for him a single sixpence in London. Let him write big dramas—the larger the better, on subjects borrowed from the earlier history of England, and as historical as possible in their character. Queen Elizabeth and Mary Stuart, for instance, are rather bores than otherwise to the irreverent play-goers of England, but the Americans look to them as their noted ancestors, much as the aristocrats of Athens looked to the mythic founders of their families. Nor must the plays be written in an anti-English spirit; for, amid all the bickerings between the two nations, the Americans harbor a deep love for their Old World, and if a date is taken prior to that of the family quarrel, this feeling can express itself without restraint—don't let King Philip conquer Queen Elizabeth, especially while Cuba belongs to the Spaniards. And so much for the stage in New York."

A comparison of the English and French stage would show an immeasurable superiority on the part of the latter.

In no country, I think, is dramatic art so much esteemed, as in France; and it is a mistake to suppose that the lascivious dances recently imported to this country from France are an index of French taste in theatricals.

Very far from it. The can-can is a dance-house institution—transplanted to the stage of what were once respectable American theatres from the dubious precincts of a public wine-garden.

The truth is, that "for two centuries the French drama

has in reality rested its whole fabric upon the development of character—upon causes which have determined certain men to do certain deeds. This school begins with Racine's 'Berenice,' which is from first to last, an inquisition into the depths of the human heart. No *roman d'analyse* of Madame Sand herself ever proved greater skill in the art of moral anatomy. And this is now the lasting principle of all the modern dramatists of France."

And the theatre in France is a key to the popular heart. For example—in spite of the general false opinion of Americans to the contrary—so strong is filial affection in France that those unerring painters of French life and morals, the French dramatists, have found, for years and years, that any pathetic allusion to "my mother" was sure of touching the right chord in the sympathetic breast ot the French audience.

A woman is depicted as about to go astray. Some one pronounces the name of her mother. She shrieks, clasps her hands,—and is saved.

A criminal is committing a midnight murder. About the neck of his victim is hung a cross, which on examination, in some mysterious way proves to have been at one time the property of the mother of the would-be assassin.

"The cross of my mother!" cries he; and wakes the sleeper and bids him go unharmed.

When those Americans and English, who so love the word "home," and what it implies, became familiar with the potent effect of such scenes as these on the sympathetic French theatre-audience, they saw therein a great cause for merriment, it seemed, and joyously bemocked the sentiment.

The French are sensitive to ridicule. By the joint efforts of these good English and Americans, who so love home, the "cross of my mother" has now fallen into disrepute among the *critics*, and awakens their merriment also, where formerly it moved them to the tenderest emotions; but with the uncritical (the real audience everywhere) the "cross of my mother" is as potent as ever.

The decline of the British stage is confessed in these terms by a distinguished English review: "We stood once highest among countries whose dramatic literature was the highest. We have entirely lost that position now. We stand, in the matter of dramatic literature, on a lower level than any other country in Europe. It will serve us as a justification to say that the taste for the drama itself has declined; for when our drama stood loftiest (in modern times), the drama was cultivated and respected in all other nations. And it is so at this moment in every other European country save England. It is in England only that the glory of the drama has gone down, and it is a fact much to be deplored, for it coincides with an undeniable degeneracy of taste, and it suppresses the noblest form of expression affected by the national tongue."

Of the power of the dramatist, the same reviewer thus speaks: "It is not true to say that a great poet has as much influence as a great dramatist; he has not, for the element of publicity is wanting; the electric action of soul upon soul, the immediate action of man upon man. It is for this that the drama in itself is the grandest form of expressed thought—it contains all others. To be a supreme dramatic poet (we will take Shakespeare, Calderon, Goethe, as the highest examples—Schiller comes long after) a man must be everything else. He must be a politician, a historian, a poet, a philosopher and an orator. He must combine two radically opposite natures, and be at once a man of action and of thought; he must conceive and criticise, but, above all, he must directly and publicly impress a crowd of other men. He must, with Egmont, teach tyrants of all times how they foolishly forfeit dominion; and with Hamlet reflect the impress of other men's deeds, and live perpetually irresolute, 'sicklied o'er' himself 'with the pale cast of thought.'"

It is stated by a well-informed person that there are in London twenty-one first-class and eleven second-class, in all thirty-two theatres, with an audience capacity of over 60,000. The largest will hold 3,923, and the smallest 360. The following are the names and numerical accommodations of the first-class houses, such as our Academies of Music, Wallack's and Booth's: Italian Opera House, Covent Garden, 2,750; Drury Lane Theatre, 3,800; Astley's Amphitheatre, 3,780; New Holborn Theatre, 2,000; New Queen's, 2,000; Holborn Amphitheatre, 2,000; Haymarket, 1,822; Adelphi, 1,500; Lyceum, 1,400; Sadlers' Wells, 2,300; Princesses', 1,579; St. James', 1,220; Olympic, 1,140; Strand, 1,081; Surrey, 1,802; Prince of Wales, 814; St. George's New Opera House, 800; New Royal Theatre, 722; Gallery of Illustration, 262; Cabinet, 370; Alexandra, 1,330. All the other theatres are called second-class, although some of them rank lower. London lovers of the drama who affect the startling and sanguinary school of art, illustrated for us in Bowery retreats, are thus distributed: Brittania, 3,923; Bower, 1,000; City of London, 2,500; Effingham, 2,150; Grecian, 2,120; Marylebone, 1,500; Pavilion, 3,500; Garrick, 800; Standard, 3,400; Victoria, 3,008; Oriental, 1,500.

Among the most celebrated playhouses of Europe is the San Carlo at Naples. This theatre was built in the time when the Kingdom of Naples was a Spanish viceroyalty. It is, with one exception, the largest theatre in Europe, and consequently in the world, having eight rows of boxes, one above another, until, to look from the uppermost, makes one giddy. Its acoustic properties are nevertheless splendid, the slightest note being distinctly heard at the greatest distance. "In its interior decorations it is magnificent, a wonderful amount of gilding being lavished on all parts of the house. As in all the opera houses of Italy, boxes take up almost the entire theatre. Besides a parquet below, and an amphitheatre running back behind the chandelier—a place reserved for the populace—there is nothing but boxes in endless profusion. The San Carlo contains 4,000 persons sitting, this plan of boxes necessarily diminishing the number of seats, while it wonderfully increases the comfort of the occupants. In such a theatre as this, if built on our plan of construction, 10,000 spectators could be easily accommodated. In this house Bellini first produced those works which have had such a world-wide popularity, 'Norma,' 'I Puritani,' etc., and Donizetti brought out his 'Figlia del Regimento,' 'Lucretia Borgia.' This was also the theatre of predilection with Mercadante, who is now ninety years of age, and blind. It was here, also, that took place a tragedy which alarmed Europe at the time. Nourrit, the great French tenor, had gone to Naples, and all expectantly waited his first night, which he confidently anticipated would be the greatest triumph of his life. 'William Tell' was the opera chosen for the occasion, Nourrit not fearing to make his *debut* in the most difficult tenor *role* known to the stage. The evening came. King and court were at the opera, and the best population of Naples filled the boxes and dazzled the eyes with their brilliancy of dress. Nourrit at his *entree* was received coldly, and so it went on until the third act, when he was hissed in his *ut de poitrinc.* It was the first time such a thing had ever happened to him. He rushed out of the theatre, not caring to finish the piece, went to his hotel, and, unable to survive such a disgrace, threw himself from his window and was instantly killed. It was afterwards discovered that those who had hissed him were in the pay of a rival tenor. The San Carlo is situated right on the bay of Naples, and for special occasions a means has been devised to open the entire background of the stage, and the beautiful bay itself takes the place of the painted canvas. The effect is magical. The Milan theatre known as La Scala is very celebrated. The building itself is homely from the outside, but inside its decorations of pure white-and-gold form a simple but beautiful effect. It contains seven rows of boxes. The two first rows have attached saloons, into which the owners retire between the acts, and in which cosy little suppers and card parties take place. It can easily be imagined that persons who go every night to the opera hardly care to give the works such constant attention as we do here, for instance, who go now and again, and for the purpose of listening. In Milan, each family of any consequence is owner of a box by the year, and each box is the exclusive property of the family that rents it. These boxes are even hereditary. The Duke of Litia, for instance, owns two boxes, for which he has been offered one million francs, but he refused to sell them. The stage of the Scala is the largest in the world, being the exact size of the theatre itself. Attached to the Scala is a Conservatory of Music, which has produced some of the most renowned singers the world has known; it also has a Conservatory of Dancing, which produces all the great dancers. Every *premiere danseuse* we have had here during the past few years received her spurs at the Scala. Morlacchi, Bonfanti, Sohlke, De Rosa, Sangali, all came from there. The largest theatre in the world is the Paliano, at Florence. It has seven rows of boxes, but they are immense, stretching in the form of a horse-shoe over a vast extent of ground. It is not a handsome theatre, and except as regarding its size is in no wise remarkable. The theatre contains 6,000 persons, seated, but, if open, like our theatres, could accommodate certainly 15,000. The Argentia, at Rome, is one of the most notable theatres in Italy, and peculiar from the fact that it exists in the very capital of the Catholic Church. Restrictive rules are applied which render the enjoyment of opera somewhat tedious at times. The Pope governs the theatre despotically, and decides whether certain artists shall or shall not be admitted to sing. One peculiar law is that no female artist shall wear anything but green tights, either in the opera or the ballet, which latter is very much liked in the Eternal City. Flesh-colored tights are considered indecent. The Grand Opera House at Vienna has been but recently constructed, having been inaugurated last summer. It surpasses anything in the way of theatres in the world, with the exception of the new opera house in Paris, which is now building. Its decorations are the colors now much in vogue—white, gold and red, and the general effect of the house is said to be very fine. The painting of the ceiling cost large sums of money, and has been done by the best artists. The exterior building is in a composite style, but is tasteful as well as elegant, and of great beauty of detail in its exterior sculptures. The inauguration of this fine theatre was a magnificent *fete*. The Emperor and Court were present, and delegates attended from all the musical societies of the Austrian Empire. The old opera house in the Rue Pelletier, Paris, is a homely building inside as well as out. It was put up in forty days, in 1811, and was merely meant to supply the want of the hour, while a more imposing building should be put up. But Napoleon's reverses came immediately after, and the great Emperor was forced to abandon his peace projects to wage war on the numerous enemies who assailed him. The opera house was therefore abandoned, and four years ago the legislative body, at the instance of the present Emperor, voted forty millions of francs for the construction of a new opera house. It was in the old house in the Rue Pelletier that Rossini brought out his immortal chef d'œuvre 'William Tell,' and that all Meyerbeer's works first saw light. It was here, also, that the attempt of Orsini to take Napoleon's life happened, in 1857. The Emperor was just getting out of his carriage, when a bomb struck it, breaking the carriage door, killing the coachman and horses, and causing a slight wound to the Emperor. In spite of the fearful emotion he must have felt, Napoleon sat out the entire opera, and he had the Empress carried up to her box, and obliged her likewise to sit next him, in full view of the enthusiastic Parisians. This event gained Napoleon more popularity than anything else he has done during his entire administration. The new opera house is situated between the Rue Auber and the Rue Scribe, facing the Grand Hotel. It occupies an entire block, and, when finished, will be the most magnificent edifice of the kind in the world. It is built of white marble, with mosaics of different colors. In every department, the best artists in France have been engaged to work on it. When finished, it will be an eighth wonder of the world. The entire inside of the auditorium is to be painted, and the decorations are to be in red, white and gold. The building is in no particular style of architecture, being *compose* in design. The doorways are on each side of the building—one for entrance and the other for exit, carriages being enabled to go through the building. The Emperor is thus enabled to drive right up to his box, and alight there. In many respects the architects have discarded old plans, and have introduced novel expedients for comfort and beauty. The old Covent Garden Theatre, in London, was burnt down in 1852, and the present one, much more beautiful, was built. The building is of white marble, and is of the Grecian style of architecture. The effect is very grand inside, rows of boxes extending, one above another, to a great height. It is a very popular theatre, but has a strong rival in Her Majesty's Theatre, in the Haymarket. When, a short time ago, this theatre was destroyed by fire, the Drury Lane was made the temporary resting place of the company which had been burnt out. This for a moment revived the prestige of Old Drury, the ancient house of the legitimate, where the elder Booth won his first triumphs. But no actor now lives who can fill Drury Lane by the sole loadstone of his talent."

With regard to the theatres of Germany, a gentleman visiting that country writes: "If a person would see a drama in its best dress, and learn to what state of perfection the theatre can be brought by wise management and a correct appreciation by the people whom it should instruct and amuse, he must come to Germany. He will find great actors very rare, but the stock companies most excellent. Throughout the year the drama and opera alternate, both companies occupying the same stage, each playing three or four times a week. A most admirable system prevails in Germany of pensioning aged actors and opera singers, provided they keep to their contracts, and remain as supports of single theatres. For example Niemann, when no longer fit for singing, will receive a pension varying with his length of service, but amply sufficient to support him and enable him to end his life in comfort. Nearly every theatre throughout Germany has this provision, and it obviates in a great measure the necessity of paying enormous salaries, as an actor, if faithful, will never be left a beggar when the public is satiated with him. The condition of their remaining by one theatre is, of course, necessary, but the tediousness of such an arrangement is relieved by the months (three or more each year) when the actor or singer travels about as 'Gastspeiler.' A great part of German play-houses are taken by subscribers, and the plays, therefore, must be constantly changed. These subscriptions are in the highest degree convenient, as one can pay for one, two or four representations a week as he pleases, and obtain his ticket at the same rate as if he subscribed for each night of the year. For example, I bought a ticket last fall which entitles me to a seat every *third* representation, whatever it may be. I have gone very regularly for five months, for the sake of learning the language quickly, as well as for amusement, and during five months have witnessed only *two* operas and *three* theatrical representations a second time. I admit that in remaining another year I should notice a great deal of repetition, but if the pieces are good, which is the case here, this is to be desired. As I said before, there are few actors who can compare with Sothern, Mathews or Kean; but too often one of these actors is supported at home with a company so miserable that it requires all their genius to prevent the play from falling lifeless upon the stage. Here, when 'Hamlet' is acted, the hero is not first-class, but his supporters, even 'Rosencrantz' and the second gravedigger, are perfect, and there is consequently a consistency and solidity about the play which more than makes up for the deficiency of *Hamlet* himself. The Germans require this—the journalist thinks it his duty to correct, in his daily critique, the humble members no less than the chief performers. The plays themselves are remarkably good, most of them native; but once a week one hears a translation from the English or French. I have only seen four broad farces during my stay in this city or in Dresden, and the only thing approaching a spectacle was a magic fountain upon the stage, upon which parti-colored light was thrown from an electric lamp. The prices are very low, and the accommodations excellent. The audiences, as a rule, are dressed as with us, neither more or less, and seated as in our theatres, with but few private boxes. A stranger would doubtless think them very stingy of their applause, and indeed that enthusiasm which takes our theatres by storm is hardly ever seen here. No singer, when encored, repeats the aria, as with us, but bows merely, and often when an actor receives an encore after fainting or killing himself, the curtain on rising discovers him in the same position in which he was last seen, and the audience is relieved from seeing a dead hero jump up and bow. This observance of common-sense rules, the excellence of the plays and actors in Germany, is owing to the interest taken in such matters by the people. The theatre is either the property of the city or partly endowed by the duke or king in whose dominion it is. As the actors are paid from the state or city, it behooves the people to see that they are good, and that the theatres themselves are as perfect as possible. As they support them, they deserve to find therein good entertainment, and gentlemen of talent and experience are always appointed to the management; those having direction of the Dresden and Leipsic theatres are noblemen. Though of course there are exceptions to this, yet, as a rule, Germans go to the opera and theatre as to a musical concert or gallery of paintings, to gratify a refined and educated taste."

CHAPTER XXX.

Literary Aspects of the Drama.—The King of Dramatists.—Shakespeare's Purity of Tone.—His Pictures of the Period.—His Contribution to General Literature.—Amusing French Blunders in Translating from Shakespeare.—"Who wrote Shikspur?"—An Amusing Travesty.—Shakespeare Reconstructed—Where Dramatists get their Plots.—High Art and Common Sense.—Patrick and the Bull.—Modern Comedy.—What it Needs.—Woman in Comedy.—Decency and Merriment.—Women Dramatists Wanted.—The Pay of Dramatists.—An Old-time Letter.—American Managers and American Playwrights.—How a Philadelphia Manager fooled the Public.—The Gentleman who improved on my "Surf" scene.—The Actor who Improved on his Improvement.—A Ghoulish Boston Notion.—Sensational Plays.—The "Lady of Lyons" Laughed at.—The Traditional Stage Sailor.

In its literary aspects, the stage illustrates at once the highest and the lowest intellectual effort.

All the way from Shakespeare, the king of dramatists, down to Boggs, the burlesque writer (who may be termed the insect of dramatists), the various gradations of human genius, talent, cleverness, so-soishness, stupidity and imbecility have from time to time found illustration on the theatrical stage.

That is of course a more agreeable and inspiring view to take of the dramatic literary world, which shuts out the insect and dwells upon the king.

The immortality of the drama, says an admirer of the theatre, "is inseparable from the immortality of poetry, music and painting. The caprice of fashion may give for a time allurement to other and very different enjoyments. The blunders which may be made from the incapacity or ignorance of directors, may so injure it that it cannot but droop and pine. Managers may be ruined by dozens, and great actors may for a time disappear; but the drama itself is not dead, but sleepeth. Each new generation must be made acquainted with Shakespeare. Editions of his works succeed each other with astonishing rapidity, and in no country has the great dramatist called forth to his illustration of late years, higher genius, profounder knowledge, or better taste than in our own. No polite education can be obtained without some acquaintance with this author; and the youthful reader will soon sigh for a living representation of the wonders of that creative pen. The student of Milton, Addison, Pope, Steel, Dryden, Young, Goldsmith, and all the chiefs of English literature, is hourly brought into feelings of interest for the drama and its actors. How absurd, then, to talk of the drama being nearly obsolete! Let a new Kean or a new O'Neal start forth into the mimic world, and the immense and deserved popularity of Rachel will soon cease to be the *latest* wonder. The importance of the stage is generally undervalued by many who do not, or will not perceive its immediate connection with morals and manners."

In spite of the sometimes objectionable language Shakespeare puts in the mouths of his characters, his teachings are singularly pure and noble. "Of all dramatists he is not only the greatest, but the most decorous and cleanly. His is a wit which never poisons our relations to humanity; his is a humor which never sinks into the slough of merely filthy imaginations; his is a broad and sunny fun, which maids and matrons, who were driven from the theatre when Aristophanes was played, can heartily enjoy without contamination. With man's highest faith and holiest hope his sympathy is constant. He approaches no sacred theme without a due sense of its holiness; the heaven of his inspiration is the heaven of our most precious revelation; he draws no ribald priests, and he casts no scorn upon religious belief, however humble or however erroneous; he has no sneer for marriage, no gibe for marital fidelity, no apology for the seducer; but, upon the contrary, a wonderful admiration for female purity, which no freak of unbridled fancy ever leads him to discard. He has left us thirty-seven of the best plays in the world, and not one of them has ever exercised an immoral influence upon young or old. Let that be at once his praise and the eternal vindication of the drama!"

Shakespeare's pictures of the period in which his plays are laid, are curiously accurate. A writer instances as one of the most remarkable of these his picture of the feeling of the days when witchcraft ruled. "When *Ford* lays his cudgel across the shoulders of *Falstaff*, supposing him to be the 'wise woman of Brentford,' he only does what all around approve. *Ford* is a gentleman and (excepting his groundless jealousy) a man of sense. In the presence of a justice of the peace, a clergyman and a physician, of his neighbor *Page*, and the several members of their families, he inflicts brutal chastisement upon an old woman, and not a word of remonstrance is uttered. There can be no doubt that Shakespeare has here given us a true picture of the feelings of his day. He has embodied the grander and more terrible idea of witchcraft in the tragedy of 'Macbeth.' There is scarcely an ingredient of the witches' cauldron for which an authority could not be found in some of the trials of that day. The details of the enchantment, the sailing in a sieve, the 'pilot's thumb,' the 'finger of birth-strangled babe,' the 'rat without a tail,' were all objects of terror in an age when it was believed that the life of the king had been endangered on his return from Denmark, by a storm raised by these very means, when the king himself had presided in person at the trials of the witches, 'taking great delight to be present at their examinations,' and had employed his royal pen to prove alike their existence and their criminality. The tailless rats were very peculiarly objects of terror. Imps, 'in shape somewhat like a rat, but without tail or ears—' 'things about the bignesse of mouses—' 'things like moles, having four feet a-piece, but without tayls,' meet us on every page of the witch trials."

Few people realize, I think, how much Shakespeare has contributed to general literature. Many of the expressions of the great poet are "household words" to those who have never seen a copy of his plays.—A very few illustrations will sufficiently prove this—for one might easily fill a chapter with examples. "Misery makes us acquainted with strange bedfellows;" "The Devil can cite Scripture;" "All that glitters is not gold;" "My cake is dough;" "Screw your courage to the sticking place;" "Scotched the snake, not killed it;" "Give the Devil his due;" "Tell the truth and shame the Devil;" "Very like a whale;" "The cat will mew, the dog will have his day;" "They laugh that win;" and so on. Besides these homely examples, many more poetic and grand illustrations of the universality of Shakespeare's genius might be given, but they are already the common property of mankind, and my readers need only wait until the next speech they hear, or not improbably—and with all due respect—until the next sermon.

The French—who have justly a most exalted opinion of their national dramatic literature—have translated many if not all of Shakespeare's plays; and some very amusing blunders in translation have passed into history. The exclamation

"Hail, horrors! hail!"

was once translated into the French of

"How d'ye do, horrors? how d'ye do?"

This is not more ridiculous than some of the blunders of a French commentator on "Hamlet." Speaking of Hamlet killing Polonius, the writer gives the English and the French translation of the words which accompany the *coup-de-grace*:—"*How how! a rat!*" "Qu'est-ce que cela? Un rien." (What is that? A nothing.) Again we have given by the same critic the following Shakesperean bit with the French translation of the meaning and of the dignity of the language:—

"Thou wretched, rash, intruding fool, farewell!
. . . . . take, thy fortune;
Thou find'st to be too busy is some danger."

"*Adieu, pauvre fou indiscret et temeraire, adieu! . . . . Subis ton sort! Tu as appris qu'il y a du danger a se trop meler des affaires d'autrui.*" (Good-bye, poor madman, indiscreet and rash, good-bye. Submit to thy fate! Thou hast learned that there is danger in mixing up too much in the business of other people.)

This does not equal the Gallic writer, who took *Macbeth* in hand, and praised Shakespeare for his great attention to particulars, instancing in proof his allusion to the climate of Scotland in the words, "Hail, hail, all hail!" *Grele, grele, toute grele!* (Hail, hail, everything is hailing.)

In the farce "High Life Below Stairs," the literary lady's maid was asked "Who wrote Shikspur?" and answered, "Why, Ben Jonson, to be sure."

In later days, there have been various efforts made to prove that somebody else beside Shakespeare wrote Shakespeare's works. A New England woman, Miss Delia Bacon, accredited Shakespeare's works to Lord Bacon, some years ago, in "Putnam's Magazine." The article failed to provoke a reply, and was not followed up by its intended succcessors. Miss Bacon went to England, and there elaborated her whole theory, publishing it in a ponderous octavo volume, which, in the words of her best if not her only apologist, Mr. Hawthorne, "fell with a dead thump at the feet of the public, and has never been picked up."

Apropos of this attempt, a wag has compiled the following patchwork—which reads like a travesty, but isn't one —and asks "*Did Shakespeare write this?*"

HAMLET (*Sol*)—To be or not to be? that is the question!
Whether 'tis nobler in the human mind to suffer
The slings and arrows of outrageous fortune,
Or,—Is this a dagger that I see before me,
The handle towards my hand—
Perdition catch my soul,
But I do—know a hawk from a handsaw!
Soft! I did but dream.—
By the pricking of my thumbs,
Something wicked this way comes.— [*Enter* FALSTAFF.]
I'll talk a word with this same learned Theban,—
The devil dye thee black, thou cream-fac'd loon,
Where got'st thou that—fair round belly with good capon lin'd?
FAL.—'Tis my vocation, Hal—
Let me have men about me that are fat.
[*To attendant.*]—Give me some drink, Titinius. [To HAMLET]—Thy father's spirit?
HAM.—No, my prophetic soul, my uncle's.
FAL.—As familiar in their mouth as household words—
Now the king—ay, every inch a king—[*drinks to* HAMLET—*Flourish.*]
Thou invisible spirit of wine,—there's lime in this sack!
HAM.—Thou canst not say I did it—
I am a man
More sinned against than sinning.
FAL. [*Aside.*]—Lord, how this world is given to lying!
HAM.—Oh, Romeo, Romeo, wherefore art thou—a fishmonger?
Most potent, grave, and therefore most valiant, JACK FALSTAFF,
Lend me your ears.—Who steals my purse steals trash,
'Tis something,—nothing.
FAL. [*Aside.*]—An infinite deal of nothing.
HAM.—I only speak right on, and tell you—
More things in heaven and earth
Than are dreamt of in—the very witching hour of night.
Be thou familiar, but by no means—very like a whale:
Take any shape but that!
FAL [*Aside.*]—A hit, a very palpable hit!
And damned be he who first cries "Hold, enough!" [*Exeunt.*]

This is Shakespeare reconstructed, I suppose—and very funny it reads.

But manager Wood, of Philadelphia, gives an account, in his "Recollections of the Stage," of a man who reconstructed Shakespeare in stupid earnest. "While my friend Wignell and myself were at our morning breakfast (the usual hour of unwelcome visitors), a well-dressed person of middle age was ushered in, as calling upon 'important business.' A ponderous roll of paper under his arm, led to a well-founded suspicion that he might prove to be an author. Such, indeed, was the fact, under some qualification, as will be seen. After briefly stating his object, he unfolded the mighty mass of paper destined for trial of poor Wignell's patience, and announced his work under this sounding title, 'The tragedy of Macbeth.' The manager delicately suggesting a doubt whether a subject treated by Shakespeare with more than even his usual genius, might not prove a dangerous experiment in other hands, was dryly answered by an assurance that the present effort was intended as a compliment and advantage to the great bard. A warm eulogy on Shakespeare's general merits followed, with, however, an essential reserve. All due praise was awarded to the general structure of his plays, his delineations of character and customs, 'but these merits were unhappily obscured by an antiquated and obsolete phraseology, wholly unsuited to modern taste. Many of his scenes and passages were barbarous and unintelligible to the masses, from the rough and ungraceful language in which they were given.' To remedy this serious defect, our friend had actually translated Shakespeare's poetry into very common-place prose, and on this novel production he demanded a trial of public judgment."

It has become so very common, in these days, to charge our modern dramatists with having stolen their plots—

> "Steal? foh! a fico for the phrase—
> 'Convey,' the wise it call,"—

that some curious references made recently by a New York lawyer, become specially interesting.

Boucicault's play of "After Dark" was in Court for some offense,—I really don't remember what it had been doing,—the principal thing I remember is that the trial was a good advertisement for the theatre where the play was running; and an effort was made to show that "After Dark" was plagiarized from the "Bohemians in Paris."

This was quite true, but how little it mattered was shrewdly shown by the lawyer on the Boucicault side—whose unlawyerlike and very theatrical name, by the way, was Booth,—in a speech as full of wisdom as an egg is of meat.

If his learned friend had ever read Milton's "Paradise Lost," said the lawyer with the tragic name, (whereupon the learned friend bridled indignantly at the insinuation that Milton was not his daily companion), he would no doubt be glad to know that it is founded on Biblical records. The description of the four rivers, the temptation of the woman, and the dialogue between the Creator and our first parents, are in Milton the same. Then take the play of "Macbeth"—no one would charge Shakespeare with being a literary pirate; but we find in *Hollingshead's Chronicle*, at pages 243 and 244, the character of *Lady Macbeth* sketched out. We find there also the greeting of the witches, which is almost word for word. We also find that the scene in the fourth act between *Malcolm* and *Macduff* was taken almost word for word from this book, which was published long before Shakespeare wrote. Let him try another. Let him take Shakespeare's "Coriolanus." In Worth's edition of Plutarch's Lives we find the germ of that play. The speech of Volumnia, in that play, commencing with "If we hold our peace, my son, and determine not to speak," etc., down for nearly a page, is from this, nearly word for word. Now, Mr. Boucicault has not taken his drama word for word, as these have done, from others. But, then, let them go on and examine "Hamlet." This is taken from *Belford's Chronicle*. The whole story of "Romeo and Juliet" is from Gerolamo's History of Venice. Then take the "Scarlet Letter," by Hawthorne, a most powerful story, and yet the whole germ will be found in *Winthrop's Chronicle*, called "Magnolia." The genius of Hawthorne stands at the head of letters, and no one will say that he was a mere plagiarist. One of Coleman's best comedies is taken from "the Spectator." Then there is a book called "Robinson Crusoe," which is believed to be gospel truth by every boy, until he attains twelve years of age, yet they could find the original of this by looking at a book published by Mr. Wood, in 1712. The story itself was written in 1719. Dampere, in his travels, relates some of the principal incidents of that book also; the prototype of the "man Friday" is to be found therein. It was never considered improper for an author to avail himself of antecedent incidents either historical or literary.

All of which is delightful information for rising authors, and most encouraging to the flourishers of borrowed plumage.

(Nevertheless I shall resist the temptation to omit quotation marks from the remainder of this work.)

I confess that sometimes when I have been obliged to sit through five weary acts of a new play by a new-fledged author, I have wished that he *had* stolen it, so that it might have been less tiresome.

If there is anything more dreary than a stilted imitation of Shakespeare (after the manner in which the frog imitated the ox) I pray to be spared experimental knowledge of it.

It is all very nice to talk about high-toned plays, but as a wiser than I has said, the dignity of a high aim cannot shed lustre on an imperfect execution, though to *some* extent it may lessen the contempt which follows upon failure. It is only success which can claim applause. Any fool can select a grand subject; and in general it is the tendency of fools to choose subjects which the strong feel to be too great. If a man can leap a five-barred gate, we applaud his agility; but if he attempt it, without a chance of success, the mud receives him, and we applaud the mud. This is too often forgotten by critics and artists, in their grandiloquence about "high art." No art can be high that is not good. A grand subject ceases to be grand when its treatment is feeble. It is a great mistake, as has been wittily said, "to fancy yourself a great painter because you paint with a big brush;" and there are unhappily too many big brushes in the hand of incompetence.

Efforts of this sort—and their lugubrious result—always remind me of the old story of Pat and the bull.

Patrick saw a bull pawing in a field, and thought what fun it would be to jump over, catch him by the horns, and rub his nose in the dirt. The idea was so funny that he lay down and laughed to think of it. The more he thought of it the funnier it seemed, and he determined to do it. Bovus quickly tossed him over the fence again. Somewhat bruised, Patrick leisurely picked himself up, with the consolatory reflection: "Well, it is a mighty foine thing I had my laugh foorst."

One of the finest discussions of the needs of modern comedy—with special reference to the place of my sex therein—which I have ever seen, is from the pen of Mr. Charles P. Congdon. "In comedy," he says, "we want women who are under the dominion, or doomed to be under it, of love, which is the paramount passion and prime necessity of the feminine nature, and not of hate, which deforms and distorts it—women whose logic is in their laughing eyes, and who are imperious by soft persuasion—women of that gentle wit which gives pleasure to its objects by the very pain which it inflicts—women of the world who are yet unworldly, and who move through the brilliant scenes of society without being unsexed by its corruptions—women whose native graces have been cultured but not conquered by conventionalities, and who, while weak in all chaste and honorable concession, are like the lioness despoiled of her young when tempted by sensual advances—women whom the virtuous need not fear to personate; upon whose personations the modest need not fear to look. What sin may not be as decorously rebuked upon the stage as in the pulpit? Have preachers always scorned the aid of wit, and of humor, and of facetious characterization, from Dr. Luther down to Sydney Smith? He who thinks that wit must be wicked makes as great a mistake as he who thinks that devotion must be dull. It is the blunder of an exceedingly coarse nature to suppose that all merriment must need be culpable, and that nothing can entertain us which is not contrary to good morals. This is a subacidulous theory which some may propound for the sake of a sour distinction, but according to which few live or affect to live. At every well-regulated breakfast table, under the ordinary circumstances of social life, there is, or should be, a new and glad comedy to inaugurate the day—an extemporized play of conversational pleasantries, of good-natured personalities, of attack without malice and retorts without anger. Whenever and whereever refined and educated men and women are gathered together, there is an improvised play enacted with a jovial and confiding sincerity, in which without exceeding the limits of good breeding, the frailties and the foibles of the company are thrown into a joint stock for the public amusement. Who finds this dull because there is a restraint upon his facetious fancies, and etiquette requires him to be decent? The man of the world, who in the drawing-room is delighted by the soft and swift repartee of a modest, and clever, and accomplished woman, would be none the less gratified could he see her, or something like her, reproduced at the theatre; for the presentation would be not only an immediate pleasure, but a pleasure of the memory. Should he wish for exaggerations or diminutions of nature's most excellent standard, he knows where the dwarfs and the giants, the very lean and the very fat are to be found. It is, or it should be, a slander upon any society to say that in dramatic representation it can relish only what is prurient. It is not too much to believe that if women wrote more frequently for the theatre they would impart to its exhibitions something of their own grace, purity and elegance; and it is certain that at the present time, under hardly any temptation to cater to the coarse and unthinking, would they venture upon the employment of those licentious baits of applause which men are not ashamed to use. She would rather seek to vindicate the dignity of her sex by presenting it in its most creditable estate, and by proving that brilliancy of mind and of manners need not argue depravity of heart. There would be a glory in the work; but there would be a consciousness of a noble service nobly performed, and of an exalting influence conscientiously exerted, which would, to an ingenuous mind, be worth all the fame and emolument which might incidentally follow. Nor can we forget that woman might in this way do something to consign to eternal oblivion those dramatic creations which reflect only discredit and dishonor upon her sex—which represent it as sensual and fickle, as thoughtless and reckless, as bent only upon pleasure, and prone only to intrigue, as fonder of winning admiration than of deserving it. In this way, moreover, she might repay the debt which she owes to those dramatic writers who have vindicated her capacity for a higher life, her fidelity for nobler intuitions, her truth, her honor and her long suffering. Out of the depths of her own womanly soul such a writer might repeat, with a new truth and uncommon vigor, the ideal heroine of poets who have celebrated not merely mortal loveliness but immortal love. Nor this alone. By dignifying the drama she would dignify that vocation which so many of her sisters follow, and would rescue from the indignation of the censor and the sneer of the scandalous those who are sometimes causelessly blamed, and sometimes not without a sufficient reason."

The pay of dramatists is so large when a real success has been achieved by a piece, that no other field of literature can offer any comparison with it.

But then—success is so very rare!

Out of ten thousand times ten thousand plays which are written, and hawked about among managers by impecunious authors, ten succeed. The others fail.

In old times, the pay of dramatic authors—though not so large as in our day—was still much larger than the pay of book-writers.

Milton's "Paradise Lost" sold for twenty-five dollars down, and a promise of as much more on the sale of thirteen hundred copies. The work sold so amazingly well that the author actually received seventy-five dollars more before he died; and after his death his widow sold out her whole interest in the copyright for forty dollars more.

One hundred and forty dollars for an immortal poem!

Why, sixty years before Milton's time, Marston, the dramatic author, received as much as a hundred dollars for a play which is almost as thoroughly forgotten as if it had never been written.

The diary of Manager Henslowe relates, under date of

September 28, 1599, that he had lent to William Borne, "to lend unto John Mastone," "the new poete," "the sum of, forty shillings," in earnest of some work not named. There is an undated letter of Marston to Henslowe, written probably in reference to this matter, which is characteristic in its disdainfully confident tone. Thus it runs:

MR. HENSLOWE, at the Rose on the Bankside.

If you like my playe of Columbus, it is verie well, and you shall give me noe more than twentie poundes for it, but If nott, lett me have it by the Bearer againe, as I know the kinges men will freelie give me as much for it, and the profitts of the third daye moreover.

Soe I rest yours,

JOHN MARSTON.

In modern days plays do not go for such sums as this, at least when played with success.

Mr. Boucicault, who labored in this country as actor and manager for many years, at the end of which he was as poor as when he began, is now, thanks to the profits of dramatic authorship, immensely wealthy.

In this country we have very few dramatic authors who have achieved really great success, though a great number who have done well enough with plays to be raised above want.

American managers have been celebrated, ever since theatres had an existence in this country, for their reluctance to produce plays by home authors.

Taking their cue from the dear public, which is so intensely patriotic, it insists on filling the pockets of foreign dramatists rather than encourage its own, managers generally prefer not to risk their money on home-made plays.

A manager who "ran" a theatre in Philadelphia as long ago as 1813, relates that on one occasion he played a very sharp trick on his friend the public.

There was a gentleman named Barker, who, as the

manager states, "had written several pieces which had no fault but being American productions. This, however, was enough to destroy their success. At my request he now dramatized 'Marmion.' The merit of the piece was positive, but the old difficulty remained. I knew the then prejudice against any native play, and concocted with Cooper a very innocent fraud upon the public. We insinuated that the piece was a London one, had it sent to our theatre from New York, where it was made to arrive in the midst of rehearsal, in the presence of the actors, packed up exactly *like pieces we were in the habit of receiving from London. It was opened with great gravity, and announced without any author being alluded to.* None of the company were in the secret, as I well knew 'these actors cannot keep counsel,' not even the prompter. It was played with great success for six or seven nights, when, believing it safe, I announced the author, and from that moment it ceased to attract."

Managers are frequently the recipients of advice from outsiders who have "brilliant ideas" which they want to see put on the stage in the shape of a play.

While my play of "Surf" was running at the Arch Street Theatre, in Philadelphia, some months since, I received a letter from a person whose name I have forgotten (though I should not, of course, print it if I remembered it), in which he commented on the scene where a child is rescued from drowning by a strong swimmer.

My adviser expressed the opinion that this scene could easily be made more effective by introducing *a shark* into the action, which shark should be made to go through divers blood-curdling antics with its tail and jaws, and finally be slain in mortal combat with the juvenile man, and be dragged out of the water dripping with blood!

A clever actor at the Arch, who wrote a burlesque on "Surf," for a minstrel show, improved on this idea by

having the shark *swallow* the little girl, after which it was caught with a boat hook, ripped open in full view of the audience, and the child extracted from its inside, alive and well.

It is related that a Boston gentleman struck a happy, though rather ghoulish idea, just after the assassination of President Lincoln. Even the modern stage has hardly reached his conception of the "sensational." Here is his letter to the manager:

DEAR SIR—As the country is now excited over the assassination of our late President, and everything connected with it, or that will give any information of the affair is caught up with great interest; I would suggest to you the propriety of bringing "Our American Cousin" on the stage, and as nearly as possible at the same place in the play, have a shot fired from a representation of the box occupied by the President, from which a person should leap personating Booth. To heighten and add effect to the scene, scenery representing mournful drapery, or his funeral, or the procession, or all combined, or whatever might be deemed most appropriate, could be introduced, the characters on the stage assuming an appropriate tableau, and the orchestra play a dirge. At its conclusion *everything could pass along as though nothing had happened.*

Respectfully yours,

It is customary to denounce the "sensational" in plays, just as if there were no "sensations" in real life for the stage to hold the mirror up to.

Shakespeare's plays are "sensational" to the core!

And whenever critics sharpen their wits at the expense of some modern dramatist, I always feel like saying, Nothing so easy, gentlemen, if you only have the mind. But it is the fate of the most telling dramas ever written to incur the contempt of the critics, very much in the proportion that they delight the great public.

Here is the way a critic deals with Bulwer's play of the "Lady of Lyons": "An ignorant gardener's son sees the beautiful daughter of his father's employer. He falls in love with her—very natural, he had a right to do so, and he doubtless displayed good taste. He becomes determined to win her—to rise out of his mean estate. He goes to work, studies hard, learns to paint and to write verses, because (as he tells you in his own romantic language), 'art became the shadow of the starlight of those haunting eyes'—(the dear boy!) He sends verses to her, which she rejects, (although there was nothing, to be sure, in the lines, as he says, that 'a serf might not send to an empress.') The young lady's father's servant beats the peasant messenger who brought the verses, for his impertinence. *Pauline*, a pretty, rich belle, a little vain and proud, was guilty of the horrid offence not only of resenting an amatory epistle from this darling boy, but she chose to reject a score of suitors and foolishly to prefer a man with a handle to his name—as which of our American belles does not?—she wanted a lord, just as Miss Brown does anybody before a mechanic. For this crime, two young gentlemen, who had been rejected by her, become co-conspirators; they determine to destroy her, and to this end furnish money to the noble *Claude* to dress and act as a prince, to win her, to marry her, to carry her to his own hovel home on his wedding night, that her mean estate may humiliate her the sooner; all of which the noble, loving, educated, chivalrous *Claude* agrees, on his oath, to do, because he swears he will be revenged on—the *girl*, (about sixteen years of age, she was, or thereabouts!) for the dreadful offence of sending back his verses and slapping the face, by proxy, of the chap in a blouse who brought them. And *Claude* does it. He wins her by fraud—takes her to his mean home—and there raves over his remorse and love, sends her to bed to sleep by herself, agrees to a divorce, and rushes off to the wars. But poor *Pauline's* 'a *goner*'—she's in love! She 'can't give it up *so*, Mr. Brown.' *Claude* changes his name, rises by magic in the army, becomes a general, returns, hears that she is about to marry, swings, with an epaulette on each shoulder, into her father's house just as *Pauline* is about to be victimized, to sell herself to save a bankrupt father, who has disposed of her for cash to an old rejected suitor, and then and there *Claude*, (having first ascertained the amount offered by his rival for the hand of his love), planks up 'thrice the sum,' clasps her in his arms, and the curtain falls—the audience draw a long breath—the sweet ones 'dry up' their eyes, and go home to dream—on *what?* 'Ay, there's the rub!' To dream, I fear, in the very drunkenness of morbid sentiment. Well is it, if on each representation of this piece, no young mind is tainted!"

Now I won't say that this is not the very acme of scholarly and delightful criticism, but I *will* say that when the same style of thing is written about—well, say about *your* new piece, friend B., or friend D., or friend F., or friend H., you can reply that if Bulwer can stand it you can.

There are certain stage creations inexpressibly dear to the popular heart, the like of which no man ever saw nor ever will, and among these is that "queer fish," the traditional stage sailor, whom a witty critic thus describes: "He tells everybody he meets to 'belay there,' which we find, by a dictionary of sea terms, is making a rope fast by turns round a pin or coil without hitching or seizing it. He calls his legs his timbers, though timbers in nautical language mean ribs, and he is eternally requesting that they may be shivered. He is always either on terms of easy familiarity with his captain or particularly mutinous, and is often in love with the same young lady as his superior officer, when, in consequence of their affections clashing, he generally cuts down to a mere hull, as he technically expresses it. He calls every elderly person a grampus, and stigmatizes as a land-lubber, every person whose pursuits do not happen to be nautical. When at sea, though only a common sailor, the stage tar is the most important personage on board, and the captain frequently retires to the side of the vessel—sitting probably on a tar barrel—in order to leave the quarter-deck to the service of the tar, while he indulges in a naval hornpipe. The dramatic seaman usually wears patent-leather pumps and silk stockings when in active service, and, if we are to believe what he says, he is in the habit of sitting most unnecessarily on the main top-gallant studding sail boom, in a storm at midnight, for the sole purpose of thinking of Polly. When he fights, he seldom condescends to engage more than three at a time; and, if the action has been general before, all retire at once the moment he evinces a desire for a combat. If he is a married man, he invariably leaves Polly without the means of paying her rent, and when he returns he always finds her rejecting the dishonorable proposals of a man in possession, who is making advances, either on his own account or as the agent of a libertine landlord. In these cases the theatrical seaman pays out the execution with a very large purse, heavily laden at both ends, which he indignantly flings at the 'shark,' as he figuratively describes the broker's man, who goes away without counting the money or giving any receipt for it. The stage tar sometimes carries papers in his bosom, which, as he cannot read, he does not know the purport of, and, though he has treasured them up, he has never thought it worth while for any one to look at them, but he generally pulls them out in the very nick of time, in the presence of some old nobleman, who glances at them and exclaims, 'My long-lost son!' at the same time expanding his arms for the tar to rush into. Sometimes he carries a miniature which, though the scene of the drama is some fifty years ago, is a daguerreotype, and finds in some titled dame a mother to match it, or pulls up the sleeve of his jacket and shows a stain of port wine upon his arm, which establishes his right to some very extensive estates, and convicts a conscience-stricken steward of a long train of villainies. At the close of his exploits, it is customary to bring in the Union-Jack or Stars and Stripes, (nobody knows why they are introduced, or where they came from), and to wave it over his head to the tune of the 'Star-spangled Banner.'"

CHAPTER XXXI.

Dramatic Critics, How They Grow.—An English Critic on Criticism.—Snarlers and Gentlemen.–Tristram Shandy's Views.—Western Critics.—Macready's Boy Critic.

The preceding chapter touches on critics in passing, but so important a class of people certainly are entitled to a chapter all to themselves.

Hinc illæ lachrymæ !

(The critics know what it means, O reader to whom Latin is all Dutch. Bless you, they know everything.)

If I am inclined to be a little facetious at the expense of dramatic critics as a class, I trust they will overlook it when I mention the reason.

The reason is, that two-thirds of them are no more fit to be dramatic critics than they are to take pupils in the art of politeness.

Not that they wouldn't take 'em as soon as not, you understand; their self-sufficiency is equal to anything.

Two-thirds of the men who, in our large cities, presume to sit in judgment on theatrical art and artists. are uneducated, vulgar, dishonorable and dissipated.

The other third is composed of gentlemen of education, ability, and integrity; and of all the wide brotherhood of literary workers none have my admiration and sympathy more heartily.

I am in some degree a dramatic critic myself, and I am as proud of some of my brethren in the field as I am ashamed of others.

Perhaps if we should divide the members of other professions and callings in a similar manner, the unworthy would outrank the worthy in about the same proportions.

That I am not alone in my opinion regarding dramatic critics—and that these persons are much the same in England that they are in America—is shown by the opinion which Mr. John Hollingshead printed a short time ago in a London magazine.

Mr. Hollingshead is a London dramatic critic, and he says: "Dramatic criticism is one of those arts that have no recognized position and no recognized principles, but plenty of too easily recognized professors. They swarm into every theatre, and are as well known as the actors or the box-keepers. They pretend that the power of preserving the anonymous would materially add to their independence of judgment, but neither they nor their employers take the slightest trouble to secure this privacy. A few beggarly pounds or shillings are allowed to stand between the critic and that which he says would aid him in doing his duty to the public. The 'free-list,' suspended at times, as far as regards bonnet-builders, dock officials, linendrapers' assistants, publicans, and that very large parish of individuals who come under the general description of 'professionals,' is never suspended, as far as the public press is concerned. Anything that bears the shape and impress of a newspaper order, any ragged reporter or printing-office laborer who represents, or is supposed to represent, a newspaper, however obscure, is admitted to all theatres and places of public amusement at all times and all seasons. A dead newspaper is treated with more respect and fear than a live public. There is no written contract in dealings of this sort, but there is an implied understanding. The manager, by these courtesies, hopes to conciliate the paper, and in some cases does conciliate it, while the critic feels the influence of transactions entirely beyond his control. He is kind and gentle to the manager, whatever he may feel it his duty to be to the actors and authors. The manager is always spirited and enterprising when he accepts a thoroughly bad piece and decorates it with splendid scenery, and he can only be spirited and enterprising when he has the judgment to select a good piece on which to lavish his capital. The worst of always pitching the key-note of praise too high, is that it makes it difficult to increase the tone when required."

When I was on the stage I once wrote an opinion of certain critics, as seen from the actress's standpoint, and what I wrote then I reprint here—with a single quotation mark at the beginning and the end, to distinguish it from what I write now.

"The evening wears on. I am on the stage at a moment when I have nothing to do but sit still; and I take the opportunity to look around for the professional critics—those who write for the press—but I don't see them.

The most of them went away in the middle of the first act, and their notices of the whole of the new play are already in type.

They get tired of this sort of thing, you know; but while cutting us up they might oftener remember that they are not so startlingly perfect themselves.

That well-known journal for the fireside, the New York *Snarler* intimates that I am pretty old, but its impartial critic who is entirely above suspicion, like Brevet-Brigadier General J. Cæsar's wife, generously adds that he has seen "much older actresses."

Let me here set this matter of age at rest by stating that I was born in 1811, and am consequently fifty-eight years old.

I am fifteen years older than the oldest inhabitant, but my front teeth are good.

Old age should be respected.

The editor of the *Snarler* is young, but I am glad to know he must be happy.

The truly virtuous are ever thus.

It would have been a proud moment for the Duke of York if he could have foreseen that this sweet young man would some time edit a paper in that city which is so closely connected with the immortal name of the duke aforesaid.

The duke died shortly before the *Snarler's* time, but it is glorious to feel that he would have received the enthusiastic support of its spotless editor, if he had got his job printing done at the *Snarler* office.

Even my *eyes* don't seem to satisfy the *Snarler*, although they have been favorably received in other cities.

At Evansville, Indiana, they got two rounds of applause (one each) and there were indications that they might be called in front of the curtain.

A gifted editor in that place stated that they were as "soft and melting as a summer's sun while ever and anon they flashed with the fury of the eagle disturbed in its eyrie heights."

It is true he called on me the next day and wanted to sell me a house-lot, but I feel confident that his admiration of my eyes was sincere.

Besides, he told me this lot would double in value in two years.

I don't know whether it is quite the thing to quote Scripture in this connection, but if it were, I should like to request the editor of the *Snarler* to pluck out the mote from his own eye before he notices the beaming in mine.

But the object of this screed is not to pick flaws with the critics.

Many of them have treated me very kindly.

Even the bitterest of those who have found fault with me wrote as he did simply because he was paid to do so.

It is pleasant to reflect that he would have praised me on the same terms.

I don't know how it is, but we are somehow expected to unite all the virtues of the angels, the beauty of the gods, and five times the learning of the erudite Edipus himself.

Our faults are magnified—our advantages are underestimated—our personal character discussed—the genuineness of our teeth and hair doubted—our dressmaker found fault with—the probabilities of her bill being paid or otherwise strongly insisted upon—vague hints thrown out in regard to the extreme likelihood of our remote maternal grandfather having been a pirate and a cutthroat robber (which supposition if true would fully account for the unsatisfactory "rendition" of our role in the last new comedy), and few other trifling personalities of the same sort help to make up "criticism" in the Metropolis of this undoubtedly extensive country.

This species of criticism, unluckily, is far more galling than the product howsoever bitter of genuine talent, and that *feu sacre* must be a perfect bonfire of tar-barrels and other rubbish which can keep blazing while the hose of the b'hoy critic is ejecting the puny stream of his milk-and-watery disapproval."

As the gentle Tristram Shandy said: "Grant me patience, just Heaven! Of all the cants which are canted in this canting world, though the cant of hypocrites may be the worst—the cant of criticism is the most tormenting. I would go fifty miles on foot, for I have not a horse worth riding on, to kiss the hand of that man whose generous heart will give up the reins of imagination into his author's hands—be pleased he knows not why, and cares not wherefore."

Badinage aside, let me say a word I tried once before to say, concerning Western critics, and did not say half as well as I wished. Practice makes perfect, and I intend to keep at this subject till I have expressed myself properly.

The general idea of Western criticism, as entertained by Eastern critics, is that it is one prolonged shriek of adulation; adjectives quite inadequate to relieve the pent-up feelings of the critic, and all the high-flown images known to rhetoric pressed into the service to describe some mediocre actor, orator, or poet.

What stuff and nonsense this all is, I well know from experience.

It is true there are some towns in the West where local dramatic companies and third-rate "Professors," lecturing on bumpology, are extolled to the skies, praise being carefully regulated by the amount of job-printing ordered. But these are always small towns, whose newspapers are as insignificant in calibre as they would be in towns of the same size East.

The only place in the West where I was attacked at column length, with a discourtesy and stupidity worthy of an enraged hedgehog, was a little city where I was engaged by a local speculator, who owed the printer and I suppose still owes him.

The rage of this little editor when he found that, in spite of my large house, there was no money left for him, was something awful. He called me nicknames, said I was a ballet-girl when at home in New York, and a good deal more of the same sort. Unable to see any excellence in me, it was a great relief to my imagination when I observed in another column a loud puff of a local actor, of the most ordinary calibre, who was boldly compared to Edwin Booth.

But to gauge Western critics, as a class, by such petty examples as this, would be thoroughly unjust. So far as my observation goes—and I think it is a pretty careful one—I should say there was really very little difference between Western and Eastern critics. The little difference consists in the Western critic being more industrious than his confrere of the East.

I know it is the opinion of some of the best judges in the East that there is scarcely a writer in the West who would be fit to write editorials for first-class Eastern journals without some months of preparation; but then the best writers on the Western press are of the opinion that Eastern writers could learn "a thing or two" about the newspaper business by coming West.

However that may be, there is only one point to which I hold, and that is that ridicule, as directed to Western critics for their "shrieks of adulation," is a great absurdity.

Western criticism often has a rollicking independence of tone about it which would horrify staid Eastern readers; like that of the Western critic who paid his respects to the great Ristori in this off-hand manner:

"As it is we have a recompense in the first of Americans if not the last of Italians, and need not starve for dramatic luxury. So, *au revoir*, Ristori! Old girl, good evening! We wish you well."

But critics do not always write for print. Sometimes they are private individuals; and apropos of this, a little story.

In the same hotel where Macready resided during his first engagement in a Southern city, lived a gentleman who enjoyed the tragedian's friendship and intimacy. Mr. S. had with him a son about four years of age, a bright, intelligent boy, who became an especial favorite of Mr. Macready. "The great actor, frequently, after delighting a large auditory with his sublime conceptions of Shakespeare or Byron, would, with a simple pleasure that did him honor, take the little Thaddy on his knee, and in friendly prattle pass a half an hour away. Thaddy, in one of these confidential moments, expressed a longing desire to go to the theatre, and see his elderly friend act. 'Very well,' said the tragedian, 'I'll ask your father to let you go to-morrow night.' Accordingly the request was duly made and granted, and on the night appointed the father and son made a portion of one of the most brilliant assemblages that ever gathered within the walls of the St. Charles. The play was 'King Lear.' Macready never acted more beautifully. The frenzy and pathos of the choleric king were faithfully delineated; and in the great storm scene, where *Lear* is exposed to the fury of the tempest, with the lightning flashing around his aged head, the frenzied gesture and sublime pathos of the great actor drew down the thunders from the front of the house, which drowned the noise of the mimic tempest on the stage most effectually. Macready left the theatre with the applause still ringing in his ears. We all have our little weaknesses, and the great actor could not feel entirely satisfied with the ovation bestowed on him by refined ladies and grey-head critics. He wanted a tit bit of admiration, a *bonne bouche*, from little Thaddy. So, on the following day, he took the first opportunity in his conversation with his young friend to elicit his childish opinion of his acting. 'Oh! it was beautiful, Mr. 'Cready,' said the boy. 'You were pleased with the play, then, Thaddy?' said the gratified tragedian. 'Yes, indeed, Mr. 'Cready,' answered Thaddy. 'Now, what do you think I was doing when I was in the rain, and when it was thundering and lightning so much?' 'Oh, I felt so sorry for you,' said Thaddy. 'You did that very well, though, Mr. 'Cready.' 'Ah! when I was throwing my arms about, you know what I did that for?' 'Oh, yes, indeed, and I wanted to help you so much,' replied Thaddy, warming up at the remembrance of the thrilling performance, 'you were catching lightning bugs!' "

CHAPTER XXXII.

The Personal and Private Lives of Players.–Social Distinctions of the Green Room.—Smoking and Drinking Behind the Scenes.—Curiosity of the Public about Actors' Private Lives.—The Wonderful Jones and Brown. —Clannishness of Actors.—A Lively Green Room Scene.—Admitting Visitors Behind the Scenes.—A Solitary Levee.—Actors' Private Habits their Own Concern.—Persecution of Actors in Former Days.—The Lesson of Charity.—Excusable Curiosity.—Actors' Ages.—Habits of French Actors.—Love Letters of Actresses.—A Funny Specimen. —A Ludicrous French Lover.—Marriage of Actresses into High Life. —General Good Health of Players.—An Actress who went Mad.—Players who Have Reached Great Age.—"Old Holland."—Dejazet.

There are as many social distinctions in the green-room as in the parlor. The "Star" is the lion of the hour, and is treated by all with the deference usually shown to lions in society.

The Star will fraternize with the manager, the stage-manager, and the leading actors and actresses; but a "utility" person—male or female—or a "walking lady" or "gentleman" who would address the Star, except on a matter of business, would be considered presumptuous.

The carpenters, property-men, scene-shifters, and machinists never enter the green-room, and very rarely hold any conversation whatever with the players. These latter consider themselves artists; the others are artisans. It is the pride of position.

The musicians have a green-room of their own, where they wile away the long moments during the acts, when they are not called upon to play, by tuning their instruments, smoking a pipe or cigar, or sipping a mug of beer. The first of these offences is considered graver than the latter; and is liable to fine, or even discharge of the offender.

"No smoking allowed," is a card conspicuously displayed behind the scenes and in the green-room of every well regulated theatre. Considering the amount of combustible matter always stowed away in theatres, the precaution is a wise one.

The curiosity of the public about the private life of player-folk is not a thing of modern growth.

The prosperous days of the profession have always been marked by this curiosity.

If you have the happiness to possess a garrulous and clear-headed old friend of eighty years of age, you will see what a hold the stage and its professors had on the generation at the commencement of this century.

"John Kemble, sir, always wore knee-breeches of grey cloth when he was in the country. Mrs. Siddons, sir, once tumbled over a stile near Coventry, and bore the mark of the accident on the instep of her right foot to her dying day. She died on a Friday, sir, and I have heard that she was married on a Thursday."

The British newspapers of 1809 are filled with more columns of discussion on the late quarrel between Y. Z., of this theatre, and X. Y. of that, than of information about the armies in Spain. "It seemed as if the moment an unlucky person, whether an Hamlet, or an aspiring Ophelia, set foot upon the boards, they were forced in all future time to dance a torch-dance down the great hall of life, like a set of princes and potentates at a Prussian wedding, and found repose and shadow nevermore. To exist forever within the glare of lamps and the smell of orange-peel was a heavy price to pay for the chance of making a palpable hit as Laertes, or captivating a marquis in the white robes of Miranda. But this suffering actors were willing to endure and the public to inflict. Once encircled with the tinfoil crown—once robed in imitation ermine—once grasping the wooden sceptre—

private existence was from thenceforth impossible to the vexed majesty of Sicily or the ill-favored King of Denmark. His ways were marked in Wardour Street—his appearance was greeted in Martin's Lane. The first seat of the gallery recognized him as he dived into a ham and beef shop to cheapen a sausage; the waiter at the Tavistock door pointed him out to the rural clergyman who was waiting for a coach. 'That's Mr. Brown, sir, of Covent Garden; he is going to appear to-night as the crabbed old gent in the Winter's Tale,' or 'That's Mr. Jones, sir, of Drury; he is to act Hamlet's uncle; a big man, and very strong. He began with gymnastics, but when he grew too heavy for the rope, he took to kings, sir; he has almost always a crown on his head. I've heard say, what with four hours' rehearsal and three hours' play, his reign would be nearly as long as George IV.'s, if they were added together, without counting the time they're both asleep.'" But the passion for dragging every one connected with the theatre before the public was not restricted, in that earlier day, to the mere wearers of the sock and buskin. "Woe befall the aspirant for dramatic reputation in any shape or form! If poverty, and beer, and vanity, and a cousin promoted to be prompter, induced a youthful Shakespeare to write a farce, he was a public character until the earth was shoveled over him, at the parish expense, in the pauper's grave. Chields were among the audience, or in the orchestra among the fiddlers, or behind the scenes among the paint-pots, taking notes; and whether the poor effort succeeded or not—whether triumphant shouts brought forward the author to the front of his private box, or indignant hisses drove him distracted from the house—the notes were printed; they were sent to a yearly volume of theatrical intelligence; they were incorporated with a thousand other records equally important; and he flourished forever in a dictionary, with all his previous life, and vaticinations of his future destiny, inscribed at full length; and, to bar all chance of immunity from the world's research, this history of him was to be found in the index, either under the initials of his name or of the title of his work. A man might write an Epic, and be laughed at for a fortnight—or a History, and be forgotten in a shorter time; but if he tried a melodrama, or a tragedy, or a pantomime, or soared into opera or comedy, it was all the same—he was pilloried in the biography of dramatic authors; and the hiss of that furious pit, the groans of that frantic gallery, never left his ears; anybody that heard his name could turn to the book; and the misfortune was, that if his cognomen happened to be a common one, or if the biographer was deceived by the identity of patronymic, the wretched subject of commemoration was credited with the doings of his double, and had follies and iniquities of every kind to blush for, as well as the failure of his literary effort."

Actors are clannish to an extraordinary degree. Usually reticent before strangers, they are very outspoken between themselves. Their style of dialogue is sometimes very amusing, being as it is a mixture of all that is most beautiful in poetic literature, culled from their different parts, jumbled up indiscriminately with technicalities, current slang, and ordinary English.

Any one who has the privilege of going behind the scenes—a privilege rarely accorded any but "professionals," in this country—has had opportunity to observe this peculiarity as it is manifested at odd times—particularly of a festive character.

Something like this, for example — the scene is the stage of a New York theatre, on Christmas day, at the close of the afternoon performance of a pantomime:

"What time is it?" asks somebody.

"A quarter to six," replies somebody else.

"My goodness! We never shall have time to go home and get dinner!"

"Dinner!" echoes Pantaloon, who is cast for the heavy parts as a general thing, and has a great contempt for himself in the Christmas pantomime, where he does little but get knocked down, and be helped up, and bawl and grimace over his petty woes. "Dinner! *You* think of dinner—I of the revenge! Ha, ha-a-a-a!" and he strides behind the wings.

"I'd like to revenge myself on a good fat turkey," says Columbine. "What is Christmas without a turkey?"

"Exactly! Also, what is home without a mother?"

Nobody seems inclined to answer these pertinent queries, and the Christmas players go thronging toward the dressing-rooms.

"Oh, say!"

Clown speaks.

"Suppose we send and get something to eat, and have it in the green-room?"

"Agreed," says a voice.

"Agreed," says another voice, in a higher key.

"A-a-agreed!" is given in the well-known strain of Hecate, and instantly joining hands the players form a ring, dancing wildly, and singing in unison for their own private diversion that which they have often sung for the diversion of the public:

"Around, around!
Around, around!
About, about!
About, about!
All ill keep running,
Running in!
All good keep out!"

"Stop!" roars Pantaloon. "By the pricking of my thumbs, something wicked this way comes!"

It proves to be the leading man, the poetical Hamlet, about whom all the Fifth Avenue girls are raving, who opens the back-door and stalks in with an umbrella under his arm, overshoes on his feet, a yellow-covered play-book in his hand, and a cold in his head.

"You're earning your sal easy," says Clown to him with some reproach.

"I earn it hard enough the rest of the year," says Hamlet; "it would be a pity if I couldn't rest when the Christmas pantomine is on."

But the Clown does not hear what Hamlet says, for the words are drowned in another wild chorus of the circling ring:

"Send down Sal!
Send down Sal!
Send down Sala-*ree!*"

"Something too much of this," says the tragedian with a frown. "What says the king?"

"The king says he's hungry. Where's the call-boy? Let's send him out. What shall it be? Oysters?"

"Ay, good, my lord."

"Fried oysters, Smirkins"—to the call-boy—"and let 'em be hot."

All adjourn to the green-room, except the call-boy, who disappears into the street.

"Boo! boo! how cold it is!" cries Columbine, who has been in her dressing-room and got a shawl. "I *do* wonder what people want to come out to the theatre for in such bitter weather as this—and on Chrismas day too!"

"To be sure," answers Harlequin, who is of English birth, and who, according to his own account, has passed the whole of his life prior to his unfortunate step of coming to America, in dancing before the Queen and the rest of the royal family. "In Hengland no one thinks of going to the theatre hon a Christmas."

"What's boxing night?" asks Clown.

"The night harfter, to be sure! And harn't they a jolly crowd then?"

No one seems disposed to answer this question, for at this moment re-enter Smirkins, with oysters fried, followed by a waiter heavily laden.

"All hail, Smirkins!"

Shout unanimous.

"You're a good boy, Smirkins."

"The labor we delight in physics pain," answers the call-boy, who is ambitious to be an actor, but whose histrionic triumphs are yet restricted to appearing before the curtain between the acts, for the purpose of taking up carpets, removing fragments of letters, and the like, on which occasions he is wildly cheered, and boisterously addressed as "Soup! Soup!" greatly to his annoyance.

The waiter having gone, it is found that there is a pitcher of beer and no glasses to drink it from.

"Why, there's nothing to drink out of!" laments Columbine, plaintively.

"There's the goblets we use in Macbeth."

This by the property-man, who stands leaning against the door-post with a paper cap on his head and a patch of gilding on his nose.

The offer is altogether facetious, for the goblets are made of pasteboard, and will hold nothing but emptiness.

"Macbeth's goblets?" roars Hamlet, who is also Macbeth as frequently as the public will possibly stand it. "Macbeth's goblets to drink beer out of? Oh, to what base uses we may return, Horatio!"

"Certainly," answers Clown. "Great Alexander stopped a beer barrel."

"So would you," returns Pantaloon, "if you could get a chance—with your mouth at the bung-hole."

"Caitiff!" roars the Clown with his mouth full of oysters fried.

"How was your house this afternoon?" inquires the tragedian in a contemptuous tone.

"Splendid," is the reply.

"Splendid, eh?" responds the leading man. "Ah well! Pleased with a rattle, tickled with a straw! The public taste is sadly deteriorating. Why won't the people rush to see my Lear for two years at a stretch?"

"Ah, that would be rather stretching good nature," says Clown.

"The public would have to be as crazy as Lear was, to do such a thing," says Pantaloon.

"Shut up!—perturbed spirit," growls the tragedian; "and give us a sup of your beer."

Spite of quibble and retort, it is easy to perceive that there is no ill-feeling here, and that a spirit of jollity such as is seldom to be met with elsewhere is prevalent.

I think the actor *chez lui*, if an actor may be said to have a *chez lui*, is a very different creature to that which he appears *chez* the superficial and unprofessional observer.

The superficial and unprofessional observer may judge the actor to be a stupid and uninteresting creature off the stage. He may wonder where that genius is hidden which shines out so brightly before the footlights. He may even doubt the existence of that genius, and be inclined to reconstruct his former opinions concerning it.

The truth is, that a good actor on the stage is generally a poorer actor off it than any man in society. He is reticent in speech, often awkward in bearing. Perkins, who is in the dry-goods line, quite eclipses him in all the small graces. Medoc, the wine merchant, who never read a play of Shakespeare's quite through in his life, spouts bad poetry among his friends till they all think he would have made a better actor than the professional now delighting the town, who sits by in silence while Medoc airs his abilities. Possibly even the professional himself thinks so.

But put the same actor among his fellows—and his fellowesses—and believe me, he will instantly become quite a sparkling and romantic creature, from whose tongue drop constant gems.

Among those who can quote back at him, the actor does not hesitate to quote freely. Give him Milton and he responds with Shakespeare. Give him Pope and he returns you Byron. And with his quotings he will mingle an everyday jargon which shall be full of humor and often even of wit.

Mrs. Siddons stabbed the potatoes. My tragic friend Uno, who plays Macbeth so well, always murders a Duncan when he carves his Christmas turkey.

But as I have said, it is not customary in this country to admit visitors behind the scenes.

In some foreign countries this practice is more common.

It is related that the manager of the Vienna theatre, at which Ada Menken once performed, stated on the play-bills that all gentlemen reserving orchestra chairs would be entitled to an introduction to Ada in her dressing-room. Nobody went in. It was a solitary levee.

To a certain extent, of course, curiosity with regard to the private tastes, habits and peculiarities of all public people is quite excusable.

But that curiosity which goes behind an actor's public life to pick faults in his private character is contemptible.

An actor's private habits, I have always strenuously contended, are his own concern, just as they are any individual's, and it is only when he obtrudes his private vices on the public in his public capacity, that there is any more excuse for saying—"There is a drunken *actor*," than there is for saying, "There is a drunken grocer," or "a drunken dealer in government securities."

When he is drunk on the stage, he is a drunken actor. Not otherwise.

As a writer remarks: "Men and women who are compelled by their vocation to move before the world in a perpetual glare of gaslight, and to submit to a surveillance which is ceaseless, and to a judgment which is seldom charitable, are sure to be suspected however innocent, and equally sure to be detected however cautious. The payment of three shillings at the box-office entitles a man to a seat, a bill of the play, and the privilege (never alas! exercised) of hissing if he be not pleased; but it does not constitute him the censor of the private manners and customs of the performers. With the actor inebriate upon the boards, shuffling and hiccoughing through his part, an enlightened audience should make short and stern work. He has broken his contract express with the manager, and his contract implied with the spectators; he has disappointed those who were entitled to an evening's amusement, and he has brought his profession, and consequently its patrons, into gratuitous disrepute. But what business had the frequenters of the London theatre to hiss Mr. Kean, in what Lord Macaulay calls a 'periodical fit of morality' because Mr. Kean had been suspected of a delicate affair with the wife of an alderman?"

The persecution of actors, as it existed in former days, has been modified in a degree to which few people give thought.

The actor of to-day is often, it is true, an object of unjust judgment, from ultra-religious people, but in the early days players were "a proscribed race, held in contempt, as pernicious to the welfare of mankind. From the very first the Fathers of the Church eyed them with suspicion, exercising every possible means to make them odious and their profession disreputable; they pursued actors with an ingenuity of persecution only rivalled by that inflicted on the Jews. Edicts were promulgated, *making it impossible for an actor to embrace the Christian faith* until he had formally renounced his calling, and received absolution; the same edicts denied him right of baptism or burial in consecrated ground. A canon of the African Church, in the third century, forbade 'such infamous persons as comedians' from making accusations in court. The Christian emperors Theodosius and Valentinian, in a prohibitory instrument, call Thespians 'that infamous race of players,' and speak of their vocation as a 'shameful trade.' Through these emperors the pious fathers procured excommunication of all renegades from the true faith who should abet or tolerate 'the children of Sathanas.'"

How horribly this contrasts with the very spirit of the Christian religion, no candid person, no true Christian can fail to see.

The lesson of charity is the first lesson a Christian has to learn: charity toward all men—and women.

Christ preached it up and down the Holy Land for thirty years. His whole life taught it; his lips taught it explicitly and often; his last act was one of *charity* to the thieves between whom he hung upon the cross.

Even his stern apostle, Paul, taught charity as the chief of virtues.

"Though I bestow all my goods to feed the poor * * * and have not charity, it profiteth me nothing. Charity suffereth long, and is kind; charity thinketh no evil."

"And now abideth faith, hope, charity, these three—but the greatest of these is charity."

However, I am not now preaching a sermon, nor even delivering a lecture.

Such information as it seems to me right to furnish to the public, I am always glad to furnish; and among the channels in which public curiosity runs, I think one of the most excusable is that which wonders *how old* an actor or actress is.

The stage arts of make-up are so confusing to our perceptions that many a young man passes for a tottering veteran, and *vice versa.*

The following ages of well-known players will be found pretty correct:

Buckstone	67	E. L. Davenport	48
Mrs. John Drew	45	Mrs. Mowatt	41
A. W. Fenno	55	J. H. Hackett	69
John Gilbert	60	Mrs. Farren	49
Jo Jefferson	40	John Brougham	53
Mrs. Fanny Kemble	58	Laura Keene	46
John Lester Wallack	49	Miss Richings	40
Edwin Forrest	63	Helen Faucit	52
Macready	76	McKean Buchanan	51
Murdoch	57	Fanny Ellsler	76
Mrs. Lander	43	George Vandenhoff	54
Mrs. Eliza Logan Wood	39	Dion Boucicault	55
Mrs. Prior	42	Mrs. Dion Boucicault (Agnes Robertson)	37
J. B. Roberts	50	Miss Lotta	21
Mrs. Skerrett	52	Maggie Mitchell	35
William Warren	52	Kate Bateman	29
Barney Williams	45	F. S. Chanfrau	40
W. J. Florence	35		

French actors are, as a rule, very different creatures from American actors, in their private lives.

With us, an actor seldom has any marked tastes aside from those connected with his profession; but French actors almost always have some pet hobby to ride, which has nothing at all to do with their profession. Thus M. Grivot, of the Vaudeville, is fond of etching, and is curious in bronzes. St. Germain collects rare books. Desrieux delights in pottery, and people go to see his specimens of old faience ware. The more famous Doche has an exquisite little museum of rare Dresden and dainty curiosities. Kopp, one of the droll coterie in the "Grande Duchesse," has a collection of pictures worth 30,000 francs. Lassouche, of the Palais Royal, collects china. One actor has a collection of clocks of Louis XIV.; another, a choice little cabinet by Meissonier; a third is a good sculptor; a dozen paint landscapes; nearly all are musicians, and most play on the violin. As for the actresses, it is not too much to say that every second one sings skilfully, and plays the pianoforte as a matter of course. Many French actors write elegant and lively verses—"proverbes" sometimes—which they act for their own amusement. All this betokens a refined tone of thought. The directors of the theatres are very often skilled and successful dramatists, and more often still trained and refined critics, who have served an apprenticeship on influential papers. The green-rooms are not like ours, bare, unfurnished apartments, but noble salons, full of busts of great players and dramatic authors, covered with pictures of scenes from great plays by great artists, furnished with presents from the kings of France.

That actresses are, as a rule, in the habit of receiving great numbers of love-letters from unhappy young men who have no better employment than to write them, is most true.

It is also true that actresses are as a rule in the habit of dropping these tender missives into the fire without bestowing a second thought on their writers.

The following is a specimen of the sort of love-letter actresses are most familiar with; for impudence and ignorance usually go together.

The letter is a real one:

Miss —— ——

New,, Orleans. La

Miss —— ——

I this mornin apply for your acquaintance if myne is acceptible I have saw your swett performance in the —— ——. Your performance suited me so well that I am not at ease until form your acquaintance I am a merchant but it is no reason that I want you to think any the more of me my Father has a large plantation. Your featers is so nice that I think that if you want a husband this is your chance let me know amediatly and I will at once to you.

Your most obident —— ——

A funny story is told about a beautiful French actress, in one of the minor theatres, who received daily, for about a month, a little penny bouquet of violets. She found the bouquet in the box or with the doorkeeper every evening as the play was about to begin, and this simple offering of an unknown love affected her in spite of herself. While acting, she looked carefully around—at the boxes, the parquet, and even behind the scenes—but to no purpose; she saw nothing. by which to recognize the man of bouquets. And thereupon she gave her imagination free rein, and the imagination of an actress is very similar to that of other folks. Was he a foreign prince who wished to captivate her heart before placing at her feet his crown and treasure? or was he an artist, too bashful to declare his passion? She interrogated the box-keeper, the tire-woman—in short, everybody employed in the theatre, bnt nobody knew anything about it. Still the bouquets came. "Do they tell us that constancy is a chimera?" murmured she. The other evening, as she entered the theatre, she received a fresh bouquet of violets, and this time the flowers were accompanied by a letter. "At last!" said she and, opening it by the light of a reflector, she read as follows:

"MADEMOISELLE—I have loved you for a long time, for is not beholding and loving you the same thing? Every day I come to admire you, to applaud you, to delight myself with the brightness of your eyes and the charm of your voice—"

"He must be in the house," thought the actress, and she peeped through a hole in the curtain. The audience had just commenced to assemble. She resumed her reading:

—"of your voice. You are, indeed, beautiful and charming, and happy are they who may approach you. What would I not give to be near you always? Would the treasures of all the world be worth one of your smiles? No!"—

"Ah, that is nice!" she sighed; and, turning the page, she continued:

"No! And yet I dare to love you—to tell you that I love you. Still more,—I venture to beg you not to reject my homage."—

"He begins to explain himself," said she to herself, "and I shall know—" and she continued:

"my homage. If this expression of my love does not offend you, place this bouquet of violets in your bosom. Oh! then I shall be the happiest of men!"

"Well," said she, "no signature, no name given; but let us see—here is a postscript:"

"P. S.—If you are curious to know who writes to you, look up to the fourth tier; my legs will hang over."

The note dropped from the hand of the actress, and her arms nearly dropped from her shoulders.

It is needless to say that the romance of the affair was quite destroyed by the reality.

Many stories are told of actresses who have married into high life, among the most interesting of which is that of Miss Mendel, an Augsbourg actress. It is related that she was considered "the most lovely woman in Germany, her beauty being of the true German type, of the peculiar fairness beheld in no other country—golden hair, in soft, silky masses, without the smallest tinge of auburn—pure gold—unburnished; a complexion delicate as the inner petals of the Bengal rose—pale pink, scarcely ever seen in nature, and almost impossible to produce by artificial means; lips of deep carnation; teeth small and exquisitely white, and eyebrows of the darkest brown, with eyes of the deepest blue. All this made such an impression on the heart of Duke Louis of Bavaria, that from the moment he first beheld her, at the Munich

Theatre, he vowed himself to the worship of this one idol. But Mlle. Mendel was valiant in defence of her reputation, and, aware of the responsibility incurred by the possession of great talent, she resisted every overture, even that of marriage, on the part of the duke, well knowing that it was almost out of his power to contract any alliance of the kind, as much was expected of him by his family. At that time Mlle. Mendel was in the habit of wearing a velvet collar with a clasp ornamented by a single pearl of great value, which had been presented to her by the King of Saxony, and in order to quell all hope of success in the bosom of her ducal admirer, she declared to him one day that she had made a vow to bestow her heart and hand on him alone who could match this single pearl with as many others as would form the whole necklace. The declaration was made laughingly, for the fair creature knew well enough the duke, living fully up to his income, which was but mediocre for his rank, could never accomplish this Herculean task, and she laughed more merrily still when she beheld the disconsolate expression of his countenance at the announcement she had made. But soon afterward she heard that the duke had sold his horses and broken up his establishment, gone to live in strict retirement in a small cottage belonging to his brother's park. That very night, when about to place the velvet band upon her neck, she found, to her great surprise, that a second pearl had been added to the clasp. She knew well enough whence it came, and smiled sadly at the loss of labor she felt sure that Duke Louis was incurring for love's sake. By degrees the velvet band became covered with pearls, all of them as fine as the one bestowed by the King of Saxony, until one evening great was the rumor in Augsbourg, the fair Mendel had been robbed; while on the stage, divested of ornament, in the prison scene, as *Bettina von Armstedt*, her dressing-room had been entered, and the velvet collar with its row of priceless pearls had disappeared from the toilet table. The event was so terrible, her nerves so shaken, that in spite of the assurance of the chief police magistrate, who happened to be in the theatre at the moment, that he was sure to find the thief in a very short time, for he had the clue already, poor Mlle. Mendel was so overcome by grief that her memory failed her entirely, so that on returning to the stage not a word could she remember of her part. The audience waited for some time in astonishment at the silence maintained by the actress; the actress gazed at the audience in piteous embarrassment, until, by a sudden inspiration, and almost mechanically, indeed, she remembered she had the rehearsal copy of the play in the pocket of her apron. She drew it forth without hesitation, and began to read from it with the greatest self-possession imaginable. At first the audience knew not whether to laugh or be angry, but presently memory, pathos, forgetfulness of all but her art had returned to Mlle. Mendel, and in the utterance of one of the most impassioned sentiments of her speech she flung the rehearsal copy into the orchestra and went on with her part without pause or hesitation. The applause of the audience was so tremendous that one of the witnesses to the scene has told us that the great monster chandelier in the centre of the roof swung to and fro with the vibration. But on her return to her dressing-room the excitement proved too much for her, and she fainted away. On coming back to consciousness it was to find Duke Louis at her feet, and the head commissaire standing by her side, bidding her take courage, for the pearls had been found. "Where are they?" exclaimed she. "Are you sure that none are missing? Have none been stolen?" Duke Louis then clasped round her neck the string of pearls, complete at last, no longer sewn on to the velvet band, but strung with symmetry, and fastened with a diamond clasp. What more could be done by the devoted lover? He had spared neither pains nor sacrifice to attain his end, and Mlle. Mendel consented to become his wife. The Emperor of Austria appears to have been much moved by the story, and suggested the nomination of the bride elect to the title of Baroness de Wallersee, which thus equalized the rank of the *fiances*, and enabled them to marry without difficulty. They live the most retired life possible in their little chateau on Lake Stahnberg. They say that the Duchess Louise of Bavaria never puts off, night or day, the necklace of pearls, the clasp of which she had riveted to her neck, and that in consequence of this peculiarity she is known all through the country round by the name of the Fairy Perlina, from the old German tale of the Magic Pearl."

The critic of a New York journal recently printed an article containing so much shrewd wisdom on this subject that I quote a paragraph from it: "Because actresses have become duchesses, it by no means follows that every actress who marries off the stage will become one. The men who solicit them are seldom lords in disguise or Admirable Crichtons. On the contrary, they are too often adventurers, who cast up with keen calculation the exact value of the actress, and propose to her as a commercial speculation. A popular actress is worth anywhere from five to twenty thousand dollars a year income, and that is no light temptation to the well-dressed idlers, loungers, betting sharps, and Bohemians who prey upon humanity. The man who marries and takes his wife from the stage is, of course, as much removed from comment as any other private gentleman who marries any lady. But the husband of the actress who remains upon the stage, even against his will, must expect curiosity and criticism, especially if his wife is a popular favorite. It is quite fresh in the recollection of play-goers that when the charming and universally esteemed Jean Davenport became the wife of Mr.—afterward General—Lander, she left the stage and remained off until after his death, and then went back in defiance of the opposition of his family. Mrs. Lander had reason for thus placing upon the play-bills the honored name of one of the most exclusive and respected of the old families of Massachusetts, in the fact that she had given up, with a noble generosity, a large fortune to our sick and wounded soldiers during the war, and had thus reduced herself to comparative poverty. Miss Kate Bateman, a lady whose private worth and social virtues have gained her the esteem of two hemispheres, married Dr. Crow, a surgeon, but remained on the stage in obedience to the protest of the world against the eclipse of her rare genius. Miss Kate Terry, of the English stage, was wedded to a rich linen-draper, who removed her at once to the wealthy sphere she is henceforth to occupy."

The gentleman who wrote the above has since married an actress himself!

Players are celebrated for the extreme age which they often reach, and the excellent health which they generally maintain.

It is rare for an actor or actress whose private habits are good, to lose his or her physical or mental powers early. The cases in which players have become insane are so few that they are celebrated.

One of the saddest of these cases was that of poor Marian Macarthy, an actress who was made insane by an excess of brain-work. Various causes of her insanity have been given; the real cause was simply overwork. She was not possessed of a naturally strong mind, but accident placed her in the position of "leading lady" at a theatre where it was her duty, in order to maintain her

position, to commit to memory a number of heavy Shakespearean parts in rapid succession. Never having been drilled by slow and healthful degrees to such prodigious mental exercise—her memory all untrained to the task—she still struggled desperately with it, and at last, poor girl! broke down completely. She fell to babbling wildly on the stage, and was taken home a maniac.

Her home, so long thereafter as she lived, was in the Indiana State Lunatic Asylum. Here she fancied herself before the public, and smiled, and sang, and spouted Shakespeare, and bowed her acknowledgments to her shadowy audience, hour on hour, day after day. It was a pitiful spectacle.

An hour or two previous to her death, reason returned. Her distorted features were restored to the gentle beauty which had so often called forth the plaudits of the gallery and the bouquets of the boxes. She opened her eyes once more on the world of reality, and then closed them forever.

"She is dead and gone,
At her head a grass-green turf,
At her heels a stone."

The asylum in which she was confined was the first retreat for the insane that I ever visited, and I shall never forget the profound impression it made upon me. I had heard accounts of the strange doings of the afflicted beings who dwell in these abodes, but they had ranked in my mind with the Arabian Nights and Æsop's fables. Did some of these poor people really deck their brows with straw, and fancy themselves like Lear, "every inch a king?" Were there really professional gentlemen there, men of great intellect, quite unimpaired except for some one mania which vitiated the whole?

Yes, there were just such poor beings here, and others who were quite as mournful to look upon.

"Canst thou minister to a mind diseased?" asked I, as I stood within these halls.

It was answered that many of the insane are cured, though many more remain permanently demented, while still others die in the asylum, as poor Marian did.

It is very rare to find professional people of any other class who retain the ability to practice their profession to so advanced an age as actors have often done.

Two notable examples of this, still living, are Déjazet, the French comedienne, and "old Holland," the veteran comedian of Wallack's theatre in New York—more lately of the Fifth avenue theatre.

Mr. Holland must be now, as I judge, not less than seventy years old; and still he plays nightly with a sprightliness and gayety which many of his juniors might envy.

Of Déjazet, one of the most interesting descriptions I ever read was that which was recently printed in the *Galaxy*. "It was about ten years ago that I first saw Déjazet, and she was then somewhat beyond the age of sixty. It was the first night of her resumption of 'Gentil-Bernard,' and half the *fauteuils* were filled with the best known representatives of literature and art. Most eager and expectant among these, I remember, was Victorien Sardou, who at that time, lost no opportunity of testifying his gratitude to the friend who had exerted herself so assiduously in assisting him to the position he had recently gained. The preliminary vaudeville was endured with less weariness than usual, the seats of Déjazet's theatre being so benificently arranged as to allow moderate freedom of action to their occupants. In most French places of amusement the accommodations provided for the spectator are pretty nearly as comfortable, not quite, as a pillory. If he dilate unduly with emotion over one of Jane Essler's tearful scenes, he exceeds the limit assigned to him, crowds his neighbors on both sides, and provokes frowns if not audible remonstrance. If he be shaken from his forced rigidity by Brasseur's mirthful influence, he chafes his knees in the most exasperating manner, or crushes contiguous ribs. Even when quiet, he is comfortless as the occupant of a Third avenue car in a snow-storm. I have no doubt that one of the reasons for the continued toleration of the claque is the frightful struggle which attends every attempt of an audience to applaud for itself. Here, however, the enjoyment of the performance is never impaired by the sense of physical inconvenience. The visitor, accustomed to other houses, on seating himself in a Déjazet *fauteuil* suddenly imagines himself lost, and passes a moment or two in extreme bewilderment before he sinks contentedly back into its luxurious depths. On the evening in question, Déjazet's reception was an event to be remembered. Her first step upon the scene was the signal for loud outcries of welcome, not only from the orchestra and parterre, but also from the more decorous boxes, whence proceeded shrill feminine tones, agreeably diversifying the chorus. Hats and handkerchiefs were waved, and for five minutes the business of the stage was suspended in order that the audience might have its jubilee out. And when quiet at last returned, it was curious to observe how the house continued to beam with silent, though not less expressive delight at the re-appearance of the dear old favorite. On all sides, little phrases of compliment and endearment were murmured: 'What grace;' 'Younger than ever;' 'Well done, *petite;*' '*Ah, la maligne.*' Pleasantly conscious of the favor lavished upon her, she glided through the representation with truly astonishing elasticity and buoyancy. Her attitudes and movements were literally like those of a young girl. Her face, closely viewed, betrayed advancing age, but by no means to the extent that would have been expected. Her eyes flashed as brilliantly as those of her youngest supporters upon the stage; and I am sure that few of them could rival her lithe and supple form. Altogether, her appearance was that of a woman of about thirty-five. It is difficult to believe that her acting could ever have been more thoroughly artistic. The timid flirtations of Bernard, his innocent wickedness, his immature attempts at gallantry, the affected bravery of his soldier life, the jaunty efforts to prove himself a man of the world, and the mischievous persistence of his last love-suit, were all expressed with inimitable grace and humor. The faculty of inventing impromptu 'by-play,' always one of her best gifts, was everywhere conspicuous, and was recognized at each new point by bursts of laughter and applause. Of course, it was inevitable that at certain moments some evidence of time's changes should assert itself; but even these were made the occasion for demonstrations of encouragement and good-will. When about to sing a rather difficult song, she would advance to the *rampe*, nod saucily, as if to say, 'You think I can't do it, but you shall see,' then pluckily assail her bravuras, comically tripping among the tortuous cadenzas, and at the end receive her applause with an odd little air of pride, indicating entire indifference as to the lost notes, or perhaps a satisfied conviction that everything had gone better than she had expected or the public deserved. Déjazet was always more famous for the *manner* than for for the *method* of her singing. It was her son, I think (a capital musician), who said of her that 'she sings out of tune with the most exquisite correctness in the world.' "

In this connection, the following bit of information, which has just appeared, has more than passing interest: "A double stroke of good luck has fallen upon the Theatre Déjazet, belonging to the celebrated actress of that name. M. Victorien Sardou, the author of 'Patrie' and 'Nos Bons Villageois,' has consented to write a comedy for it, and Baron Haussmann has determined to demolish it next Summer, to run a new street over its site. The effect of the first of these measures will be to give Mademoiselle Déjazet a full house during all the winter season, and that of the second to put ten thousand pounds in her purse as indemnity. Truly, Providence is never kind by halves, for, had neither M. Sardou nor M. Haussmann turned their thoughts toward the Theatre Déjazet, it must inevitably have come to grief before long. The public had quite forgotten the way to it. Mdlle. Déjazet, it should be remarked, is seventy-three years old. She first appeared on the stage during the first Empire, and still acts now in the parts of *soubrettes*—that is, young servant maids!"

CHAPTER XXXIII.

Successful Actors.—George Frederick Cooke.—Success not always the Guerdon of Merit.—E. L. Davenport and Miss Lotta.—Jefferson, Booth and Forrest — Booth's Wealth.— Booth as Hamlet.—Forrest.— The Sock-and-Buskin View of Nature and Emotion — Forrest's Debut.—Jefferson and Ristori.—Foreign and Native Actors.—Jefferson and Eliza Logan.—Jefferson's Home.—Wealthy Actors.—Ups and Downs.—Macready.—The Great Riot in 1848.—Julia Dean and Eliza Logan.

I have always believed that the energy, the perseverance, the "vim" required to make a fine position as an actor would be enough to make any person successful in other less precarious pursuits. For all *art* is precarious. The painter, the sculptor, the poet, the musician, all these lead exactly as visionary lives as the actor. But the very same spirit, the passion, which induces the painter to stick to his easel in spite of starvation, is what lures many a "poor player" on,—love of the art.

George Frederick Cooke, whose popularity was so great in England that he had to be fairly kidnapped to get him over to this country, never had his talents recognized until he was forty-five years of age. It may be that he did not reach perfection until that time; if so, this is a strong argument against those who claim that genius alone—and not study and application—makes an actor. If this idea could once be effectually scouted, it would drive many men who now are a disgrace to the theatrical professlon, either to hard study, as a means of possible distinction, or to an abandonment of an art for which they are obviously unfitted.

But I know many writers, many painters, many sculptors, who labor under a delusion—exactly as some actors do—that one fine day the world will discover them to be great geniuses, and they have only to wait for that day, which will inevitably come, without exertion on their part. And the consequence is, they live and die in poverty, and perhaps drunkenness and vagabondage.

Cooke was called, in his day, the king of actors, the genius of geniuses. On the stage he was one man, another off it; as Cooke the actor he bore scarcely any resemblance to Cooke the man. Off the stage he was nervous, awkward, and embarrassed; on the stage impassioned, graceful, and "monarch of all he surveyed." Off the stage he had no voice, but spoke in a disagreeable, indistinct whisper; on the stage he had a fine, mellow and powerful voice. In short, off the stage nothing but his grand eyes gave earnest of what he could perform upon it. And, as I have said, he did not attain eminence until he reached middle age, the period of youth being spent in the ordinary drudgery of a theatre.

Every actor who has not achieved fame and fortune will be quite willing to concede that success is not always the guerdon of merit.

There are, it is undoubted, numberless actors now performing in comparatively humble capacities in stock companies, who are far more meritorious than numberless others who display themselves as "stars," and make large sums of money.

Actors like E. L. Davenport, who have never created any marked sensation, and, in spite of rare abilities and conscientious effort, see themselves outstripped in the race for fortune by people far below them in all the qualities which should deserve success, may be excused for sometimes feeling that the theatre-going masses need educating.

And apropos of this actor, there is a story which is good enough to print, for its own sake, as well as for the subtle truth which it suggests.

A lady in Chicago asked Mr. Davenport to write his autograph in her book, with some sentiment or quotation added. He wrote the line from Shakespeare:—

"A poor player."
E. L. DAVENPORT.

When little Miss Lotta came along, the lady made the same request of her. With ready wit, she inscribed beneath the first:—

A good banjo player.
LOTTA.

Lotta, by the way, is said, by those who know her, to be a very estimable little creature in private life,—not at all given to the frisky eccentricities which characterize her on the stage, but quiet, modest, and ladylike.

Doubtless the three most prominent names in the list of successful actors of our day are Jefferson, Booth, and Forrest.

In the autumn of 1867, it chanced that Joseph Jefferson and Adelaide Ristori were playing engagements at the same time in New York, and I then made the fact a theme for comment as regards foreign and native actors.

These players may be taken as representatives of the American and foreign schools of histrionism. Mr. Joseph Jefferson represents the former no less forcibly than Madame Ristori represents the latter; and, by the latter, I mean to indicate the histrionism which deals with a foreign tongue. English players speak our native tongue, and the criticism which separates acting into these two classes cannot well avoid the seeming solecism of including mother England under the native banner. An English actor, in an American theatre, becomes an American actor.

In the season just previous to that which I am now speaking of, Mr. Jefferson appeared at the Olympic

Theatre, after an absence of many years, during which period he had received enthusiastic praise in England and elsewhere where our tongue is spoken. But Mr. Jefferson's engagement at the Olympic that season was, comparatively speaking, a failure, the prestige of which followed him, like a ban, to the other cities of the land.

The reason of this failure was, that the public eye was then filled with Ristori, the great Ristori, the wonderful Ristori, as her skilful advertisers gave her to us *ad nauseam.* Her houses were crowded from night to night, her praise was a parrot-cry on everybody's tongue, and he who praised her most was thought the most capable of appreciating high art.

Afterward she sailed through the provincial towns, like a line-of-battle ship, and made a fortune out of a public which was determined to prove its admiration of high art.

The people were, *entre nous*, sadly bored by Madame Ristori, whose language they could not understand, but they endured it bravely, thinking, good souls, that after all it would soon be over, "and there an end."

"Oh, how *lovely* she was," cried society, "when—ah—she—ah—said to him—ah," hastily consulting the *libretto*, and not finding the place, "*You* know what I mean."

Of course, everybody knew at once, and everybody said "extraordinary!"

But Ristori came again, and, to her own astonishment, perhaps, and to the astonishment of Manager Grau, the fickle Yankee public did not rush to see her after the old fashion.

No doubt it is a debasing evidence of our want of taste for high art that we don't know Italian, but it is fair to presume the people of Italy are as ignorant of English. If Mr. Edwin Booth, or Mr. Forrest, or Mr. Jefferson, were to play in Italy, I doubt if he would make the money or meet with the enthusiasm that Ristori made and met here during her first season.

It was not Ristori's fault that the American public had had enough of her. Neither was it the American public's fault. It was, however, Ristori's misfortune. The fashion her first season was to try and make yourself believe that you were overwhelmed with awe and admiration of Ristori; and next season the fashion changed. There were moments, certainly, when the power of her undoubted genius forced itself upon us and won our admiration in spite of our ignorance of what she was talking about. But those eyes which can be on the stage and on the *libretto* at once are so rare that I have never yet seen any.

Besides, the *libretto* was often so very funny in its English translation that one felt like bursting out laughing at the most serious part of the play. The actress herself was also a source of laughter sometimes, and her Italian brethren oftener.

Nothing in the way of burlesque, it seems to me, could be more provocative of merriment than the spectacle of those grimacing, shoulder-shrugging foreigners mouthing their absurd translation of Macbeth. If any one ever saw a funnier stage creation which was intended to be gravely impressive, than an Italian Scotchman, I beg to be informed of it.

The florid Italian school of acting, with its wild, nervous, tempestuous-teapotty gesticulation and articulation, is unsuited to the American stage—or so, at least, it appears, when we are witnessing gestures which to us emphasize nothing, and hearing words which to us have no meaning.

While a foreign actor is a novelty, it is natural that we should rush to see him, as we should rush to see any other curiosity. But we soon get familiar with his "classic poses," his "artistic drapery," and his mouthed thunder, and he is lucky if he do no more than bore us—he is lucky if he do not become food for laughter.

I have no experimental acquaintance with the Italian stage, but no doubt all countries are alike in loving their own language best in an actor's mouth, and I can easily imagine the effect of Forrest, for instance, on a *French* audience. Fancy his shouting at the *Comedie Francaise* his

> The world is out of joint—oh, cursed spite
> That ever I-I-I-I was bor-r-rn to set it right!

Or his

> Cade the bon-n-ndman!

"*Grand Dieu!*" I fancy my next neighbor remarking; "*mais* it is the giant of the fairy tales, this-one-here! He makes fear to the children—he is an Ogre."

I doubt if the *Comedie Francaise* would long draw crowds with Forrest, spite of his fine declamation, his fervid force of style, his muscularity, his superb pantomime, his statuesque attitudes, his speaking eye, and, in a word, his genius. Nor would Mr. Jefferson, I think, fare better.

Mr. Jefferson's *Rip Van Winkle* is triply American, in that it is an American actor's presentation of an American author's story of an American legend. We all understand the language *this* actor speaks, Dutch though his accent be, and we can only admire utterly the great skill with which he makes a character so simple in itself a medium for stirring the most varied emotions of which the human heart is capable.

Joseph Jefferson, like Edwin Booth, comes of a theatrical family. His father was a comedian of high ability; and so were his grandfathers for three or four generations.

Jefferson's *debut* was made in New York, when he was a lad six years old.

He spent a large part of his childhood in the West,

however; and, while they were both still children, he and my sister Eliza used to sing little comic duets together on the stage of various Western towns.

Mr. Jefferson is now very wealthy, the foundation of his large fortune having been laid in Australia, through which country he made a tour when it was "as ripe fruit for the gatherer," and his profits were enormous.

He resides in a charming villa at Hoboken, a romantic and beautiful spot in the Saddle River Valley, within a short ride by railroad from New York city. His house is a delightful combination of the old with the new, being an old-time Jersey brown-stone mansion, metamorphosed by a well-known architect, under whose hands the house, outbuildings and grounds assumed most picturesque forms and faces. It is surrounded by handsome grounds, with shrubbery, and the lawns are fronted by a transparent and lovely little lake.

Edwin Booth, like Jefferson, is to the stage manner born.

Unlike his father, Edwin is a model of morality and irreproachable character. He has no bad habits, is careful and conscientious, and his great success is chiefly due to an unremitting industry and assiduity in the practice of his profession.

He is very wealthy, and possesses many of those "solid citizen" qualities which were in former days supposed to be impossible to an actor.

Jefferson and Booth are both married to estimable young ladies—both Chicago girls—and both belonging to theatrical families.

Booth's wife is the daughter of the manager of the same theatre in which Jefferson's present father in-law has for many years acted as treasurer.

Thus, out of one little theatrical circle, in a Western town, the two greatest actors of America have chosen their life-companions.

This is one of the best bits of testimony that could be offered of the appreciation in which theatrical people hold their own class.

Jefferson or Booth had, as no one needs to be told, a very wide world of ladies before them where to choose. Booth, particularly, might have made a very grand match with a high-life dame, if he had chosen. But he chose from the little circle whose merits he knew.

Every present-day theatre-goer may be supposed to have seen Edwin Booth in his most celebrated part—*Hamlet.*

The existing history of the American stage is so identified with him in this character that I quote from one of the most delightful of our critics—George William Curtis—his comments on this creation: "Mr. Booth looks the ideal Hamlet. For the Hamlet of Shakespeare is not the 'scant of breath' gentleman whom the severer critics insist that he should be. He is a sad, slight prince. It is, indeed, a fair question, how much John Kemble and Sir Thomas Lawrence are responsible for the ideal Hamlet. The tall figure, preternaturally tall in the picture, clad in the long black cloak, with one foot resting upon the earth from the grave, the skull in the hand, and the fine eyes uplifted to the chandelier—this is the imperious tradition of Hamlet. We see it in youth, and it remains forever. But Mr. Booth disturbs this tradition a little. When he appears, we perceive at once that a certain melancholy youthfulness is wanting in the stately Kemble. He represents the Prince, but he is not identified with him. But Mr. Booth is altogether princely. His costume is still the solemn suit of sables, varied according to his fancy of fitness, and his small lithe form with the mobility and intellectual sadness of his face, and his large melancholy eyes, satisfy the most fastidious imagination that this is Hamlet as he lived in Shakespeare's world. His playing throughout has an excellent tone, like an old picture.

The charm of the finest portraits of Raphael's Julius or Leo, of Titian's Francis I. or Ippolito di Medici, of Vandyck's Charles I., is not the drawing nor even the coloring so much as the nameless subtle harmony which is called tone. So, in Mr. Booth's Hamlet, it is not any particular scene, or passage, or look, or movement that conveys the impression; it is the consistency of every part with every other, the pervasive sense of the mind of a true gentleman sadly strained and jarred. Through the whole play the mind is borne on in mournful reverie. It is not so much what he says or does that we observe; for, under all, beneath every scene and word and act, we hear what is not audible, the melancholy music of the sweet bells jangled out of tune, and harsh. This gives a curious reality to the whole. Most acting is as superficial as the costume of the actor. It may be carefully and even exquisitely studied, but you touch bottom all the time. 'I can see how A's and B's and C's poetry is made,' said a famous critic, 'but I lose my breath when I read D's, for I cannot see how it is done.' If the acting is merely in the mouth or on the back, it is like the Western wines, which have so delicious a bouquet, but are thin aud sharp to the taste. So with singing. If it is only in the throat of the singer, it cannot get to the heart of the hearer. If it is in the soul of the singer, the hearer is not so much conscious of the beautiful voice as of the sense of it, so to speak. If you heard Cinti Damoreau or Persiani, you listened with smiling wonder and delight, as to a musical box or a canary. If you heard Jenny Lind, there was an expansion and satisfaction of soul. Afterward it was remembered, not merely as a pleasure you had enjoyed; it was a revelation you had received. It was genius."

The same polished and genial pen tells a story of a friend who was on a visit to New York, and who "had never seen Forrest! He had been in New York I know not how often, every autumn and winter when Edwin Forrest has been playing—and when, pray, was Edwin Forrest not playing?—and yet he had never seen him! If he had said that he had never seen Trinity Church, or the Astor House, or the Hospital, it would have been strange; but to aver that he had never seen Forrest was to tax credibility. The street was full. Upon a pleasant autumn evening how pleasant Broadway is! There is such a gay crowd swarming up and down. The stress of the day's work is over. There is an air of festivity, not of business, in the groups that pass. The absence of almost all carriages but the omnibuses, decreases the loud roar of the daytime, so that you can hear the sound of conversation and light laughter. It is even tranquilizing to move slowly along the street. The shops are not yet very pretty, but they are very bright. Then people are going to and from the theatre, and eager, happy children are with them. Every warm, pleasant autumn evening in Broadway is a glimpse of Carnival. We paid our money at the little hole, where the strange being within must have a marvelous opportunity for studying the human hand, and entered the theatre. It was crammed with people. All the seats were full, and the aisles, and the steps. And the people sat upon the stairs that ascend to the second tier, and they hung upon the balustrade, and they peeped over shoulders and between heads, and everything wore the aspect of a first night, of a debut. And yet it was the thirty or forty somethingth night of the engagement. And every year he plays how many hundred nights? And people are grandfathers now who used to see him play in their youth. Yet there he is—the neck, the immemorial legs—the ah-h-h-h-h, in the same hopeless depth of guttural gloom—if gloom could be guttural; which, indeed, any rustic friend may fairly doubt until he has heard Forrest. But the crowd is the perennial amazement; for it is not to be explained upon the theory of deadheads. The crowd comes every night to behold Metamora, and Spartacus, and Damon, and Richelieu, because it delights in the representation, and shouts at it, and cries for more, and hastens and squeezes, the next night, to enjoy it all over again. Certainly there was never a more genuine or permanent success than the acting of Forrest. We may crack our jokes at it. We may call it the muscular school, the brawny art, the biceps æsthetics, the tragic calves, the bovine drama, rant, roar and rigmarole; but what then? *Metamora* folds his mighty arms, and plants his mighty legs, and with his mighty voice sneers at us, 'Look there!' until the very ground thrills and trembles beneath our feet; for there is the great, the eager, the delighted crowd. He has found his *pou sto*, and he moves his world nightly. To criticise it as acting is as useless as to criticise the stories of Miss Braddon, or of Mr. Ainsworth, as literature. That human beings, under any conceivable circumstances, should ever talk or act as they are represented in the Forrest drama and the Braddon novel is beyond belief. The sum of criticism upon it seems to be that the acting is a boundless exaggeration of all the traditional conventions of the stage. After ten minutes' looking and listening the rustic friend turned and said, 'Why, I seem to have seen him a hundred times.' It was true to the impression; for there is nothing new. You have seen and heard exactly the same thing a hundred times, with more or less excellence. I say excellence, because it is certainly very complete in its way. The life of 'the stage,' was never more adequately depicted. It is the sock-and-buskin view of nature and emotion; and it has a palpable physical effect. There were a great many young women around us crying, in the tender passages between *Damon* and his wife. They were not refined nor intellectual women. They were, perhaps, rather coarse; but they cried good hearty tears, and when, upon the temptation to escape, *Pythias* slapped his breast and, pushing open the prison-door, with what may be termed a 'theatrical air,' roared out, 'Never, never!—death before dishonor!' the audience broke out into a storm of applause."

Few people are familiar with the circumstances of Forrest's *debut*, the general impression being that he never made any "first appearance," but, as *Topsy* phrases it, "jest growed" on the stage, and in his earliest infancy played with tragedy instead of a rattlebox.

Forrest, however, made his *debut*, in due form, in the city of Philadelphia, fifty years ago. An old manager thus relates the particulars of the "first appearance of a young gentleman of Philadelphia, Master Edwin Forrest. This youth, at sixteen years of age, was introduced to the managers, by Col. John Swift, as a person who was determined to be an actor, and had succeeded in obtaining the slow leave of his family. We had been so unfortunate in the numerous 'first appearances' of late, that the young aspirant could hope for little encouragement of his wishes, the drooping state of theatricals furnishing another and stronger reason for our course. The usual arguments were strongly urged against embracing a profession at this time so especially unpromising. The toils, dangers, and sufferings of a young actor were represented with honest earnestness, but, as was soon discovered, in vain. Forrest was at this time a well grown young man, with a noble figure, unusually developed for his age, his features powerfully expressive, and of a determination of purpose which discouraged all further objections. He appeared on the 27th of November, 1820, in *Douglas*, with the following cast: *Lord Randolph*, Mr. Wheatley; *Glenalvon*, Mr. Wood; Old *Norval*, Mr. Warren; *Lady Randolph*, Mrs. Williams; *Anna*, Mrs. Jefferson. So much disappointment had been expressed by the public at many late first appearances, to which I have already alluded, that no great excitement was perceptible on the present occasion. The novice, however, acquitted himself so well as to create a desire for a repetition of the play, which soon followed, and with increased approbation."

Mr. Forrest's popularity has been such that he is now said to be worth $500,000—perhaps more. He owns a magnificent residence corner of Broad and Master streets, Philadelphia, a summer residence near Chestnut Hill, and is the possessor of several valuable paintings, and, above all, delights in the ownership of perhaps the finest Shakespearian library in the country—a library, too, carefully and daily studied by the great tragedian, who, despite his eminence, does not regard himself above the necessity of improvement.

Among other wealthy actors and actresses may be named Mr. Barney Williams, who is said to be worth $400,000, invested chiefly in real estate. He resides in elegant style on Thirty-eighth street, near Murray Hill, boasts a picture gallery and a collection of imported statuary, keeps five carriages and any number of horses, sports servants in livery, and owns a country residence near Bath.

Mr. John E. Owens, of "Solon Shingle," celebrity, is believed to be worth about $300,000. He owns a fine place near Baltimore.

Mr. Chanfrau, an excellent comedian and estimable man, is deemed worth about $100,000. He is one of the most economical, industrious, careful actors living. He resides in a modest but substantial house in a quiet street west of Sixth avenue, New York.

Mr. W. J. Florence is generally believed to be quite wealthy. He resides at the Fifth Avenue Hotel when in New York, but spends his summers almost invariably in Europe, accompanied by his devoted wife.

Lester Wallack is another wealthy actor. He resides in a house in Thirtieth street, for which he paid $49,000.

Actresses of great wealth are not so common as actors. Perhaps this is because so many wealthy actresses are married to actors—as in the case of Mrs. Florence, Mrs. Williams, Mrs. Chanfrau, etc.—and their wealth is included in their husband's!

Charlotte Cushman is believed to be worth a quarter of a million. Maggie Mitchell is worth at least $100,000. Mrs. John Drew is probably worth as much. Mrs. Lander was at one time very wealthy, but her wealth was nearly exhausted by her husband, Gen. Lander, in patriotic uses during the war of the rebellion. Little Miss Lotta is supposed to be worth a fortune.

But such are the ups and downs of theatrical life, that many an actress now living, who was once the possessor of large fortune, is now worth nothing but what she can earn from season to season. Miss Lucille Western, for example, has seen two or three fortunes slip from her possession during the past fifteen years. So with her sister Helen—at one time worth probably $100,000; at her death she was not worth as many cents.

Mr. Macready, the great English tragedian, has probably earned as much money as any actor living—but he retired from the stage, some years ago, a confirmed misanthrope.

Mr. Macready is sometimes quoted by the opponents of the stage as one who testifies to the wickedness of theatrical life—because he says no child of his shall ever be an actor, if he can help it.

Setting aside the fact that Macready is a soured, misanthropic, world-weary man of genius, I would ask if it is not a very common thing for fathers who have pursued a toilsome profession through long years, to declare that there is *no* profession so unsatisfying as theirs, and that their sons shall never follow it?

A gentleman at my elbow answers that *his* father was a physician, and that he warned all his sons against a physician's life. This gentleman had a strong inclination to be a doctor, but his father said, "No—be a farmer—be a carpenter and joiner—be a day-laborer—in fact, *anything* but a doctor." So this gentleman became a printer, and subsequently an editor and author.

Macready's misanthropy is said to have dated from the time of his visit to this country, when he was mobbed.

The story of the Astor Place riot, in 1849, is one of the most interesting in the history of the American stage. It is stated that there was a feud between certain partisans of Edwin Forrest, who at that time was endeavoring to ride into Congress upon the Native American excitement, and the adherents of Macready, the English tragedian. A reckless crowd—led by E. Z. C. Judson (Ned Buntline), who was secretly supported by Capt. Isaiah Rynders, Mike Walsh, Ed. Strahan, and other disturbers of the peace—filled Astor-place, and assaulted the Opera House with a storm of paving-stones. The Seventh Regiment had been called for, but when they arrived on the ground they were ruthlessly assailed by the rioters, and for some time were in great disorder. Prominent citizens urged the Sheriff to order the military to clear the streets, but he had not the nerve. Then they appealed to the Mayor, but he was even more useless than the Sheriff. The excitement, meantime, was spreading, the police were useless, and the military was powerless for want of orders. Finally, Recorder Tallmadge, having proper authority, ordered the military to fire over the heads of the crowd. They did so; but, as no one was hurt, the rioters gave a yell of defiance, and again rushed up to the lines, hurling all manner of missiles upon the soldiers, who, to their credit be it said, held their lines, with no perceptible wavering, though many of their men had been taken to the rear, disabled by the missiles hurled upon them. At this juncture Recorder Tallmadge gave his second order, to "fire low," and within three minutes nearly twenty of the rioters were killed, and more than thirty seriously wounded.

It is very interesting to read the newspaper accounts of this celebrated riot, as printed at the time. The following account is compiled from various journals:

On Wednesday night, on the first appearance of Mr. Macready on the stage, he was received with the most vociferous groaning, hisses, and cries of "off! off!" A portion of the audience were warm in their plaudits, and waved their handkerchiefs, but they were overborne by the horrid and uncouth noises which continued almost without intermission (except when Mr. Clarke appeared, and he was cheered) until the end of so much of the tragedy as was performed. Mr. Macready walked down to the footlights, and abode "the pelting of the pitiless storm" of groans and shouts of derision and contumely with wonderful firmness. A placard was hung over the upper box, on which was inscribed, "You have been proved A LIAR!" Then arose louder yells, and these were accompanied with showers of rotten eggs, apples, and a bottle of asafœtida, which diffused a most repulsive stench throughout the house. Mr. Macready endured all this without flinching for some time; and at length commenced his part, which he went on with, in dumb show, through two acts, and a part of the third. But as the play proceeded the fury of the excitement seemed to increase; until the mob began to shout to the *Lady Macbeth* of the evening to quit the stage; and on Mr. Macready's next appearance, a heavy piece of wood was flung from the upper tier, which fell directly across Mr. Macready's feet. The curtain then fell, and there was a long intermission. During this time several of the gentlemen undertook to remonstrate with the rioters, but without avail. Mr. Chippendale then came forward, but could not obtain a hearing. He then advanced, with Mr. Sefton, bearing a placard on which was written, "Mr. Macready has left the theatre." Meantime, another placard had been displayed by the mob, on which was inscribed, "No apologies! it is too late!" Mr. Clarke was then called for, came forward, expressed his thanks for his reception, and said he had accepted this engagement as his only present means of supporting himself and family by his professional exertions. This over, the rioters slowly left the house.

Early in the morning of the following day, placards were posted up through the city, stating that the crew of the British steamer had threatened violence to all who "dared express their opinions at the English Aristocratic Opera House," and calling on all working men to "stand by their lawful rights." In consequence of this and similar threats, a large body of police was ordered to attend at the Opera House, and in case this should not be sufficient to preserve order, the Seventh and Eighth regiments, two troops of horse, and the hussars attached to Gen. Morris' brigade were held in readiness. They formed in two bodies, one of which was stationed in the Park, and one at Centre Market. In anticipation of a riot, the rush for tickets was very great, and before night none were to be had. For some time before the doors were opened, people began to collect in Astor place, and the police took their stations at the doors and in the buildings. The crowd increased every moment, and at half-past seven the square and street, from Broadway to the Bowery were nearly full. There was such a tremendous crush about the doors, in spite of a notice posted up, stating that the tickets were all sold, that several of the entrances had to be closed. The police used every exertion to maintain order, and succeeded in preventing all attempts to force an entrance. Inside, the house was filled, but not crowded, and the amphitheatre was not more than half full. The general appearance of the audience was respectable, and it was hoped, at first, that there would be no serious attempt at disturbance. The windows had been carefully boarded up, and the doors barricaded—the object of which was afterwards made manifest. The first two scenes passed over with a vociferous welcome to Mr. Clarke as *Malcolm.* The entrance of Mr. Macready, in the third act, was the signal for a perfect storm of cheers, groans, and hisses. The whole audience rose, and the nine-tenths of it who were friendly to Macready cheered, waving their hats and handkerchiefs. A large body in the parquette, with others of the second tier and amphitheatre hissed and groaned with equal zeal. The tumult lasted for ten or fifteen minutes, when an attempt was made to restore order by a board being thrown upon the stage, upon which was written, "The friends of order will remain quiet." This silenced all but the rioters, who continued to drown all sound of what was said upon the stage. Not a word of the first act could be heard by any one in the house. The policemen present did little or nothing, evidently waiting orders. Finally, in the last scene of the act, Mr. Matsell, Chief of Police, made his appearance in the parquette, and followed by a number of his aids, marched directly down the aisle to the leader of the disturbance, whom he secured after a short but violent struggle. One by one, the rioters were taken and carried out, the greater part of the audience applauding as they disappeared. Before the second act was over, something of the play could be heard, and in the pauses of the shouts and yells, the orders of the Chief and his men in different parts of the house could be heard, as well as the wild uproar of the mob without. Mrs. Coleman Pope, as *Lady*

Macbeth, first procured a little silence, which ended, however, immediately on Mr. Macready's reappearance. The obnoxious actor went through his part with perfect self-possession, and paid no regard to the tumultuous scene before him. As the parquet and gallery were cleared of the noisiest rioters, the crowds without grew more violent, and stones were hurled against the windows on the Astor place side. As one window cracked after another, and pieces of bricks and paving stones rattled against the terrace and lobbies, the confusion increased, till the Opera House resembled a fortress besieged by an invading army, rather than a place meant for the peaceful amusement of a civilized community. The policemen were constantly engaged in nailing up the boards dashed from the windows by the stones cast by the mob. The attack was sometimes on one side and sometimes on the other, but seemed most violent on Eighth street, where there was a continual volley of stones and other missiles. The retiring rooms were closed, and the lobbies so "raked" by the mob outside, that the only safe places were the boxes and parquet. A stone thrown through an upper window, knocked off some of the ornaments of the large chandelier. The fourth and fifth acts were given in comparative quiet, so far as the audience was concerned, a large number of whom assembled in the lobby, no egress from the building being possible. At these words of *Macbeth:*

> "I will not be afraid of death and bane,
> Till Birnam *forest* come to Dunsinane."

An attempt was made to get up a tumult, but failed. The phrase,

> —"Our castle's strength
> Will laugh a siege to scorn,"

was also loudly applauded. But, in spite of the constant

crashing and thumping of stones, and the terrible yells of the crowd in the street, the tragedy was played to an end, and the curtain fell. Macready was called out and cheered, as was Mr. Clarke. Towards the close, a violent attack was made by the mob on one of the doors, which was partly forced. A body of policemen, armed with their short clubs, sallied from it, and secured a number of the leaders, who were brought in and placed in a large room under the parquet with those who had been previously arrested. These rioters, to the number of thirty or forty, battered down the partition of the room with their feet, and attempted to crawl out at the bottom by the holes so made. A strong guard was therefore placed to watch them, and not one succeeded in making his escape. After the play was over, the noise being apparently diminished somewhat, the audience was allowed to go out quietly by the door nearest Broadway. The crowd was not dense in the middle of the street, a body of troops having just passed along, but the sidewalks, fences, and all other available positions, were thronged, and a shower of stones was kept up against the windows. Two cordons of police in Eighth street kept the street vacant before the building, but the shattered doors and windows showed how furious had been the attack on that side.

The crowd refusing to disperse after the reading of the riot act, a volley was fired by the troops, the quick, scattering flashes throwing a sudden gleam over the crowd, the gas-lights in the streets having all been extinguished. The crowd seemed taken by surprise, as, on account of the incessant noises, very few could have heard the reading of the Riot Act. Many assert that it was not read, but we have positive testimony to the contrary. Presently a second volley was fired, followed, almost without pause, by three or four others. A part of the crowd came rushing down Lafayette place, but there was no shout nor noise except the deadly report of the muskets. After this horrid sound had ceased, groups of people came along, bearing away the bodies of the dead and dying. The excitement of the crowd was terrible. Most of those who were killed were innocent of all participation in the riot. An old man, waiting for the cars in the Bowery, was instantly shot dead. A little boy, eight years old, was killed by a ball at the corner of Lafayette place, and a woman, sitting in her own room, at the Bowery, was shot in the side. Some of the bodies were carried into Vauxhall, others into Jones' Hotel, and others to to the City Hospital and the Ward Station House. Groups of people collected in the streets and in front of Vauxhall; some of which were addressed by a speaker, calling on them to revenge the death of the slain. The troops for a time anticipated another attack, in consequence of this, but none was made.

After the performance of Macbeth was finished Mr. Macready passed through the crowd with the audience who were leaving, on foot and unrecognized, and made his escape. He left the city during the night, and was seen at New Rochelle the following morning at five o'clock, where he breakfasted and took the early train to Boston. He soon after left the country.

I need make no further comment on this disgraceful event than to say that while it was nominally a theatrical riot, it was in reality nothing more nor less than a *political* disturbance, with a foreign actor as the scapegoat.

Mr. Macready could come to New York to-day and meet with the most cordial welcome on the stage, the political feeling of that time having entirely subsided. Enmity to foreigners is no longer the basis of a political party in America; and against Mr. Macready professionally or personally there is no prejudice.

During the starring career of Julia Dean and Eliza

Logan, there was supposed to exist a bitter feeling of rivalry between the two young actresses, though in reality the young ladies were excellent friends from their childhood, which friendship was uninterrupted till the death of Julia Dean Hayne, which occurred in New York city some two years since.

But being the only candidates in the Western country at that period for the same dramatic favors, the dear public at once concluded that they must necessarily be bitter rivals and foes.

The whole valley of the Mississippi engaged in a sort of theatrical war of the red and white roses. Each lady had her separate and ardent set of admirers. Miss Dean was admired for her beauty of face, my sister for her beauty of mind.

Excitement was intense when either appeared at the theatres in the different cities.

Omnibuses, steamboats and race-horses were named after the young ladies by their different admirers. They had bands of music to escort them from the steamboat landings to the hotels, and serenades given them after the play.

If Miss Dean had a service of silver given her, Eliza's friends at once presented her with a set of diamonds. Clubs were formed—the Deanites and the Loganites, and party feeling ran very high.

Of course the newspaper critics had their feelings enlisted, and their columns teemed with the subject during the engagement of one or the other, their preference for their own favorite being given in earnest words, with very frequently a comparison of the merits of the two actresses.

One enthusiastic admirer of both said in describing their acting that Julia Dean in her efforts was like beautiful flashes of lightning, while, on the other hand, Eliza Logan's voice was like the thunder of Heaven's artillery.

Apropos of this, George D. Prentice said: "If Miss Dean lightens and Miss Logan thunders, what a stormy time the audience must have of it!"

Stormy times like the Macready riot, are, however as rare in the annals of the stage as in those of any other profession.

The noisest audience that I ever confronted was one which was gathered, one holiday evening—I really don't remember now whether it was Christmas or the Fourth of July—in Burton's Theatre, in Chambers street, New York.

It was, I believe, in the year 1856. Edward Eddy was then in the zenith of his fame, and upborne on the tiptopmost wave of popularity.

He had taken Burton's theatre on speculation for a season, and the night in question was one of the most profitable that ever occurred to him in his whole career.

The play was "Pizarro," and I was representing the faithful *Cora.* Eddy himself was the *Rolla* of the hour.

There was a crowd so dense in the theatre that night, that anything like order or quiet was entirely out of the question.

The whole house, from pit to gallery, literally swarmed with humanity, and although there was no occasion for excitement, except the mere fact of the throng being so immense, such was the steady uproar of the night that no one in the audience could have heard a word that was uttered on the stage.

We went through the performance almost in dumb show. Instead of raising the voice to a pitch which should make it audible to the audience, one and all of the players spoke the words in the quiet tone of a private conversation.

It was all the same to the spectators. They could not have heard us if we had bellowed ourselves hoarse.

Cooper, the famous tragedian, was fond of telling the

story of his triumph over a noisy and belligerent English audience, on the occasion of his debut in Manchester. "Of all actors Cooke had long been the first favorite, particularly in *Richard*—a part suited to rather a rough audience, who had coldly received Kemble, and were not disposed to favor a young American actor (which Cooper always claimed to be), a title at that time far from being a recommendation. The determination was formed to oppose any actor in Cooke's great part, when Cooper unconsciously selected it. Upon his appearance, a large audience greeted the stranger with every kind of noise and insult. He was soon, however, made fully aware of the cause and motive of the attack, by yells for 'Cooke! Cooke!' 'No Yankee actors!' 'Off with him!' and other more offensive cries; but, summoning his accustomed fortitude, he acted with his best ability through three entire acts, without seeming conscious that not one word of his speaking could be heard. Whether from fatigue, arising from their brutal exertions, or respect for the constancy which no outrage could shake, they suffered the fourth act to commence in comparative silence; when Cooper, taking advantage of the momentary lull, played his part so well, that the act was scarcely disturbed in its progress, and its conclusion marked by a long-continued applause, lasting nearly to the commencement of the fifth, which began and ended in a tumult of applause. He frequently adverted to this triumph over unfair opposition as one of the brightest scenes of his life."

CHAPTER XXXIV.

Curiosities of the Lecture Field.—The Comic and the Pathetic in Lectures. —False Ideas about Western Audiences.—Doctor Charletan—How I Chanced to Turn Lecturer.—My First Trip.—Amusing Incidents.—Wabasha.—What the American Lecture System is.—Its Perpetuity.—Women Lecturers.—Anna Dickinson.—Descriptions of Everett and Emerson as Lecturers.—The Requisites for Success.

One of the most curious curiosities of the lecture-field is that, being the most intellectual of all the branches of the "show business," it should include among its votaries so many numbsculls, whose only idea of success with an audience is involved in making it laugh.

It is the pathetic touch of nature, and not the humorous, which makes the world kin.

The strictly comic speaker is not to be envied; for one man to laugh at his pet joke he will find twenty to remain perfectly stolid under it, fifty to be disgusted with it, and perhaps double that number who will extend their disgust of the joke to the joker himself. Notwithstanding this fact the pervading impression among tyros in the lecturing business, is that for a speaker to meet with greatest success he must appeal altogether to the comic taste of the crowd; and especially is this idea prevalent in regard to Western audiences. The conviction is based, to speak truly, on a firmly-grounded opinion that audiences in the West are exclusively composed of giggling louts and their red-handed feminine companions, who desire to be entertained, and comprehend entertainment in no other wise than as an evening's roaring with insensate laughter.

The immediate result of this idea is that the whole Western country is flooded with traveling lecturers (comic of course), migratory "theatres comiques," itinerant minstrels with their immensely ludicrous Billy Bummum and Bobby Bobbem in their excruciatingly laughable drolleries, and many other comicalities too humorous for minute recapitulation.

The consequence of the influx of this mirthful crowd of merrymakers has been to draw to them the rough and uncouth element in every town they visit, and to shut out all the culture and refinement of the same town until, not seeing any, these wanderers have concluded that no refinement existed there.

If it be but one step from sublime to ridiculous, it is no less than that from the "comic" to the coarse and vulgar. This it is, no doubt, which has caused what may be called the aristocracy of the small towns of the West to look with distrust upon every species of "entertainment" which comes to their town and puts its colored bills up; which has set up a law which makes it a loss of caste to be seen witnessing the comicalities of the comical Bobby.

The popular lecturer who has tears in his voice and pathos in his soul can appeal to all classes in a way which the comic man looks at aghast. He can play on the feelings of his audience, be it composed of the louts or the aristocracy, as easily as if he were a skillful musician touching ivory keys with practised fingers. Only this first; himself must be honest. The tears which sob through his voice must really be wetting his eye-lashes; the pathos of his story must really be born in his own soul. Otherwise, he may go his ways with the comical Bobby.

Of all audiences in the world, I think, the Western audience is keenest alive to humbug. It scents it from afar. It will have none of it. Why it is that the impression prevails in New York that Western audiences are not critical, that they go into boisterous exclamations of delight over coarse and vulgar performances, is quite inexplicable to me. As a rule, New York audiences are far less difficult to please than those of the West, when the performance is of an intellectual character.

Artemus Ward once told me that before a Western audience he always felt like a mountebank. In New York he never had any such uncomfortable feeling.

It is clear then that the comic element is least attractive to Western audiences; pathos is appreciated by them; but above all attractions the most attractive is that which furnishes information of a valuable sort. Never was known a people more hungry for knowledge. They also care much for strong and clear expressions of individual opinion on vital topics. They are a thinking people—far more deeply thinking than the generality of the people of the metropolis—and they have their own opinions, which they like to compare with those of the lecturer, and do so with the utmost good-nature while perhaps contradicting him point-blank. For applause, they do not give much at the best; consequently they are never guilty of that horrible delinquency—applauding in the wrong place; but the speaker who can read the faces of his audience will find appreciation there, even if hands and umbrellas are silent. It is true that one who has been speaking to a New York audience misses these noises of approbation at first. The metropolitans are such a well-educated body of amateur claqueurs! With what admirable exactitude they always send down a ripple of applause at the very proper moment! Wise young judges!

The patience of Western audiences has been tried for years with impostors. A curious class of these are traveling "physicians," graduates of Query College, with a diploma unfortunately left at home. These men come into a town, engage the hall, get their colored bills out, and hang up a photograph of somebody with a good deal

of hair on his head and face, and a written inscription to know all men by these presents, that this is Dr. Charletan, the "lecturer."

Dr. Charletan lectures for a night or two free of charge; and the consequence is that all the louts in town and all their red-handed companions go *en masse* to hear him. He then proceeds to frighten them very nearly to death by prognosticating the most fatal consequences in case they do not immediately put themselves under the treatment of some one who knows how to cure them of the ills which flesh is heir to; and he mentions casually at the close of his lecture that he may be consulted every day at the principal hotel of the place between such and such hours. In a night or two he begins to charge an admission fee for his lectures; and generally makes a handsome thing of his charlatanism all around, for poor human nature is especially weak when it comes to a question of keeping this mortal body in order, and sick people are like the drowning who clutch at straws.

One of the coolest operations I ever heard of was that performed by a self-styled "lecturer on mesmerism," who announced "that he would hold forth at fifty cents a head, and exhibit the wonders of clairvoyance. The hall was well filled, as the newspapers say, 'with a highly intelligent and appreciative audience.' The money for admission having been counted over, and salted down by the lecturer, the latter locked the door to keep dead heads out, put the key in his pocket, and mounting the platform, commenced the performance. Having selected a subject from the audience, subject to their approval, he made a few remarks upon the wonderful science, and then, after a few passes, the subject passed into a deep sleep. 'Now, my friends,' said the operator, 'you can ask the sleeper any question you please,' and so saying he left the subject and passed behind the screen. A couple of gentlemen went upon the platform, and though they propounded questions of the most simple nature, the subject failed to respond in a single instance. In fact, he was oblivious to all around him; he was as mum as an Egyptian mummy. They turned to look for the lecturer, but he had passed away; behind the scene was a back window, from which dangled a rope, showing how the lecturer had disappeared; a sponge, saturated with chloroform, was discovered on the stage at this stage of the proceedings, which told the story of the subject's slumber. Before the audience could obtain egress, the lecturer was off on a railroad train."

I have sometimes been asked how I chanced to "turn lecturer." It was by a very gradual process. I turned writer first. Then it occurred to me that, having left the stage behind me, I might still turn my stage training to advantage in the literary field by appearing in public to speak my own pieces—so to speak.

I wrote a lecture about theatrical life; committed it to memory, line by line; delivered it in public; and finding it was well received in New York, accepted an offer to deliver it elsewhere. Thus, little by little I became a regular laborer in this field.

There were some amusing incidents connected with my first essay in a field with which I was so little acquainted then.

Any one who starts on a lecture tour must, of course, be under the impression that he or she has sufficient reputation to draw audiences.

Lecturers are not generally so attractive in themselves as to awaken provincial enthusiasm to any great extent, and to crowd uncomfortable halls on unpleasant and stormy nights.

Therefore, the point is to get persons who have already a name in some one of the fields of art, science or literature.

There is scarcely a young writer in the East but imagines he has enough reputation as a *litterateur* to be immensely attractive on the rostrum.

And about the most effectual means I am acquainted with, of convincing him of his error, is to send him "out West" to try it.

"Seeking the bubble reputation at the cannon's mouth" is a trifle compared to seeking it in the lecture field, "out West."

We are wont to speak and think of the West as if it were a potato field in size. We forget that New York is a very small island, while the West is a vast continent; and that while the brilliancy of your metropolitan reputation may have extended to portions of the West, it must be very great renown indeed if it has penetrated everywhere.

In the green and flower-perfumed village of Monmouth, Illinois, I was engaged to lecture in aid of the Baptist Church.

I arrived at night, and awoke in the morning to find the rain coming down in a deluge. I sat at my window drearily looking out.

Presently I heard a rap at the door, and in answer to my "come in!" in rushed a girl of about sixteen, with her hair dragged off her face by a round comb, and her whole visage expressing the keenest interest.

She closed the door carefully, and then, after assuring herself that there were no listeners, pounced down upon me and popped into my ear this momentous question:

"*Do* you tell fortunes?"

Fortunes! Tell fortunes! Why, what in the world had put that in her head?

"Not I," I replied.

She was wofully chopfallen. Not, I think, so much on account of her *faux pas* as because it was a dire disappointment to find I was not the seventh daughter of a seventh daughter, and born with a caul.

"Why," she explained, standing on one foot, and twisting the first joint of her forefinger round and round in her mouth, "Sarah said you was a—a—something, and I thought it meant a fortune-teller. There was a lady (!) around here six weeks ago, 'ut told Sarah's fortune, and I thought you was another."

Clearly my literary renown had not reached the young lady's ears. I saw her afterwards with a Mrs. Southworth novel before her, lost in the witchery of its pages.

Poor Artemus Ward, whose reputation one would have thought had penetrated the length and breadth of the land, told me that it often happened to him to be gravely called "Professor," when he was out lecturing; and one intelligent creature actually addressed him as "Doctor!"

At Piqua, Ohio, I lectured in the High School.

A pretty, old-fashioned town, delightfully quaint, where a stranger was a curiosity to be stared at; where the citizens, for the most part, were born and reared, and the lawyer, the doctor, the bookseller, and the preacher call each other Bill, and Joe, and Tom, and Harry.

Before the door of the hotel where I was stopping there were suspended two pictures of myself in different "Stage-struck" attitudes, and the manager was ticketing up on their frames an announcement of

"OLIVE LOGAN TO-NIGHT."

While he was still at work, a long, lank, gawky specimen of backwoods humanity strolled up to the pictures and stared at them, apparently in the greatest astonishment.

As the manager was moving off, the specimen took his hat from his head, ran his fingers through his hair, and drawled out in an incredulous tone,

"Sa-ay!"

A long pause—his fingers outstretched toward the pictures curiously.

"You—don't—mean—to say—how't you're goin' to show them folks ALIVE that way?"

What insane conceptions were in that man's brain, as to the kind of creature "A Live Logan" might be, who can tell?

And what's in a name?

Nothing—not even an indication of sex, sometimes; for, in another place, a misguided enthusiast was one day loudly congratulating the assembled crowd on the good luck that was in store for them.

"What's the matter?" asked the country editor, elbowing his way in amongst the knot of assembled friends.

"Matter!" answered the ringleader, contemptuously, "why, haven't you heard? Olive Logan is coming next week."

"Gosh! IS HE? Hooray!"

As the funny papers say, "comment is unnecessary."

St. Paul is a delightful town. My audiences there were among the most select and brilliant I anywhere addressed. My lecture was very extensively announced there, and generously received. I gave a Reading from the Poets on a subsequent evening.

A gentleman *from the East* got in quite late at the Reading, under the impression that he was to hear the lecture on theatrical matters.

The next morning he was asked how he liked it.

"Capital," said he. "Never thought so much could be said on that subject. *She's* been there!"

Where? thought I, when I heard of it. I had simply occupied the evening with selections from different authors, without the slightest connecting links of my own contriving.

Like the man who read the dictionary through, this

auditor must have thought the subject changed very often.

A German paper there got the lecture and the readings and the reader mixed up in the most incomprehensible way.

There was a selection from Dickens in the readings, and it is to this fact, no doubt, that I am indebted for being called, in the queer German type of the *Volksblatt*, "Miss OLIVE DICKENS, diese talentvolle Dame, das eloqenteste und schönste Frauen-zimmer in America."

One of the most picturesque towns on the upper Mississippi is Wabasha, Minnesota. Here I was engaged to lecture by a committee headed by the editor of the local newspaper—a genial and kindly gentleman, as true a wag as ever lived, and known far and wide in the Western country by the *soubriquet* of "642."

It appears that the editor weighs 246 pounds—a very snug weight indeed; but some brother editor commenting on it made a slight typographical mistake, so that the announcement read, "642 pounds!"

The item about the editor in Wabasha who weighed 642 pounds, traveled all over the country, until it met the eyes of the alert Barnum.

642 pounds! What a figure!

The first mail after that carried a letter to the editor from Barnum, offering to negotiate with the 642 man for his moral museum.

The great showman wrote that he had had men who weighed 600 pounds in the museum, but 642 was a little the highest figure he had ever heard of.

Well, "642" headed my committee. "Stage-struck" was announced in Wabasha.

The weather was intensely hot. The little town lay on the Mississippi bank, and sweltered. The mosquitoes were as thick as hops. Windows and doors were protected by netting, but the musquitoes and the heat triumphed.

I was lying on a lounge, in the afternoon, fanning myself, and wondering who would be tempted to come to a hot hall and listen to a lecture on such a night, and coming to the conclusion that nobody would, when I heard the brazen blare of a brass band thundering on the dead stillness of the heated atmosphere the beloved strains of Yankee Doodle.

What could it be?

Could it be a circus?

It must be. I arose to look at the "pageant."

There, on the parched lawn before the door, was drawn up a huge cart, fantastically decked with white cotton drapery, in which were seated a dozen or two Teutonic musicians, blowing away lustily, while the perspiration rolled off their faces; and on each side of the cart was hung a flaming canvas banner, announcing to the expectant world that there was to be an "OLIVE LOGAN TO-NIGHT"—a "STAGE-STRUCK TO-NIGHT."

And even while I looked the big cart creaked over the roasting gravel, and sped away on its mission of drumming up customers for the evening "show."

All that long afternoon it rolled around, visiting wondering people who lived a half a dozen miles off, blowing its patriotic tunes and persistently exhibiting its astonishing banners.

At length night threw her sable mantle over the earth, and pinned it with a "star" (meaning me).

There was a fine audience assembled in the close little hall. That is to say, fine in point of numbers.

There were about a dozen really congenial and appreciative ones present, among the rest, "642," who sat at the door taking tickets, and laughing till he cried, at his first effort in the "show" business.

Ah, such a funny crowd as that was to deliver such a lecture as "Stage-struck" to! A crowd which had been drawn like flies to molasses, by the cart and the brass band, and which, I truly believe, had no more idea what an Olive Logan was than what a "Stage-struck" might be!

A funny crowd of farmers in heavy shoes, and nondescript beings in moccasins, and women in cotton sunbonnets, which completely obliterated them—covered them out of sight; and the German musicians, with their caps on and their brass instruments clutched affectionately in their arms, sitting on the top boards of some rough, raised seats at the back, listening earnestly, and striving to be amused, and failing dismally.

I left Wabasha that same night. The boat was expected along at about nine o'clock, and I did not think I should catch it. But after the lecture was concluded, and "642" had laughed again over his wagon feat, and patiently endured my reproaches for the brass band, I learned that the boat had not yet come, and I might still leave that night.

So I hastened to don traveling dress and pack baggage, and was soon ready on the levee, where we—a small party of us—sat down upon the trunks and waited.

The moon had risen by this time in glorious beauty. The wide Mississippi lay placid in her light, and the bluffs looked down like dark, enchanted castles.

And we sat there three hours!

How we managed to kill the time I hardly know. I have a dim recollection of falling asleep on the trunk, and waking up again with a start, and giving an impromptu "reading" to my little audience with those noble "Lines on the Mississippi," written by my father:

Sweep on! sweep on! thou Empress of the World!
Upon thy rolling tide thou bear'st the wealth
Of youthful nations—richer far than all
The gorgeous gems which sparkle in Potosi.
Thou hast a gem—a peerless gem—
Whose ever-radiant corruscations flash
A thousand leagues along thy sunny banks.
'Tis brightest in the heavenly diadem,
Blood-stained, but dimless. Men call it freedom!"

Or, did I dream it?

At any rate, there was the Mississippi, and here was I, and there was ——

Suddenly "642" brightens up, and points to two far-off jewels in the distance:

An emerald and a ruby, dancing high in air over the still waters below.

We watch them as they approach, and then we see a weird monster ploughing the water, with dancing torches flickeringly reflected in the mirror-like river, and strange black men, half clad, running about and arranging weighty objects, and shouting unintelligibly, with full reverberation on the heavy air.

"Chu! Chu! Chu!" The boat has arrived.

Good-by, "642." Good-by, Wabasha, good-by.

One of the best explanations I have ever seen of the peculiarities of our American lecture system, is furnished by that veteran lecturer, Mr. Curtis: "Lecturing, in the sense that we understand it, is a purely American affair. The scientific themes, or papers, and the literary essays which are read in England to select audiences, and called lectures, are as different from ours as the Earl of Carlisle or Professor Faraday are different from Mr. Gough or Mr. Beecher. An American popular lecture is a brisk sermon upon the times. Whatever its nominal topic may be, the substance of the discourse is always cognate to this people and this age. It may be a critical, a historical, or a moral discourse, but it is relished by the audience just in the degree that it is applied to them. The public does not object to be scored, even, if it is done with spirit and by one of themselves. Naturally, we don't care to hear John Bull's criticism, although it is often valuable. He tells the truth so sourly that it sounds false. But we take our flagellations from native hands kindly, and there can be no doubt that the tone of the best and most popular lecturing, in this country, has been for a long time of the greatest service as national criticism. With some exceptions, the favorites of the platform are those who have by no means coddled the national vanity; who have insisted that money-making was not all; that if it were made so there could be no true national glory; that trade and a huge prosperity were muddling us; that, hair by hair, by each unimportant detail, we were being bound and delivered to the power of the tormentors, Liliputians though they might be; and that great people could spring only from the same principles which bore a great manhood in the individual case. The Lyceum in this country is emphatically what it has been so often called—lay-preaching. Its experience, and the constant success of certain men, shows that the heart of the nation is an earnest, manly heart; that it asks and willingly hears candid and considerate opinions of every kind; and while in our church we are sure to hear the doctrine we believe, and at our party caucus the policy we approve, the Lyceum is a common ground for all fair and capable men. The only change in the character of the speakers which an observer would be likely to remark, is that the Lyceum is becoming less a system of sheer lionizing. Half a dozen years ago, if a man had done anything, from inventing a mermaid to writing a history, he was instantly bagged by the lecture committees, and carried through the country. There was a natural and simple curiosity to see the men of whom so much had been said; and the shortest and easiest way was to ask them to lecture. For an hour they were thoroughly inspected; then, if they could say something in an agreeable way, as well as be looked at, they were very sure to be called again. When you reflect that every Lyceum lecturer in good practice speaks to fifty thousand persons, at least, during the season, and that they are the most intelligent men and women in the country, the power of the system is evident enough. It may well allure ambition, for it brings the orator into the direct personal presence of all those people. Probably the chief Lyceum lecturers are personally more widely known than any other class of public men in the country."

Regularly, each year, as the lecture season draws nigh, there comes up a cry from certain people and presses, that the lecture system is dying out. On the contrary, its perpetuity is as positive as that of the drama itself.

The same influence, as a gentleman well informed in this matter recently said, "which is doubling the number of theatres is increasing the bulk of lecturers and of Lyceum organizations. Accurate statistics are impossible. Lecture associations are largely intermittent. Probably not more than seven hundred regular courses exist in the country, and perhaps even this number is overstated. But of fresh lecture organizations; of towns which had no course last year and will have one during the present season; of charitable courses; of individual lectures for special objects, the number is very great, and we presume that, taking all the lecture-patronizing communities through, not less than three thousand of them may be enumerated. Between two and three millions will be spent this year on lecturers' fees and contingent expenses; indeed the chances are that this will prove an altogether inadequate estimate. New England was the old foraging-ground in the transcendental epoch; to-day, however, the West disputes the palm, and the Middle States have a very large proportion of lyceums. For individual cities, Boston, Hartford and Providence are the strong points East, Albany, Troy and Buffalo are the great New York cities, although our own metropolis, Brooklyn, and the adjacent cities and towns have every year a vast number of irregular courses. Newark is the banner lyceum city of New Jersey, and, with due respect to Philadelphia, Pittsburgh holds the same position in Pennsylvania. At the South, the lecture-field is still fallow, and Delaware and Maryland alone of the old slave States have established associations. From Ohio to the line of the Pacific Railroad, and far up in the North-west to the extremest towns of Minnesota, there is scarcely a village of a thousand inhabitants which will not be visited by at least one member of the lecturing fraternity. The Associated Western Literary Societies alone include a hundred distinct courses, and this league numbers scarcely a fourth of the established lecture organizations in that section. It will readily be imagined that between these various societies—sometimes three in the same city—the sharpest rivalry exists, and the fiercest fight is made to secure the best possible talent. Our lecture committees are thoroughly American. They want the best that is going. The lecture agency in this city frequently receives applications from localities consisting scarcely of more than a blacksmith shop, a meeting-house, and a grocery and post-office, combined with an order for Wendell Phillips, Anna Dickinson, John B. Gough, at 'any price and any date they will come for.' It is much the same with all. They want the cream, and they are willing to pay, or, at all events, promise to pay good, sound, cream prices."

Harper's "Easy Chair," some seasons ago, said: "A pleasant friend politely asks whether the 'humbug lecturing business is not about run out?' Why this polite question should be put to an Easy Chair, which, reposing quietly here, in Franklin square, upon four good solid legs, profoundly pities the 'itinerants' as they go rushing about the land, is incomprehensible. 'Itinerants' is the withering sarcasm hurled at the unfortunates by newspaper editors who, as the clergymen say, have no 'call.' 'Itinerants'—the word has a sound of tin peddler in it which is overpowering. These wretched 'itinerants,' who are paid a hundred dollars a night, with their expenses, how pitiful their case must seem to the luxurious editor of the ——, who gets home to bed at three o'clock in the morning. However the question is not itineracy, but lecturing. Why, then, not address your remarks to Demosthenes and Cicero, who are familiar with the whole matter, and suffer the Chair to remain Easy? Of course, we have all been wondering when the public would tire of hearing certain people talk—prose, the wise call it—through an evening hour or two. Thackeray used to wonder in the same way. One evening he lectured in Philadelphia, in a terrific storm. He expected to find nobody in the hall. 'But,' said he, 'I went, and lo! eight hundred mild maniacs awaited my coming!' The further he went the greater his amazement grew. 'It is incredible,' he exclaimed, 'but, my boy! let us make hay while the sun shines, for presently they'll find us all out.' There are some who have not been found out yet. No, and it is doubtful whether the first lecturers of all, those who began twenty and thirty years ago, are not the most sought and liked. They are the planets, the fixed stars in the Lyceum sky. Comets, meteors, shooting stars, flash and dash and dazzle and expire around them, but their steady, lambent light beams cheerfully on. It is an interesting and curious study, even for an Easy Chair, to remark how faithful the Lyceum is to men who not only amuse but instruct, and not instruct only but inspire. No, the lecturing business is not about run out. It will not run out so long as men are men. What is lecturing? It is teaching, or it is oratory. It has its dull examples, of course, as every human pursuit has, and must have. But it has its great powers and its profound influences. That old 'itinerant' upon the Grecian shore who defied Philip, and the other in the Roman Senate who accused Cataline—they are not outgrown yet. Their business was moving, controlling, inspiring the human mind. Is that 'about run out'? * * * * * * It is fashionably *de rigueur* to go to the opera and applaud the public singing of women. It is fashionably *de rigueur* to recoil in horror from the hall where there is public speaking by woman. Does any one quarrel with fashion? Does any one rail indignantly with the virtuous fair of both sexes who do not advise Jenny Lind, or Medori, or Bosio, or Grisi, or Pasta, or Malibran, or Sontag, to stick to their nurseries and mind the cradle, but who sneer that Lucretia Mott, or Lucy Stone, or Anna Dickinson, unsex themselves? If any one does lose his temper for this reason with the moral censors who haunt the opera, this Easy Chair will not be disturbed so easily. Until very lately many a parent who would have sternly forbidden his daughter to hear the most earnest of women speaking most eloquently for justice, or temperance, or liberty, would have thought it perfectly proper for her to go and enjoy an evening with the spurious 'negro minstrels.' For fashions change. Then there is the ancient argument put in the interrogative form, How would you like to have your sister talk in public? The reply is like unto it, How would you like your sister to sing in public? And why, whenever a woman speaks about something, is there such a general feeling that something indelicate has been done, and the newspapers—those sturdy moralists—cry fie, while, if a woman sings about nothing and makes a spectacle of herself, there is no such shudder in the morning, and the sturdy moralists of which we spoke do not find it necessary to laugh, or satirize, or solemnly condemn, but simply criticise as if nothing extraordinary had occurred. If Jenny Lind or Malibran were your sisters, would you be sorry to have them sing in public? Or if Charlotte Bronte were your cousin, would you be sorry if she wrote a novel? Or if Rosa Bonheur were your niece, would you be sorry if she painted animals? But it isn't customary for women to speak. True; nor is it the habit for us men to write epic poems. Shakespeare is not the habit. God gave one man the genius to be Shakespeare; to a few men to be great painters; to others to be sculptors, poets, singers. In all it was the genius that justified the work; and whenever the genius to do is given, what do you think of a fashion or a habit which insists that the thing shall not be done? Kind souls who sit splendid in opera boxes, with bare necks and arms, and hanging gardens in your hair, who so sternly frown upon the 'female orator,' speak her more fairly. Have no fear that your little sister must paint because Rosa Bonheur paints—nor study the stars because Mrs. Somerville is an astronomer—nor address the public because Miss Dickinson does it. These women do these things because they have the gift. It is for the same reason that you do not sing—for the same reason that you do not dance gracefully—for the same reason that you do not look as Helen of Troy looked, nor more like Juno—dearest lady, it is because you cannot, not because you would not."

The same delightful gossiper thus pictures the lecture-room on the occasion of an eminent lecturer's appearance, and comments on Edward Everett and Ralph Waldo Emerson: "The audience is now waiting, both upon the stage, and in the boxes with a kind of expectation. There is little talking, but a tension of heads toward the stage.

The last nose is blown there, the last joke expires; all attention is concentrated upon an expected object. The edge of eagerness is not suffered to turn, but precisely at the right moment a figure with a dark head, and one with a gray head are seen at the depth of the stage, advancing through the aisle toward the footlights and the audience. They are the president of the society and the orator. The audience applauds. It is not a burst of welcome; it is rather applausive appreciation of unquestionable merit. The gray-headed orator bows gravely and slightly, lays a roll of MS. upon the table, then he and the president seat themselves side by side. For a moment they converse, evidently complimenting the brilliant audience. The orator also, evidently says that the table is right, that the light is right, that the glass of water is right, and finally that he is ready. In a few neat words 'the honored son of Massachusetts' is introduced, and he rises and moves a few steps forward. Standing for a moment, he bows to the applause. He is dressed entirely in black, wearing a dress coat, and not a frock. The first words are clearly cut, simply and perfectly articulated. 'It is often said that the day for speaking is past, and that of action has arrived.' It was a direct, plain introduction; not a florid exordium. The voice was clear, and cold, and distinct; not especially musical, not at all magnetic. The orator was incessantly moving; not rushing vehemently forward, or stepping defiantly backward, with that quaint planting of the foot, like Beecher; but restlessly changing his place, with smooth and rounded but monotonous movement. The arms and hands moved harmonious with the body, not with special reference to what was said, but apparently because there must be action. But the first part of the discourse was strictly a lucid narrative of events and causes; there was no just opportunity for action. It seemed therefore superfluous, tending to alienate attention. The discourse itself, so far, was a compact and calm history by a man as well versed in it as any man in the country; and it culminated in a description of Sumpter. This was an elaborate picture, in words of a perfectly neutral tint. There was not a single one which was peculiarly picturesque or vivid; no electric phrase that sent the whole dismal scene shuddering home to every hearer; no sudden light of burning epithet, no sad elegiac music. It was purely academic. Each word was choice; each detail was finished; it was properly cumulative to its climax; and when that was reached, loud applause followed. It was general, but not enthusiastic. No one could fail to admire the skill with which the sentence was constructed; and so elaborate a piece of workmanship justly challenged high praise. But still—still, do you get any thrill from the most perfect mosaic? Then followed a caustic and brilliant sketch of the attitude of Virginia in this war. In this part of his discourse the orator was himself a historic personage; for it was to him, when editor of the *North American Review*, that James Madison wrote his letter explanatory of the Virginia resolutions of '98. The wit that sparkled then in the pages of the *Review* glittered now along the speech. It was Junius turned gentleman and transfixing a State with sarcasm. The action was much the same. But after, in one passage, describing the wrongs wrought by rebels upon the country, he turned with upraised hand to the rows of white-cravated clergymen who sat behind him, and apostrophized them: 'Tell me, ministers of the living God, may we not without a breach of Christian charity exclaim,

"'Is there not some hidden curse,
Some chosen thunder in the stores of Heaven,
Red with uncommon wrath to blast the man
That seeks his greatness in his country's ruin?'

This passage was uttered with more force than any in the oration. The orator's hands were clasped and raised; he moved more rapidly across the stage; it was spoken with artistic energy, and loudly applauded. Thus far the admirable clearness of statement, and perfect propriety of speech, added to the personal prestige which surrounds any man so distinguished as the orator, had secured a well-bred attention. But there was not yet that eager fixed intentness, sensitive to every tone and shifting humor of the speaker, which shows that he thoroughly possesses and controls the audience. There was none of that charmed silence, in which the very heart and soul seem to be listening; and at any moment it would have been easy to go out. But when leaving the purely historical current he struck into some considerations upon the views of our affairs taken by foreign nations, the vivacious skill of his treatment excited more than vital attention. There was a truer interest and a heartier applause; and when still pressing on, but with unchanged action, to a glance at the consequences of a successful rebellion, the audience was for the first time really wide awake. Let us suppose, said the orator, that secession is successful, what has been gained? How are the causes of discontent removed? Will the malcontents have seceded because of the non-rendition of fugitive slaves? But how has secession helped it? When, in the happy words of another, Canada has been brought down to the Potomac, do they think their fugitives will be restored? No; not if they came to its banks with the hosts of Pharoah, and the river ran dry in its bed. Loud applause here rang through the building. Or, continued the orator, more vehemently, do they think, in that case, to carry their slaves into territories now free? No, not if the Chief Justice of the United States (and here a volley of applause rattled in, and the orator wiped his forehead), not if the venerable Chief Justice Taney should live yet a century, and issue a Dred Scott decision every day of his life. Here followed the sincerest applause of the whole evening; and the Easy Chair pinched his neighbor, to make sure that all was as it seemed; that these were words actually spoken, and that the orator was the one he came to hear. The hour and a half were passed. The peroration was upon the speaker's tongue, closing with an exhortation to the old men and old women, young men and maidens, each in his kind and degree, to come as the waves come when navies are stranded; come as the winds come when forests are rended; come with heart and hand, with purse and knitting needle, with sword and gun, and fight for the Union. He bowed: the audience clapped for a moment, then rose and bustled out. * * * Many years ago the Easy Chair—a mere footstool in those days—used to hear Ralph Waldo Emerson lecture. Perhaps it was in the small Sunday-school room under a country meeting-house, on sparkling winter nights, when all the neighborhood came stamping and clattering to the door in hood and muffler, or else ringing in from a few miles away, buried under buffalo skins. The little low room was dimly lighted with oil lamps, and the boys clumped about the stoves in their cowhide boots, and laughed and buzzed, and ate apples and peanuts, and giggled, and grew suddenly solemn when the grave men and women looked at them. In the desk stood the lecturer, and read his manuscript; and all but the boys sat silent and enthralled by the musical spell. Some of the hearers remembered the speaker as a boy, as a young man. Some wondered what he was talking about; some thought him very queer; all laughed at the delightful humor, or the illustrative anecdote that beaded for a moment on the surface of his talk; and some sat inspired with unknown resolves, and soaring upon lofty hopes as they heard. A nobler life, a better manhood, a purer purpose wooed every listening soul. It was not argument, nor description, nor appeal. It was wit and wisdom, and hard sense and poetry, and scholarship and music. And when the words were spoken, and the lecturer sat down, the poor little foot-stool sat still and heard the rich cadences lingering in the air, as the young Priest's heart throbs with the long vibrations when the organist has risen. The same speaker had been heard a few years previously, in the Masonic Temple in Boston. It was the fashion among the gay to call him transcendental. When some one said that, he had the air of having said something he understood. It was uttered in the same tone with which certain lovely beings declare that they are not strong-minded! And, dear lovely beings, was it ever suspected that you were? Grave parents were quoted as saying, I don't go to hear Mr. Emerson; I don't understand him. But my daughters do! Extinction of the lecturer was supposed by many to have been achieved by that remark."

The requisites for success in the lecture-field are imperative in their nature. "It is a career, a profession; yet how shall a man fit himself for it? How can he, unless he is naturally called to it, as a singer is called to sing, by certain natural gifts?"

These natural gifts are the first requisite to success. And to these must be added culture, a thorough acquaintance with the subject handled, and an energetic industry which knows no defeat.

CHAPTER XXXV.

Curious Stage Anecdotes.—The Mad King and the Drunken Actor.—Eliza Logan and the Creole Belle.—The Irish Greek in *Ion*.—An Actor who had Lived long Enough.—A Disgusting Glass.—The Cushman Sisters and their Bed-spread Balcony.—Queer Verbal Trips.—Playing Behind a Ragged Curtain, the Audience Looking through a Hole in it.—Kemble and the Apple.—A Horrified Auditor of Booth in Othello.—A Saucy Stage King.—A Boston Notion.—A Blonde's Wig on Fire.—An Amateur who Determined to Do Himself Justice, no Matter for the Part.—Not Dead Yet.—The Slipped Garter and the Dropped Skirt.—How Shakespeare Picked up a Glove while Playing.—A Luckless Lad.—Shaking Dangle's Head.—Tickling a Stage Ghost. Fainting on the Stage.—A False Alarm.—Snow on Fire.

There are numberless curious stage anecdotes in circulation among the members of the profession, which in themselves would suffice to fill a volume. Some of the less hackneyed ones I propose to devote the present chapter to telling.

Let the reader imagine himself one of a circle of players "off duty," sitting about a pleasant parlor fire on a wintry afternoon "telling stories." The scene opens with a story about the "little giant" tragedian, Junius Brutus Booth, which I think has never been published, and which is strictly true.

During one of his visits to the West on a starring tour, Mr. Booth was engaged to appear at the Louisville, Ky., theatre, and my sister Eliza, who was then the "leading lady" at the National theatre, Cincinnati, was summoned from the Queen City to support him.

Mr. Booth, who was, as is well known, somewhat given to hard drinking, kept religiously sober throughout the week, until the night appointed for his benefit, when it was evident that he had taken a little stimulant. From some unexplained cause his benefit night always seemed to be fatal to his sobriety, and to bring out his weak point.

The tragedy of "King Lear" was the play selected by the tragedian for the occasion. During the first three acts his acting was uncommonly brilliant. This actor often indulged in the utterance of *sotto voce* "asides," for the benefit of his fellow actors, rather than for his audience. My sister says she has frequently been at his side at the footlights when she has been moved to tears by one of his magnificent and pathetic touches of nature, and in one minute after has been convulsed with laughter at a side-speech given "up stage" and as a sort of sequel to the sentiment delivered to the audience. It may not be generally remembered that Mr. Booth essayed farce as well as tragedy, and was equally successful in both. He excelled in the power of making you laugh and cry in the same sentence.

The play of "King Lear" had progressed to the fifth act, on the night referred to, and the tragedian's intoxication increased palpably as the tragedy progressed. Before the opening of the last scene, where *King Lear* and his daughter *Cordelia* are discovered in prison, the frantic *Lear* has a wreath of straw about his head. Eliza (the *Cordelia*), and Mr. Booth were arranging themselves as father and daughter for a touching posé as the scene opened, when suddenly the crazy king—or rather the intoxicated actor—demanded the presence of the property man of the establishment, before he would allow the scene to be drawn.

"Miss Eliza," said he "the straw that they have made this wreath of don't suit me."

"Indeed," said Eliza, who had *supported* him in more senses than one during the play, and trying to humor him till it could be got through with; "what is the matter with the straw, Mr. Booth?"

"Why," he replied, "it is *wheat* straw and I require *rye*

straw for the wreath! I won't finish the scene without it! I always demand *rye* straw for this mad scene."

Here Pratt, the property man, made his appearance.

"Ned," said Booth; "what kind of straw d'ye call this?"

The reader will bear in mind that before the footlights the audience were waiting impatiently while this absurd colloquy went on behind the scenes.

"Wheat straw, Mr. Booth," replied the property man.

"Well, sir, I want *rye* straw."

"Ah," rejoined the man "I know you do, and I tried to get it for you but couldn't."

"Couldn't! why not, sir?"

"Because they didn't have it, sir."

"Did you go to Jonson's stables?"

"Yes, sir."

"Didn't they have it there?"

"*No*, sir."

"Did you go to the *jail?*"

"Yes, sir,"

"Didn't have it there?"

"No, sir."

"Well," said Booth, turning to Eliza, "ain't that singular? When *I* was in that jail, five years ago, they had plenty of rye straw!"

At that instant the prompter's whistle blew, the scene drew, and discovered *King Lear* flinging his wreath of wheat straw at the unhappy property man, and Miss Logan, the fair *Cordelia*, in a most unmistakable fit of laughter.

The old Latin proverb, *in vino veritas*, was never more fully illustrated than in this case. The truth was that Booth had been in the Louisville jail exactly five years before. He had got through a very profitable engagement and was on a big spree. A man in town was charged with petty larceny; he was a person whom Booth had known in better days, and having nothing else to do, he went to jail in the man's place; but only for a few days, and as he said "simply because he didn't like his boarding house."

During one of the many successful professional visits made by Eliza Logan to the city of New Orleans, a scene not set down in the bills occurred on one occasion which will never be forgotten by her, and no doubt made a lasting impression on every member of the goodly assemblage present.

The night was set apart for Eliza's benefit, and the play selected was "Lucretia Borgia."

The grand old Saint Charles theatre was filled to overflowing. The seats had been sold at auction in the morning, and the choice places were filled with the beauty and aristocracy of the flourishing Crescent City—the "Paris of America," at that time. In those days ladies dressed *en grande toilette* when they appeared in the dress circle of their favorite Saint Charles, and on the present occasion the array of beauty and youth in brilliant colors, and all ablaze with diamonds, was a sight not often witnessed now-a-days.

The play had progressed to the last scene, when the bloody *Borgia* is about to be stabbed—stabbed by her own son.

The acting had been fine throughout the evening, for in those days pieces were cast with great strength. The interest and excitement of the audience had become intense, and as the unrelenting *Gennarro* raised his arm with the glittering dagger ready for its work, with the word "*die!*" on his lips, a beautiful Creole belle who had been worked up to a state of entire forgetfulness by the natural acting, appeared and almost threw herself out of a private box, shrieking,

"Oh! oh! don't kill Miss Logan, she's going to be my bridesmaid to-morrow!"

The effect on actors and audience can be more easily imagined than described.

The excited young lady in a moment recovered herself and shrank back in her box, much embarrassed. *Gennarro* was stayed for a moment from his deadly purpose, but recovering himself, he gave the death blow to the fair *Lucretia*, and as her prostrate form lay upon the stage, the same lovely girl was seen to stand up in her box and to lower from it to the stage a pair of beautiful carrier doves bridled with white ribbons, bound together with an immense diamond bracelet, and in their mouths a billet-doux for Miss Logan, containing cards for the wedding of the Creole belle. As the curtain descended, they perched their snowy forms upon the lifeless *Lucretia*, while shouts and bravos went up from the enthusiastic audience.

An incident of a somewhat similar character occurred one night in a Washington theatre where Eliza was playing. The occasion was her benefit, and *Ion* her character.

A more elegant or cultivated audience than was present on that evening never graced the inside of a theatre. Henry Clay occupied a box, and at his side sat his then protegè, John C. Breckenridge.

The part of *Clemanthe* was assigned to a lady who, besides being a novitiate, had evidently at some period of her life visited the Emerald Isle, and had carried away with her a most unmistakeable brogue.

Throughout the tragedy the audience seemed "wrapt" with the language of a play which took its author twenty years to complete. The last scene was reached, when the "devoted youth" plunges the consecrated knife into his own bosom, when *Clemanthe* rushes on and throws herself upon the body of her heroic lover.

Fancy the effect on the audience when the excited *Cle-*

manthe burst out with, "Arrah, honey, and is it killin' yourself you'd be?"

Down came the green curtain amid shouts of laughter, while Henry Clay, wiping the tears of laughter from his eyes, said to Breckenridge, in the broad Southern dialect he often used,

"Whar did that woman come frum?"

"Why," returned Breckenridge, "evidently she is a Greek—and as *Ion* is a Grecian play, nothing could be more appropriate!"

That estimable actress, Mrs. Farren, was once delighting her audience with her fine impersonation of *Adelgitha.*

The villain of the play, *Michael Ducas*, was allotted to one of those stage bores who generally has at least one representative in every theatre. He proceeded in his part—annoying the audience, mutilating the author, and torturing the lady star—till he finally *met his fate* at the hands of the heroine, who plunges the dagger he intended for her bosom into his own.

A sigh of relief escaped from the breast of the lady, and a shout of joy went up from the audience as she held up the knife stained with the stage-blood of the murdered *Michael.*

At this juncture his stage daughter appears, and in tears and lamentations bewails the death of her father.

On the instant a matter-of-fact gentleman rose up in the audience and said, "Don't cry *much*, Miss, he wasn't killed a bit too soon!"

Many years ago Edwin Forrest was playing an engagement in the good city of Albany.

The company was rather limited as to numbers, and during the rehearsal of "Macbeth" it was found necessary, in theatrical parlance, to "double" some of the minor characters. Accordingly the "Bleeding Captain," who appears only in the first act, was pressed into double duty, in the fourth act, to appear as one of the eight apparitions who cross the stage at the back (sometimes behind a gauze) during the scene of—

> "Double, double, toil and trouble;
> Fire, burn; and cauldron, bubble."

Upon the appearance of the first apparition, the language runs thus—

> "Thou art too like the spirit of Banquo; down!
> Thy crown does sear my eyeballs," &c.,

till the appearance of the eighth apparition, when *Macbeth* exclaims—

> "I'll see no more;—
> And yet the eighth appears, who bears a glass,
> Which shows me many more."

Mr. Forrest was always very particular about the so-called "*business*" of this scene, which is somewhat complicated, but exceedingly effective in his hands when the actors engaged did their duty as directed by him. He stopped in the rehearsal to give particular instructions to the party who was "number eight" of the apparitions, and who "bore a glass."

"Be particular, if you please," he said, "respecting the instructions I have given you concerning the part you take in this scene, when you appear with the glass in your hand."

"It will be all right at night, Mr. Forrest," responded "number eight."

Night came, and so did the play; likewise the appearance of the apparitions. Mr. Forrest commenced the line—

> "And yet the eighth appears, who bears a ——"

"In the name of mercy, what is *that?*" exclaimed the first witch.

The three witches began to laugh; so did the audience; so did *not* Mr. Forrest, who was livid with rage.

Lo! "number eight," "who bore a *glass*," which should have been a small mirror, held in his anti-Shakespearian hand a *tumbler*—a large-sized cut-glass tumbler!

Forrest rushed off the stage, closing the scene in a perfect phrenzy. The play was all but spoiled, and it took all the genius of the actor to restore the audience to anything like gravity, and get them at all *en rapport* with him during the closing struggles and final death of the bloody Thane of Cawdor.

One summer, several years ago, when the city theatres were all closed, and dull times prevailed generally, Charlotte Cushman and her sister Susan found themselves (for want of a better) members of a little traveling company.

The first town visited was the pretty little one of Trenton, N. J.

Charlotte had not then been to England and "made her mark." She was simply a stock actress belonging to the Walnut Street Theatre, Philadelphia, and if she had any fame at that period, it was for her homely face, albeit she always possessed the "light behind the eye." On the other hand her sister Susan was celebrated for the beauty of her face.

The scenery, property and appliances generally of the Trenton theatre were limited as to quality and quantity. The theatre was simply the ball-room of the village hotel at which the ladies were staying.

Shakespeare's "Romeo and Juliet" was the play selected, and, as a great novelty, Miss Charlotte assumed a man's role, essaying the character of *Romeo*, while her sister Susan was really an embodiment of the fair maid of Verona.

Who could have foretold at that time that these two

sisters should have acquired such fame as that which attended their representation of these same characters, throughout the United States and Europe, but a few years following the date of this occurrence?

They met and conquered many obstacles in the way of scenery, until the balcony scene was reached, at the rehearsal. The balcony for the gentle *Juliet* was the one thing needful, but where was it to come from? how be manufactured or built?

After much perplexity, an old-fashioned bed-spread, or patch-work quilt, of many colors, appeared to be the only thing that could be found to answer the purpose (!) and the manager declared it to be "the very thing." But, to this day, I presume, Miss Charlotte has failed to see it with the manager's eyes, or to discover any positive resemblance in that faded bed-quilt to the wall of *Juliet's* balcony.

The immortal bard has said, "Sweet are the uses of adversity," but I have heard very few agree with him on this point.

It was arranged that the bed-spread should be stretched across the form of *Juliet*, and be held up on one side by the manager, while it was supported on the other (from behind, of course,) by a little colored boy belonging to the hotel, whose duty it was to answer the bells.

When night came, the balcony scene had progressed as far as where *Juliet* addresses her lover with the words—

"At what o'clock to-morrow shall I send to thee?"

Romeo replied—

"At the hour of—"

Here they were interrupted by the appearance of the little darkey who, tired out with holding up the bed-spread balcony, stuck his head out from the side, and, turning his shining ebony face up at *Juliet*, said—

"Miss Cushing, I hear my bell ringin', and I is obleeged to let my side of de house DRAP!"

And he did!

The remainder of that balcony scene has never been played.

Among queer verbal trips which have been made upon the stage, none is more extraordinary than that related of John Kemble, who was once playing *Shylock*, and instead of asking, "Shall I lay perjury upon my soul?" overturned the text by exclaiming, "Shall I lay surgery upon my poll?" This is said to be—what Miss Edgeworth used to emphatically affirm of incidents in her stories—"Fact!"

There is a better and better-known story about the soldier who levels his halberd to prevent *Richard* from impeding the progress of *Henry's* funeral, with the remark, "My lord, stand back, and let the coffin pass!" exclaiming, in his hurry and confusion, "My lord, stand back, and let the parson cough!" Such a mistake, however, has many a parallel. On the French stage a young actor having to shout "Sonnez, trompettes!" knocked all the majesty out of the command by his shout of "Tompes, sonnettes!"

There is a curious story told in the correspondence of the Princess Palatine, under the date of 1719. She was then at Dunkirk, where the players acted in the presence of the court. One of them, performing Mithridates, happened, by unlucky change of a letter, to address to Monime a word that conveyed great offence in the utterance. The unlucky actor, in his confusion, made matters worse by turning to the royal box, in which the Dauphiness was the most conspicuous personage, and saying with great contrition, "Madam, I most humbly ask your pardon; my tongue unwittingly tripped me up!" The Dauphin was so tickled by the incident that he not only fell into an uncontrollable fit of laughter, but fell backwards from his seat. To save himself, he grasped at the cord which kept the curtain up, and the curtain coming down by the run, struck against the lamps and caught fire. The flames were immediately extinguished, but the curtain could not be raised, and the play was acted out, the audience looking at the performers through the gap caused by the fire.

A magazine writer says: When we consider the inevitable and ridiculous interruptions, and constant blunders which characterize the most careful of stage representations, we find it to be a cause of wonder that the illusion is even partially preserved. Whatever may be the merits and skill of the prominent performers, every stage maintains a squad of awkward and ignorant persons, to whose mercy the minor parts are committed, and by whose stupidity they are continually murdered. It matters not whether Alexander the Great be a hero, or a very ordinary person, to his *valet de chambre;* but it does matter a good deal whether the valet affect military airs and a parody of the royal sequipedality, or is content to deliver messages in a modestly aggravated tone. A very small matter suffices to disenchant us. Some gallery god once cast an apple at John Kemble while he was stalking through one of the stateliest scenes in Coriolanus. He came down to the foot-lights, holding the pomonic missile in his hand, appealed to the kind consideration of a British audience, and concluded, amidst great applause, by offering a reward of fifty pounds for the discovery of the tasteless malefactor. It must have been hard for the most enthusiastic spectator to get back "before the walls of Rome" that night. It was a little curious that the pippin came down just as Coriolanus was kneeling in the speech beginning:

> "Like a dull actor now,
> I have forgot my part, and I am out,
> Even to a full disgrace."

An amusing incident is related, which occurred at the

old Winter Garden theatre two or three years ago, during a performance of "Othello," by Edwin Booth. "When *Othello* comes to smother *Desdemona*—one of the most painful and repulsive scenes in all the dramas that keep the stage,—there is a prolonged silence. He stands over her, completing his fearful work, and the audience sit spell-bound with horror. There was not a sound in the theatre. Nobody whispered, nobody coughed, nobody talked behind the scenes, and there was no rumbling and knocking of scenery. The profound silence had lasted for a few minutes, when a voice proceeding from our immediate neighborhood made itself audible, as it seemed to me, to the uttermost extremity of the house, perfectly calm, and clear, and resonant: 'What! is he a slaughtering on her?' The spell of fearful silence was broken. The audience laughed and clapped. The actors resumed their parts. *Iago* came on to say that he would never speak more. The curtain fell. But the play had been already ended by the ludicrous interpolation."

Some years ago, when Macready was performing in Chicago, he was unfortunate enough to offend one of the actors. This person, who was cast for the part of *Claudius* in "Hamlet," resolved to pay off the star for many supposed offenses. So, in the last scene, as *Hamlet* stabbed the usurper, that monarch reeled foward, and after a most spasmodic finish, stretched himself out precisely in the place *Hamlet* required for his own death. Macready, much annoyed, whispered:—

"Die further up the stage, Sir!"

The monarch lay insensible. Upon which, in a still louder voice, *Hamlet* growled:—

"Die further up the stage, Sir!"

Hereon *Claudius*, sitting up, observed:—

"I bleeve I'm King here, and I'll die where I please."

A funny "Yankee notion" was that of the Boston

editor who announced that, "last evening, at one of the theatres, an actor had his clothes burned off with a turpentine thunderbolt, which descended on a theatrical ship, of which he was the romantic and desperate commander, during a sheet iron tempest."

At a theatre in Troy, New York, last summer, an actress in a burlesque, who was to all appearances a pretty blonde, was suddenly transformed into a good-looking brunette. She had occasion, in the character of a Peri, to hold a lighted torch in her hand, and was engaged in the lively dialogue of the piece, with Miss Sophie Worrell, when the flames caught her flaxen wig, which immediately was in a blaze. Miss Worrell, with great pluck and presence of mind, seized the burning tow in her hands, and then finding it impossible to extinguish the flames, snatched the wig off the head of her companion and threw it on the floor, discovering that young lady's own hair neatly tied up in a conical mass at the back of her head. She skipped off to the wings, and returned almost instantly, amid thundering applause, with her own hair untied and falling with graceful negligence down her back. The poor girl was very much frightened, as her palpitating bosom plainly showed. With the exception of having slightly scorched her face, she escaped uninjured.

In a town in Michigan, the play of "London Assurance" was announced to be played one night by a strolling theatrical company; but the actor who was to play *Max Harkaway* was suddenly taken ill. At the last moment, a young amateur belonging to an association in the town was recommended as having played *Max Harkaway* before a "select audience," with great success. The manager found the gentleman, and he "kindly consented to volunteer," if his name was not placed on the bills. On the evening of the performance, Mr. Amateur appeared in the green-room, and taking one of the company aside, told him that he felt very nervous. The actor advised him to "stiffen up" on a glass of brandy. He did so. Up went the curtain, and the would-be *Max*, after receiving his cue, went boldly on. But alas! he wouldn't come *off!* He actually stood there and not only spoke the lines set down for *Max*, but recited "Sheridan's Ride," part of "Shamus O'Brien," and the "Address to the Roman Senators," all mixed into highly worked up melo-dramatic and romantic-novel style of speeches, amidst the applause of the audience, who evidently considered it all in the play line.

In a Philadelphia theatre, some years ago, a slight, dandified young man, fortified by numerous influential recommendations from persons of reputed judgment, made a bold attempt at fame as *Romeo*. Well educated, and evidently conscious of the value of his text, he indulged himself in the most strange and eccentric illustrations of it. New readings occurring in every scene, were sheltered from uncivil notice by the apparent zeal and enthusiasm of the young actor. In the last scene, at the death of the hero by poison, he appeared to resign himself to his fate, and his death-scene was duly applauded, according to custom. *Juliet*, who, in despair, was about to throw herself upon the lifeless body, was startled by a sudden restoration of the "seeming dead," accompanied by a loud whisper, "I'm not dead yet." This unexpected announcement was followed by a renewed series of expiring evolutions, which continued until abruptly ended by the jeers of an exhausted audience.

There are other slips on the stage than those made by words. At the beginning of the last century, on the French stage, the slipping of Barton's garter led to a traditional action observed in the part by every succeeding player; and one night, at a French theatre, the slipping of Mdlle. Chaumont's petticoat produced an amusing unrehearsed effect. "In the first case, the great French actor was performing the *Earl of Essex*, and his garter slipped from below his knee, in the scene where only he and the traitor Cecil were on the stage. Such a person *Essex* might treat with indifference or contempt; and accordingly he replaced the dropped band round his leg, while he continued to address *Cecil* in a disdainful tone. The effect was so successful that succeeding actors adopted the incident of affecting to tighten the garter as a good 'bit of business,' and the tradition continued to be observed as long as 'Le Comte d' Essex' continued to be acted. Mdlle. Chaumont's slip was of another character. It taxed her readiness in an emergency, and did not find her wanting. She was playing *soubrette* in '*Nos Gens*,' and was engaged running to and fro to collect and burn the presents of various old lovers. In the very middle of her action she was impeded by her petticoat suddenly falling about her feet. Of course it was a very pretty article of its sort, and she got out of it, and out of the embarrassment which had come with it, by describing it as a tribute of admiration from one of her old admirers, which must be sacrificed like all the rest; and she thrust it into the stage fire accordingly, with a merry laugh, and amid the general hilarity of the house."

There is a pleasant story which relates how Queen Elizabeth, when Shakespeare was once acting in her presence, endeavored to put him at pleasant perplexity between his sense of stage discipline and that of his royal gallantry. After many a vain attempt, we are told that Elizabeth, crossing the stage whereon the poet-actor was enacting the counterfeit presentment of a king, and engaged in royal work, dropped her glove. Shakespeare, without departing from the character he was illustrating, interpolated the original text with words to suit the action of his homage. He paused in a processional movement of which he made a part, exclaiming—

> "And though now bent on this high embassy,
> Yet stoop we to pick up our cousin's glove"—

and rendering it to her with a profound bow, proudly strode off the stage.

Old Pepys makes record of having gone to see "All's Lost by Lust," in which the musical effects had been so ill rehearsed that singers and orchestra were all at odds, and universal discord reigned. One vocal lad was so out of tune and memory that his "master"—which may imply either the stage manager or the leader of the band—"fell about his ears, and beat him so that it put the whole house into an uproar."

It is related of Moody, the Irish actor, that he was the original *Lord Burghley*, in "The Critic," and that when Sheridan selected him for the part, the manager declared that Moody would be sure to commit some ridiculous error, and ruin the effect. The author protested that such a result was impossible, and, according to the fashion of the times, a wager was laid, and Sheridan hurried to the performer of the part to give him such instructions as should render any mistake beyond possibility. Lord Burghley has nothing to say, merely to sit awhile, and then, as the stage directions informed him, and Sheridan impressed it upon his mind, "Lord Burghley comes forward, pauses near Dangle, shakes his head, and exit." The actor thoroughly understood the direction, he said, and could not err.

At night he came forward, *did* pause near Dangle, shook his (Dangle's) head, and went solemnly off!

A humorous story of a stage ghost is told in Raymond's "Life of Elliston," aided by an illustration from the etching needle of George Cruickshank, executed in quite his happiest manner. Dowton, the actor, playing a ghost part—to judge from the illustration, it must have been the ghost in "Hamlet," but the teller of the story does not say formally that such was the fact—had, of course, to be lowered in the old-fashioned way through a trap-door in the stage, his face being turned to the audience. Elliston and De Camp, concealed beneath the stage, had provided themselves with small rattan canes, and as their brother actor slowly and solemnly descended, they applied their sticks sharply and rapidly to the calves of his legs, unprotected by the plate armor that graced his shins. Poor Dowton with difficulty preserved his gravity of countenance, or refrained from the utterance of a yell of agony while in the presence of the audience. His lower limbs, beneath the surface of the stage, frisked and curvetted about "like a horse in Ducrow's arena." His passage below was maliciously made as deliberate as possible. At length, wholly let down, and completely out of sight of the audience, he looked around the obscure regions beneath the stage, to discover the base perpetrators of the outrage. He was speechless with rage, and burning for revenge. Elliston and his companion had of course vanished. Unfortunately at that moment Charles Holland, another member of the company, splendidly dressed, appeared in sight. The enraged Dowton, mistaking his man, and believing that Holland's imperturbability of manner was assumed, and an evidence of his guilt, seized a mop at that moment at hand, immersed in very dirty water, and thrusting it in his face, utterly ruined wig, ruffles, point lace, and every particular of his elaborate attire. In vain Holland protested his innocence, and implored for mercy; his cries only stimulated the avenger's exertions, and again and again the saturated mop did desperate execution over the unhappy victim's finery.

It is not often that players give evidence of sickness on the stage, but it sometimes happens; and I remember a case where a lady fainted so opportunely that some of the audience thought it a part of the play.

It was at the New York theatre, in the play of "Cendrillon." Mrs. Marie Wilkins was playing *Madam de Houspignolle*, the wife of *Pinchonniere*. In the fourth act, where *Pinchonniere* (Lewis Baker) subdues his wife, he had seized her by the wrist, to force her to her knees; "you hurt me," she says, according to the text, and was soon in a kneeling position. Suddenly she commenced to groan, then fell prostrate in a swoon; two or three of the performers rushed to Mr. Baker's relief, who was endeavoring to raise her, and she was carried back a little way, and the curtain was closed. Mr. Baker subsequently appeared, and stated that she had left a sick bed to play her part, but the effort was too much for her, and she was obliged to succumb. For a time, the event created quite an excitement in the audience, although some of those who had not before witnessed the play supposed it was a part of the business of the character, and commended her for the natural manner in which she did it.

A curious panic once took place among the audience at Barnum's Museum, during the performance of the "Christian Martyrs." The wild animals, soldiers, and auxiliaries had just left the stage, when a dull, heavy sound was heard, followed by a crash. The audience, believing that one of the wild animals had broken loose, made a rush for the doors, jumping over seats, benches, and railings. Several persons were bruised more or less. Quiet was not restored until the actors returned upon the stage. The noise was occasioned by the breaking of a rope, to which was attached a heavy piece of wood. None of the animals escaped from their cages, and the excitement was wholly causeless.

During the performance of "Pauvrette" at the Park Theatre in Brooklyn, on one occasion, a circumstance occurred which might have resulted disastrously had it not been for the coolness and courage displayed by those on the stage. The scene of "the hut on the mountain" was on the stage. The snow is represented by masses of raw cotton, which are thrown from the flats. *Maurice* and *Pauvrette* were in the hut, and the terrible avalanche began to crumble. By some means or other the light snow (cotton) took fire, and in a moment the roof of the hut and the floor of the stage were covered with the flaming material. The actors, supernumeraries, and others connected with the theatre, rushed upon the stage, and the curtain was rung down. In about five minutes it was hoisted again, and the hut was discovered with the avalanche, the only thing that reminded one of the fire being the disagreeable smell of the burnt cotton. The first words of the text uttered by *Maurice* and *Pauvrette* were very suggestive.

Maurice.—We have escaped a great danger.

Pauvrette.—Yes, but thank God it is all over.

CHAPTER XXXVI.

Amusements Sixty Years Ago.—Old Times and New.—The Foul Plays of Dryden's Time.—Vitality of the Drama.—Former Better Accommodations for Players.—The Marked Changes which Theatres have Undergone of Late Years.—Better Scenery and Costumes.—Better Music.—The Reserved Seat System.—Early Introduction of Private Boxes.—Opposition to Aristocratic Distinctions.—A Curious Resemblance.—The Greek Drama and the Muse of Lecturing.—An Old Playbill.—Seats on the Stage in Early Days.—The Indecent Old Theatres.—The Vile Third Tier.—What Worked a Cure of this Horrible Evil.—Power of Public Opinion.—Proof that the Theatre can be Elevated and Purified.

It is curious in these days when theatres open at seven o'clock, balls begin at ten or eleven, and late hours are the rule instead of the exception, to read that sixty years ago theatres opened their doors at five o'clock, and the performance commenced precisely at six o'clock p. m., and the audience were thus enabled to return home not far from nine o'clock, seldom later than ten o'clock. Evening parties commenced at seven o'clock, and among the ladies of fashion the midnight hour found the guests departed.

The differences between old times and new are shown in nothing more strikingly than in theatres.

For my part I do not wonder, when I read the annals of the stage, that in the "good old days" we hear so much about, morality and religion were always at war with theatres and players.

If I had been alive in the days of Milton and Dryden, with my present ideas of right and wrong, I feel very forcibly that I should have been a Puritan, and should have had a wholesome horror of the player folk.

For I read that in the "good old days" the theatre was cursed with plays more vile and indecent than anything known to the present day, and I am quite ready to agree that "it is not wonderful that the honest Puritan, who wished to educate his children in the love of God and the practice of virtue, was unwilling to carry them to such an entertainment as this. If he were a tradesman, he would hardly care to have his progeny taught that the patient and plodding pursuit of a competence argued a low and mechanical nature, and that it would be far finer and more manly to live by the gains of tavern-dice, and upon the sufferance of extortionate money-lenders. If he were a member of a dissenting congregation, how would he have relished the ridicule of swaggering swash-bucklers, who with profuse profanity, swore that he was a hypocrite, and that the wife of his bosom was always in the market when the fops of the court were seeking such light commodity? How the people of the play-house regarded the Puritan may be gathered from Sir John Vanbrugh's preface to 'The Relapse.' 'As for the saints, your thorough-paced ones,' said he, 'with screwed faces and wry mouths, I despair of them: they are friends to nobody; they love nothing but their altars and themselves; they have too much zeal to have any charity; they make debauchees in piety, as sinners do in wine, and are as quarrelsome in their religion as other people are in their drink; so I hope nobody will mind what they say.' And this is in the preface to a play, which, to borrow a line from Fielding, is but a ragoût of smut and ribaldry. The sober citizen who knew that upon the stage he was libeled, slandered, ridiculed, and maligned—that the Scriptures which he held in awful reverence were quoted with unscrupulous license, to make him a laughing-stock—that the plays of his time were full of gratuitous oaths and indecorous jests to which we could not listen without horror—that the actors were usually loose men about town, needy and unscrupulous, some of them wenchers, and some of them dicers, and some of them bullies—that the actresses were half of them kept mistresses of gentlemen of quality, and a moiety of the remainder at the service of the first comer with a golden Carolus in his pocket—the honest man, we say, who knew all this, might well refuse to become the patron of the polluted boards. His was an indignant disinclination which no right thinking man can blame. The clergy who lashed the vices of the play-house—and many such were ornaments and guardians of the Established Church—had not only Christian truth but common good taste upon their side; and it was a side which they showed themselves amply able to defend against all comers, as Congreve found to his cost when he heedlessly grappled with Jeremy Collier, the great non-juror, and came out of the conflict mauled and bruised as never playwright was before. The Puritan had no horror of what was really excellent in dramatic literature, when its degrading connection (for such he considered it) with the play-house was severed. The first hearty recognition of the real greatness of Shakespeare came from the pen of John Milton, who was himself the author of the beautiful 'Masque of Comus,' which, until a few years, kept its place as a musical afterpiece upon the English stage. The most sturdy and resolute, and persistent sneers at Shakespeare, on the other hand, came from John Dryden, who found no relief from his torturing hatred of the Puritans, until he was safely lodged upon the bosom of the Roman Catholic Church, which, if he had but played in his own productions, would have refused him at that time a Christian burial."

That the theatre has not been utterly destroyed and swept from existence, under the influence of the baleful evils that have so often fastened upon it, is only due to the wonderful intrinsic vitality of the drama. For twenty-four hundred years it has existed. It was invented at Athens, Greece, twenty centuries ago. It has survived the rise and fall of empires, the change of the Greek and Latin languages from living to dead tongues; the downfall of kings, emperors and nations.

But above all it has outlived the destructive influences of vice and shamelessness, brought against it by wicked and worthless men, who have from time to time been its representatives and defenders.

A writer in the Cincinnati *Gazette*, in a mistaken conception of my position toward the drama, and a severe criticism thereon, said some things which I could not say better, if I tried. "We read of the time when people of rank attended the theatre, and we read of noble and other literary celebrities writing for it, and of the literary circles that went together to see a new play, and to approve or denounce it; and from this we have fancied that in those days the theatre must have been much more respectable than now, and that the actors and actresses were reputable and virtuous. But the manners of the time were coarse. The plays which they witnessed are mostly banished from the stage now, because of their indelicacy. Even the plays of Shakespeare, whom we have lately seen written down a Christian dramatist of the time when the theatre was a school of pure morality, have to be much 'cut' to suit the delicacy of our degenerate times. Literary men themselves were not considered a very reputable class at that time. And to be the mistress of a man of fashion was regarded as the natural relation of a favorite actress. The honest *Dame Quickly* expresses naively the common report, when, in admiration of *Falstaff's* acting of the heavy father in reproving *Prince Hal*, she exclaims, 'O rare! he doth it as like one of these harlotry players as ever I see.' If we place the palmy age of the stage at the time when it was most prolific in the great celebrities of its traditions, such as Garrick, Quin, Barry, Colley Cibber, Kemble, Cooke, and Foote, we shall find it a time when the drama was grossly licentious; when audiences were coarse and often turbulent; when the pit made free remarks upon the actresses, and they often replied; when the men of fashion frequented the 'tiring room' of the actresses, and freely commented on what was revealed and concealed, and when the great actresses generally were mistresses to men of wealth and fashion, and it made no difference in their reception by their royal patrons. In the list of the great actresses of the eighteenth century, whose names are now greatest in the traditions of the stage, they are very rare exceptions who lived according to the ordinances; while the list of our time and country has such as Julia Dean, Mrs. Mowatt, Miss Davenport, Miss Cushman, and many others who achieved success on the stage and maintained good social repute. If we place the palmy or the virtuous period of the stage at a time other than that when it produced its greatest historical celebrities, where shall we put it? In all later times it has been lamenting its decline. The stage has so much improved that a woman may be an actress without its being thought a matter of course that she has sacrificed modesty and chastity. That is a great improvement upon the 'pure age' of the drama. Actors and actresses are regarded as a peculiar people, on account of the atmosphere of fiction in which they are always seen by the public; but man or woman may now follow the stage and still maintain a social standing. Many American women have done so who were admirable in all the relations of life. In fine, the stage, though by no means perfect, has improved, and is improving in every respect—decency, reputability, remuneration, artistic ability, public appreciation and professional respectability."

In one respect it is undoubtedly true that there has been a retrograding movement on the part of our theatres. I refer to the accommodations provided for the players.

In former days, when the theatre was almost invariably a building from ground to attic, entirely devoted to theatrical uses—to the theatre, in fact—the comforts of the players were greater than they are in this progressive and utilizing age. But, now that ground is so very valuable in our large cities, and as theatres must always be situated in the most populous and fashionable quarters of the town, stores below and offices above encroach upon the theatre's space, and "behind the scenes" is a more cramped and crowded world than ever. Every available inch is given to the auditorium and the stage. In many theatres there no longer exists a green-room—that time-honored rallying ground of the players—and the dressing-rooms are bare and beggarly little cubbyholes, ill-lighted, damp, and foul-smelling.

But this is counterbalanced in numberless particulars, wherein the march of improvement has been steadily onward. A writer in one of our theatrical journals thus brings up several of these: "As a rule," he says, "our actors now take more pains to understand their parts than they did at a former period—this with regard to little ones as well as big. We have known the time when a professional having a part under what is technically called a 'length' (forty-two lines), was either careless about it, or exerted himself to render it ridiculous, deeming it below his deserts. Then, as to the dressing and scenery of plays—both betrayed the utmost ignorance on the part of managers who could pay for better. A gratifying evidence of the improvement we speak of, is afforded us on the occasion of Mr. Edwin Booth's appearance at the Winter Garden as *Hamlet*. How this tragedy used to be given, we need not inform our readers. If there was a tolerable performer in the principal character, it was considered quite enough. The rest might be below par—a *Ghost* that was husky instead of solemn, a *Polonius* senile and not courtly, a *Grave-digger* a buffoon in place of a quaint fellow, a *Claudius* who was a regularly ticketed villain instead of a very passable monarch, and an *Ophelia* who was an affected walking lady. Then, the costumes and the scenery! There was *Hamlet* himself dressed like a rope-dancer in mourning, the daughter of *Polonius* like a modern Miss done up for a ball, and the rest to suit; exteriors and interiors not known for many centuries after the represented race—the whole constituting a ludicrous hash. Where and when we saw Mr. Booth in the part all this was changed for the better. All the scenery was antique, also the costumes—the long, flowing habits of the era being the general wear. Often in our time had we seen *Claudius* seated on a throne bearing the English insignia of royalty; but it was different on the occasion in question, when, in place of the golden lions of Albion it was the mysterious raven of Denmark that met our view, and the banner of Odin in place of that of St. George. As 'Hamlet' used to be acted, the churchyard scene, instead of being one of the most solemn in the whole play, was usually changed into one of low fun. The idea of those who were sent on as the grave-diggers was that they were intended to show as the lowest sort of buffoons. To do this they tried their best in style of speech, in look and in action. What old play-goer can forget the bottle of supposed Rhenish from which the chief clod-shoveler has several pulls, the red nightcap on his head and the sixteen vests his companion helped him to take off? Another change for the better perceptible in plays, as they *are* acted, in contradistinction to that in which the *were* acted, is the grand music we have between the acts. This was a particular which used to be entirely neglected, or observed in a very careless way. It too frequently happened that we had no music save that preceding the first piece and that which followed, if there was a second, and this was of so lugubrious a quality as to remind us of the famous and oft-mentioned piece of our younger days, said to be 'tune the old cow died through.' Plays other than 'Hamlet' have suffered through negligence in the respect we have spoken of. There was 'Richard the Third,' wherein the actor, first as *Gloucester* and then as *King*, was a mass of tinsel and high calves. 'Othello,' wherein the *Moor* looked more like an Indian juggler than a military chieftain and the governor of an island; 'Romeo and Juliet,' in which young *Montague* showed, in the earlier scenes, more like a tight-rope dancer than a gentleman of Mantua, and in the latter more like the usual *Hamlet* than anybody else; 'Macbeth,' where the ambitious *Thane* and his associates were fancy ball Scots and nothing beside, and the *Witches* so many scavengers; and 'King Lear,' wherein the old monarch reminded us of some of the prints of Moses. Only fancy plays dressed like this, scened in a similar manner, carelessly acted, and preceded and followed by melancholy tunes from a shabby orchestra, and you will confess how different a thing a dramatic entertainment *was* to what it *is*. In the Old Country, it took a long time to bring the change about; but on this side of the water, from obvious causes, a comparatively brief period was required. We hear that in Shakespeare's time great improvements were introduced on the stage, but after then there must have been a retrograde movement, until the stage had little aid. It is a matter of authenticated record, that Garrick played *Hamlet* in 'smalls,' and a straight coat and vest; *Macbeth* in similar fixings, with the addition of a plaid scarf over his breast, with Mrs. Pritchard as his wife, in a high head dress and hooped skirts, such as were worn by ladies of that time. But

Garrick made many improvements in the dressing of plays, and was followed in the good path by the Kembles. Still, these improvements were confined to only a few of the principal parts—the honor of clothing an entire *dramatis personæ* with propriety being reserved for Mr. Macready and Madame Vestris—to the former in his association with historical plays; to the latter, in respect to comediettas and mythological pieces. It has been the same with the music at theatres; jingling tunes, and not many of them, have been succeeded by a liberal supply of fine pieces; and so have the qualifications for actors and managers been enhanced, till it requires very accomplished persons to fulfill the respective duties as they ought to be fulfilled. In the ornamentation of theatres, in the seating of the audience, and in the facilities for seeing, the people on this side of the water have the start of those on the other. It was at one time expected that care in what is called the 'mounting' of pieces would, in devoting so much attention to the material, detract from the efforts of actors and cause audiences to be less critical than it was proper they should be. In our time we have had objections like these piled up till they formed a perfect Ossa. But we never placed faith in them, and the sequel has shown how well we judged in assuming that the greater the pains taken in the direction of illusion by means of scenery and costume, the greater would be the endeavor of actors to perfect the illusion of *character*. One of the most obvious improvements in our theatres is their having numbered seats. This we derived from the French, who have their seats separate as well as numbered. This prevents crowding, and assures every person buying a ticket of the facilities for seeing and hearing. But simple and meritorious as the plan is, it is often sought to be abused by persons whom nothing on earth or in heaven will satisfy. For example, there is Mr. J. and Mr. A., who have taken two tickets, which entitles them to a couple of seats. They have a friend, Mr. B., who has bought an ordinary ticket at the box office in the evening. It does not provide him with an exact location; but he sees Mr. J. and Mr. A.; he wants to be near them, and so takes a seat next to one or the other. All well for the time; presently, however, the person who has bespoken the seat presents himself with his proper check, and the interloper is politely requested to give it up. He does so, though not with a good grace; in fact, we have often seen gentlemen very angry on the occasion, and heard them say something terrible about the manager and the theatre—even to go so far as to threaten the entire withdrawal of patronage therefrom. At the Boston theatre they have a very neat arrangement by which the time is told every five minutes. Two little compartments in the centre of the proscenium, above the stage, attract notice, the one on the right showing the hour, that on the left the figures five, ten and upwards to fifty-five, the change next ensuing gives the new hour and so on. There is a great deal of cleverness in this idea, and credit is due to the person who first conceived it."

It is curious, in these days when the reserved seat system is so universal at all places of amusement, to read an account given by manager Wood in his "Recollections," of the troubles following the introduction of private boxes into the Philadelphia theatre. The difficulty attaching to this innovation, he relates, came to him with the very opening of the theatre in 1793. "Mrs. Bingham, a lady, in her day the chief leader in the fashion of Philadelphia, the wife of an early and valued friend of Wignell himself, a lady of great social and family influence, and very extensively connected, proposed for the purchase of a box *at any price to be fixed by the manager.* She had passed much of her early married life in France and England, where she was uncommonly admired, and being a woman of exclusive and elegant tastes, was desirous to have the privileges which were allowed in the theatres with which she had been familiar abroad. She offered to furnish and decorate the box at her own expense; but it was an absolute condition that the key should be kept by herself, and no admission to it allowed to any one except on her assent. Mr. Wignell had many strong inducements to accept this offer. He was undertaking a new enterprise. *He could name his own sum.* It was a certainty. It would gratify an early friend, whose large fortune might prove of great value to him. He knew that it was probably the only condition on which he was likely to have either the presence, or perhaps the very cordial wishes of a fair, elegant and influential woman, whose house was the rendezvous of the distinguished and really elegant foreigners whom the French revolution had brought here. Her voice in the small world of fashion which Philadelphia then acknowledged, would be quite potential. He looked at the matter, however, with much more comprehensive and philosophic regards. He knew that the theatre in a country like ours must depend entirely for permanent success, not upon individuals, however powerful, not upon clubs, cliques, factions or parties, but upon THE PUBLIC alone; that in a country where the spirit of liberty is so fierce as in ours, such a privilege would excite from an immense class a feeling of positive hostility; and it made no difference in his view that the expression of it might be suppressed, which it was doubtful whether it would be, as the suspicion would be fatal. He saw that it must be a cardinal maxim of any American manager to act on the principles of his country's government, and on the recognition of feelings deeply pervading the structure of its society; to hold, in short, all men 'free' to come into his house, and 'equal' while they continued to be and behave themselves in it. This country he well perceived has not, and cannot have any class which, as a body, possesses even the claims to exclusive privileges which exist abroad, and which give a prestige impossible and unfit to be asserted or allowed for an aristocracy here; an aristocracy which, with occasional exceptions, must be one of money merely, the most despicable and poorest of all grounds of distinction. He therefore with great address, and with many expressions of polite regret, declined the offers of his beautiful friend, and stuck steadily to his wisely settled system. The result was just as he anticipated. The lady, though not capable of resentment, and expressing her acquiesence in his views as a sound one, scarcely ever visited the theatre again; but the theatre itself was filled by a constant and satisfied public. It was pleasantly intimated by some persons that Mrs. B. fixed on some occasions of extraordinary benefits at the theatre for evening entertainments at her house. But though exceedingly caressed, she was not an unamiable woman, and her house was very often open. This coincidence was probably accidental. Another case occurred at a later day. A gentleman of Baltimore, a proprietor in the theatre, and a constant supporter and true lover of the drama, made a proposal nearly in these words: 'I wish to secure a box in which I shall always be certain of seats for my family. I will give at once $3,000 for an ownership of this box for the term of my life. No fashionable box is desired. One of those in the second tier, not more than four from the stage, will satisfy me. I will engage that on any day at twelve o'clock, when I may not be able or willing to occupy the box, the key shall be sent to the office, and the box be at the service of any you may choose to accommodate.' Nothing could be more liberal than this; nor would anything have been more convenient to us than the receipt of so large a sum as $3,000, at a moment when we were making great expenditures in the opening of our house. A short consideration of the subject settled the answer of the managers, and a few words of explanation satisfied our liberal friend that a compliance with his wish would be injurious to us. He saw the case, and withdrew his proposal with all the kindness and liberality with which he had first offered it."

It has lately struck me with peculiar force, in looking back upon the history of the drama, that in its early days it presents an interesting resemblance to the American lecture system of our time — which, when it was first set on foot, was intended solely as an instructor, without any idea of amusement. But year by year the popular lecture has taken on more and more of the character of an entertainment, until in the present day the most popular "lecturer" is John B. Gough, whose lectures are little more than a series of dramatic performances, with a sort of moral and instructive background.

So we read that "the Greek drama, being solely a religious ceremony, never had for its object the *amusement* of the people, but their instruction. It never contemplated *illusion* as its object. *Suggestion* was all it aimed at; consequently its adjuncts, in the shape of dress and scenery, were severely simple. The words, the acting, the tones of the voice were its chief study; and Shaw, in his 'English Literature,' observes: 'In comparison with the Greeks, we, with our painted scenery, shifting scenes, and complicated machinery, are as a painted and dressed waxen figure to a marble statue.'"

This sounds curiously like a remark made by the Boston *Advertiser*, in criticising my lecture on "Girls." "The Muse of Lecturing," said this critic, "as we paint her to ourselves, is clad in the simplest robes, and is direct, unartificial, and severely simple in manner."

But the "Muse of Lecturing" (conceding the existence of this new goddess), according to the critical pattern here set up, is going rapidly out of fashion.

The lecture is becoming, as the drama has become, a

means of innocent intellectual diversion for the long winter evenings.

May it be long ere the faults which have cursed the theatre shall attach themselves to the lyceum!

The play-house of a hundred years ago was brought before me in vivid colors by an old playbill which I lately saw, and of which the following is a copy:

By Particular Desire.

FOR THE BENEFIT OF MISS BRICKLER.

THEATRE ROYAL, IN COVENT GARDEN.

On Saturday next, being May 16th, 1767,

"THE BEGGAR'S OPERA."

Captain Macheath by Mr. Beard, Peachum by Mr. Shutter, Locket by Mr. Dunstall, Filch by Mr. Holtom, Player by Mr. Gardner, Beggar by Mr. Bennet, Mat-o'-the-Mint by Mr. Baker, Lucy by Mrs. Baker, Mrs. Peachum by Mrs. Stephens, Diana Trapis by Mrs. Copin, Mrs. Slammekin by Mrs. Green, Polly by Miss Brickler; with a hornpipe by Miss D. Twist; and a country dance by the characters in the opera.

End of Act I. Miss Brickler will sing a favorite song from "Judith," accompanied by Mr. Dibdin on a new instrument called Piano-Forte.

To which will be added a farce called

"THE UPHOLSTERER."

The Barber by Mr. Woodward, Feeble by Mr. Murdin, Bellmour by Mr. Perry, Rovewell by Mr. Davis, Watchman by Mr. Weller, Quidnunc by Mr. Dunstall, Pamphlet by Mr. Shuter, Harriet by Miss Vincent, Maid by Miss Cockayne, Termagant by Mrs. Green.

Tickets to be had of Mr. Sarjant, at the stage door, where places for boxes may be taken.

It was a curious custom in that day to permit a portion of the audience to sit upon the stage, and it is easy to understand how these spectators must have incommoded the actors.

In an early number of the *Spectator*, Steele, describing a visit to the Haymarket Theatre, makes mention of his surprise at seeing a "well-dressed young fellow in a full-bottomed wig appear in the midst of the sea, and, without any visible concern, take snuff."

The *Fine Gentleman* in Garrick's little comedy of "Lethe" describes to *Æsop* his manner of spending his evenings: "I dress and go generally behind the scenes of both playhouses—not, you may imagine, to be diverted with the play, but to intrigue and show myself; I stand upon the stage, talk loud and stare about, which confounds the actors and disturbs the audience, upon which the galleries, who hate the appearance of one of us, begin to hiss and to cry, 'Off, off!' while I, undaunted, stamp my foot so, loll with my shoulder thus, take snuff with my right hand, and smile scornfully thus. This exasperates the savages and they attack us with volleys of sucked oranges and half-eaten pippins." "And you retire?" *Æsop* inquires. "Without doubt," replies the *Fine Gentleman*, "if I am sober; for orange will stain silk, and an apple disfigure a feature."

It is almost incredible to us, with our present-day ideas of the sacred illusions of the stage, that it was long a custom in the London theatres, on special occasions or particular benefits, to accommodate an overflowing house by means of benches erected across the stage, rising one above the other, until sometimes the spectators were perched up higher than the trees of the scenery, and hats and bonnets were beheld fastened to the clouds. The playbill of Garrick's benefit in 1742, contains an announcement that "the stage will be formed into an amphitheatre, where servants will be allowed to keep places." In the following year it was stated that "the stage will be formed into side boxes, and seven rows of the pit will be railed into boxes." The entrances were oftentimes on these occasions so choked up by the spectators that the players could hardly come upon the scene; "and," says an authority, "the feats of Bosworth Field, amidst drums, trumpets, battle-axes and spears, were enacted between two audiences, while *Richard* spoke his tent soliloquy and his dying lines upon a carpet no bigger than a table-cloth."

Tate Wilkinson relates that he had seen Mrs. Cibber, as *Juliet*, prostrating herself on an old couch covered with black cloth to represent the tomb of the Capulets, with at least two hundred persons behind her, and that when Quin returned to the stage for one night to play *Falstaff* for Ryan's benefit, notwithstanding the impatience of the audience to see their old favorite, it was several minutes before he could force his way on to the stage through the numbers that wedged him in. "But this arrangement, however remunerative to the actor whose benefit was thus so liberally patronized, was very unsatisfactory to those among the spectators who came to the theatre for entertainment and with an eye to scenic illusion. Moreover bickerings and jealousies ensued between the audiences before and behind the curtain. Thereupon arose a practice, especially favored by the less popular comedians, of inserting at the bottom of their advertisements and playbills, by way of an additional attraction, a notice in the following terms: 'N. B.—There will be no building on the stage.' Thus, on the occasion of Mrs. Bellamy's benefit in 1753, the bills of the night announced, 'No part of the pit will be railed into boxes, nor any building on the stage.' The presence of the spectators behind the scenes was for a long period a grave inconvenience and annoyance to the players. Efforts were made from time to time to abate what had become a real nuisance. In 1738, on the production of 'Comus' at Drury Lane, there was a notice in the playbills: 'To prevent any interruption to the music, dancing, etc., 'tis hoped no gentleman will take it ill they cannot be admitted behind the scenes or in the orchestra.' In the following season another notification appeared: 'The audience having lately been much disgusted at the performance being interrupted by persons crowding on the stage, it is humbly hoped none will take it ill that they cannot be admitted behind the scenes in future.' When 'King John' was revived in 1745 there appeared a somewhat similar announcement, the reason alleged being that the play was so full of characters that company behind the scenes would be of great prejudice to the performance. A few years later appears another notice: 'As the admission of persons behind the scenes has occasioned a general complaint on account of the frequent interruptions in the performance, 'tis hoped that gentlemen won't be offended that no money will be taken there for the future.' Garrick, when he became manager, was much bent upon a thorough reform in this matter; but thorough reforms, as we all know, are not easy of accomplishment. The actors, in many cases, would not venture upon the expense of taking benefits if they were to be deprived of the privilege of crowding their friends upon the stage. The building on the stage sometimes put as much as a hundred or even a hundred and fifty pounds into the pocket of the 'beneficiare.' Then the young men of fashion, steady patrons of the drama, claimed the right to 'go behind' not merely on benefit nights, but on all other occasions as well, and questioned the manager's power to control their wishes; while he, on his side, had some natural compunctions about offending such very constant supporters. It was not until the theatre was enlarged in 1762, and the space before the curtain made to contain as many persons as formerly filled the boxes, pit, galleries and stage, that the actors were appeased, the excuse for going on the stage was removed, and the inconvenience and evil of the proceeding in a great degree suppressed. From that time only a very privileged few were admitted to the 'arcana' of the playhouse."

The changes which have taken place in the theatres themselves are as great as those which have taken place in the plays which were represented therein. We seldom see on our stage to-day any such absolute defiance of good morals as was exhibited by the dramatists of the Restoration.

Even our blonde burlesquers make a *pretense* of respecting public opinion, and offer "appeals to the public" in defence of their nude "innocent amusements."

Not so in old times. The dramatists of the Restoration were frankly and confessedly wicked. "If they were devoid of virtuous instruction, they did not pretend to proffer it; if their plays were one long-drawn sneer at female chastity, they did not affect to believe in its existence; if they gibed at the sober citizen, they vowed that they thought a rake-helly life the only one for a man of spirit, and money of no value except to squander in the brothel or at the basset-table, upon loose ladies of quality or upon tailors of a brilliant taste. The refined corruptions of the court and the stolid virtues of the city were the constant themes of playwrights, who professed an easy familiarity with the one and an impudent contempt for the other. They laughed at their monarchs, and they libelled their merchants. They borrowed money, and repaid the obligation by ruining the lender's wife. It was a rare joke, at which the whole theatre roared, to bilk a banker of his cash, and then to destroy his domestic happiness. It showed wit and good breeding to gibe at his honesty, to caricature his religion, to sneer at his punctuality, and to burlesque the formality of his manners. Yet the men who were thus systematically subjected to derision not merely laid the foundation of the commercial greatness of England, but were continually called upon to supply the necessities of a poor yet extravagant court. The palace depended for food and raiment upon the counting-house, when it did not more ignominiously depend upon the subsidies of Louis XIV. There is a laughable story in Pepys of the lamentable shifts to which Charles II. was driven in the matter of clean linen, through the peculations of his valet and the badness of the royal credit with the draper. A fine lady in the comedies which we are considering was a hybrid of French levity grafted upon English coarseness. After her marriage—and sometimes before it—she felt herself at liberty to swear, to gamble, to drink, and to intrigue. The chief business of her life was to irritate and mortify and ruin her husband; to pass all day in bed reading romances, and all night at a drum dancing minuets; to play high and to paint high; to divert herself with ratafia, the spleen, or coarse talk over a raking pot of tea; to disseminate scandal about her dearest friends, and to cheapen old China at an auction. Virtue did well enough for parsons' wives and dowagers in their decadence. But virtue could not satisfy the wants of a fine lady. 'Can virtue,' sneers Sir Harry Wildair, 'bespeak a front row in the boxes? No; for the players cannot live upon virtue. Can your virtue keep you a coach and six? No, no; your virtuous woman walks afoot. Can your virtue hire you a pew in the church? Why, the very sexton will tell you, No. Can your virtue stake for you at piquet? No; then what business has a woman with virtue?' Yet this very homily comes from gallant, dashing, delightful *Sir Harry*—a part often played by a woman, as a print of pretty Mrs. Greville in the character, in our possession, attests. It is strange that this vulgar type of tainted women should, for so many years, have kept possession of the English stage, from which it has now, and, as we trust, forever, almost entirely disappeared. The character of *Lady Teazle,* which is but a faint and tolerably modest copy of her predecessors, was the last specimen of it upon the London boards."

Coming down to more modern days, and to American theatres, it is noteworthy that changes of the most thorough and sweeping character have taken place in the dramatic temples of our days.

It is within my own recollection that the hideous abomination known as the "third tier" was in existence in our theatres. I can only speak from hearsay, of course, concerning the wickedness of this shameful evil; but I well remember, in my early girlhood, having looked up from my place on the stage, to the brutal exhibition of faces in the gallery, with something such a feeling as one might have in looking over into pandemonium.

That dark, horrible, guilty "third tier!" How dreadful it seemed to me that the theatre should be cursed with such a monstrous iniquity!

I well remember the newspaper war which was waged upon the last lingering remnant of this shameful thing in the Cincinnati theatres. There was but one theatre left where the loathesome wickedness of the "third tier" had failed to yield to the onward march of public opinion. And on this theatre a determined attack was made by the press, with the settled purpose of breaking up the wickedness.

I cannot better place on record this foul shame than by quoting one of the articles which appeared at this time in the Cincinnati *Daily Enquirer*,—an article which at once tells my readers what the vile old third tier *was*, and illustrates the vigor of the war which was made upon it when public opinion was once turned against it.

"From the bills of this house," says the *Enquirer*, alluding to the old National theatre, "the public learn that its doors will be closed for the time being, for the purpose of re-decoration, etc., and that it will again open, in a few days, with a powerful company. It is to be hoped that if its polluted doors are again to be opened to the public, the management will pursue a different course from the one which has characterized his conduct during the whole season, and give us dramatic entertainments worthy the patronage of the citizens and the public, and not of the 'exclusiveness' which has been exhibited nightly on its boards, and which was of such a 'powerful' character, in connection with the scenes enacted in the 'third tier,' by drunken cyprians, as to drive the more respectable and order-loving portion of the lovers of the drama from the house. The time was when a 'third tier' for prostitutes in a theatre was looked upon as a matter of necessity; and as long as these prostitutes were prevented from exhibiting themselves to those in the lower tiers of boxes, it was thought nothing of. The parent saw no impropriety in taking his sons and daughters to the theatre. The precepts inculcated by the great bards, in the productions of the stage, were considered of a salutary character to the young mind. It made no difference to him how many cyprians were admitted to the third tier, so long as his children were not brought under their contaminating influence, and were not aware of the fact. But the times have changed. We are progressive, and have learned to the contrary. Many a parent has learned from sad experience that he was in error when he permitted his children to visit places of amusement where free license was given to prostitutes of the most abandoned and degraded character, for we believe it is admitted on all sides that none but the most degraded of prostitutes visit the theatre, and they only to entrap and deceive the unwary. Some three months since, the press of this city in the most unqualified manner, denounced the National theatre as the vilest of 'assignation houses,' and advised their readers to discountenance the house unless the third tier was closed. The appeal to the people was too strong for the management to resist, and the third tier *was closed*,

with a promise that it should not be opened again,—at least we were so advised by the stage manager. What was the result? It was announced in the bills and through the press, that the third tier would be *closed in future.* The better portion of our citizens took the manager at his word, and once more graced the theatre with the beauty and fashion of the city. The third tier being closed, everything was orderly and quiet; the ear of the wife and daughter was not shocked by the profanity of language and licentious actions that nightly before descended from that sink of iniquity, the 'assignation house' of the National. The warm season coming on, and the greater portion of our theatre-going public leaving the city on tours of pleasure, the attendance at the theatre necessarily diminished. The cause was natural, but the management thought not. They thought the people must be brought out; if they could not bring the respectable portion to the theatre when the thermometer stood at 95, the rabble must be induced to come; and to do this, the third tier was again opened, and an officer despatched to the low dens of prostitution, to invite their inmates to revel once more within the luxurious bar-room of the assignation tier of the National. Reader, think for a moment on the idea of the management. Is it not horrible, revolting, and diabolical? He seeks to fill his theatre and put money in his pocket, by placing prostitutes in the third tier, that they may, by their temptations, allure the youth of our city from the paths of rectitude. It is nothing more, disguise it as you will, but opening an assignation house on a large scale, and in a public manner; for do not the abandoned women who visit there nightly do so for the purpose of carrying on a trade in the prostitution of their bodies and souls? Most assuredly they do. Our laws are stringent on this subject, and yet, although the police have been busy, within a few days past, in ferreting out houses of a lesser magnitude, the National theatre is permitted to continue on in its infamous career. Some one says the management has the police in his pay, and for fear that they may be deprived of the paltry pittance he pays them, they keep mum. It is, however, always the case in law,—the rich escape, no matter how guilty, and the poor, no matter how innocent, suffer. The rule is applicable to the National. The sovereigns—the people—are, however, becoming awakened to their great error in supporting a theatre whose only qualification lies in a desire to pander to vice and immorality, and are rapidly withdrawing their patronage from it. A case in point. Some six weeks since, the Italian Opera Troupe, under the management of M. De Fries, was, through motives which we do not propose here to discuss, induced to take the Lyceum theatre, an establishment which had been closed for some time on account of the disreputable character of the house, produced by a course of action similar to that being pursued by the management of the National. However, on that point our readers are perfectly conversant. Every lover of opera was pained to hear the announcement that the opera troupe were to play at the Lyceum, and the universal prediction was, their performances would be a failure. 'No one who has any respect for themselves or family will go to the Lyceum!' was a common remark, and the poor artists, with misgivings of their success, commenced their season with a comparatively small house. Everything passed off orderly and quietly; no prostitutes were admitted to the house, nor was the ear of the virtuous female insulted by the coarse ribaldry of the wanton. The next day the words passed rapidly from mouth to mouth, 'The opera troupe sing well, and deserve patronage. You can take your wife and daughter without fear of having their feelings shocked by indecencies.' What was the result? The next evening the Lyceum was crowded, and numbers were turned away, unable to gain admission, and so the attendance continued. The troupe left our city for Louisville, where they also played a most successful engagement. On returning to this city, the management of the National effected an engagement with the troupe, thinking that as they had crowded the Lyceum, under all disadvantageous circumstances, they would certainly crowd to overflowing the great National. But here they reckoned without their host. The opera troupe came, but the *people* did not follow them. The edict had gone forth, 'We will not patronize an institution that insults our wives and daughters by making a portion of its edifice a common assignation house, no matter how great the attraction. The man who seeks to put money in his pocket by catering to the base passions of man, is no better than the most degraded cyprian.' The opera troupe, after playing to comparatively empty benches, left our city, we are informed, fully convinced of the unpopularity of the management of the National, and with the consciousness that the manager was one thousand dollars worse off in pocket than when they entered it. The people would not visit a house like the National after the exposition that had been made of the doings of its management by the Press of this city, no matter what the attraction. If the management of the National wish to make their theatre such as it should be, let them close their third tier, and put a good company on its stage. Unless they do this, we assure them all their efforts to draw respectable houses will be futile, and the result will be that they will have again to close their doors, at a heavy loss. The people will not countenance an attempt to play on the baser passions of man to fill their theatre. It is an insult to their good sense to cater to their amusement in a theatre by placing apart a portion of the house as a place of assignation."

It was such bold and outspoken expressions as this which, backed up and supported actively by the people, resulted in the complete extinction of the third tier, until to-day no vestige of it remains, so far as I know, in any theatre in the land.

When we reflect that no more than twenty years ago this thing was a common and usual attachment of all theatres, it is easy to see what tremendous power there is in public opinion, and in newspaper attacks on the abuses of the drama.

It is my unflinching faith in the power of public opinion to elevate and purify the theatre, which causes me to "keep up a good heart and labor on."

Reading an article from the pen of George William Curtis, two or three years ago, I seemed to find in it the inspiration to my subsequent course in writing and speaking of the theatre and the drama. "Work upon public opinion," it said. "Make that true, healthy, robust, and it will put forth noble, and purifying, and energetic laws. And each good law will mark the high-tide point of the nation in that direction. It will not have been forced up by artificial means, and be sure to fall to-morrow; but it will be the calm level of general conviction. The presentation by the Grand Jury of the snares and pitfalls of Broadway is an influence brought to bear upon public opinion. In due season they may be suppressed upon precisely the same grounds that certain books and pictures are seized, and their sale forbidden. Every honest citizen owes the Grand Jury thanks. Every scoundrel in the country will call them Puritans."

This was apropos of an effort made to suppress certain disreputable and baleful places of amusement in Broadway.

Public opinion, its attention aroused by the press, demanded the suppression of these places.

They are suppressed!

It was public opinion, moved to action by the press, which demanded the abolition of the vile third tiers in our theatres.

They are abolished!

It was public opinion, awakened and inflamed by the press, which recently demanded the return of the theatres of New York to the proper walks of the drama, and the banishment of the blonde jiggers.

They are banished!

Wherever and whenever public opinion has directed its tremendous force steadily against an evil, that evil has disappeared.

And the best proof that the theatre can be kept free from the orgies of leg-performers, and the degrading influences of foul and immoral plays, is afforded in the above instances of public opinion's work.

CHAPTER XXXVII.

Opera Going.—Interesting Reminiscences.—Kellogg.—Susini.—Brignoli. Old Times.—Truffi and Benedetti.—Bosio.—Steffanoni—Operatic Expenses.—Salaries of Singers.—A Curious History.—Palmo, the Operatic Manager.—French Opera in America.—Offenbach.—English Opera.—Mrs. Richings-Bernard and Madame Parepa-Rosa.—Behind the Scenes at the Opera.—The Singing Green-room.—An Operatic Rehearsal.—Rachel and La Marsellaise.—Music as a Medicine.—An Orchestra consisting of a Single Violin.

About everything pertaining to the opera, there is to me a special charm.

Music is a passion with me; and while I have no ability either as a vocalist or an instrumentalist, my technical and critical knowledge of music is very thorough.

I have no patience with musical mediocrity. It is so painful to my sense to hear false singing or playing—to listen to the bellowing of some coarse fellow with a voice like a bull, and no culture, or the frantic squallings of the average young lady singer who haunts the parlors of the period—that I would rather pass an equal length of time with a raging toothache, than bear the pangs these creatures inflict.

For many years I have never missed any favorable opportunity to attend the opera; and I have heard the finest singers of either sex, in this country and Europe, but especially those who adorned the Parisian operatic stage during my residence there.

In this country opera-going is far from being the matter-of-course that it is in France.

The only operas that have ever been pecuniarily profitable in this country, I think, are the operas bouffes which were originally brought out here by Mr. Bateman; and these representations had so many objectionable features connected with them that they were religiously tabooed by a very large class of people with whom the grand opera ranks first among all amusements.

The genial gossiper of the Easy Chair, whose cultivated reminiscences are always fraught with the truest artistic sense, chats about opera in New York—and what he says of New York is mainly true of Philadelphia, Boston, Chicago and all American cities—in these terms: "The opera is always a lottery in New York. Since Grisi and Mario did not surely and always fill the house, it is in vain that the city talks of taste, and knowledge and enjoyment of music. It has its metropolitan degree yet to take. For if it had known itself better it would not have built so huge a house; and if it insisted upon the opera from knowledge, and not from fashion and imitation of other capitals, it would have recognized the great singers when they came. What wonderful singing was that of Grisi, in her resolute moments, upon this very stage! When she saw the impassive audience, and determined to conquer, by the force of superb disdain, she recovered her old splendor and swept the stage and thrilled the house with great bursts of lyric passion. They had slight response, and she drooped again, and everybody said 'What a pity such an old woman does not sink into private life!' Well, she did persist too long. Her voice in New York was not what it had been in Paris twenty years before. But the grandeur of her style was still the same; yes, it was finer. And Mario was in his prime when he was here. One evening when he sang in 'Lucia,' the last scene was the most marvelously sung of any in the annals of the Academy stage. It is hard to believe that Rubini could have surpassed it. Thus it is part of the fascination of a theatre as of a ball-room that the associations are so vivid. The ghosts and the living mingle in almost equal distinctness. Perhaps it is the scenic, half-spectral, unreal appearance of the persons upon the stage that summons the wholly spectral figures of the departed. But when I sit and hear an opera I hear at the same time all the other operas I ever heard. It was 'Martha,' the other evening, and Anschutz, director, and Susini was the *Plunkett.* But as I sat it was thirteen years before and the opera was 'Martha,' and it was the opera house at Berlin, and it was Flotow the composer, who directed, and it was Botticher who was *Plunkett;* then it was Formes who was *Plunkett,* and the whole thing seemed shadowy and languid, and the singers to be indifferent, and they and the audience to be in a musing trance of memory. It was not so, of course. For with Miss Kellogg, the prima donna, it was a very serious task of the present time. She was making her impression, and she knew that she had certain other impressions to unmake or overlay. And it was equally serious with Susini who knew that Formes used to be funnier than he, disproportionately funny, indeed. And it was serious with Brignoli who had a cold and constantly expectorated and was glum because the house was not full. Was it less serious with the gay groups in the boxes and gallery, or balcony as they call it? The youth of the year eighteen hundred and sixty-two is not less fresh than that of a century ago, and it was just as fresh and pleasant and exciting to the new eyes as it used to be to the old ones. So it was only you that were musing and remembering; and that peculiar bloom of enjoyment which you cannot help thinking is gone from all fruit because it is rubbed off your particular plum, is just as soft and lovely and perfect as ever it was. 'Boys having now become men,' said the Afghan prince when he became two dozen years old, 'it is ordered that all rocking-horses in the realm be destroyed.' The only really fine singing was Brignoli's. He is not in the least magnetic. He is even more of a lay-figure than tenors generally are. He has all the childish whims and absurdities of the tenor. But his voice is exquisite, and he sings much more easily than he walks. We have had no such voice except Mario's. Antoquini I did not hear. Salvi had to pump up his voice, and it was a thin trickle when it came—thin, but very clear and sweet. Bettini's voice was inadequate for the house and his own size. But Brignoli's has the charm and quality which make a tenor voice the luxury of kings and the enthusiasm of fashion. A king gives enormous sums to tempt a tenor to his theatre, as the Emperor of Russia tempted Rubini. But he does it as he would give a fortune for the rarest flower or the most brilliant gem. And Nature hides all these treasures in queer places. You shall find the flower in a lonely, noisome marsh, or the pearl in the oyster, or the voice in Alboni. It is well worth a fortune when you find it. * * * The opera with us began properly in Chambers street. There was the old National, indeed, where Miss Sherriff sung; and we do not forget that Malibran herself had sung in the old Park. But as an institution of our fine society it dates from Palmo's in Chambers street. They used to sing 'Belisario' there, and we all looked knowing, and said that it was really very well. They sang, too, the plaintive, pathetic 'Puritani;' and then some people for the first time felt the character of Italian music. The theatre was very small. It was prodigiously uncomfortable. But dear me! in white gloves and white waistcoats (they were actually worn then), who could be conscious of anything but bliss? Then came the flight up town to Astor Place. Palmo was submerged, and Patti and Sanquirico appeared as managers. The golden age of the Astor Place Opera was the brief and beautiful epoch of Truffi and Benedetti. No operatic success in this country was ever so entirely satisfactory, probably, to the audience as theirs. We all went mad with the loveliest of *Lucias*, and died in tuneful agony with the most delicious of tenors. Poor Benedetti lost his voice. The climate was too sharp, or he had his tonsils cut, or some sad mishap befell; in any case he lost his voice, and all we Easy Chairs of both sexes, our joy. Truffi herself faded after Benedetti failed. She never seemed quite the same, and gradually she disappeared from the scene. A multitude of singers followed, chief of whom was Bosio, whom some of us—that is, we who made up the truly wise part of the opera-goers—knew to be as fine a singer as she was afterward declared to be in Europe. But the poor Astor Place house floundered along in its latter days, attempting to believe Parodi a tolerable prima donna, and flying white doves to her from the gallery on the night she appeared, with sonnets of adulation and ecstacy tied round their necks and showered about the house. But Steffanoni came, took snuff, and carried the town by her ample self-possession and unctuous voice. She had the dowdy air and pure good humor of Alboni, and she sang with a richness and fire that charmed and surprised."

The expenses of grand opera are very large. It is unnecessary to go into details; the chief expenses arise from the fact that the director has to pay leading artists high salaries; has to appropriate a considerable sum nightly for a numerous and imperative orchestra; has to satisfy the perpetually craving appetite of a clamorous chorus; has to feed and clothe a more or less brilliant ballet; has to employ "supers" who will not work for nothing, although the work is light; has to purchase the assistance of prompters, stage managers, machinists, and scene-shifters; has to keep a well stocked wardrobe; has to provide new scenery and have the old frequently retouched; has to see his best seats occupied by dead-head stockholders; and has to pay a dividend to the same stockholders in the shape of a heavy rent. He has, in short, to meet the usual expenses of a first class theatre, with a very large amount of additional expense for his peculiar attractions.

When it is remembered that even in foreign cities, where certainly the opera is more popular than with us, its expenses are largely met by governmental appropriations, the wonder is, that here—where the government has enough to do to pay its own expenses, and does little or nothing for art—we should have ever had any opera at all.

The Parisian Grand Opera, since its foundation by Louis XIV., has constantly been—except during the reign of Louis Philippe and the ephemeral Republic of February—a strictly governmental establishment, "founded and sustained to advance national musical genius, and, perhaps, it should be added, to attract and retain strangers in Paris. Louis XVIII. is reported to have said to one of his courtiers who remonstrated with him on the enormous amount of money annually expended on the opera, 'Do you think the receipts of the opera are taken in at the door? No, they are received at the frontier.' The royal remark was just, for it is these intellectual appeals which allure the roving traveler, who, after 'doing' a score or so of cathedrals and museums, is but too glad of a decent excuse for retiring from sight-seeing and closing his 'Murray' forever. But it is rather difficult to suppress a stare, when we learn that this decoy-duck requires annually sums varying from a hundred to a hundred and fifty thousand dollars above the receipts at the door. Even after we are told that there is an orchestra of eighty performers, some seventy choristers, eighty dancers, seventy machinists, and we know not how many supernumeraries, all living on the opera-house treasury, it is hard to avoid resorting to the use of the pedagogue's safety-valve, and relieving our astonishment with a deep-fetched 'Prodigious!' The keeping of a white elephant is a trifle by the side of the alimony of this syren. All this, however, is the business of the taxpayers on the other side of the ocean, and is of no more concern to us than the tortures of the man who rests hours, salamander-like, in a red-hot oven, or of the beast-tamer mangled by his pet lion or darling tiger. We may have our private opinion on the matter, but so long as the eleemosynary hat is not intruded into our face—play, opera! roast, mountebank! bleed, tamer!"

The salaries paid to singers are sometimes enormous. Prima donnas, especially, are often in receipt of very high salaries. "No one among women receives a larger income, apart from property, except she be an empress or a queen. There is only this difference: the income of the sovereign is for life, while that of the prima donna is only for the life of her voice, which, however, may fairly be reckoned at twenty-five years. Among men, no minister of state is so highly paid as Madam Patti was last winter, at St. Petersburg. The salary of a first-rate prima donna is about equal to that of an ambassador (say $50,000 a year), and she retains the right denied to the unfortunate ambassador, of receiving presents. Alboni receives equal terms with Patti, from the Emperor of Russia. Mlle. Christine Nilsson, for a few concerts in the provinces, receives $20,000. Rarity and excellence are always well paid. When the Empress Catherine heard the terms demanded by a popular prima donna, she exclaimed that that was more than she gave to one of her marshals. Thereupon Gabrielle advised her to get one of her marshals to sing."

The history of grand opera in America is forever inseparably associated with the name of Ferdinand Palmo.

The history of this once wealthy and successful impresario is one of the most curious known to the annals of the "show" world—of which, of course, even grand opera is a branch.

Palmo was born in Naples, about 1785. When he was a young man of twenty-five, he came to this country, and settled in Richmond, Va. "There he remained in business for six years, when he removed to New York city and opened a confectionery store on Broadway; but he was not successful, and he returned to Virginia. After paying two visits to Europe he once more settled down in New York, built an establishment known as the *Cafe des Mille Colonnes*, made quite a snug little fortune. In 1835 he opened a saloon on Chambers street, afterwards known as Palmo's Opera House, Burton's Theatre, and now used by the United States Courts. When he first opened this place it was a sort of concert saloon, but unlike those of the present day. In 1844 Mr. Palmo, naving a great desire to introduce Italian opera on a firmer basis than had yet been attempted in America, altered his establishment, at an expense of $100,000, and called it Palmo's Opera House, which he opened Feb. 2d, 1844, for a season of Italian opera, presenting 'Il Puritani.' Vattelina was the director of the company, and Rapetti leader of the orchestra. During the season he produced the best operas of the day. The venture proved an unlucky one for Palmo, in a pecuniary sense. 'High art' was not cultivated, or, in fact, really appreciated in those days, and, after three years of managerial experience, Palmo found himself reduced to poverty. Assisted by a few friends he opened a hotel, which he kept nine months, when he returned to New York and became cook for Mr. Chris. Williams, who kept the 'Waverly,' corner Fourth street and Broadway, where he might have often been seen wearing his white apron and square paper cap, and engaged in preparing the delectable dishes for which that establishment was noted. The death of Mr. Williams some years ago, threw Palmo out of a situation, and reduced him to very straightened circumstances. He was now, too, well advanced in age, and unable to perform much manual labor. The theatrical managers and many members of the dramatic and musical professions were determined that one who had done so much for art (who may, in fact, be justly styled the father of opera in the United States), should not be reduced to want. Accordingly they formed into an association for the purpose of creating what was known as the Palmo Fund, each member paying $13 annually, which money was devoted to the support of their old friend and co-laborer. On this fund Palmo was ever afterward enabled to live comfortably. He was a mild and genial gentleman, whose affable manner and natural goodness of heart made for him hosts of friends. He never relinquished his love for the opera, and whenever a 'season' was being given in New York he was sure to be among the most constant attendants on the performances."

Palmo died in September, 1869, aged eighty-five. His funeral was a very quiet one; and it is a curious commentary on the vanities of life, and the forgetfulness of the world, that no musical or theatrical celebrities attended his funeral.

The world had rolled on, and poor old Palmo was forgotten!

The history of French opera in this country is brief but brilliant.

Mr. Bateman, the well-known theatrical manager, conceived the idea of bringing a troupe of French singers to America.

They came; they sang; they conquered. The Bateman pockets were filled. The newspaper welkin rang with praises of French operatic jollity and jingle; Offenbach was a prince; the can-can was piquant, if naughty; and the crowds went to see, to hear, to laugh.

Then other managers caught the fever. Other French troupes were brought over. The thing was overdone, and the rage died out, just about the time Bateman sold out.

Grau, with his troupe at the French Theatre, and Fisk, with his troupe (bought off Bateman's hands), at the Fifth Avenue Theatre, floundered along into the slough of despond, sinking money by the bagsfull, and finally giving up in despair.

The French singers packed their trunks, sold their greenbacks for gold, and hied them merrily across the sea, leaving the French Theatre and the Fifth Avenue Theatre alone to gloom and desolation.

Since then, both these theatres have returned to their legitimate uses. The Fifth Avenue, under the management of Augustin Daly, the author-manager, has undergone a thorough purification; and Shakespeare and Colley Cibber have taken the place of Offenbach.

And thus be it ever.

Apropos of Offenbach, a mixture of reminiscence and criticism by an English writer is interesting. "Mr. Offenbach made himself originally known in London as in Paris, some forty years ago, as a graceful but not vigorous violoncello player, who wrote pleasant music, not merely for his instrument, but for the voice. Nothing much more meek, nothing much less marked, than his playing and his music, is in the writer's recollection. His was the appearance of a slender talent—if there was ever such a thing—a talent which for many after seasons could make but a languid assertion of its existence in the concert rooms and theatres of Europe. The composer's life was advancing, and such success as artists love appeared as far distant as ever, when some demon whispered in the musician's ear that there was a field yet to be trodden, because heretofore disdained by any artist of repute. There had been coarse comic singers without voices at the cafés, there had been comic actors of no less value than Verner and Odry, who could condescend to such coarse travesties as Mme. Gibou and Mme. Pouchet; but for an artist of any pretension to turn their unmanly and unwomanly vulgarities to account by setting questionable stories to music which could be eked out by their *un*questionable pranks, was left to the gently insipid writer under notice, who had been just, and only just able, to keep his name before the public. To-day the name commands Europe, and commands, too, such gains as in his prime the composer of 'Il Barbiere,' 'Il Turco,' 'Corradino, 'La Cenerentola,' 'Otello,' 'Le Comte Ory,' 'Moïse,' 'Guillaume Tell,' and many another serious and sentimental opera, never dreamed of. The iron age has come; the exchange of mirth for the base excitement of prurient allusion and appeal. It is not pleasant to have to insist that M. Offenbach has amassed a large fortune and an universal reputation by his late recourse to the bad device of *double entendre* in the stories selected by him, and in the execution of his favorite interpreters. His music, in itself trite and colorless, as compared (to rise no higher) with the comic music of Adam, though ingeniously put together and neatly instrumented, would die out because of its nothingness, were not the action it accompanies spiced with indelicacy by women and men of the most meagre musical pretensions. His 'Grand Duchesse,' Mlle. Schneider, salaried as Sontag never was in her best days, a pretty actress, content, some ten years ago, to display her less matured charms and more timid impertinences in that 'dirty little temple of ungodliness,' (as Mrs. Gore called it,) the Palais Royal Theatre, would never have passed muster in opera had it not been for certain airs and graces which, till the opportunities afforded for their display in the prurient stories which M. Offenbach has set to colorless music, were confined to such singing and smoking houses as the Paris Alcazar, to the significant gestures of Mlle. Theresa, or her shabby imitators in the open-air shrines of the Champs Elysées."

English opera has a very different history among us from that of the brief and rather dubious career of opera bouffe.

We have had English opera for a number of years, and its reputation has always been of the most irreproachable character.

Thousands of people have listened to English opera in this country who never saw a play of any kind, nor attended an evening of Italian or French opera, and who would be shocked at the idea of so doing,—many of the ultra-religious seeing something about English opera to save it from the stigma which is cast upon all other amusements of a theatrical character.

There are, at this writing, but two English opera companies in existence, so far as I know,—one, that which Mrs. Richings-Bernard has labored for so many years to establish; the other, that more recently organized by Madame Parepa-Rosa.

Parepa-Rosa ranks deservedly high as one of our most delightful singers—especially in simple soulful ballads—but no higher than Mrs. Richings-Bernard does as a rare and thorough musician. Besides being a fine singer, Mrs. Bernard is a good pianist, and is capable of going into the orchestra and seizing the baton herself, directing the opera with a skill and precision which has few parallels.

Madame Rosa is an English woman by birth, but is very fond of America. Her husband, Carl Rosa, the violinist, took out naturalization papers in New York last winter, thus to become a voter, as becomes a man.

Life behind the scenes at the opera has its own peculiar features, some of which are thus set down by a sprightly writer: "I am going to initiate the reader into the mysteries of the Grand Opera—to carry him behind the scenes, into the green-room, up to the loft, down to the cellar, and to exhibit the physiology of fabric and inhabitants. Knock at this door, leading from the opera-house to the stage, and show this bit of paper, your 'open sesame' to the stage, else you could not pass that threshold; for silken as are the porter's manners, official claws are concealed beneath such softness, which is indeed the oft-vaunted *suaviter in modo, fortiter in re*, and unless one has an especial *laissez-passer*, or is enrolled on the book he holds in his hands, and which contains the list of the favored mortals entitled to ingress, egress, and regress from, in, and to the stage of the Grand Opera, he had better go his way,—'there's no use knocking at *that* door.' Were you ever behind the curtain? Then don't go, if you have never been. Don't earwig actors and newspaper editors for an initiation into those mysteries of canvas and paint, spangles and paste, rouge and pomatum, if you would retain one jot or iota of romantic delusion, the least vestige of youth secure from the attrition of those terrible bronze effacers, the 'bills payable,' 'protests,' 'due-bills' and 'accounts-current' of life, which seize us at the threshold of existence. Shun the 'slips' as you avert your eyes from the skeleton of the beauty, last night danced with, and loved to-day, as you would shun the shambles where beeves enter on the first stages of the process which gives us noble sirloins, as you would shun the compost heap which paints on the tulip its most gorgeous colors. The stage of the Grand Opera is not unlike some vast ship leaving port, whose 'confusion worse confounded' has not been reduced to order. Ropes, blocks, hatches, broken canvas, unwieldy scenes, keel-long grooves, balance-weights, lamp-racks, curtains, clouds, gothic cathedrals, public squares, groves of trees, broad-oceans, bed-chambers, light-houses, palaces, cloisters, cemeteries, lie or stand jumbled up together in 'most admired disorder,' which is heightened by screams, orders, counter-orders, 'aye-ayes,' from the upper, nether, and surrounding voices. Here men sweep (what a cloud of dust they manage to raise!) and water the stage floor; scene-inspectors cry and push to keep the stage clear, and bellow their eternal 'take care,' to warn actors and the curious of impending dangers; singers and songstresses in costume, trill and quaver, to be ready for the 'call;' dancing girls are bounding about in every direction, practising their steps; firemen, with sponges, or wet blankets, or buckets of water, are standing everywhere, to wage war on fire, if that terrible mar-all should show its least sinister glance; and machinists are running, like sailors, up and down the ropes. There's a fellow making thunder by beating a suspended bass-drum, and there's another burning licopode powder, to imitate lightning, while, hard by, a party is tossing rapidly large plates of sheet iron on each other, to represent the striking of the bolt, and their neighbors are whirling watchmen's rattles with wonderful energy, to persuade the audience that a terrible 'fusillade' is going on in the streets. It is not so much the stage as the green-room of the Grand Opera which the astute pleasure seeker tries to attain. There are two green-rooms, the singing and the dancing, both popular, but the dancing green-room is incredibly so,—'why,' we shall, perhaps, enable the reader to understand. Very thin partitions divide the feminine corps of singers and dancers, but they are separated from each other by a different physiology, a different constitution, we had almost said a different conformation. This difference is visible even in their respective green-rooms. The singing green-room, which occupies the 'salon' of the old Hotel Choiseul, is decorated with the universal white and gold, the alpha and omega of French architects, and is of aristocratic spaciousness. A piano stands in the centre, surrounded on every side by benches. It is used as the audience-chamber, where actors and choristers give touches of their quality when they seek an engagement. There it is the actors and choruses study the scores of new operas. At the first rehearsals, the composer himself presides at the piano, and points out the time of the part-pieces to the singing masters and artists. And there the leading actors study separately, with the composer, the airs, duets, trios, they have to sing. When one act has been mastered, the quatuor rehearsals commence, under the supervision of the leader of the orchestra, where all of the stringed instruments successively execute the score. And as soon as the whole work,—words and score,—is known by the chorus and actors, the general rehearsals of the orchestra begin. All the singers rehearse sitting. During these three or four rehearsals, (they rarely exceed this number,) the mistakes of the copyists are corrected, and the whole of this arduous, severe, and long labor (six months, at least, are required to perfect the studies of a grand opera,) is ended by new quatuor rehearsals (with a piano to accompany the recitative,) with the scenery, and at last by rehearsals with full orchestra, lights, scenery, and costume. The singing green-room is a place of study. It is consequently calm and tranquil. The songstresses are obliged to pay a constant attention. They are never seen extravagantly dressed, nor full of noisy coquetry. Most of them go to the theatre in overshoes, and with umbrellas under their arms, and are proverbial for their punctuality and zeal. Some of them are married and live modestly; some of them are excellent musicians, and eke out their pay by giving music lessons."

The combination in the same person of true genius for both acting and singing, is a most rare and precious one, but it has existed in several instances. One of the most striking of these was furnished in Rachel, the tragedienne, who was also a singer of fine powers.

Among the interesting remembrances of my sister Eliza, few are more interesting than her account of Rachel and *La Marsellaise*, the stirring French hymn which almost every patriotic heart is familiar with. I give my sister's recital in her own words.

"To my mind," said she, "Rachel's utterance of the French hymn of liberty contained more of the *feu sacre* than all the rest of her acting put together. If ever a woman was *inspired*, it was she when she appeared dressed for *La Marsellaise.* She first was seen standing like a marble statue in the centre of the stage, far away in the distance. Her dress was white, composed of some fabric which clung in graceful folds to her form. As the band struck up the symphony, she advanced with rapid strides to the footlights. Her face was livid with emotion, and marked the strong contrast with her eye, which was black as night, and brilliant as the stars. At the close of the short prelude, she extended her right arm towards the audience, as if to impose silence. The vast multitude, assembled in the large Boston theatre, held their breath as one person. A death-like stillness prevailed. When she tremulously uttered,—

"'Sons of FREEDOM! awake to glory!'

I felt myself getting cold to the very tips of my fingers. Words can never describe the emotions that took possession of my innermost soul as she half spoke half sang these patriotic words. The close of the first verse runs thus:

"'To arms! to arms ye brave!
The avenging sword unsheath!
March on! march on! all hearts resolved
On victory or death!'

"The words seemed unparalleled in patriotic fire. She raised her arms, and disclosed in full her slender, exquisite form. She looked a giantess in height and majesty of presence. She could have commanded an army with her eye. The orchestra followed her as they would a commanding officer. Talk of the acting of Ristori, in comparison with this mighty effort! The triumph of the whole of Ristori's life would not make up the crowning glory of that one burst of enthusiasm which shook the walls of the building. A young French girl fainted at my side. The members of the band dropped their instruments, rose to their feet, waved their hands, and with one general, deafening, maddening *brava!* joined the audience in their thunders of applause. Not to speak it profanely, I thank God that I was there to see, and am now here to remember, that Hymn of *La Marsellaise;* and it rings in my ears now, as a requiem for Madame Rachel."

Among interesting anecdotes of musicians, is the story of the invalid whom Felicien David, the composer, cured of fever by his piano-forte performances. "The sick man at the sound of the instrument felt his fever leave him, and when it threatened to renew its attacks, David would chase it away by a few preludes. In a week the man was well. This was not unlike the genuine original David playing before Saul. This fact is worth receiving the attention of the faculty. To treat people by music would be an excellent method of introducing harmony into the conflicting medical systems. A dyspeptic affection would probably be cured by three days of the cornet-a-piston. Nothing has yet been advanced to prove that neuralgia could resist an hour of violincello; and an attack of cholera, however violent, would not stand more than twenty minutes of ophicleide. Half an hour of bassoon would drive away the headache, while deafness could be effectually cured by the united efforts of these instruments in one of Verdi's finales."

A curious story is told of Cooper, the tragedian, which occurred when he was manager of a New York theatre, many years ago. The occasion was the production of the pantomime of "Cinderella." "Much labor and expense were lavished upon this beautiful dumb piece, which, relying solely on music and action combined, demanded nicety and care. The band, however, had on several occasions exhibited the most insolent neglect of the rehearsals, and Cooper placed a notice in the music-room, to the effect that all absentees from rehearsal would in future suffer such fines and forfeits as were designated by the orchestra rules and their several contracts. The notice was in vain; the fines were exacted, and a conspiracy determined on. On the first night of 'Cinderella,' an audience, forming a receipt of fifteen hundred dollars, was assembled, and on ringing the orchestra bell for the overture, Mr. Hewitt, the leader, was informed by the ring-leader that the whole orchestra was determined not to play a note until the whole sum forfeited by their absence should be refunded. Here was a situation! He rushed almost speechless to Cooper's room, and unfolded the plot. Cooper coolly asked, 'Can you play the music?' 'Why, yes sir; I have been practicing it before your eyes for three weeks; but how am I to get through a pantomime without aid?' 'We shall see,' said Cooper. He at once went before the audience, stated the full particulars, with much regret at the position in which the theatre was placed. He then frankly proposed two alternatives for the decision of the audience; the first, to receive back their entrance money, if desired; the next,—and a droll one it was,—that as there was so large an audience, and many doubtless, were unwilling to be deprived of their amusement by the freaks of underlings, he offered to them 'Cinderella' led and played solely by Mr. Hewitt, with the assurance that on its next representation the orchestra should be full and certain. This proposal caused a momentary titter, but was followed by a good-natured acquiescence on the part of the audience. He also promised the dismissal of all the offenders, and rigidly fulfilled it." The performance passed off with great spirit; the leader, in solitary state in the orchestra, playing his single violin throughout the evening. The piece was then withdrawn for two or three days, and reproduced with a splendid band, to a long series of full houses.

CHAPTER XXXVIII.

About Ballet Dancers.—What the Ballet is.—A Reminiscence of Paris. —The Dancing Greenroom.—The Ballet Girl's Miseries and Tortures. —The Story of Mlle. Eulalie.—Beauty and Ugliness at Odds.—Religion among Dancing Girls.—Their Love of Mourning Robes.—A Ballet at Rehearsal. — The Ballet in its Influence on Morals. — The Results of Observation.— A Romantic Western Story.— Celebrated Dancers.— Cubas, Fanny Ellsler, Vestris, Taglioni, etc.—Serpents and Devils.

There is no branch of my subject more difficult to deal with than that with which this chapter has to do; for there are numberless people—for whom personally I have the greatest respect—who are utterly unable to see any difference in decency between the dancing of a ballet-girl and the caperings of a jigging burlesque woman.

Yet dancing is an art. It is not necessarily coarse. It can be degraded—and we all know it has been very much degraded, in this country, by groveling and conscienceless speculating managers—but so can any art be degraded.

This, however, is art's misfortune—not its fault.

In this country dancing has never taken its proper grade as an art—with the public, that is; for with the dancers themselves there is no branch of art ranking higher. The professional dancer has a high opinion of the value of her efforts in an artistic sense, and she resents with pain and indignation the low estimate placed upon them by American audiences.

But it is also true that here in America the highest manifestations of the artistic sense—painting, sculpture, even music—have not yet received one tithe of the admiration and appreciation which they meet in foreign lands.

And if this be the case with the noblest of the fine arts,

in how much greater degree must it be with dancing—which has something more than indifference to contend with, in the disposition of low-toned managers to make the ballet a pander to vice and sensuality.

No one who has ever visited foreign capitals—Paris, London, St. Petersburg, Vienna—can have failed to observe that the terpsichorean art is placed very little lower than the lyric, and its great exemplars—Cerito, Taglioni, Fanny Ellsler—are named in the same breath and with as great admiration as Malibran, Sontag, Bosio, and Caridora Allen.

A woman who selects the vocation of dancer, must be endowed with great physical endurance, a passionate devotion to the poetry of motion, and a keen appreciation of graceful poses.

Many of the ballet women are thoroughly familiar with the great masterpieces in painting and sculpture, and strive to recall them to the audience by poetical posturing. Among thoroughly cultivated audiences such efforts are instantly recognized, but when they are presented to uninformed bodies of men and women, they fail to see the poetic value of what is passing before them, and look on it merely from the grosser side.

I remember one evening, in Paris, being inside the Grand Opera House, on an occasion which the most unobservant person could not have failed to see was one of great interest.

The street on which the opera house was situated was literally jammed with gorgeous vehicles resplendent in golden trappings, velvet hangings, emblazoned panels, drawn by thorough-bred horses richly caparisoned, and bearing the very flower of the beauty, wealth and distinction of both hemispheres—fair women, laden with diamonds blazing like stars; brave men, equipped in brilliant uniform and glittering with orders, stars, crosses and garters to proclaim their valiant deeds or gentle blood; the graceful Eugenie, Empress of Beauty and of the French; Louis Napoleon, proud and happy; German princes, English dukes and duchesses; the young and graceful lad with the red hair which has run through the race for generations, the Marquis of Douglas; generals, magistrates, statesmen, merchant-princes from New York, scholars from Boston, celebrated beauties from all parts of the globe.

What was the occasion of this great gathering? Was it a council of nations, an opening of Parliament, the reception of a foreign potentate?

No; it was simply a first appearance in public of a young girl less than seventeen, and whose only claim to attention was that she was a dancer.

Her name was Emma Livry. From her earliest childhood she had been devoted to the art of dancing—though this was no extraordinary thing, for there are a large number of girls always in training for the Grand Opera, in Paris, who are taken at the age of four years, and kept in constant practice until they reach womanhood, when they appear in public.

But this girl had shown extraordinary genius. In her later years the celebrated dancer Marie Taglioni, Countess de Voisins, hearing of the new dancer, left her villa on the Lake of Como and her palace in Venice to come to Paris and give the girl lessons.

Her improvement was miraculous. Taglioni said she would renew the triumphs herself had won in former days.

And now she glided upon the stage. The brilliant audience ceased their chatter as she appeared. The occasion took the character of what it was afterwards called in the newspapers—"a great solemnity."

She was very young, and was just at that period in the

life of a girl when her figure is apt to be what old-fashioned people call raw-boned. She was tall, thin and pale.

Her face was not handsome. Her form gave no evidence of physical strength.

She was received in a hush of silence. "Let us see," this great audience seemed to say, "what you really can do in this poetic art."

Any one who could have connected sensuality, grossness, with this girl, would have been baser than a sybarite; and yet her dress was the conventional dress of ballet-dancers—short to the calf of the leg, but thickly clad above.

She began. O grace, you never found a prototype till now! O painting, sculpture, you paled before this supple, elastic, firm yet dainty tread!

At the conclusion of her first movement, when with a gush of sweet music she sprang like a fawn to the footlights, and extending her slender arms and delicate hands towards the audience, as if to ask, "Come, what is the verdict on me now?" a burst of enthusiastic applause, loud shouts of "brava," "bravissima," "c'est magnifique," wavings of perfumed handkerchiefs, a deluge of sweet flowers, formed the response.

The whole evening was a series of triumphs. The Emperor and Empress sent an aid-de-camp behind the scenes to offer her the imperial congratulations. Marie Taglioni, accompanied by her noble husband, sought the girl also, and taking from her breast a magnificent diamond star, which had been given her in former days by the Emperor of Russia—"Here," said she, "take this—the queen of dance, Marie Taglioni, is dead—long live the Queen, Emma Livry."

As I passed out amongst the dense crowd which composed the audience, I saw a woman of middle age, and respectably dressed, leaning against one of the marble columns in the vestibule. Her face was flushed, and she was wiping tears from her eyes.

"You weep, Madame?" said a gentleman who was passing.

"Yes, monsieur," she replied, "but it is with joy. Who would not be proud of such a daughter, and of such a tribute to her genius?"

The early death of this young artist was a sad event. If she had lived she would have conferred honor upon an art which has so much to degrade it—so much to contend against.

The life of the ballet girl is far from being that roseate and delightful thing which many people picture it to be.

A peep into the dancing green room of the opera, or of a theatre in which a ballet is progressing, will show the life the ballet dancer leads.

One striking peculiarity of her public life is that a ballet dancer can never sit down *for one minute* either on or off the stage, after she is dressed for the evening's performance. This is the standing rule with dancing girls. If they sat down even once, their tarletan skirts would be crushed, their silk leggings (known as "tights") would be wrinkled about their knees; in short, they would be unpresentable fairies, untidy Undines, or whatever they personate.

The audience sees these pretty creatures dancing away for dear life to rapid music, with beating chest aud flushed face, and no doubt some charitable souls say to themselves, "Ah, well, she will rest as soon as she gets off the stage. She will sit down and have a good rest."

Nothing of the kind. She will stand up till midnight if the performance lasts so long, leaning her aching back against a canvas scene or a damp stone wall; laying her hot forehead against some iron clamp; but never once sitting down—never while she is behind the scenes.

One who visited the dancing green room of the grand opera in Paris relates that "at night it is brilliantly lighted, and the effects of the gas-jets is greatly increased by the numerous large mirrors which almost conceal the walls. In front of each of these mirrors a wooden post a little higher than one's waist, is securely planted, and before a dancing-girl 'sets off,' she raises one foot after the other until she places it horizontally on one of these posts, where she keeps it for some time, then quitting this position and taking hold of the post with one hand, she practices all her steps, and after having in this way 'set herself off,' she waters the floor with a handsome watering pot, and before the large mirrors, which reach down to the mop-board, she goes through all the steps she is about to dance on the stage. The leading dancing-girls commonly wear old pumps and small linen gaiters, very loose, in order to avoid soiling their stockings or stocking-net. When the 'call-boy' gives his first notice, they hasten to throw off their gaiters and put on new pumps, chosen for their softness and suppleness, whose seams they have carefully stitched beforehand. The 'call-boy' appears at the door, 'Mesdemoiselles, now's your time! the curtain is up!' and the flock of dancing-girls hasten to the stage. Among the ballet-corps one sees the strangest vicissitudes of fortune, the most wonderful 'ups' and 'downs' of life. Some who yesterday were glad to receive the meanest charity of their comrades, who joyfully accepted old dancing pumps, and wore them for shoes, and faded bonnets and thrice-mended clothes, appear to-day in lace, silks, cashmeres, with coachman, valet, carriage and pair! The sufferings, the privations, the fatigue and the courage of these poor girls, ere the miserable worm, the chrysalis, is metamorphosed into the brilliant butterfly, cannot be conceived. Bread and water support the life of more than one of them; many would be glad to feel sure of it regularly twice a-day. A great number live three or four miles from the Grand Opera, a distance which they trudge almost shoeless to their matutinal dancing lesson, rehearsals, and evening performances, and on their return home, long after midnight, in the the summer's rains and the winter's snows, nothing buoys them up but that bladder which kept Trotty Veck afloat on the stream of life: 'There's a good time coming, Trotty; there's a good time coming!' They laugh and say, 'I suffer to-day, but perhaps I shall be rich to-morrow.' "

The story of Mlle. Eulalie is related by a Boston writer, who had it from a friend in Paris. "They had just brought out," said the friend, "a great spectacular piece, of rare attraction, requiring a very large *corps du ballet.* The sub-manager, a friend of mine, invited me behind the scenes the first night of representation. I went and had my usual chat with my favorites in the corps, in the green room, before the rising of the curtain. While in the green-room, I noticed, sitting quite apart from the girls, a young dancer whom I had seen before a few times, and whom I had always spoken to in vain; she never would answer me; and I always noticed that she treated all the other gallants in the same way. On this evening she was sitting apart, and I observed tears were rolling down her cheeks, which were heavily rouged. She was dressed, very sparsely, in pink gauze. I approached her, and, touched by her evident depression, asked what the matter was. She shook her head and turned away. One of the girls, a bold hussy, on this came up, and said, 'Can you guess what's the trouble with our fine little Mademoiselle Eulalie? Why, she's crying because she has got to appear in that light dress, and offer the king, in the play, a goblet of wine, kneeling. *Mon Dieu*, how terrible! *Comme c'est affreux!*' And the speaker bounded off laughing. We Frenchmen are so hardened by our devil-me-care life, that we are seldom susceptible to pity. But I was really touched by Mlle. Eulalie's emotion; perhaps it was because she was unusually pretty, and so wonderfully fresh and innocent. During the play I saw her on the stage. The poor thing was forcing a smile through the first acts; when it came to the place where she had to kneel and thus expose herself to the rude gaze of the *parterre*, she hesitated, and trembled like a leaf; and the tears came once more, and by an agonizing effort were forced back again. When she arose her modest color so mounted to her face as to quite conceal the rouge paint; and after the last act she went into the green-room again —and fainted. I felt interested, and, *roue* as I am, did from my heart feel for the poor thing. This wasn't sham, and I'm a good judge. In about a week, after a good deal of effort, I managed, by getting the sub-manager to introduce me, to get acquainted with Mlle. Eulalie. After an acquaintance in which I had to win her confidence by the most gradual steps—for she was most timid, as well as modest—I learned her history, and, with it, to respect and venerate this same simple ballet girl. Her real name was Françoise Tellier—Eulalie was her fancy stage name. She was eighteen. Her father was dead; her mother had re-married a man who had till within a year been a joiner, but meeting with an accident, had become imbecile, and was the inmate of an asylum. Her mother was a very sickly but pious Protestant woman, and by her second husband had a family of three small girls. Since her husband's misfortunes she had hardly been able to work at all; what she did was to copy documents for lawyers and libraries; for she had had a good education, and you know that this has always been a regular occupation for many French people of the lower bourgeois order. Mme. Reynard, whose father had been poor, had learned it in her younger days, and had since taught Françoise to write a 'lawyer-like hand.' It appears that a nephew of the unfortunate stepfather was acting in scenic pieces at the Châtelet, and was an enthusiast in his art; and he, observing the advantages which the young Françoise possessed—her grace of movement, etc.—proposed that she should take lessons for the ballet. This shocked the mother, who refused her consent; but the heroic daughter, although she shuddered at the prospect, was so earnest in favor of the plan, that she at last won Mme. Reynard's consent. The girl saw the difficulties her mother had in providing means for her subsistence and for the support of the unfortunate invalid in the asylum, and was ambitious only to aid in earning enough to support them. Her cousin was able to be of great assistance; he engaged a master at less than half price, to be paid from the future earnings of Françoise; and when she had become a proficient, which she did very quickly (owing to her zeal and natural brightness), he procured her a situation at one of the smaller theatres, where she at first, of course, only appeared *en corps*. She rose rapidly, had the satisfaction of carrying home a goodly number of francs every week, and of seeing both her mother and her poor imbecile stepfather supplied with many comforts of which they had long been deprived. When she came to the ballet, rehearsal mornings, she was observed to carry a little parcel of papers, most neatly tied; and in the intervals, when she was not wanted on the stage, she was seen writing with great rapidity at one of the tables in the green-room. She was doing her mother's copy work. And more. Immediately after rehearsal, which lasted till twelve or more, she hurried home and continued her copying, working three or four hours at it; then she went to the market and bought a basket of fruit, with which she rode in an omnibus to the asylum, and gave her purchases to the imbecile stepfather. Then she returned home, took a slight dinner, and was off again buying provisions for the next day. At six she returned to the theatre, where she was till after midnight. When the play was through, her cousin always came to escort her home. She rose at six in the morning, made breakfast, and fell straight to writing. And working thus, excellent Françoise managed to gather, toward the end of her stage career, (for she was, happily, near its end when I got acquainted with her), about one hundred francs a week, which was a capital income for poor people in Paris. And there never was a word spoken against her; but it was remarked by all how modestly and uprightly she bore herself in all her toil and trouble. Such a girl was sure to be found out and appreciated. A young lawyer's clerk, a Protestant, of highly respectable family, and a sufficiency of money, was struck by her heroism, her zeal, and her modesty. She became his wife six months ago, and is studying under his affectionate tuition."

That beauty is valuable to a ballet dancer no one need be told; but it has been shown in numberless cases that this is not an indispensable requisite to her success.

In the first place, it is easy for a very ugly woman to conceal her ugliness and pass for a presentable person, if she understands the use of the appliances of modern adornment; and, on the other hand, if a woman is really a fine dancer,—if she possesses both a keen artistic sense and a thorough training to her profession,—her personal defects will always be overlooked in the appreciation of her performance.

Some years ago, as the story is told, there was a dancer at the Grand Opera, at Paris, who had advanced considerably in years, and was conspicuous among her fellows by pre-eminent ugliness. She was so ugly that she excited the same wonder which the amber-mummied fly

raises—"how the dickens did she get there?" No one knew; but there she stayed. The manager ordered her to be discharged time and again, but nobody would consent to discharge her. At last, one day when the manager became more peremptory in his orders, she went to him. "Don't dismiss me, I beg of you," she said, "for if you do, I shall fall into the deepest poverty; I am very punctual, I know how to dance, and I supply the place of anybody who fails to attend the rehearsals in the morning or the evening's performance; I stand behind everybody, that no one may see me; do take pity on me." The manager was touched, and retained her among the ballet corps. Some months afterwards, she again spoke to the manager. She thanked him for his kindness, and told him he might get rid of her whenever he pleased; that she had succeeded in inspiring an attachment in a gentleman whom she had now married. The silks and lace and watch she wore showed that she had married one above the reach of the surging wave of poverty.

The ballet dancers of the Parisian Grand Opera are many of them devout religionists. It is a very common thing to see them with amulets on their necks, and other symbols of the Roman Catholic Church—this being the prevailing religion in France.

It is related that when Mdlle. Fanny Cerrito was offered her first engagement at the Grand Opera, her first act after signing the contract was to hasten to an eminent silversmith and order a splendid silver chalice, which she had vowed to the Blessed Virgin if she ever received an engagement at that theatre.

The ballet corps have, too, an ardent longing for cloister life. A retreat to a convent is not an unusual occurrence among them.

Another morbid taste among great numbers of these girls is their fondness for mourning robes. They will wear mourning for months on the death of a friend or relative, and even sometimes without this excuse.

To their sufferings and tortures I have already referred; and a writer who has familiarized himself with their lives says: "Little as the raw spectator may suspect it when they retire smiling from the stage, the dimpled cheek is clouded by pain the moment the audience lose sight of them. They suffer most from a chronic cold in the head, which obliges them to breathe almost constantly through their mouth, and consequently prevents their smiling, except with very great pain. 'O! mother, how much I do suffer!' is their first exclamation when they reach that mother, who always stands behind the scenes, holding for them a handkerchief, a warm wrapper, and a cup of cold beef tea or sugared water,—and then, at the command of the call-boy, they bound forward again upon the stage, looking as gay and smiling as ever. O life, life, how the obverse and reverse of thy medal doth differ!"

The same writer says: "The rehearsals of the ballet corps take place on the stage, which then presents the strangest imaginable sight. It is a miniature Babel! The extremes of wealth and poverty jostle each other. In the same group are tatterdemalions, ragged even to the soles of their shoes, and beauties who seem to have stepped out of the plate of the last fashions; by the side of paste and pinchbeck are diamonds and all the art of the goldsmith; the rack exhibits in the closest neighborhood greasy bonnets, of faded colors and dirty ribbons, and the most fashionable hats, wonders of the milliner's art, gay with the fairest flowers, the costliest lace, the freshest ribbons. Here a modest dancer embroiders, under her mother's eye, during the moments of rest; there two confidants recount their heart-aches, their happiness, and their hopes; there is cake or candy munched in every corner; some are over head and ears in a novel; children are making a parody on the last pantomimic scene they have just witnessed; in some dark recess is a beauty poring over a love letter the stage porter has just given her; altogether presenting a varied, gay, picturesque scene, which baffles alike the pen and the pencil."

As to the ballet's influence on morals, it must be admitted by its most earnest defender, unless he be steeped in the prejudices which discredit manhood, that in its degraded state in this day and country, it must be often pernicious.

To this the common reply is, that none but a depraved nature could be influenced perniciously thereby; and the question is thus argued: "Bailey's lovely statue of Eve at the Fountain, in which there is not the slightest pretense of drapery or concealment of the divine form fresh from the hands of the Creator, is purity itself; and any one who sees impurity in it has the impurity in his own heart. In the same manner, there is no indelicacy in the display of the pretty bare legs of little maidens of from four to five years old, or in the bare feet and ankles of the bonny Scotch lassies, innocent alike of shoes and stockings and of evil intent, though there would be indecency in the display of a naked leg and foot in the streets of London or Edinburgh by full-grown damsels, who made the display for a meretricious purpose. There are statues and statuettes to be seen all over Europe in which nudity is as complete as it is beautiful; but when such statues or statuettes are imitated by purveyors of obscenity, and crowned with a modern bonnet, wrapped in a modern shawl, and encased in modern stockings, and nothing else, their vile intention becomes apparent, and they fall properly under the cognizance of the police. The display is not indecent *per se*, as when an actress of high attainments and genius, in default of an actor of truthfulness and talent enough to undertake the part, appears as *Romeo*, any more than it is indelicate or improper for a man to hide the form by appearing in petticoats to play the part of one of the witches in 'Macbeth.' The intention is everything, just as it is in killing. If you intend to kill, you are a murderer, and deserve the murderer's fate. If you kill in self-defense, and in a just and patriotic cause —like a soldier—you are not blamable, but virtuous. In like manner, the scanty drapery of the ballet, for the purpose of art, and art alone, is no offense against good taste or good manners; but if the ballet girl—not for the sake of art, but for the sake of attracting lewd attention—overdoes the scantiness, and betrays the immodesty of her mind by her motions or gestures, she commits an offense, and ought to be hissed from the stage which she disgraces."

An American artist—a well-known painter,—who at one time in his career passed a period of four months on the stage, as an actor, gave the result of his observation in the *Atlantic Monthly*, and, regarding the ballet, testified as follows: "The 'supes' and ballet-girls formed a class by themselves, the actors' contact with which was confined to the stage. I never saw in their conduct anything offensive, or that I would not have permitted in my own house. The ballet was made up of young women who had their living to make, and when not on the scene they were generally engaged in embroidery, sensation novels, or quietly watching the play. So far as my observation went,—and I kept my eyes open,—there was no greater amount of immorality among them than among the same number of sewing-girls of our great cities. They were always treated with respect."

An incident occurred in a western city some time ago, which, as stated by the person who tells the story, belongs to the realm of fiction, although it is an actual fact. Fanny Casserly was a ballet dancer. Her mother had been an actress, and guarded her daughter's character with all a mother's solicitude. "But the mother became a victim to disease, her scant earnings were soon expended, and Fanny, obliged to support herself and invalid mother, joined a traveling ballet troupe as a dancer. While performing in Chicago, a young 'Captain Tom,' a hero of the late war, and a son of a well-known clergyman and editor of Chicago, fell in love with the girl. He was struck with her modesty, simple manners, and the air of purity which surrounded her. Like a frank, open-hearted fellow as he was, he mentioned his love and his intentions to his parents. They, of course, were shocked,—it was useless to plead with them,—they threatened to disown him, and appealed to his family pride. Captain Tom left his parents angrily, went directly to the ballet-girl, and offered to make her his wife. To his astonishment, the strong-minded ballet-girl, who fully reciprocated his affection, said 'no,' very emphatically. She declined to wed him against his parents' consent, and under circumstances which would bring him and his family into disgrace. He pleaded hard, but she refused firmly, and granted no appeal. The mother of the young man called soon after, and was informed by Fanny of her decision. She was pleased, and offered her presents, which she proudly refused. After the troupe left Chicago, Captain Tom became gloomy, melancholy, and careless in business. They forced him into society, but found it all useless. They were sensible parents, and accordingly came to a sensible conclusion. The people of Milwaukee, in the mean time, noticed a young girl among the dancers at Music Hall who modestly retired from view whenever her duties would permit her. She would edge behind her companions, and retire from sight as often as possible. Last Friday night, at the end of the third act, the manager informed her that, as she was not very well, she might go back to the hotel, and he would see that her place was supplied. He led her to a carriage, and when she arrived at the hotel she hurried to her room and lay down to rest. She was in low spirits, and was having a good cry when she was called to the parlor to meet a gentleman. She declined at first; but was informed of the urgency of the case, dried her eyes and went down. Of course she met Captain Tom. He clasped her in his arms—she protested—scolded him for following her. Tom's father appeared—'Bless you, my children.' He married them on the spot. Ex-Mayor Kirby, of Milwaukee, gave the poor ballet girl away. The manager released her from her engagement, and the party started for Chicago. The bride has education and winning manners. She will make a good wife and will adorn the circle to which she has risen."

Such marriages as this are far from uncommon. I have known of several similar cases in my own experience.

There is a gentleman now connected with the New York press, an editor very highly esteemed, not only in New York but throughout the whole country, whose wife was formerly a ballet dancer; and a more devoted wife it would be hard to find.

Many celebrated dancers have from time to time appeared on the stage in this country, and among the ever-delightful reminiscences of Mr. G. W. Curtis, I find the following about dancers: Apropos of Cubas, "a friend, who in a few months had been more entirely saturated with Spain than most of us would be in many years, or in all our lives, said that to see Cubas was to see very Spain—not languor and sunshine only, or chiefly, but fire and passion and the glittering snake that always coils in the south. The half-wild, barbaric, gypsy intensity and strangeness and fearlessness, all were to be felt in the dancing of Cubas. It was the most characteristic of all the dancing we had ever seen. It was the language spoken by a native with all the native asperity. It was not softened, and modified, and adapted, and flavored to different national tastes, as when Ellsler, or Cerito, or Lucille Grahn, or Taglioni danced a Spanish dance. It is Spanish, he said, as the Tarantella, danced by a Neapolitan girl upon the shore, is Italian. Bata cosi, amico mio, let us go and see Cubas. It was certainly all that he had said. Years ago, at the old Park Theatre, where we used to be boxed up in those frightful red boxes, and look with cramps and stitches in every limb, and envy in the heart at the free movement of actors or singers, or dancers upon the stage—years ago, Fanny Ellsler came, danced and conquered. She danced Spanish, and Polish, and Italian, and Hungarian dances, and all with such stately grace that the brains ran out of some people's heads, and they became asses, and drew her in a carriage. Jenny Lind made no more intense, although a much more lasting and extended impression upon the public mind than Fanny Ellsler. We had Celeste and Augusta before, and Augusta in the Bayadere was beautiful; but Fanny Ellsler fascinated the town, and triumphed. Remembering this, recalling her in the Cachuca, the Jaleo, and the Haute Arragonaise, there was a curious expectation in the mind of the Easy Chair when he saw the black-eyed Cubas in her gold skirt, dashed all over with huge flaunting black bows, standing at the side scene, and then clicking her castanets, with a few rapid bounds leaping to the front. The coal-black hair, eyes and eyebrows, the glittering grin, and the powerful, rapid, darting, snake-like quality of her movement, amazed rather than pleased the audience. But the dancing was wonderful. Her partner thumped and rang the tamborine, and she rattled her castanets, while she flew and bounded about him with marvelous muscular agility and a litheness like that of a blade of grass. She darted and fled, scorning the ground like Shakespeare's lapwing, then erect as a crested snake she glared and glittered at him till you looked to see the forked tongue. It was a fierce pantomime of passion, of jealousy, of scorn, of all the savagery that hides in coal-black coils of hair and the tawny skins that cover dusky natures. The audience was surprised, repelled, cold. They applauded, but not heartily. They even encored the second dance, but simply as a freak, and when she ran stooping to the front, instead of a louder burst of welcome, the applause died away. The most extraordinary and effective points passed unrecognized. She had none of that responsive fervor of applause which stimulates and intoxicates a dancer. The audience did not help, it hindered her. But she danced magnificently. Fanny Ellsler would have so modified the dances as to enchant the spectators; but she could not have shown so perfectly the dance of Spain exactly as it is danced, and with all the characteristic gypsy ferocity. The coffee of Mocha, when you drink it in Arabia, is thick and muddy, and your little cup is half filled with slime when you have drunk the liquid; but it is sweet and delicious beyond description. The same coffee in Paris is strained to dusky transparency; but it is thin, and metallic and changed. Yet it is French coffee which is thought to be perfect. Nobody shall quarrel with different tastes; but the Mocha berry browned with care, immediately bruised in a coffee mortar, then made almost a paste from which you drink the liquid, is as different from the beverage of the Boulevards as the dancing of Cubas from that of Ellsler."

Fanny Ellsler's career as a dancer was a short but very brilliant one. The history of her first engagement in Paris is rather curious. "Fanny, with her sister Therese, was playing at London when her fame reached France, and the manager of the Grand Opera posted over to see on what foundation the rumors were raised. He came, saw, and was conquered. Mlle. Fanny Ellsler was very anxious for an engagement at Paris, but Mlle. Therese was afraid of that city, and these indecisions rendered the manager's negotiations a very delicate affair. While they were vacillating between a small salary, very irregularly paid, at London, and eight thousand dollars and punctuality, in Paris, he gave them a grand banquet at the Clarendon Hotel, and served them up, with the dessert, a silver dish containing forty thousand dollars' worth of jewels and diamonds, which was handed round to the guests as if it contained but so many pea-nuts. The sisters selected each one of the most modest trinkets in the dish—though these bagatelles were worth two thousand dollars a-piece—and, to the gratification of the manager, signed an engagement, after Mlle. Therese's fears had been satisfied by the insertion of a provision that the engagement of three years might be ended at will at the expiration of the first fifteen months. Mlle. Therese did not come to America with her sister, and we are informed that we lost a great deal by her absence, as Mlle. Fanny was never so brilliant as when her sister was at her side. The two different talents completed each other, and made a harmonious group of an exquisite perfection. Both of these eminent dancers have retired from the stage, the possessors of very large fortunes. Mlle. Therese has been the wife (by a morganatic marriage) of the Prince Royal of Prussia, and Mlle. Fanny Ellsler married a wealthy physician of Hamburg."

Taglioni is celebrated as the founder of a more modest and pure style of dancing than that which Vestris had popularized in Europe.

Taglioni, the father—whom we only know in these days through the fame of his daughter—would never allow his pupils to make a gesture wanting in modesty. He was wont to tell his daughter, "Dance in such a way that any lady and any maiden may see you dance without blushing; take care and dance in a style full of austerity, delicacy and taste." He was "severe to harshness, inflexible to cruelty with his pupils, and especially with his daughter. He made her work three or four hours a day, and her utter exhaustion of body and bitter sobs could not induce him to abate one jot or tittle of her daily exercise. This celebrated name is a new instance of the truth of the vulgar observation of the futility of omens cast in youth, and founded on precocious developments or tardy promises. At the first dancing school to which she was sent, her comrades constantly jeered her. 'What!' they would say, 'can that little hump-back ever learn how to dance?' In the course of time the little 'hump-back' founded the most brilliant school of dancing, and was acknowledged, by universal consent, to dance better and differently from all her predecessors; and she numbered as her enthusiastic admirers the most aristocratic ladies and the very best society. The nick-name 'hump-backed' probably arose from the peculiar narrow and short conformation of her breast. Satirists have said that dancers have no intellect except in their legs. This general rule does not apply to Mademoiselle Taglioni, who is an exceedingly sprightly woman and an adept in playful raillery."

CHAPTER XXXIX.

The Leg Business.—The Blonde Burlesquers, How they Grew.—History of the Nude Woman Question in America.—The Black Crook.—The White Fawn. — Ixion. — The Deluge. — Padded Legs Wriggling and Jigging all over the New York Stage.—Obscenity, Vulgarity and Indecency Running Riot. — The Wild Orgies of the Hour. — The Effect on the Theatrical World.—Managers Lose their Senses. —Decent Actresses thrown Out of Employment.—The Temptations of Debauchery. How I came to attack this Shame. — The First Results of My Attack. Abuse, Threats and Contumely; Praise, Encouragement and Words of Cheer.—The Religious World *versus* the Nude-Woman World.— A Despairing Poet.—The Final Results.—Flight of the Foul Birds. — The Stage Returning to its Legitimate Uses.

The "leg business" is a branch of the show business which I have labored with some earnestness to render infamous.

Those who have read my various magazine articles bearing on this question, or my little book entitled "Apropos of Women and Theatres," (published in New York by Mr. Carleton), do not need to be told what the "leg business" is; but as these pages are expected to fall into the hands of thousands of people who will need the information, I will explain that the "leg business" is a term in common use among theatrical people, and means the displaying in public, by women, of their persons, clad in close-fitting flesh-colored silk "tights," and as little else as the law will permit.

Considering it a burning disgrace to the theatrical profession that there should be in its ranks a class of so-called actresses, whose claim on public patronage lay in their boldness of personal display, I have persistently made war upon them for several years past.

My first *printed* attacks on this class of performers were made in the *Galaxy* magazine, in the summer of 1867. At that time the chief exponents of the "leg business" were women who made a specialty of such rôles as *Mazeppa*, in which they represented, at one point in the play, a naked man strapped on the back of a horse.

These women's power lay confessedly in their exhibition of their persons, (the ostensible object being to represent an unclad man), and no woman who could have enchained an audience otherwise would ever have descended to this baseness. But such women were never actresses in the true sense, and among the reputable members of the profession were, as a rule, tabooed and avoided in private—even by those who were compelled to appear on the same stage with them in public.

But these leg-performers were so few in number, and so confessedly low, that the evil did not assume such frightful proportions as it subsequently did, when it took the shape of burlesque.

There were burlesque actresses in those days, too, but they were never very successful—for the simple reason that they did not so outrage decency as to draw the staring crowd. Such were the Worrell sisters, the Webb sisters, the Leffingwell troupe, and others of their class. Their chief attraction was the fun they made, and the actresses who presented this class of entertainment were not infrequently young women of irreproachable private character.

The spectacular play of the "Black Crook" was the desperate resort of a manager who had been losing money in alarming amounts for several months, and at the end of a disastrous season was forced to close his theatre.

The resolve was made to create a sensation which should startle the town, and revive the drooping fortunes of the theatre.

Great preparations were made; the newspapers were

"worked" for weeks in advance with the most indefatigable persistence; wonderful rumors were set afloat; public curiosity was excited to the utmost; and at last the doors of the theatre were flung open and a dense crowd rushed for seats.

The play was a mass of dreary twaddle, magnificently mounted, superbly costumed, and presenting a troupe of French and Italian dancers in costumes which at that time were startlingly scant.

The piece created a furore. The leading dancers became the town talk; their portraits, hung about town in public places, were surrounded by crowds of gaping men; they were exalted to the pinnacle of public favor, and men raved about Bonfanti, Sangali, Betty Rigl, etc., as if they had been demi-goddesses instead of being merely ballet girls.

But there came a time when this highly spiced sensation palled on the masculine appetite. The French and Italian demi-goddesses were dethroned; and were destined to behold their subjects rally in great force around the flag of "perfidious Albion," on the arrival from England of a troupe of blonde-haired burlesque women, to whom the fickle public transferred its devotion, and over whom it went wild.

The "Black Crook" was withdrawn, and a piece of the same character, entitled the "White Fawn," appealed in vain for favor.

The burlesquers came, and "Ixion" was the rage. This was a burlesque which contained a great number of British novelties, whose chief piquancy was derived from the fact that the women who performed in it talked slang and sang coarse songs with a very good imitation of that English accent which had hitherto been associated in our minds with ideas of culture and refinement. There was something very rib-tickling, as it seemed, in hearing a blonde-haired woman sing,

"Wokking in the Pawk!"

or—

"I took up the baeuf baeuone
And shied eet at hees head."

At first, these burlesquers were modest, in some degree, and maintained that indescribable air of respectful deportment toward their audiences which they had been forced to preserve in Europe.

But as time passed on, and the young noodles of New York fast life began to shower them with bouquets, and take them to drive in Central Park, and give them late suppers at fashionable hotels, and generally lionize them in a way that made them open their eyes in amazement at American folly, they began to think there was nothing too bold and impudent for them to dare. They grew brazen and saucy, leered at men in the boxes, and generally exhibited a disrespectful regard for the audience, or what it might think of them.

The echo of their success reached English shores and set all British burlesquedom agog with the eager desire to share in the glories and profits of the wild fever raging in this "blarsted country."

Then came the Deluge. An army of burlesque women took ship for America, and presently the New York stage presented one disgraceful spectacle of padded legs jigging and wriggling in the insensate follies and indecencies of the hour.

Rivalry grew so sharp that it seemed to be a scrub race with these women as to who should sing the vilest songs, dress with the greatest immodesty, dance the most indecent dances, and indulge in the supremest vulgarity and license of gesture.

The effect upon the theatrical world was such that managers lost their senses, became crazy to share in the profits of burlesque, and turned off decent actresses by scores, that they might fill their theatres with the coarse women who had now come in fashion.

I was then, as now, separated from the stage, and following the profession of literature; but I was still in frequent association with reputable actresses in private life, and I stood appalled at the state of affairs.

I saw beautiful young women, whom I loved and honored, tempted by the offers of managers to go upon the stage in the most immodest garb, and engage in the all-prevailing orgies of the "leg-business." It became a question with actresses seeking a situation, not whether they were good actresses—not whether they had stage training and histrionic talent—but whether they were pretty and were willing to exhibit their persons, and do as the burlesque women did.

It was this which, more than anything else, made me attack this shame; and I set about it with my purpose clear before me—to make this class of performances *odious*. I resolved that I would never cease to wage war upon the prevailing grossness, until this end was accomplished.

I wrote one article. I called it "The Nude Woman Question," so that in its very title it should strike a hard blow; and the article contained many another plain word, simple in its meaning, and certainly without a trace of squeamishness.

Some people found fault with me for having spoken so plainly; but I knew the enemy, and how as well as where to strike.

The first blow "told." I was astonished at the effect. I saw at once what a reeking muck I had stirred up, and congratulated myself on the speedy effects produced.

The primary result was, a tempest of abuse and defamation, poured upon my head by a class of newspapers with whose names I should be sorry to sully the pages of this book. One, however, I will mention—unwillingly and reluctantly, but because I want my readers to judge of the whole class by its type: *Pomeroy's Democrat.*

A paper which called Abraham Lincoln an ape, and cheered on his assassin, can only compliment Olive Logan by the basest thing it can say of her.

And as for the remainder of the rabble of which *Pomeroy's Democrat* was the fitting leader, it is enough to say that they lacked only one thing to make them rank alongside of that leader—to wit, circulation.

But, as an evidence of the faithfulness to truth and purity prevailing throughout the reputable journalistic world, I am going to reproduce here a few of the things said by the press apropos of "The Nude Woman Question."

Among the New York dailies, good words were spoken by the *Herald, Tribune, Times, World, Evening Post* and *Telegram*, from some of which I make extracts.

Said the *Tribune:* "It is cheerful to see a woman of Miss Logan's stamp, young and elegant, and the centre of an admiring circle, doing battle so bravely for so good a cause. The loose drama can be reformed by woman, we believe, and by her alone. Let the priestesses of fashion put the wild license of opera bouffe and the orgies of the leg drama under the ban, and such performances will soon be swept from the theatres. It may be said that if respectability holds aloof, a lower class of sensualists will rush in, and the plays get worse instead of better. But experienced managers will tell us how mistaken is this fear. The bulk of our places of amusement must depend upon the respectable classes for support. The feverish passions of the viler sort of men are hard to satisfy, and their patronage is always an unstable dependence. The theatre offers a grand field for the exercise of woman's reforming abilities. * * * We observe that the lady has been pretty soundly abused for what is called an attack on 'the profession.' *What* profession, we should like to know, is insulted by such a protest? Nobody attacks the stage in attacking a brazen imposture, reeking with vice, that has mendaciously assumed the stage's form and function. Acting is an honorable art, and the people who worthily pursue it and live by it are honorable people; and it is in their interest, and not against it, that rebuke of all this frivolity and vice is directed. The bare-legged women who tramp over the boards in burlesque, and kick up their heels in the can-can, have—with here and there an exception—no more title to be regarded as members of the dramatic profession than they have to be regarded as members of the French Academy. They are a sort of fungus upon the stage, and the fungus has now become excessive and intolerable. We do not mean to say that, in all this flock of pantomimes, burlesques, and ballets, existent or yet to come, features of merit may not be found. Nonsense has its graces and its rights, as well as sense. But it is needful to remind theatrical managers that there is such an institution as The Drama, for the development of which theatres exist, and that intelligence, taste, refinement and morality—matters of great import to the welfare of society—have rights that theatrical greed cannot safely violate. Licentiousness and reckless thirst for gain have gone very far, of late days, to ruin the American stage as a vehicle of art and a school of acting; and strong measures are justifiable to combat the evil. * * * The stage is overwhelmed with mummers and dancing girls, variously ridiculous or vulgar, who are striving, with all the little gifts they have, to win the reward of prosperity by pandering to the sensual instincts of the people. And this medley of bombast and dirt proclaims itself as the drama; while, in more than one theatre roués and courtesans, sometimes consorting with a manager himself, flaunt in the boxes, in their gilded trappings of brazen vice. It is a revel of Cyprians, on the money of prosperous counter-jumpers."

Comments like these do not derive their chief value from the mere fact that they sustain my course. They are specially valuable for the purposes of this work, in being excellent reading, strong and pure argument and statement, and a valuable part of the history of this question, which I wish to preserve in my book for the amazement of coming generations.

The *World* said: "We incline to think that the remedy for the evil lies in the drawing of a rigid line between the several walks of the dramatic art. Spectacular nonsense may, or may not, be very well. But, certainly, very little is requisite for an actress to make a hit in it beyond the purely physical qualifications which Miss Logan enumerates. Of this class of actresses it will be generally conceded that we have quite enough. But the real profession of acting, the portrayal of character, and the holding up of the mirror, not to factitious calves, but to nature, is very remote from this, and deserves to be classed as a distinct profession. And of actresses of this latter sort, every one who has any knowledge of the stage will admit that there is by no means a glut. On the contrary, there is a deplorable scarcity of them. Good 'leading ladies' are precisely the rarest birds in the theatrical land. That there are not more of them on the stage is, perhaps, partly due to a public apathy which it is to be hoped will not endure forever, but in a much greater measure to the fact that there are very few of them extant anywhere. If we have not these artists, and if we really need them, we must go to work to produce them. And the only way to do this is by careful and systematic training. If acting is a legitimate business, its followers should be regularly bred to it, although, as Joseph Miller remarked of the law, and as Miss Logan complains of the stage, it cannot always be relied upon to be regularly, bread, to them. The German stage, undoubtedly the highest morally and æsthetically, in Europe, was brought to its excellence by this means. Goethe did not disdain to charge himself for a term of years with the drudgery of managing the little theatre at Weimar. And our own dramatic authors ought not to expect a proper production of their performances unless they are willing to take similar pains. Nor ought our play-goers to expect an improvement, either in the ways of actresses or in the goodness of their acting, so long as they are willing to forgive any ignorance of her business and any impudence in the actress who bestows upon them the boon of a pretty face and a pretty figure."

Said the *Times*: "For a considerable time the many in this country who regard the drama as one of the noblest and most elevating branches of art, have seen with sorrow that while all the other arts are advancing, the drama alone, in spite of some noble exceptional efforts, is in decline, and that the theatre, instead of being dedicated to its proper province of proffering a high intellectual or, as might be, a gay and graceful amusement, had become in many instances a place of licentious exhibition and demoralizing resort. This feeling, born in the 'Black Crook,' has grown and strengthened with this blonde business, and if this style of art is permitted to ride rampant much longer, must eventually make extinct, as it is now doing, the old school of artists, and apply the torch to the dramatic pile."

The *Evening Telegram*, which, in a facetious way, was unsparing in its goadings of what it called "the blonde angels," said: "Our people have no difficulty in investing the paint and gewgaws of the stage with the special charms which we attribute to Mahomet's paradise. Under such circumstances it seems a pity that they should be dispossessed of their fond delusions—that they should be made to shudder and loathe where they now grin and worship. Under these circumstances the press has all along withheld its full knowledge of the characteristics of the blonde moss growing swamps of London, but only out of compassion for the poor infatuated noodles who aspire to live in a dramatic heaven, where houris will pirouette for all time before them, and twinkling legs will keep time with seraphic orchestras, while they, the princely noodles aforesaid, enjoy the unbounded delight of throwing them bouquets by the bushel. The first who has dared to take a step towards breaking down this radiant fallacy is a woman—a strong-minded woman—and no less a person than Olive Logan, herself an actress, who is supposed to be well posted in regard to all the arts of make-up, with the modern improvements in leg pads, 'symmetries' and all the mechanics of angel manufacture. Olive comes out heavily against sylphs and blows their gossamer figures to atoms with a few left-handed but powerful puffs from the lecture platform. She declares that the yellow-haired fairies are brazen, painted, dyed, padded, homely, inartistic, ignorant, uneducated and immodest. And she tells the plain, unvarnished truth."

Among the religious papers which spoke good words on the subject, the *Independent* said: "Doubtless some of her language is startlingly plain and direct; but we honestly think she has done a service to art as well as to morals by her denunciation of the base degeneracy at which her efforts are directed."

The *Bulletin of the Brooklyn Young Men's Christian Association* said: "It is really refreshing, in these days when principle is trimmed down to fit expediency, and giant sins are clothed in jeweled phrases, till their hideous character is quite concealed, and plain Anglo-Saxon words full of force and vim, are substituted by foreign dishwater importations, and in danger of being crowded out of our vocabulary altogether—it is truly refreshing in these days, we say, to read an article like that of Miss Olive Logan where a naked subject is pelted with naked words. We bespeak for Miss Logan, in her brave battle with the devilish forces at work to ensnare our young men, what she claims to be her due—the hearty support and co-operation of every righteous soul in the land. We are glad to learn that her first trenchant blow is not to be the last; that she intends, if we may use the hackneyed phrase, 'to fight it out on that line, if it takes all summer,' aye, and winter, too. We understand that Miss Logan is deluged with imprecatory letters from the hounds who fatten and grow rich on the profits of their lascivious shows. So much the better. It proves the strong purgative properties of the dose she has administered. It shows, too, the nature of the broth in this unclean cauldron, that such a little stirring should produce so large a stench. And if the cry of one woman can make such a flutter among the carrion crew of vultures and buzzards that are pecking out the vitals of the drama, what might not be accomplished if every friend of public decency would rally around the standard which she has set up? Meanwhile, wield your trenchant pen without mercy, Olive, and the more imprecations the better. None but galled jades wince."

The *Christian Recorder* even went so far as to say: "The article by Olive Logan on 'The Nude Woman Question,' deserves to be put in tract form and circulated far and wide."

But the comments of the press were as nothing when compared to the private letters which poured in upon me at my business headquarters, the Authors' Union, in New York.

Abuse, threats and contumely from the angry advocates and defenders of indecency and vice, vied with praise, encouragement and words of cheer from the better classes of society—from ladies in every sphere of life, from Fifth avenue luxury to struggling virtue in the shape of discharged actresses—from New England wives and mothers to those in far Western homes—and especially from clergymen of every denomination.

It really seemed as if I had become a *medium* through which the religious world stood arrayed against the nude woman world.

Many of the letters I received might well bear publication, but perhaps the most entertaining thing was a doggerel poem which was sent to me after having been (as I judged from certain marks it bore) rejected by some editor to whom it had been sent.

I take compassion on the unfortunate author of this work, and print it in my book, promising him, if he will send me his address, that I will enclose him a soup ticket in payment for it.

The poem is "despairingly dedicated to Olive Logan by a poor young man who has spent his last cent for bouquets," and reads thus:

"What in the world is coming to pass?
Since the days of Balaam and Balaam's ass
There never was heard such noise, nor, alas!
Beheld such curious antics
As the women are making on every side,
Till one is ready to get astride
Of a wild Velox, and away to ride
With a pace all fierce and frantic.

"Over the hills and over the dales,
Thorough sunshine and thorough gales,
Till the flying Dutchman his glory pales,
And everything is spinning.

Away to China by Central Park,
Whirling along long after dark,
Gracious goodness! what a lark,
And all because of the women!

"In the good old days, when a girl said 'No,'
The man was voted a 'muff,' and 'slow,'
Who didn't quite well at the bottom know
That 'yes' was the darling's motto.
'You really must n't,' meant 'kiss me quick,'
And the fellow was voted a perfect brick
Who'd battle his way through thin and thick
To do what a lass said 'No' to.

"But now the lasses, alas! declare
On poor hu-man-ity desperate war,
And vow they'll vote, though they never will wear
The trousers or any such nonsense.
'The woman's rights doctrine is upside down,
Says Olive Logan with charming frown,
'I'm going to vote in a trailing gown,'
And the girls all chorus '*Bon* sense!'

"Each belle by her chignon swears she'll vote,
And chatters a lot of stuff by rote,
About suffrage, amendments, and how to promote
The highest good of the species;
The duties of every *citoyenne*.
The case of rooster *versus* hen,
And vow they are going to leave the men
To cooking, and washing the dishes.

"Oh, horrible hullaballo of—well,
Amidst this hurly and loud pell-mell
A mere male man scarce dares to tell
The full extent of his feelings.
As the chorus echoes with loud hurrah
The voice of the speakers expounding the law,
Till the air is vocal with echoing jaw
And a babel of feminine squealings.

"But Anna Dickinson roasting the press,
And Stanton calling for fierce redress;
And Susan Anthony making a mess
By snubbing each male who rises

To open his mouth ; and Livermore, she
Of the inches many, and fierce array
Of facts to deafen and quite dismay
The caviler of the crisis—

"These and the chorus all combined
Less dangerous are to our peace of mind
Than the Logan with face so fair and kind,
And words so fierce and cruel ;
Slashing fiercely here and there,
Allez an diable ! filez ! guerre !
Assailing the angels debonaire
Of burlesque water-gruel.

"Vote if thou wilt, thou Logan tall,
Roll on the woman suffrage ball,
In chorus cry we *jeunesse* all,
But in pity spare our leg-gers.
Take all we have, but leave us these;
We ask it on our bended knees ;
Take brains, take costumes, what you please,
But do not make us beggars !

"Take that we eat,—we still can drink;
Take that we wear,—but leave the wink,
The jig, the joke,—O, Olive, think !
Without our legs we perish !
Go blow your trumpet through the land,
Raise up a petticoated band
Of voters fair on every hand,
But leave the legs we cherish !

'And '*filez ! guerre !*' the Logan cries,
'Before my sword the invader dies !
Look ! bleeding there the Drama lies,
By naked *mollets* trampled !
Clog-dancing girls with yellow hair,
And brazen cheeks, and saucy stare,
No longer shall pollute the air
Of Thespis all her temples !'

"She swoops upon our chickens sweet,
Half-naked girls unfit to meet
Such onslaught, cowering at her feet,
Awed by the bold proceeding.

'*Et filez! guerre!*' she cries again,
While round her fall our tears like rain;
'Doomed is the dirty drama's reign,'
And vain is all our pleading.

"Alas! alas! what times are these!
No longer we can take our ease,
For battle-cries on every breeze
Are echoing and pealing.
As round and round the warriors prance
In robes of lace, with diamond lance,
And floating plumes, and shout *avance!*
Until our sense is reeling!

"With hideous din on every hand,
No longer peace is in the land,
But vengeful sword and flaming brand
Are flourished madly o'er us.
The female cohorts scour the plain,
And sweep us down with sweeping train,
Till in despair we shriek again,
And swell the hideous chorus!"

The effect of the combined attack made upon this evil by the more reputable press generally, was quick and decided.

With my lance still quivering with the shock of the first blow, I saw the enemy retreating, demoralized and overthrown. There was no need to strike further blows.

In a time so brief that as I look back upon it now it seems almost marvelous, the theatres turned the burlesque women adrift and set about providing a more reputable style of entertainment.

The change was as magical, as sudden, as if worked by some dramatic Aladdin, with the wonderful lamp of public opinion—whose power to control theatres as well as other public institutions, is one which no wise manager will dare to resist.

It was public opinion which wrought this work—public opinion, aroused by the press, which is mighty in its power when it seeks to stir up the public love of purity and morality—and whatever the results upon the drama itself, one thing is certain, our theatres no longer present the disgraceful spectacle of Virtue, Respectability and Decency crowded to the wall by Vice, Vulgarity and Indecency.

This chapter stands as a record of a period in the history of the drama which will long be remembered as an extraordinary one, and which I have no hesitation in prophesying will not find a parallel in the experience at least of the present generation.

Burlesque will no doubt have more or less place in our theatres, as it has always had, but it will not be the indecent thing it was, nor create the wild fever it did, in the first half of the year 1869.

CHAPTER XL.

The Moral Aspects of Life Behind the Scenes and Before the Footlights. Can the Theatre be Purified at all ?—Arguments on Both Sides.—The Views of Dr. Channing. — The Error of Wholesale Denunciation. — Nothing on Earth Utterly Bad. — The Bad should be Denounced, and the Good Recognized. — Candor the Great Requirement of our Moral Censors. — Twaddle Fit for Babes. — Men Laugh at It, and Satan Chuckles.—Some Divines who have Spoken with Candor.—Dr. Bellows's Defense of the Stage. — Grave Mistakes.—Vices Not Amusements.—A Baleful Feud.— Amusement Defensible. — Advice to Players. — The Perils of Theatrical Life. — Preaching and Practice.—A Noble Demand.—CONCLUSION.

The moral aspects of life behind the scenes and before the footlights have often been the theme of writers and speakers, and the usual tone of the religious press is, I need not say, one of wholesale condemnation.

The effect of wholesale condemnation of anything which is not utterly and wholly bad, is worse than useless —it is pernicious. It injures the cause of morality and religion, and steels the heart against those who are guilty of this grave error.

"It is difficult," says a thoughtful writer in Harpers' Magazine for June, 1863, "for an honest and simple-minded gentleman, who in his youth went to the theatre with his grandmother, and in his old age still goes to the theatre with his grandchildren, to comprehend the heavy charges of immorality which sober and serious people have made so long and with so much earnestness against the drama. He feels that his love of the mimic art has not contaminated his own nature; and he will not, with equanimity, be told that he is a degraded creature because he relishes the exquisite repartee of Congreve, and likes Shakespeare better in the show than in the printed sheets."

I know that many people are firm in the belief that it is impossible to ever purify the theatre itself, and that the only course for good people is to frown it down without stint or mercy.

And if it could be frowned down, why, then—

But it can't.

Its evils can be worked upon, modified, and perhaps eventually eradicated altogether. To *that* end, I join heart and soul and brain with all good people; but I shrink back appalled when it becomes a question of trying to frown down THE DRAMA!

I should as soon think of undertaking to frown down laughter, because, forsooth, laughter is often associated with scenes of drunken riot, and finds provocation from obscene jokes in the mouths of wicked men..

In the Springfield (Mass.) *Republican*, some years ago, I read an editorial article, in which it was remarked: "The attempts now made to stem the current so strongly setting towards amusements once considered worldly and harmful, if not decidedly sinful, are few and feeble. They fail, perhaps, more from wholesale and indiscriminate denunciations of all amusements than from any perversity in those to whom they are addressed. There is, of course, moral peril connected with recreations, as there is, indeed, with the more serious business of life. But it does not follow that all amusements, or all fun and frolic even, are therefore to be avoided. The accepted philosophy of the world, if not of the church, now, is that sport is as legitimate as work, recreation as rightful as worship. The old maxim that the Christian must not engage in anything which turns his mind from serious things is discarded, and the common belief is that the man who enjoys a dance, a game of chance, or any other innocent recreation, can be quite as devout at the proper time and place as one who considers everything vain and sinful that is not positively religious. It is difficult to draw any exact line, and to set down this amusement as sinful and that as innocent, but our Christian casuists should not find it impossible to state the general principles governing all such matters so plainly that their application to particular cases will be obvious. In games of skill and chance, chess, checkers, backgammon, and such like, have long been tolerated in the most puritanical circles, while cards were formerly tabooed, for the then sufficient reason that gambling was chiefly done with cards, and there was consequently danger that whoever should play them might fall into that vice. If that objection has disappeared, cards are in themselves as innocent as chess or jackstraws. The practical question is, does card playing naturally lead to gambling? So of theatricals; religious people formerly opposed them because of the loose morality of plays and players, and the bad associations of the theatre. The prevalence of tableaux, exhibitions and parlor theatricals, and the growing tolerance of the theatre proper among our most precise Christians, show that the real objection is not to the stage, but to the abuses connected with it. It is very evident that the church is now educating its children to be theatre-goers, and that in the next generation the theatre is to be more universally patronized than ever before. In principle there is no more objection to the theatre than to the exhibition of tableaux, and there are necessarily no greater moral exposures there than in any other place where all classes meet for instruction or amusement. The same may be said of all amusements not intrinsically wrong. What specially needs to be considered by those who endeavor to direct Christian opinion is this: If the church (by which we mean all who accept Christianity) does not think it necessary or possible to check or turn aside the current now setting so strongly towards public amusements, if it has tolerated them, it should take the direction of them and make them safe, by excluding all that is impious and indelicate. The stage will slough off its grossness if its best supporters come from the church, and insist upon decency and morality in the performances. But if the church will not attempt to reform and control popular amusements, then it must keep away from them altogether, and leave them wholly to the publicans and sinners. This is the manifest alternative."

About the same time there appeared in the Philadelphia *Ledger* an article containing these wise words: "Popular tastes are founded on the instincts and affections of the human heart. With such a foundation, they are capable of effecting great good and great evil, just as their tendencies are directed. The wiser course of the moralist would be to avail himself of influences so powerful in their operation, to give them the right direction, and thus have the powerful assistance of the stage in forming virtuous habits, and correcting vicious tastes inimical to good morals. Next to the pulpit and the press, the stage has the greatest capabilities in itself of influencing the masses of society. Why should so powerful an agent be neglected, or why should not its capabilities be cultivated for the good of society? How long would grossness of speech or of thought be tolerated in places where intelligence and refinement are accustomed to resort? How is a good standard of taste created except by the best examples? And where are vice and vulgarity, always more or less allied to brutal instincts, so completely abashed as in the presence of virtue and refinement, or at least of those who in their outward conduct observe all the decencies and proprieties of life? Let respectable and moral people encourage a proper public taste by their presence at our popular amusements. The stage reflects the manners of society, but it is the manners of the society which visit the theatre. It is, therefore, in the power of those who condemn such amusements as gross and immoral, to make them as moral and refined as themselves."

All my experience of theatres and managers goes to assure me that this view is practically a sound one.

I feel absolutely certain that if it were the common habit of clergymen to go regularly to theatres, and to regularly hiss indecency and immorality there, their influence would be utterly irresistible. Players and managers alike would learn to stand in awe of such a body of determined moral censors, and the effect would be positive and permanent for good.

But while clergymen and religionists, as now, stand afar off and denounce the theatre in wholesale terms, actors and managers will reply indignantly, "What do *they* know about us and our business? They never visit the theatre—many of them never saw a play in their lives—how can they judge of that of which they are confessedly ignorant?"

Mr. Lewis Tappan once gave an interesting account of a meeting he attended thirty or forty years ago at the house of Rev. Dr. Channing, of Boston, composed of lawyers, clergymen, physicians and merchants, at which the question was discussed of encouraging the Tremont Theatre, then projected as a reformed place of amusement. Dr. Channing stated that he had long thought that religious persons should interest themselves more than they had done in public amusements, with a view to elevate their character, allure the young men from corrupt pleasures, and make amusements subservient to good morals.

The truth probably is, that there is nothing on earth wholly bad, and the true principle for the earnest and candid reformer is to carefully separate the good from the bad, recognizing the former while denouncing the latter,

Candor is the great requirement of our moral censors. The stupid twaddle which well-meaning men often utter is a positive injury to good morals, as well as an insult to intelligence.

As a specimen of this baneful twaddle, a writer in the *Atlantic Monthly* mentions a "Lecture on Popular Amusements," delivered to young men by a celebrated preacher at Indianapolis, in 1846. "With admirable perspicuity, the lecturer places 'vagabonds, fiddlers, fashionable actors, strumpet dancers, dancing horses, and boxing men,' in the same category, and with a naiveté truly refreshing asks his hearers if they ever knew a theatre in which a prayer at the beginning and at the end of the performance would not be considered an intrusion. The only term fit to apply in characterizing such extravagance is 'bigoted intolerance,' and many will think opposition useless and unprofitable. But this tirade represents the opinion of a very large and important part of the community, who think twice before making such a compromise with conscience as to go to the theatre themselves, and who would never dream of permitting such lapses from grace on the part of their children. The feeling is illiberal, and evidence of incomplete culture."

In one of the very best and most ably conducted of Boston's religious papers, I once read this silly mess:

"Not many months ago a coffin bore from the Tuileries the body of Count Bacciochi, cousin of the Emperor, the first chamberlain and *superintendent of the theatres.* He had seventeen grand crosses of the highest orders in Europe. He saw *all the splendid sights,* and heard *all the wondrous music of the stage,* and by those whose taste was in that direction, he was thought the *happiest of men.* But alas! *not to speak of religion,* there was one thing which cost him more hard daily labor than the hardest worker usually performs, and that was the getting of a little rest in sleep."

Truly, when one reads such awful examples of the evil effects of theatres, one is forced to say that there is no reply to make to such an argument.

Lack of the power of getting sleep, as everybody knows, is a peculiarity unknown to people who never go to theatres,—who never see the "splendid sights" and hear the "wondrous music."

I had some acquaintance with Count Bacciochi when I lived in Paris, and I chance to know that he was so *blase* about these things that he cared about as much for the "splendid sights" and the "wondrous music" of the theatres as a railroad superintendent would care for the "magnificent scenery" he advertised on his road as an inducement to travelers to go that way. So, if for his sins the Count Bacciochi could not sleep, it certainly was not for the sin of being too "happy" over the theatres which his duties made him oversee.

It is twaddle like this which makes wicked men laugh and Satan chuckle.

Some enthusiastic enemy of the theatre once printed the appalling statement that "It is estimated more money is expended in the United States for theatres than for all the Sabbath-schools in the country."

This astounding intelligence drew forth from an irreverent wag the counter statement that "It has been estimated that the cost of washing linen that might just as well be worn two days longer, amounts to enough, in this country, to defray the expenses of the American Board of Foreign Missions. The expenses of buttons on the backs of our coats, where they are of no earthly use, is equal to the support of all our orphan asylums. It is estimated that the value of old boots thrown aside, which might have been worn a day longer, is more than enough to buy flannel night-gowns for every baby in the land. Also, that the cost of every inch on the full shirt collars of our young men is equal to the sum necessary to put a Bible in the hands of every Patagonian giant."

But there have been, and are, many divines who treat this subject with candor,—men who believe that

> —"There have been more in some one play,
> Laughed into wit and virtue, than hath been
> By twenty tedious lectures drawn from sin
> And foppish humors."

So fully impressed with this opinion was a Cambridge divine of twenty years ago, that he preached four sermons in the University Church in support of them. Before his day Archbishop Tillotson was not backward to give testimony in their favor, by declaring, "they put some follies and vices out of countenance, which could not be so decently reproved, nor effectually exposed and condemned any other way."

Among later utterances from clergymen, one of the most notable is that of Rev. Dr. Bellows, in the New York Academy of Music, a few years ago; and with a few extracts from this able and earnest address, my book will find fitting conclusion.

"There is no graver mistake in the world," said Dr. Bellows, "than to imagine that, taking society together, the love of amusement is an overweening passion of humanity. Doubtless it is the ruin of a class. But selfishness, the root of depravity and the mother of human evils, finds its chief outlets and manifestations in the serious and anxious passions of men,—in cupidity, the love of power, envy, jealousy, and malice. Out of the grand desire to appropriate wealth, power, place, or to avoid want, submission, and injury, spring the worst characteristics of society. Falsehood, fraud, violence, anger, cunning, slander, meanness, apathy, vice, and crime, originate in selfishness, which is ordinarily unsocial, stern, sober, laborious, and far as possible from pleasure or diversion. Instead of being self-forgetful, disposed to relaxation, playful, or gay, it is sullen, introspective, tightly girded, and in no mood for delight. For certainly we must not confound things different, and call the grim satisfaction with which the miser pursues his gains, the tyrant his victims, the rogue his prize, with which envy surveys the mortification of a competitor, or hatred the misfortune of an enemy, or jealousy the pangs of a rival,—amusement. Nor are the vices of society, drunkenness, lust and gambling, to be placed among the relaxations and amusements of mankind. They are the serious and horrible outbreak of lawless appetites, which do nothing to recreate, but only to destroy. If they are found in connection with the pleasures of the world, they are just as often found in absolute separation from them. Indeed, the lack of the wholesome excitement of pleasure is commonly seen producing the noxious excitement of vice; and intemperance, lust, and gambling have devastated communities in which public diversions have been scrupulously forbidden. It is a terrible fact, that the first hundred years of Puritanism in New England was marked alike by ascetic public manners, and the prevalence of vices almost unheard of in our free and more indulgent society; and it is even now asserted that the soberest of our sister States contributes more than any other State in the Union to the sad catalogue of female frailty. There is hardly a more baleful error in the world than that which has produced the feud between morality and amusement, piety and pleasure. By presenting as the mark for reprobation the recreations instead of the sins of society; by confounding amusements with vices, the moral feeling of the world has been wastefully diverted from its opposition to absolute wrong and depraving affections, into opposition to things innocent, indifferent, or hurtful only in excess; and thus a very mischievous confusion has been introduced into the natural and the Christian conscience of evil. Consider the thick darkness, the absence of interior light and moral order, which is likely to reign in a soul that has been instructed to put dancing and the frequentation of shows, spectacles, and balls into the same category in which lying, slander, hatred, and unchastity are kept, and to reckon the love of fun, gayety, and social excitement as a depraved and Satanic affection! What but moral confusion, secret protest, insidious revenges, private vices, latent skepticism, and laxity in directions not open to observation or suspicion, can result to many, from such unwarranted and unnatural classifications? It is true the second generation often pays the penalty of the asceticism of the first, but the first usually has a ruinous pity on itself, and treats its resolution in dark and deadly ways. We cannot afford to waste our moral feeling, our sensibility to sin, our powers of self-control and of resistance, upon false issues or on artificial sins."

The sum of his argument as to the defensibility of amusement is found in this sentence: "The best things are most open to abuse, and amusement, like food, love, power, money, requires to have the dangers of its pursuit pointed out, but not its lawfulness or its innocency, in its place and degree, denied or concealed."

Some of the reverend doctor's words of advice to players and managers are worthy to be painted in letters of gold, framed in frames of silver, and riveted to the walls of every green-room in the land, an ever-present preacher.

For instance these: "Be sure you gain nothing by the grossness or immorality of the plays you present. People will go to see great talent and great dramatic triumphs, in spite of the indecency or viciousness of the plots and incidents; but they would go a great deal more to see genius and power united with purity and truth. I take no narrow, squeamish view of the range of subjects proper for the stage, but plays which make light of moral distinctions, excuse vice, reward crime, or ridicule religion, are essentially mischievous, and cannot be defended anywhere. If managers wish to place themselves on the same catalogue with pimps, they have only to continue to quote the public taste as an apology for producing immoral and depraving plays. All honor is due to those among them who strive to produce the legitimate drama, and I know and believe that some managers feel a laudable and artistic loyalty to their profession, and make sacrifices to the exactions of taste, propriety and purity, which the public do not sufficiently appreciate."

Speaking of the perils of theatrical life, Dr. Bellows said: "I have spoken of your life as a peculiarly perilous life—perilous to the moral nature; and before I explain particularly why it is so, let me say that the post of moral danger may be the post of moral honor. It by no means follows that because a line of life is hazardous to virtue, it is a life forbidden to a moral being. There may be reasons for adopting it which are imperative—such as a strong constitutional proclivity, making any other course exceedingly difficult; an early education fitting for nothing else; a powerful combination of providential circumstances leading up to that path; or a parental will which had shaped that course before responsibility began. If the theatre be a social necessity, the profession of the actor is a lawful one; and its moral perils, while they should make it a calling slowly and reluctantly adopted by those who have a choice, are not such as to excuse any want of virtue, probity, or the strictest decorum, in any of its professors. If they were such, the calling would be self-condemned. Perils and temptations are not of the nature of compulsive forces, and we are none of us, having adopted a morally perilous vocation, to claim on that account any larger charity than other men of other callings. Only we are to put forth a greater and more constant effort to counteract these dangers. The life of a player is a morally perilous life, chiefly because it is a public life; and public life in every form is trying to the character. The actor shares with the politician, the clergyman, the dangers of a career in which he is continually appealing to masses; where he is an object of interest to masses; where strong temptations exist to substitute immediate reputation for self-respect, and to make fine words and skillful manœuvers to do the work of sound principles and patient performance of duty. Public life, in all its forms, is surrounded with flatterers and fawners, and tempted to the bargain and exchange of its opportunities for the opportunities of others. All men who live by the tongue, whether it be in the utterance of their own thoughts or those of others, whose reputation and livelihood is in the ear of the public, are greatly exposed men; and it would be a long step in self-knowledge, if the members of the clerical profession recognized the fact that the seriousness of their subject does less than they think to save them from the dangers which essentially belong to the talking vocations. The error of mistaking the glow of composition for the flame of faith; or the pleasure of uttering generous sentiments, for the honor of holding them; or natural sympathy with eloquent passion, for the courage and resolution of a good heart and life; this is a danger which rostrum, pulpit and stage may equally share, and the consciousness of which, I confess, increases my sense of fraternity with your calling. And yet it remains solemnly true that your profession is a dangerous profession, however lawful and necessary it may be, and sharing in some respects its perils with others. It is peculiarly open to vanity, levity and sensuality—more dangerous than it need be, on account of the present state of public opinion—but necessarily dangerous in any state of public sentiment. Aiming to please, and finding its chief incentive in the applause it nightly excites; peculiarly exposed to jealousy; required to affect sentiments and personate characters not its own; usually in contact only with its own class; feeling deeply the need of animal spirits and physical energies, most conveniently supplied by artificial stimulants; working chiefly in the night; vacillating between long seasons of leisure and short periods of excessive labor; at the mercy of a capricious public, here very kind, and there very cruel; overpaid in its favorites and underpaid in all who are not; splendid for its *stars* but dull for its *stocks*—what elements are wanting to make your profession one of very singular moral trial?"

Such words as these are listened to by players with respectful attention. They are seen to be the voice of candor, and not of cant; and they have an influence therefore for positive good.

And in the following passage is involved a demand, from the preacher on behalf of the player, which is noble and just: "What I demand for you, in the name of Christian brotherhood and of universal morality, is a complete restoration to the common rights and the common protection of society. Your calling is a lawful calling; lawful, in that it is the exercise of providential gifts and talents for the gratification and well-being of society—itself a divine order; lawful, in that its highest and best fulfillment involves necessarily not the least infringement of one of God's laws or Christ's precepts; lawful in that it is recognized by the law of the land. Not only so; it is an intellectual and artistic calling, demanding a somewhat rare organization—physical and mental—for its pursuit, and requiring for high success a degree of general information, culture and self-discipline, which should elevate it to the rank of the liberal professions. It is your duty, therefore, to claim, and our duty to concede to you, precisely the same kind of justice and charity, the same kind of severity and censure, which the other honorable pursuits of life are visited with. You have a duty and a right to demand that your private character shall be held as sacred as that of other public persons; your virtues and discretion as readily admitted; your weaknesses as truly deplored, and your guilt as resolutely punished."

This is the true principle. By this principle I can labor straight on in the path I have marked out for myself, and reach forth my hands for sustainment to all good and true men and women—to the enemies and opponents of all that is vicious and injurious in theatres—whether they be ministers of the gospel, strict religionists, stern moralists, or members of that gayer throng which I have indicated in the words THE MIMIC WORLD, AND PUBLIC EXHIBITIONS.

THE END.

THE PHYSICAL TRAINING OF CHILDREN.

By P. H. CHAVASSE, Fellow of the Royal College of Surgeons of England; author of "Advice to a Wife," etc., etc., with a *Preliminary Dissertation* by F. H. GETCHELL, M. D., Clinical Lecturer on the Diseases of Women and Children at the Jefferson Medical College; Fellow of the College of Physicians, Philadelphia; Corresponding Member of the Gynæcological Society, Boston; author of "The Maternal Management of Infancy," etc., etc.

No other work can take the place of this one. It is worth its weight in gold to all—single, married, parent and child. It presents *the Highest Type of Authorship known in England or America.* It is a convenient book of reference, a timely and sensible friend, a wise counselor—intelligible, economical, practical and indispensable. It is a work no one keeping house can afford to be without. It will save time and money; will lighten the trials of daily life; and will instruct the moral, physical and intellectual nature. It is a book which, when its contents are known, nothing will prevent the introduction of into the family.

QUESTIONS AND ANSWERS.—A highly interesting feature in this work is the use of questions and answers. An intelligent mother calls upon an eminent physician and asks apparently *every question which it is possible for a mother to ask* in relation to the subject. Everything, *from the first washing of the infant to the choice of a profession, or proficiency in household affairs,* is portrayed.

The FATHER, MOTHER and FRIEND are told: How to Save Lives—How to Strengthen Delicate Minds and Bodies—How to Amuse, Influence and Instruct—How to Beautify, Refine and Elevate.

ILLUSTRATIONS.—These are by celebrated engravers upon STEEL, and are among the most beautiful in conception and execution ever published. Of themselves they create a demand for the book.

The bindings are highly *ornamental, artistic* and *durable.*

CONDITIONS.—The work will be printed from new electrotype plates on fine tinted paper, and will be furnished at the following low rates:

In fine English Cloth	$3.00
In Leather, Library Style	3.50

THE NATION;

ITS RULERS AND INSTITUTIONS.

The intimate knowledge of the subject possessed by the author, Hon. JUDGE WILLIS, of New York, his legislative and judicial experience, embracing many years' duration, his literary attainments and profound scholarship, and his general capacity, have peculiarly fitted him for the task undertaken. Wherever he is known the work will be deemed accurate, reliable and indisputable.

An accurate account of the organization and mode of operating the United States Government is here furnished, with an insight into the machinery by which it is done. In their appropriate places the names, dates and terms of service and compensation of every President, Vice-President, Cabinet Officer, Chief Justice and Associate Judge of the United States Supreme Court, and Senator from every State, from the beginning to the present incumbent, are given, with the name of every candidate for President and Vice-President, the votes cast for each, and the result. It tells the tax-payer to whom and for what his money is paid, how collected and how expended ; it tells of the office, the office-holder and his duties, and of the citizen and his rights; in short, it tells about Ambassadors, Foreign Ministers, Consuls, National Banks, Naval and Military Academies, the Army and Navy, Patent Rights, Copyrights, Naturalization, Neutrality, Elections, Pensions, Prisons, Hospitals, Asylums, Indians, Passports, Compromises, Treaties, Revenues, Duties and Tariffs, the Census of 1870, the Declaration of Independence, Constitution and Amendments, Parliamentary Rules, and the *whole list of other subjects* which are important to every inhabitant of this great Republic. The work also affords a very complete chronological and historical compendium of the leading events in our national career.

This *gem* among useful publications embraces within a convenient compass the very essence of the knowledge necessary to constitute an intelligent citizen. It is admitted, by all competent to judge, to be *the most complete and reliable epitome of our institutions* which has ever been published. It is unrivaled in its peculiar field, and covers the ground so thoroughly as to leave no room for competition.

No one who is alive to his interests will fail to keep this work within his reach, and none who desire the education of those around them will be willing to dispense with it at any reasonable cost.

CONDITIONS.—The book will be printed from new electrotype plates, and will contain fine full-page steel plates, and thirty-seven small engravings of the "Coat of Arms" of each State. It will have over 500 pages.

In fine English Cloth, Sprinkled Edge.................................. $2.00
In Leather, Library Style, Sprinkled Edge.......................... 2.50

www.ingramcontent.com/pod-product-compliance
Lightning Source LLC
LaVergne TN
LVHW021100110826
845150LV00001B/137

* 9 7 8 1 4 2 5 5 6 6 1 6 6 *